SECURITY AND ARMS CONTROL

SECURITY AND ARMS CONTROL

Volume 1:
A Guide to National Policymaking

Edited by Edward A. Kolodziej
and Patrick M. Morgan

Greenwood Press
NEW YORK • WESTPORT, CONNECTICUT • LONDON

Library of Congress Cataloging-in-Publication Data

Security and arms control : a guide to national policymaking / edited
  by Edward A. Kolodziej and Patrick M. Morgan.
    p. cm.
  Includes index.
  ISBN 0–313–25257–2 (lib. bdg. : v. 1 : alk. paper)
  ISBN 0–313–25258–0 (lib. bdg. : v. 2 : alk. paper)
  1. National security. 2. Security, International. 3. Arms
control. I. Kolodziej, Edward A. II. Morgan, Patrick M., 1940–
UA10.5.S38 1989
355′.03—dc19   88–7224

British Library Cataloguing in Publication Data is available.

Library of Congress Catalog Card Number: 88–7224
ISBN: 0–313–25257–2

First published in 1989

Greenwood Press, Inc.
88 Post Road West, Westport, Connecticut 06881

Printed in the United States of America

The paper used in this book complies with the
Permanent Paper Standard issued by the National
Information Standards Organization (Z39.48–1984).

10 9 8 7 6 5 4 3 2 1

Contents

Preface

The unifying notion for this two-volume reference work is that national and international security and arms control studies are an interdisciplinary field of study. It seeks to give more precise form and profile to this emerging area of study than what exists in the literature today. Volume 1 focuses on the broad analytical perspectives that are relevant to the security and arms control considerations of any national government. Volume 2 attempts to clarify and define selected current issues and problems from an international perspective.

These volumes seek to fill three needs. First, they attempt to define the scope of the emerging interdisciplinary field of security and arms control studies as a serious field of systematic inquiry. The chapters identify major problems, key concepts, methods, disciplinary approaches, intellectual styles, and data sources associated with the principal sub-fields of international security and arms control studies. It is very difficult to coherently order the multiple literatures and disciplines appropriate to the study of security and arms control. These volumes present one way—by no means the only way— of handling this sprawling material and diverse activity.

Second, both volumes provide a critical review and evaluation of the most important literature associated with each sub-field to assist more extended analysis by interested students and policymakers than can be attempted in these brief evaluative surveys. Contributors were recruited specifically because of their acquaintance with a broad range of interdisciplinary literature relevant to each sub-field and, where appropriate, because of their experience in policymaking.

Third, the volumes can be used as texts for courses in international and national security and arms control. Each may be used as the framework for a year-long, two-semester course or be used separately as need dictates. The literature or sources evaluated in each chapter may be used to supplement these volumes.

In meeting these needs, these volumes seek to achieve several objectives. They can assist the further development of interdisciplinary programs in international and national security and arms control at universities and colleges. A liberal education implies knowledge of the world around us, not simply that of bygone eras. The possibility of war, nuclear holocaust, or terrorist attacks now weighs so heavily on human consciousness that serious and systematic study of the determinants of force and the mechanisms to control it needs to be part of the formation of the educated citizen in an open society, as much as history, art, or science. How else can the imperatives of using, threatening, and controlling force be reconciled with those associated with democratic norms, requiring broad public consent and informed support of governmental strategic policies?

Next, policy analysts and decision-makers will be aided in their effort to extend their special areas of responsibility to include concepts, methods, criteria, and data used in other fields. They should also find the volumes helpful in learning about the broader dimensions of the specific security and arms control problems which they are responsible for managing or resolving.

Finally, the volumes provide a provisional agenda for further research and analysis by indicating where more work needs to be done to advance security and arms control studies and policymaking.

These volumes are based on two conflicting assumptions arising from the strategic problems confronting national decision-makers: (1) that force and coercive threats are fundamental features of the behavior of states and (2) that the utility of force, given the increasingly lethal power in the hands of nations, has never been more questionable and problematic. There is no reason to believe that in the immediate future states will eschew force or threats in pursuing their objectives. Yet thoughtful analysts and decision-makers are aware of the costs and risks of arms races and the danger of prodigal and improvident use of force in supporting a nation's aims and interests. We need to understand the problems associated with making national and international security and arms control policy and how states are attempting to relax, if not resolve, the dilemmas posed by organized violence today.

Rationalizing the use of force has never been as difficult or fraught with danger as it is today. Not only the nuclear arsenals of the superpowers, but also the sustained and unremitting development of centers of military power around the globe threaten to envelop the world community in war. If states demonstrate little interest in rejecting force in support of their political objectives, they are no less confronted with the imperative of determining how their assembled military power can be prevented from toppling their regimes and of calibrating its use to ensure its subordination to legitimate political and moral purpose. Using and controlling war as an instrument of state policy are, therefore, only different aspects of a single imperative confronting national decision-makers. The nation's response to this imperative constitutes its strategic policy.

Volume 1 has four parts. Part I identifies those characteristics of the international system that condition the use or threat of force and that also prompt the need for ways to control violence and to discipline it to national purpose. It also stipulates what might be termed twelve functions of national strategic policy. Eight refer to the use or threat of force and are covered in Part II. Part III discusses three other functions associated with controlling the adverse feedback from efforts or threats to kill, hurt, or maim others, to destroy what an adversary may care about—material well-being, culture, or form of government. A final part reviews the twelfth function—ways that might be used to go beyond violence or threats in coping with human conflict. This is a counterbalancing function or check on those functions covered in Parts II and III. A bibliography at the end of the two-volume work provides guidelines for developing a core reference library.

Volume 2 has five parts. The first surveys the contending contemporary perspectives on the international system itself as the source of conflict and war. The second examines various facets of nuclear deterrence, including implications for the possible use of nuclear weapons. In the third part the focus shifts to conventional military power in the system, including arms transfers. The incidence of sub-conventional or low-intensity conflicts, including the practice of and possible responses to terrorism, is given attention in Part IV. In the concluding part strategic arms control, nuclear proliferation, and the study of crisis decision-making are discussed.

Two important caveats are in order. First, these volumes cannot hope to cover all of the relevant topics, literature, and approaches appropriate to the study and practices of national and international security and arms control. They are designed only as a start toward identifying and synthesizing some of the major components of this vast, sprawling, and still uncharted field. They are an initial and provisional inventory of what is known, what is not known, and what needs to be known about the behavior of states as they seek, alternatively, to use, threaten, and control force. The editors expect that others will be stimulated to improve on our effort in clarifying the parameters of strategic studies and the methods and approaches relevant to them. The editors freely admit that much has been left out as a consequence of funding shortfalls, space limitations, the availability of analysts, and the exigencies of cloture and publication schedules, to mention only some of the constraints under which these volumes were produced.

Second, the editors have emphasized problems and problem-solving. We believe that theory-building in international relations must proceed in part by concentrating on what decision-makers are concerned about and about what they say and do. For students of international relations, the task is to describe, explain, and ultimately predict the behavior of states and decision-makers. One way to approach this problem is to begin with *their* problems and to assess whether or not they see them clearly rather than simply substitute our own paradigms in the dubious hope that they are relevant to serious human concerns.

Third, the division between national and international security and arms control problems is a convenient distinction, though hardly the only one that could be employed. The perspective of Volume 1 is that of the decision-maker who is obliged to develop strategies for the use, threat, and control of force to support national objectives. He or she has an interest in determining the outcomes of conflict relations in favorable ways where coercion or violence act as arbiters. The second volume assumes more the perspective of the analyst who is interested in defining security and arms control issues from global perspectives. The problems are by and large system-wide in their impact and assume some level of international cooperation if they are to be managed or resolved. We hope the volumes complement each other since the problems addressed in Volume 2 will be solved, if at all, by policymakers responsible for strategic policies rather than by analysts who can warn, criticize, or cajole but who cannot take initiatives to strike workable, albeit tenuous, balances between the competing requirements of national and international security. Through these volumes, analysts can speak but cannot dictate to power.

Edward A. Kolodziej

Patrick M. Morgan

PART I

INTRODUCTION

Functions of Strategic Policy Within a Global Environment

EDWARD A. KOLODZIEJ
AND PATRICK M. MORGAN

The terms *strategic policy* or *national strategy* as used here refer to the plan for the use of organized violence or coercive threats to control the behavior of other actors, principally nation-states, and, more generally, to shape the international environment in preferred ways. The possibility of war and the pervasiveness of coercive threats to achieve nationally desired aims remain intrinsic to the global political system, as it has evolved since the emergence of the nation-state several centuries ago. Less clear have been the likely outcomes of using or failing to use force or threats to accomplish national purposes. The mindless carnage of World War I demonstrated that war is too important to be left to generals, despite the efforts of strategists like Karl von Clausewitz (1976) and the creation of the General Staff to plan war by marshalling a nation's resources and by ostensibly placing them under strict political control.

The experience of World War II, arising from the expansion of Hitler's Germany and Imperial Japan, suggests that war is also too serious a matter to be left even to national leaders. Would either state have resorted to war had it known the consequences of its decision, including the enormous costs in men and material and the eventual frustration of national goals, not to mention the incalculable number of deaths and the destruction visited on other lands and peoples? Despite these hazards, nations still have powerful incentives to use force, although, paradoxically, they have no certainty that the strategic policies they are pursuing will yield the desired results at acceptable costs.

National leaders operate today under unparalleled conditions of complexity, uncertainty, and risk to core values in resorting to force or threats to ensure intended outcomes in conflicts with other states or internal adversaries. The first part of these introductory remarks outlines some of the principal characteristics of the international system and the security regimes comprising it which condition the use or threat of force. These characteristics and conditions sharply limit the ability of states to predict what will likely happen when force is used or threatened. No empirically based theory exists to guide strategic policy and decision-making, notwithstanding the claims of political leaders and strategists that, say, nuclear deterrence has kept the peace or standing firm has compelled an adversary to capitulate to one's demands. We have at best partial theories of only partial elements of the broad field of activity that may be properly subsumed under the heading of strategic studies, whether viewed from a national or international perspective.

The second half of this introduction provides a rationale for the chapters of Volume 1. They represent a first-cut effort to systematize the interdisciplinary study of strategic policy as a branch of the social sciences. We need better theory as well as relevant data and information before we can begin to speak with some confidence about explaining or predicting outcomes where force or threats are employed to resolve differences between adversaries. These chapters identify some of the key substantive and methodological problems that must be addressed in making strategic policy. They also evaluate, through a selective review of the relevant disciplinary literature, what we know and what we need to know to make progress in using force, as an instrument of policy, disciplined to legitimate human purpose, and in devising realistic strategies to control and to surmount violence when it no longer serves rational choice.

CHARACTERISTICS OF THE INTERNATIONAL SYSTEMS: CONDITIONS DEFINING THE USE AND THREAT OF FORCE

A Multipolar World Society

The spread of the nation-state after World War II, as the principal unit of political organization of an imperfect and divided global society,[1] has generated incentives for the use and threat of force. There exists no common body of laws or ethical principles that are universally accepted to guide the behavior of states or arbitrate their differences. The incipient anarchy of the international system creates a security dilemma (see Stein, Vol. 1, ch. 2). States alone, or with allies, must provide for their own security and marshall military forces to underwrite their objectives. But in raising armed forces, they threaten—or are perceived to threaten—other states, which, in response, arm also to check a real or potential adversary. As Kenneth Waltz argues, following a line of analysis sketched earlier by Jean-Jacques Rousseau, the absence of a central authority capable of enforcing rules on the other states of the system provides the occasion for states to use force or to threaten coercion in pursuit of their interests (Waltz, 1959, 1979; Butterfield, 1951).

The efforts of major powers to dominate the international system by imposing their will on other states and by attempting to create a unipolar system have almost without respite for half a millennium inclined the international system toward war (see Modelski, 1980, and Thompson, Vol. 2, Ch. 1). Beginning first with Spain and Portugal in the fourteenth and fifteenth centuries and later with Holland, Austria, England, Prussia, Russia, and France, the nations of Europe struggled for regional hegemony. Gradually, they extended the European system of rival states to the rest of the globe, creating for the first time in history a truly global order, however precarious its constituent elements (DePorte, 1979). By the end of the nineteenth century, Germany and Japan emerged as new contestants for hegemonic status. Their defeat in World War II ushered in the United States and the Soviet Union as the latest rivals for primary status of the world system. The Cold War may be viewed as an extension of the past by means other than a direct military confrontation between the principal antagonists, each seeking to create an international environment congenial to its aims and interests.

The nation-state system, animated since 1945 by the superpower struggle and the decolonization process that destroyed the Eurocentric order, has been imposed on preexisting communal, ethnic, national and socio-economic differences within the world society. These provide additional outlets for armed conflict that work their way through the nation-state structure which itself is the occasion for attempts by different groups to capture or use state power to impose their will on rivals. Ethnic, ideological, and religious splits still count. Witness the U.S.–Soviet struggle or the rise of Muslim fundamentalism, which currently focuses on the emergence of a revolutionary Iran bent on limiting superpower intervention in the Persian Gulf and Middle East and dominating regional secular and religious opponents (respectively, Iraq and Saudi Arabia). The Arab–Israeli conflict is similarly rooted in communal differences, as is the civil war in Lebanon. The South Asian struggle between Pakistan and India pits Muslim against Hindu and, within India, Hindu against Sikh. Tribal strife further divides the African continent. Racial differences convulse southern Africa. Ethnic tensions are woven deeply into the social fabric of Sri Lanka, Burma, and the Indo-Chinese peninsula (Vietnam, Cambodia, and Laos).

Disparities in wealth and socio-economic development also sharply divide the world. The developed sector, including the Soviet Union and the Communist bloc, accounts for 80 percent of the world's wealth and productive resources, but only a quarter of its population. The coalescence of the so-called Group of 77 within the United Nations, composed of most of the developing states, gives an institutional form to the North-South split. Their demand for a redistribution of the globe's wealth is being played out in trade talks (Lomé convention), in debt rescheduling and monetary reform (World Bank and the International Monetary Fund), and in pressures on developed states for greater economic assistance. Bargaining over base rights, particularly with the superpowers, is negotiated in the coinage of military aid, principally arms, and economic assistance (see Harkavy, Vol. 1, Ch. 7). At stake is not only the global distribution of economic wealth and productive resources, but, as Stephen Krasner (1985) and David Baldwin (1985) demonstrate, the acquisition or retention of political power and strategic advantage. Economic progress and technological development (see Reppy, Vol. 1, Ch. 4, and Bellany, Vol. 1. Ch. 6) are prerequisites of a modern military establishment and indispensable components of national strategy.

These sources of conflict—an anarchical nation-state system, communal and ideological strife, and tribal as well as socio-economic differentiation—appear to be symptoms of even deeper cleavages within the world society and the product of more fundamental forces. For the Marxist-Leninist, war has been identified with the emergence of a capitalist system based on the private and corporate ownership and control of economic resources. The state arises as a coercive instrument to protect private wealth and power. Wars erupt as a consequence of the struggle between capitalist states over imperial domination (Lenin, 1939). This classic Marxist-Leninist formulation continues to command the intellectual allegiance of many theorists (Wallerstein, 1974, 1980; Kaldor and Eide, 1979). Conversely, others identify the primal causes of war with the emergence of warrior classes and self-perpetuating military systems, as the product of national atavistic forces, which institutionalize conflict in the world society. These forces are alternatively condemned (Schumpeter, 1955) and praised (de Gaulle, 1970) as the inspiration for global differences and the primary sources of armed conflict.[2] Still others, like Woodrow Wilson, identify war not only with the absence of a free market and a capitalist international economic system, but also with authoritarian political regimes and their purported inclination to expand toward imperial systems, at once anti-democratic and protectionist as well as illegitimate, in frustrating the expression of national sentiment and the creation of independent nation-states (Levin, 1968).

Diffusion of Military Power

Whatever the primary or secondary causes for conflicts may be in the global society, they are the occasions for an appeal to force or coercive threats to resolve state and group conflicts on terms favorable to the contesting parties. The decentralizing, centrifugal forces operating within the international system have been matched by an unprecedented expansion of global military power and by its diffusion throughout the world system. This diffusion has crystallized at four discernible, overlapping levels: (1) the superpower nuclear balance paralleled by enormous conventional military strength, capable of being projected around the globe; (2) the East-West military balance centered in Europe, the only region where superpower forces and those of most other developed states directly confront each other; (3) the enhanced military capabilities of developing states; and closely associated with the growth of Southern Hemispheric arsenals, (4) the emergence of new regional balances of power and the rise of local hegemonies. Accompanying this diffusion process has been, paradoxically, the increased interdependence of states and groups at each of these levels of military activity. In addition, today there is a more widespread capacity than ever before for new centers of military power to decide outcomes between warring states or groups within a state. They also dispose assets of strategic value that, as in bargaining over bases (see Harkavy, Vol. 1, Ch. 7), be traded for military, economic, or political advantage.

Superpower Balance of Terror and Global Reach. Viewed in absolute military terms, the superpowers dominate the international system. Their commanding status is a function of their nuclear forces and their developed techno-scientific capacities to modernize and deploy ever more efficient and effective offensive and defensive systems. Their prowess also rests on the progressive growth of their conventional warfighting forces which can be projected, overnight, around the globe. The size and complexity of their nuclear forces are too extensive to be more than summarized here (see SIPRI, 1987; IISS, 1986). Each superpower has about 12,000 strategic, that is, long-range, nuclear warheads capable of reaching the homeland of its adversary. Together, they possess another 25,000 non-strategic or so-called tactical or regionally designated nuclear weapons. Both possess a triad of platforms to launch these weapons. About two-thirds of Soviet warheads are carried by ground-based intercontinental ballistic missiles (ICBMs); one-fifth of U.S. capabilities are similarly stationed. Half of American strategic warheads are based on submarines; approximately one-quarter of comparable Soviet warheads are sea based. The remaining proportions for long-range bombers— U.S. B–52s and F–111s and Soviet Bears and Bisons—are 33 and 8 percent, respectively. Each superpower is deploying or developing new missiles to replace those in their inventory as well as new bombers, armed with stand-off cruise missiles. As these offensive programs go forward, both are devoting increasing resources to developing anti-missile defensive capabilities against ground-launched ballistic systems (President Reagan's "Star Wars" proposal), anti-submarine warfare (ASW), and anti-satellite systems (ASAT).

Superpower nuclear capabilities are matched by the maintenance of large conventional forces, many of which are based outside their national boundaries. Both also possess long-range air- and sea-lift capacity. These logistical capabilities afford both the option of sending armed forces, their own or those of allies and clients, to almost any point in the globe. While both superpowers retain a worldwide base network, their long-range sea and air transport capabilities make them increasingly independent of the kind of extended and vulnerable base network that undergirded the European imperial powers up to World War II. Their non-nuclear forces are also specialized to fight in different terrains and climates, to engage in amphibious operations, or counter-insurgency operations, while being directed from national command centers in touch with local forces by equally global communications systems. Thanks to these non-nuclear capabilities, both powers have been able to intervene around the world where other states, lacking such forces, have been precluded from entry. The Soviet Union occupies Eastern Europe and maintains Communist governments against insurgents in Afghanistan, Ethiopia, Angola, and Nicaragua. Similarly, the U.S. operations in Vietnam, the Persian Gulf, and the Middle East would have been impossible in the absence of large conventional forces and lift capacity.

East-West Balance. The European nuclear and conventional balance between East and West represents the largest concentration of military forces in the globe. Spending by both blocs was approximately $600 billion in 1983 (in constant 1982 dollars), equally divided between the two (U.S. ACDA, 1985, p. 48). The armed forces of both sides were also approximately equal, totaling 5.6 and 5.8 million, respectively, for the North Atlantic Treaty Organization (NATO) and the Warsaw Pact and including the forces of both superpowers. In 1983, these totals represented almost 80 percent of the world defense expenditures and 40 percent of the forces under arms (U.S. ACDA, 1985, p. 47). Complementing these forces are regionally based nuclear weapons. Despite the dismantling of nearly 2,000 warheads by both sides in approximate ranges between 300 and 3,000 miles, in accord with their signing of a treaty on medium- and long-range missiles in 1987, both superpowers still possess several thousand tactical nuclear weapons backed by their respective strategic forces as well as land- and sea-based aircraft and cruise missiles.

NATO and the Warsaw Pact forces have developed elaborate doctrines for regional warfare in Europe (see Mearsheimer, 1983; Dean, 1987). Managing bloc competition and overseeing the European arms race are quite distinct strategic tasks from those associated with either the superpower struggle or regional conflict in the developing world. Also included in the European theatre are the nuclear forces of Great Britain and France. Although the warheads at their disposal are only approximately 5 percent of the superpower arsenals, they will, alone or together, soon approach a lethal capacity sufficient to place at risk at least a quarter of the population of the Soviet Union and over half of its industrial resources in the prompt effects of nuclear weapons (see Kolodziej and Morgan, Vol. 2, Ch. 5). (A total of twenty-two Soviet cities with a population of 1 million or more will be within reach of British warheads; a smaller number will be within reach of the French.)

Diffusion of Military Capabilities in the Developing World. The growing military strength of developing states is one of the most notable features of the emerging global security environment. This diffusion process, accelerated by decolonization and given impulse by massive arms transfers from developed states, principally the superpowers, creates serious obstacles for any state seeking global hegemony as the experience of the United States in Vietnam and that of the Soviet Union in Afghanistan suggest.

In the decade between 1973 and 1983, the developing states outpaced the developed world in the rate of growth of expenditures for military forces, in percentage increases in GNP devoted to the military, in per capita military expenditures, and in the number of personnel under arms (U.S., ACDA, 1985, pp. 47–51). Since these states started from a lower base, one should expect a higher rate of growth in their defense spending. Their overall inferiority, measured in absolute terms vis-à-vis industrial states, is also likely to continue for some time. Even with these reservations, the expansion of military capabilities in the developing world is impressive. Like the developed countries before them, they are creating their own military forces and are assuming the traits and trappings of modern states at a rate consistent with their resources and the level of their socio-economic and techno-scientific advancement (see Ross, 1987; Ball, 1988; Neuman, 1984; Kolodziej, 1987, Vol. 2, Ch. 6).

Between 1973 and 1983, the developing world increased spending on arms from $95.3 billion to $162.6 billion in constant 1982 dollars. Men under arms rose from 15.1 million to 17.5 million. Arms imports rose, measured in constant 1982 dollars, from $20.1 billion to $27.5 billion (U.S. ACDA, 1985, pp. 47, 89). What is particularly striking about these increases is that they were made possible by devoting a gradually decreasing share of central governmental expenditures (CGE) to military purposes while essentially holding constant the ratio of military expenditures to GNP. Over the decade under examination, the ratios of military spending to CGE fell from 22.5 to 18.4 during this period. The ratio of military expenditures to GNP remains annually, with few exceptions, slightly below 6 percent (U.S. ACDA, 1985, p. 47).

A more revealing trend in the military expansion of developing states is the incorporation of advanced military systems in their inventories. In 1950, few states had any advanced aircraft, missiles, ground armor, or warships. By 1985, 55 had supersonic aircraft; 71, tactical missiles of all kinds; 107, armored fighting vehicles; and 81, modern warships, primarily small but speedy and (proportionate to size) well-armed ships (SIPRI, 1978, pp. 238–53; IISS, 1981).

The increasing sophistication of developing state military inventories is paralleled by the growth in indigenous arms production and in the gradually rising arms sales activity of these states. In four main areas of arms capability, the developing states have registered considerable progress. In 1960, only seven states could produce fifteen different types of aircraft, largely through licensed production. Twenty years later, eighteen states had entered the field and were able to mount sixty-seven types of aircraft. Over this twenty-year period, the number of developing states capable of building naval vessels rose from thirteen to twenty-five, and the number of types of ships that they could produce more than doubled from eighteen to forty-five. Similarly, the figures for manufacturing armor and ground equipment as well as tactical missiles of all kinds show an expansion of developing state arms production capacity. By 1980, six states could produce seventeen varieties of ground equipment and nine states twenty-six different types of missiles, whereas twenty years earlier almost no state in the Southern Hemisphere had this capability (Ross, 1981; SIPRI, 1974, pp. 250–58 and 1980, pp. 168–73; Broszka and Ohlson, 1986, pp. 16–17).

Meanwhile, between 1973 and 1983, the value of the developing states' arms exports increased from $600 million to $4 billion (U.S. ACDA, 1985, p. 89). Over this period, these countries increased their share of the world market from 2 to 11 percent. While still far behind developed states in the value of arms production and sales, the developing states have made great strides in expanding and modernizing their military forces and arms production capability. However dependent these states are on developed states for arms, there is no reason to believe that improvements in the military capacity of developing states will not continue. This is especially likely to proceed in key regional states like China, India, Brazil, Argentina, the two Koreas, and Israel, which are among the current leaders in arms production and sales (see Ross, Vol. 1, ch. 5).

The impact of growing developing state military capabilities and arms production capacity cannot be fully measured by gross measures. Most armed conflicts since World War II have been in the developing world. According to one estimate, of the twenty-five interstate wars and thirty-two intrastate wars between 1945 and 1980, the overwhelming majority were initiated in the developing world. Most prominent among these have been successive Arab-Israeli and Indian-Pakistani flareups and the thirty-year Vietnam War, stretching from the decolonization war with France to the national integration struggle waged against the United States and its South Vietnamese allies (Singer and Small, 1982).

Rise of Regional Powers. With the breakup of the Eurocentric system, the diverse regions of the Southern Hemisphere have been the principal centers for armed conflict in the postwar period. The decolonization process, linked closely to the expanding global conflict of the superpowers, initially fostered regional strife as national peoples struggled toward independence. These conflicts were often simultaneously accompanied by civil war, as was the case in Vietnam or Malaya. As new states and regimes were established, they joined in the age-old struggle for regional dominance as the Indian-Pakistani, Arab-Israeli, and Iran-Iraq conflicts evidence.

Accompanying the enlargement of armed forces, the expansion of military activities, and the growing complexity of foreign and economic relations, the states of the Southern Hemisphere have also been widening their roles in defining regional and global security regimes. Developing states increasingly (1) decide the outcomes of interstate and intrastate conflicts and (2) grant or deny their strategic assets to other states, including most notably the superpowers, and thereby influence how regional conflicts and the superpower global competition are conducted (Kolodziej and Harkavy, 1982, pp. 331–68).

The outcomes of interstate and intrastate wars have been increasingly influenced or determined by developing states. Vietnam rules over Laos and Cambodia and holds China at bay in Southeast Asia. In the Middle East, Israel remains the dominant military power, as is India in South Asia and South Africa in southern Africa. Cuba bolsters regimes in Ethiopia, Angola, and Nicaragua. Until recently, Libya frustrated French efforts to resolve the civil war in Chad. Israel and Syria, and a revolutionary Iran, define Lebanon's fate as a nation. Pakistani forces helped defeat Palestinian forces in Jordan in the 1970s. In 1977 Moroccan troops played a decisive role in maintaining the Mobutu regime in Zaire in power against insurgents in Shaba province. Examples can be multiplied to illustrate the growing importance of key developing states in influencing the outcomes of regional conflicts.

Developing states also possess strategic assets useful to other states. Cuba and Vietnam are valued Soviet allies, as are Israel and Egypt, key American partners in the Middle East. The oil-producing states, most notably Saudi Arabia and Libya, finance arms purchases for other states and rebel forces. Algeria has played a key diplomatic role in negotiations between the United States and Iran. Brazil supplies armored vehicles to Iraq. Israel has supplied arms to Iran and to states in Central America, Asia, and Africa, including South Africa. Vietnam, North Korea, and China have also reportedly sent arms to Iran, while Libya delivered French Mirage aircraft to Egypt during the 1973 Yom Kippur War. As outer space becomes a region of military competition, developing states around the globe play a key role in communications, transmission, and relay networks, as well as in intelligence gathering of all kinds (see Harkavy, Vol. 1, ch. 7). These assets place these states in a favorable bargaining position vis-à-vis the superpowers and enhance their relative influence on regional and global arrangements.

COPING WITH COMPLEXITY, UNCERTAINTY, AND RISK

Never before has military force been more pervasive or more problematic as an instrument of policy. Never has it appeared more needed or useful to check armed adversaries, yet less reliable and even counterproductive in deciding outcomes in regional conflicts or civil wars. National leaders can neither be indifferent to the external and internal threats to their regimes and objectives, nor sure that the military strategies they devise will yield planned and prescribed results.

The system-wide conditions under which military force must be used or threatened account for much of the unprecedented complexity, uncertainty, and risk surrounding national military strategy today. First, as sketched above, the current international system—a product of the superpower struggle, the decolonization of the Southern Hemisphere, and the reemergence of the European states and Japan as major economic and military powers—is truly global in its dimensions, yet remains politically divided into over 150 competing nation-states. The conflicts generated by these states overlay more traditional—yet still unresolved and by no means no less intensely pursued— ideological, communal, ethnic, tribal, and socio-economic conflicts.

Second, the multiplication of centers of political authority has led to the diffusion of military force throughout the system. New centers of military power are now capable of affecting outcomes of interstate and intrastate conflict. There are now more actors than ever before whose reliance on force or threats has not only local but larger regional and global repercussions as well. The interdependence between the superpowers, the East-West bloc, and regional security regimes in the developing world creates new uncertainties about the likely effects of using or threatening force. Armed conflict begun at one level may spread to others in unforeseen ways. No state at any level possesses sufficient military power to fully control events or outcomes at other levels, or even to assure control over those within its own primary sphere of interest.

Third, the destructiveness of modern weapons and the multiplicity of contingencies under which force might be employed place a premium on force in being over those that might be mobilized after hostilities have erupted. War is so costly that it must be prevented. Under these conditions, deterrence has progressively become a preferred posture. The rapidity with which military force can be applied, nuclear or conventional, and the decisiveness that surprise can bring to disarm and overpower a foe's military forces reinforce incentives to be prepared before a war begins to deter an attack, or, if an attack is imminent, to launch a preemptive strike to destroy enemy forces before they can be launched.

But how much is enough to deter by threatening damage or loss in excess of any desired adversary gain? That question raises profound difficulties about properly assessing adversary intentions and capabilities; detecting threats in timely fashion to respond to them; estimating the opportunity costs to the economy in terms of investment, growth, income levels, and distribution of different levels of defense spending; accurately projecting the scientific and technological requirements of force modernization; and eliciting public and allied support for strategic policies that are costly to other valued aims and interests. Once assembled, how are military forces to be controlled and their costs held to tolerable levels? How can they be reconciled with international controls? As Thomas Schelling asked (1960), how can adversaries cooperate for mutual benefit while pursuing strategies to gain military advantage and even superiority over an opponent? Finally, are there ways to surmount the zero-sum strategies of using and employing force and transforming a lethal conflict into socio-economic and political competition, and even cooperation?

These problems advise a broad, systematic approach to strategic policy-making that attempts to specify more precisely than we have so far the outcomes of conflict behavior involving force or coercive threats. No state can escape the responsibility of developing a comprehensive strategic policy, although it may almost certainly lack the military capabilities to impose its will on an opponent or to control allied or third-party behavior. It is with these notions in mind that we turn to the second part of these introductory remarks and survey the chapters that follow.

FUNCTIONS OF NATIONAL STRATEGIC POLICY: USING, THREATENING, CONTROLLING, AND SURMOUNTING FORCE AND COERCIVE THREATS

Under contemporary conditions of international relations, all states are obliged to develop a comprehensive strategy for using, threatening, controlling, and surmounting force and coercive threats in their attempts to influence or determine the behavior of other actors, principally states, and to shape the international environment in preferred ways. These tasks may be conceived as a set of twelve functions: perception and communication of threats; estimates of enemy capabilities; economics of national security; arms acquisition and transfers; science, technology, and military power; basing; public support; force posture limits; arms control; domestic controls; international controls; and creation of alternative security systems. These functions must be simultaneously and continually performed within the decision-making process of those elements of the government concerned with strategy. In that way, a stable equilibrium can be struck that balances the conflicting requirements of these functional tasks while effectively responding to external strategic imperatives. As the chapters below suggest, this is no easy responsibility to discharge.

In Chapter 2, Janice Stein identifies some of the principal perceptual barriers to accurate reception or communication of threats. These barriers arise from unconscious cognitive and motivated error rooted in the needs and interests of leaders—and their peoples—within an international environment that fosters reliance on threats and force. Cognitive and unmotivated errors either magnify or minimize, unduly and in unanticipated ways, real threats or find threats where none exists or was intended. The sources of cognitive error are multiple: belief systems; absence of empathy for real or potential adversaries, that is, lack of concern for their problems as a way of understanding their initiatives or reactions; simplistic representations of an opponent's behavior; egocentric focus; overconfidence in explaining the complex thinking and moves of others; denial of alternative, less threatening, explanations of opponent actions; biased attribution wherein one's behavior is described as situationally dictated while an opponent's is viewed as volitional and malevolent; and greater policy coherence being imputed to other states than is warranted.

Clusters of these cognitive errors conspire with motivated misperceptions to falsify an adversary's intentions or distort his or her capabilities. Because of real or apparent fears or deeply held interests or convictions, leaders engage in defensive avoidance, selective attention (retaining information that supports their position while dismissing or ignoring data that conflict with what they want), informational distortion, and just plain wishful thinking. Misperceptions arising from these cognitive or motivated errors are inextricably merged with real threats rooted in the security dilemma of an anarchical international system or in shifts of power balances or in the needs of the domestic struggle for power. Although leaders may be confident in proclaiming that threats do or don't exist, it is apparent from Stein's evaluation of what we know of their behavior that neither they nor we, as analysts, have a theory of misperceptions that can distinguish between the real or the apparent which may assume a life of its own.

Even if we assume that a threat is real, that is, that an adversary intends to use force under certain conditions, it is far from clear either that he will be able to carry out his threat or that we are able to determine the true material dimensions of the military threat being posed. Problems of calculation and estimation arise at many levels. As Robert Butterworth suggests, three problems are especially relevant. First, there are no reliable measures for estimating the effectiveness of aggregate forces. Firepower values can be assigned to individual weapons or small units, say, fighter aircraft or a tank crew, but serious estimating problems arise when one attempts to evaluate these forces when they are combined in a single military capability. Adding to these problems are weights to be assigned to logistical capabilities—the proper ratios of "tooth to tail"—and the relative performance of variously defined modular forces against different enemy formations. And how does one assess leadership, experience, training, or command, control, and communication (C^3I) capabilities? Do the C^3I capabilities, for example, divide or multiply forces? These questions only scratch the surface of the imponderables confronting the analysts.

As one moves from static to dynamic analysis of assessing the operational effectiveness of rival forces, one faces a deeper dimension of uncertainty. Do new weapons systems, such as homing ordnance, or military reorgnizations with greater firepower, say, above corps level for ground forces, change the elasticity and density of a fixed front? Are breakthroughs now possible in the European front by means other than attrition? Using scenarios as an analytic technique helps to "game" the use of variously packaged forces under shifting environmental conditions, but it is bedeviled by serious flaws: deficient information, focused and inflexible limits to the analysis, and failure to anticipate the dynamics of real military operations marked by unforeseen and often chance circumstances.

Finally, the measures used may be misleading. What Butterworth calls the Heisenberg principle may be operating: The analyst or strategist may substitute a flawed or even irrelevant measure for what the adversary is really doing. One may have balanced forces, as a necessary condition for deterrence, but they may not be sufficient because an opponent may value them differently or, as Stein suggests, an opponent may build around deterrence—what Anwar Sadat's Egypt did in launching its Yom Kippur attack in 1973. Similarly, the

United States believed that deploying the Pacific fleet to Pearl Harbor would deter Japanese expansion in the western Pacific. What was a deterrent for Washington was a target for Tokyo. The Japanese secretly developed a shallow torpedo and a fighter bomber with a longer range, thanks to greater fuel efficiency, and used surprise in destroying most of the moored U.S. ships in harbor.

The heavy material burden of modern defense creates yet another set of dilemmas. In Chapter 4, Judith Reppy analyzes the problem of opportunity costs in spending on defense and the preservation and promotion of a vigorous economy as a necessary condition of national security. There is, first of all, the issue of resource mobilization. Should mobilization be through command or market mechanisms? Which are the least burdensome and most effective mechanisms? Volunteer armed forces provide a useful measure of the market value of such elements, but can a society afford such a policy and is it militarily effective? To what degree can weapons development be considered—or be made—disciplined to market demand? Can those with leverage—sole suppliers or buyers—exercise their economic advantage without adverse impact on security or the growth potential of the economy? If limits must be placed on defense spending because of pressures for less taxation (more personal and corporate discretionary income) or for civilian investment, how is the defense industry to be sustained at a sufficient level to provide for efficient full employment or for surge capacity when security needs abruptly arise?

Then there are the questions of who pays and profits. Gross national product (GNP) is a useful measure for determining the proportion of public spending devoted to military purposes, but it is not as useful in assessing the factors that produce growth. Here data are needed on investment patterns and impact on industrial development and employment. Reliable estimates of the impact of public expenditures on national or sectoral economic growth are also absent. Similar to the predicament of those concerned with detecting or estimating threats, strategic analysts interested in explaining or predicting the reciprocal impact of military spending on the economy and economic development on military prowess lack a satisfactory theoretical framework and an adequate empirical base to address and answer these questions.

The issue of "guns versus butter" is directly posed as national leaders attempt to reconcile the conflicting imperatives of security and welfare. In Chapter 5, Andrew Ross examines this function of strategy within the question of whether a state should indigenously produce its own arms, procure them from abroad, or pursue some mixed strategy. Except for the superpowers and, arguably, France and China, most states lack the resources to be autonomous in making arms to meet their security needs. Conversely, they have powerful incentives to reduce their dependency either on arms or military technology abroad by developing their own arms industry. This import substitution policy correspondingly increases pressures to sell or even dump weapons in foreign markets to decrease unit costs and to cover the rising expenses associated with research and development. Meanwhile, the emergence of a techno-scientific military-industrial arms complex impedes reversal of an initial decision to create an independent arms production and development capacity. As Michael Broszka suggests in Volume 2, an international arms production and sales network arises. Although the superpowers still dominate this system, they are confronted by the multilateralization of production and supply within the system. While each nation must devise its own optimal strategy, deciding on what mix of indigenous production and external acquisition is best for it, the systemic effect may be damaging and ultimately counterproductive. What may be good, say, for France (Kolodziej, 1987) may have deleterious effects on global economic growth, particularly in developing states, or may encourage arms competition (Ball, 1988) regionally and globally.

Ian Bellany next addresses the proper relation of science and technology to security and arms control policies as an intrinsic part of a nation's strategy. It would appear that scientific discovery and technological advances are independent factors shaping the global security environment and defining the specific strategic problems confronting nation-states. So-called sweet technological solutions like the development of multiple, independently targetable reentry vehicles (MIRVs) could not be resisted, although they seriously complicated efforts at arms control between the superpowers. The development of cruise missiles raises additional obstacles to developing rules for modernizing arsenals. They are cheap, easy to conceal, launchable from the air, ground, or sea, and capable of delivering nuclear or non-nuclear warheads. These characteristics pose almost insurmountable problems for verification. MIRV and cruise missiles illustrate the difficulty of defining strategies for military technology that simultaneously anticipate all potential threats arising from an uncertain future while precluding uninhibited weapons modernization that may unwittingly undermine national security in its pursuit.

Making and marketing arms is also closely related to a sixth function of national strategic policy, that is, access to foreign bases and facilities. While this is particularly important for the superpowers, their need for bases abroad necessarily engages other states in their acquisition schemes. Arms transfers and military and economic assistance have been the principal media of exchange for superpower access to foreign territories, especially with states in the developing world. As Robert Harkavy shows in Chapter 7, the analyses of Reppy, Ross, and Bellany converge in their implications for base acquisition. Economic and military assistance as well as arms transfers entice other states to place national territory or air and sea rights at the disposal of the superpowers or other states, like France. This draws them inevitably into the superpower competition. Their security needs become enmeshed in the superpower struggle, creating a network of potential hot points that could flair into regional or global conflict. The technological complexity of modern warfare reinforces incentives for base acquisition or extraterritorial access to service C^3I systems, to monitor and track satellites, and to extend surveillance or ASW operations.

Decisions at all of these strategic levels do not evolve in a political vacuum. They imply, particularly in open societies, public support for the military strategies, economic burdens, and political entanglements that arise from each of the foregoing levels of strategic policymaking. In Chapter 8 Richard Eichenberg outlines the parameters of the systematic study of public opinion as both the object and subject of a nation's security policy. Domestic opinion sets limits, which vary over time, on the kinds of security regimes that are politically acceptable. It would seem that values and attitudes have considerable staying power over time, with ideological (or party) commitments, age, and educational levels being key indicators and determiners of a nation's security and arms control policies.

How then does a state develop a coherent strategic doctrine, as well as force levels and weapons systems that respond to real or potential threats, within a framework of scarce economic and technological resources, bounded by often conflicting public and elite values and fixed attitudes toward the use of force, alliances, and acceptable modes of using or threatening to use force? These constraints, including the complexity, uncertainty, and risks surrounding them, produce national plans that invariably fall short of needs. There are more contingencies that are susceptible to management or resolution by force or threats than there are resources or vision to cope with them. In preparing for certain contingencies, states are often undone because their planning is irrelevant or mischievously heightens their security problems. It may decrease their security and well-being via the too active pursuit of military solutions to political and socio-economic problems. In Chapter 9, John Rainier describes some of these difficulties in his review of U.S. efforts to devise force levels under conditions of material and political constraints and uncertainty.

In constructing military complexes and national centers under the direction of what Samuel Huntington terms "specialists in organized violence" (Huntington, 1957), a state runs the risk of undermining the objectives and interests that were to be promoted by an appeal to force. War or military force may be an extension of politics, as Clausewitz' much cited aphorism indicates, but disciplining military force to legitimate political authority and purpose is, as the following chapters evidence, far more difficult than he anticipated. The globalization of the nation-state system, the proliferation of centers of organized violence, the increasing number of potential incidents that may lead to the outbreak of hostilities, and the variety, complexity, lethality, and interdependence of armed conflict prompt thinking about ways to regulate and reduce the role of force and coercion within the world society.

Since war as much sustains as it threatens core values, states must incorporate at least four other functions into their strategic policy processes. Three concern related but conceptually and operationally distinct levels of control. These functions are discussed in Chapters 10 through 12. Finally, the cost and risks of war urge reexamination of its utility and the search for ways to diminish its role in setting disputes and in replacing it by alternative conflict resolution and cooperative processes.

In Chapter 10, Michael Intriligator and Dagobert Brito advance a strong and spirited defense of arms control as a regulatory mechanism. Much of their argument and its persuasiveness depends on their understanding of arms control. For them, it refers essentially to all efforts to control weapons development and deployments that "reduce the chance of war, especially nuclear war." Such efforts cover the quantity and quality of weapons as well as their configurations and the rules governing their use. Such an expansive definition implies that any change in the military environment that may decrease the probability of war is an arms control measure. Even increases in the number and quality of some arms may help reduce the chances of war, particularly nuclear war, where vulnerably deployed weapons are an invitation to pre-emptive attack.

A host of approaches and methods have already been tried to control organized, institutionalized violence. These approaches are not restricted to bilateral agreements between the superpowers, a common view that narrows the scope and possibilities of arms control to the vicissitudes of the superpower struggle. Tables 10–1 and 10–2 in the Intriligator-Brito chapter sketch a broad field of activity for arms control. Unilateral and multilateral approaches, such as the declaration of nuclear-free zones and nuclear test ban accords, respectively, are significant additions to the development of measures initiated by the nation-state to inhibit the outbreak of war and to reduce its damaging effects.

Perhaps the most controversial and certainly counterintuitive aspects of the Intriligator-Brito conception of arms control is the notion that some arms races may actually contribute to arms control. The authors see great value in large superpower nuclear stocks and diverse delivery systems and warhead payloads as supports for deterrence. That theirs is not a universally held view is suggested in their citation of alternate viewpoints. Few, however, would disagree that preventing inadvertent warfare is a critical priority. Opponents, as Schelling suggests (1960), have incentives to cooperate to avoid a mutually adverse situation, a war that no one wants (e.g., World War I) but that no one appears capable of preventing. The urgency of the problem stems precisely from the growing incidence of warfare occasioned by increasing global interdependence and weapons proliferation, the prospects of escalation arising from local conflicts, and the delicate complexity of warning mechanisms and C^3I systems which may fail when they are most needed. The Challenger crash and the Chernobyl nuclear accident suggest the hazards of relying on flawed instruments, imperfect control procedures, and fallible humans. The authors also advance some intriguing suggestions to improve arms control procedures by enlarging the nuclear arms control forum to include nuclear powers other than the United States and the Soviet Union and to extend arms control to regional security and even to the regulation of destabilizing features of domestic politics.

Chapter 11 by Sam Sarkesian focuses on the impact of the military on civil society. As Harold Lasswell recognized over a generation ago and, as the authors of the American Constitution understood even earlier (Federalist Papers, 1961), an open society may lose its liberties in pursuit of external strategies presumably designed to protect them. A standing military, which is now a seemingly indispensable requirement of the nation-state, raises the issue of what role the military is to play, and, specifically, the appropriate division of authority and responsibility between the professional officer corps, the state, and civil society.

As long as war is not imminent and as long as it can be prevented by maintaining a political stance of neutrality, civilian-military relations can be managed by positing a rigid professional code to which military officers are expected to adhere and then by essentially isolating them from politics and the democratic policy process. This purist approach characterized the United States before World War II. With the need for a standing army to deter war, to respond to conflicts, or to promote U.S. interests, the size and burden of military preparedness inevitably increased both the role and the incentives of the military to participate in governmental decision-making vitally affecting the resources available to the armed forces, the political authority that they could legitimately exercise, and the discretion that they might enjoy in using or threatening the forces under their command. The purist model neither accurately describes the behavior or role of the military in open societies, especially the military in the developed world, nor suggests what should be the proper boundaries between the military and the civilian spheres. Conversely, so-called fusionist models that would expand the military's role to capture what it is already doing or what needs to be done (depending on the analysts' diagnosis) to meet strategic imperatives beg the question of what should be the proper balance between military and civilian authority and power. There is growing awareness of what elements should be in the civilian-military equation. These include political control over the military; value compatability between the military, especially the professional officer corps, and society; internal control of the armed forces; and appropriate cultural integration of the military to patterns prevailing in society. But what should be the measure of each element in striking a stable and tolerable balance remains unclear. It is a key problem to be tackled by future research and analysis, whether viewed from the perspective of open, authoritarian, or even totalitarian political systems.

External controls complement internal mechanisms to prevent war from shattering the fragile political structure of the world society. Reformers have dreamed for centuries about devising schemes to forestall the outbreak of armed hostilities and to contain its damaging effects. These efforts, traced by

Professor Harold Jacobson in Chapter 12, crystallized in the creation in this century of the League of Nations and the United Nations. Jacobson evaluates these initiatives, as well as other indirect approaches, and identifies some of the principal strengths and weaknesses of international governmental organizations (IGOs) as means of control. He concludes that proposals aimed at substituting global organizations for the current nation-state system are not likely to succeed. This is not to say that they have no role or that they have uniformly failed to mediate and moderate armed conflict in specific instances and regions. If one evaluates the record and prospects of IGOs from a horizontal, not vertical, perspective, the case for IGOs as an instrument of conflict management and peace is strengthened. If IGOs give little prospect in the near future of surmounting the conflict-prone tendencies of the current system, they can be expected to make the system work better than they would otherwise in their absence.

But controls may not be enough to prevent war and its institutionalization as a governing mechanism in international society. One may, so to speak, be moving chairs on the *Titanic*—exercising controls within a system that is itself sliding toward its demise. As Francis Beer suggests in Chapter 13, controls on violence that are even more extensive than those outlined by Intriligator and Brito may be needed to impede the outbreak of war and to inhibit its debilitating effects. These include crisis and war management, restraint in opposing real or perceived threats, and active non-violence. These are minimalist approaches. More ambitious efforts to replace the current war-prone international system would involve the creation of new balances of power and political legitimacy within global society at several levels through the strengthening of world order, functionalism, and human rights (group and individual) and through a corresponding reduction in reliance on the nation-state as a guarantor of security. These changes would have to be supplemented by enlarged participation of peoples and individuals in determining international security arrangements and in promoting demilitarization. These visionary developments may not be as unrealistic as they may first appear. As Quincy Wright never tired of arguing in response to critics animated by a conception of history based on power and realpolitik, human vision and the goal of a better tomorrow in which force or threats may have less sway and play in deciding events are themselves potential causes or forces shaping the future (Wright, 1955).

The enterprise of using or threatening force intelligently, that is, of disciplining it to legitimate human purposes, of controlling its harmful and undesired effects, and of devising ways to surmount it will require the assistance of government leaders, military officers, elites associated with national security communities, and interested and informed publics everywhere. All will have to learn to think like strategists. This volume and its companion represent one small step toward achieving this ambitious goal.

NOTES

1. The notion of a single but not unified global society that has been able to order its affairs, however provisionally, is drawn from Hedley Bull, *The Anarchical Society: A Study of Order in World Politics* (London: Macmillan, 1977).

2. For an analysis of de Gaulle's theory of international relations, see Edward A. Kolodziej, *French International Policy Under De Gaulle and Pompidou: The Politics of Grandeur* (Ithaca, N.Y.: Cornell University Press, 1974).

REFERENCES

Baldwin, David A. 1985. *Economic Statecraft*. Princeton, N.J.: Princeton University Press.

Ball, Nicole. 1988. *Security and Economy in the Third World*. Princeton, N.J.: Princeton University Press.

Broszka, Michael, and Thomas Ohlson, eds. 1986. *Arms Production in the Third World.* London: Taylor and Francis.

Butterfield, Herbert. 1951. *History and Human Relations*. London: Collins.

Clausewitz, Carl von. 1976. *On War*. Edited and translated by Michael Howard and Peter Paret. Princeton, N.J.: Princeton University Press.

Dean, Jonathan. 1987. *Watershed in Europe*. Lexington, Mass.: Lexington Books.

De Gaulle, Charles. 1970. *Discours et messages*. Paris: Plon, 5 vols.

DePorte, Anton. 1979. *Europe Between the Superpowers: The Enduring Balance*. New Haven, Conn.: Yale University Press.

Gulick, Edward Vose. 1955. *Europe's Classic Balance of Power*. New York: W. W. Norton.

Hamilton, Alexander, James Madison, and John Jay. 1961. *The Federalist Papers*. New York: New American Library.

Huntington, Samuel P. 1957. *The Soldier and the State: The Theory and Practice of Civil-Military Relations*. Cambridge, Mass.: Harvard University Press.

International Institute for Strategic Studies (IISS). 1985. *Military Balance 1985–86.* London: IISS.

Kaldor, Mary, and Ashborn Eide, eds. 1979. *The World Military Order*. London: Macmillan.

Kolodziej, Edward A. 1987. *Making and Marketing Arms: The French Experience and Its Implications for the International System*. Princeton, N.J.: Princeton University Press.

———, and Robert Harkavy. 1982. *Security Policies of Developing Countries*. Lexington, Mass.: Lexington Books.

Krasner, Stephen A. 1985. *Structural Conflict: The Third World Against Global Liberalism*. Berkeley: University of California Press.

Lenin, V. I. 1939. *Imperialism: The Highest Stage of Capitalism*. New York: International Publishers.

Levin, Norman Gordon. 1968. *Woodrow Wilson and World Politics: America's Response to War and Revolution*. New York: Oxford University Press.

Mearsheimer, John. 1983. *Conventional Deterrence*. Ithaca, N.Y.: Cornell University Press.

Modelski, George. 1980. The Theory of Long Cycles and U.S. Strategic Policy. In Robert

Harkavy and Edward A. Kolodziej, eds. *American Security Policy and Policy-making*. Lexington, Mass.: Lexington Books.

Neuman, Stephanie G. 1984. International Stratification and Third World Military Industries. *International Organization* 38:167–97.

Ross, Andrew L. 1981. *Production in Developing Countries: The Continuing Proliferation of Conventional Weapons*. No. N–1615-AF. Santa Monica, Calif.: Rand Corporation.

———. 1987. Dimensions of Militarization in the Third World. *Armed Forces and Society* 13:561–78.

Schelling, Thomas C. 1960. *The Strategy of Conflict*. Cambridge, Mass.: Harvard University Press.

Schumpeter, Joseph. 1955. *Imperialism*. New York: Meridian Books.

Singer, David, and Melvin Small. 1982. *Resort to Arms: International and Civil Wars 1816–1980*. Beverly Hills, Calif.: Sage Publications.

Stockholm International Peace Research Institute (SIPRI). 1987.

(Publishers vary as do the years of these yearbooks.)

———. 1974. *World Armaments and Disarmament*. New York: Crane, Russak.

———. 1978. *World Armaments and Disarmament*. New York: Crane, Russak.

———. 1980. *World Armaments and Disarmament*. New York: Crane, Russak.

U.S. Arms Control and Disarmament Agency. 1985. *World Military Expenditures and Arms Transfers*. Washington, D.C.: U.S. Government Printing Office.

Wallerstein, Immanuel. 1974. *The Modern World System I*. New York: Academic Press.

———. 1980. *The Modern World System II*. New York: Academic Press.

Waltz, Kenneth. 1959. *Man, the State, and War*. New York: Columbia University Press.

———. 1979. *A Theory of International Relations*. Reading, Mass.: Addison-Wesley.

Wright, Quincy. 1955. *The Study of International Relations*. New York: Appleton–Century–Crofts.

PART II

USING AND THREATENING FORCE

2

On Perceiving and Communicating Threats

JANICE GROSS STEIN

This chapter examines the misperception of threat in international politics and its implications for strategies of conflict management, such as deterrence, that rely heavily on the accurate perception of threat to achieve their purposes. It looks first at the impact of cognitive and motivated error on the misperception of threat. Next, the impact of schematas, heuristics, and biases that culminate in unconscious cognitive error are considered, and then the consequences of need, fear, and interests resulting in unacknowledged motivated error are examined. The deliberate and self-conscious manipulation of threat by political leaders is excluded from this analysis. When leaders deliberately minimize or exaggerate the threat an adversary poses, they do not unconsciously misperceive but deliberately distort. We then consider cognitive and motivated error as mediating variables and examine the political and strategic factors that may either make these errors more likely or compound their impact.

The chapter assesses the strengths and weaknesses of theoretical explanations of the misperception of threat and concludes with a consideration of the implications of the evidence for theory and policy. Despite the grave consequences of the misperception of threat for the management of international conflict, explanations of the processes of misperception are weak. Current theories do not consider systematically the critical interaction of a range of cognitive and motivated errors or the political and strategic factors conditioning the likelihood of misperception. Politics must be built back into psychological explanations of threat perception in international politics.

THE PROCESSES OF MISPERCEPTION

In international relations, threats are broadly of two kinds. When leaders use strategies like deterrence, for example, they signal their commitment and resolve in part by issuing threats to a would-be challenger. This kind of threat, by its nature, is conditional. One leader threatens another with harmful consequences that are under the control of the threatener if the target does not comply with its wishes. What is relevant to the success of the strategy is not the threat itself but its perception; there is often a considerable gap between the intentions of the leaders who issue the threat and its perception by another.

Leaders perceive not only those threats that are communicated by another party, but also those that inhere in the environment. We term these situational threats (McClelland, 1975, p. 19). Accuracy in the perception of situational threats is even more problematic for policymakers to achieve and for scholars to establish. People may read their environment very differently: one may perceive a situation as threatening, whereas another will consider the same set of conditions to be benign. Even analysts, who are less immediately involved than policymakers and often have the advantage of hindsight, can subsequently disagree among themselves about the substance and scope of the threat leaders confronted.

In order to assess the scope of misperception, a standard of accurate perception is required. Even with the advantage of hindsight, assessment of accuracy is seldom obvious. Although threats that are issued by one party to another are often communicated explicitly and their content is known, leaders and analysts can still debate the intentions that underlie the threat. Assessment of the perception of situational threats is still more troublesome; the dangers inherent in a situation are rarely unambiguous. Senior American officials, intelligence analysts, and political leaders varied widely, for example, in their estimate of the threat inherent in the political crisis in Iran in the autumn of 1979.

Where good documentary evidence is available and the intentions of those who issue the threat are well established, we can compare leaders' perceptions of threat to the intentions of those who threatened and to their capabilities and make a judgment of accuracy (Levy, 1983, pp. 73–80). Where such evidence is not available or, as frequently happens, is open to multiple interpretation, assessment of the accuracy of threat perception is far more difficult. Under these circumstances, we treat threat perception as a process rather than as an outcome and consider deviations from generally accepted norms of inference and judgment (Jervis, 1986a). Again, since standards of rationality vary and leaders rarely approximate these norms, evaluating processes of perception can also create controversy (Jervis, 1976, pp. 117–42; Stein and Tanter, 1980, pp. 3–20). Nevertheless, because the perception of threat is in its essence a psychological process, the explanation and evaluation of misperception as a process is useful.

Four sets of factors can contribute to the underestimation or overestimation of threat. We look first at the explanations provided by cognitive psychologists who examine the impact of central cognitive constructs and biased processes of thinking on threat perception. Second, we examine the impact of leaders' needs, fears, and interests on their perception of threat; here the crucial explanatory variable is the motivated errors leaders make. Third, attributes of the international strategic environment may contribute to the process of misperception; the workings of the international "security dilemma," for example, where the security of one requires the insecurity of another, encourages the overestimation of threat. Fourth, we look at the additional impact of the political and institutional context on leaders' definitions of their interests and on their processes of threat perception. Strategic threat is perceived in a political context that shapes leaders' expectations, their needs, and their interests. Very little systematic work has been done on the impact of critical political processes that can define the parameters of threat perception.

Before beginning the analysis of the misperception of threat, some important caveats are in order. First, any explanation of misperception must be tentative until it is validated through the systematic analysis of cases where the perception of threat was relatively accurate. Some of the important contributory factors to misperception may be present as well when leaders perceive threats with minimal distortion. In looking primarily at cases of distorted threat perception, we can identify the necessary conditions of misperception, but we cannot establish their importance.

Second, we seek to explain two kinds of misperception, the *underestimation* and the *overestimation* of threat. As will become apparent, the same explanatory variables can result at times in one kind of distortion and at times in another. Stalin's expectations about Hitler, for example, were a major factor in his underestimation of the threat of German attack, whereas Anthony Eden's beliefs about President Gamel Ab'dul Nasir of Egypt contributed to his overestimation of threat. Similarly, leaders' needs can at times induce them to minimize or exaggerate threat. President Carter, operating in a harsh domestic political climate created in part by the Soviet invasion of Afghanistan, responded unwittingly with an exaggerated estimate of the Soviet threat. Israel's political leaders, on the other hand, faced an imminent election in the autumn of 1973; although they did not do so consciously, it was very much in their interest to minimize the threat posed by Egyptian Army maneuvers that October. In assessing the contribution of explanatory variables to processes of misperception, it is important to try to specify, insofar as possible, when and how each is likely to lead to the minimization or the maximization of threat.

Third, we look at each of the explanatory factors in sequence. Each of these variables—cognitive predispositions and biases, motivated error, the strategic environment, and domestic political processes and politics—can independently confound threat perception. These factors, however, are often interdependent. Political and strategic factors can interact with cognitive processes and motivated error to multiply the obstacles to accurate threat perception. Domestic and international pressures can encourage leaders unconsciously to minimize or exaggerate their estimates of threat to achieve their political purposes. In explaining the processes of misperception, the interaction of these variables may be more important than the independent impact of any single factor.

Cognitive Sources of the Misperception of Threat

Belief Systems. Cognitive psychologists have examined the distorting impact of cognitive "schemata" and "scripts" as well as a series of heuristics and biases that color threat perception. The most important is the overwhelming impact of leaders' expectations and beliefs on their perceptions. Individuals who think, reason, and learn impose structure on a complex world by the concepts they develop of themselves and others. Any acquisition of knowledge involves categorization and the use of "schemata" that relate new information to prior knowledge (Abelson, 1973; Anderson, 1982; Edelman, 1977; Kelley, 1972; Lau and Sears, 1986; Reder and Anderson, 1980; Schank and Abelson, 1977; Thorndyke and Hayes-Roth, 1979). These belief systems or "schemata" are essential; without them, no individual could organize or interpret the enormous amount of information that might be relevant to any problem. Yet these belief systems constrain and condition how and what leaders perceive.

In October 1973, Israel's leaders believed, first, that Egypt would not attack until the Egyptian Air Force could strike at Israel in depth and at Israel's airfields in particular, and second, that Syria would attack only in conjunction with Egypt (Stein, 1985, p. 64). Using these beliefs as the organizing concepts to interpret a great deal of evidence about Egyptian military activity, intelligence analysts discounted the possibility of preparation for an attack and interpreted the activity in the field as annual military maneuvers. Their low estimate of the likelihood of attack was reinforced by their confidence in Israel's military superiority; beliefs reinforced one another. The "theory" of analysts in military intelligence drove the interpretation of the evidence and led to a serious underestimation of threat. In this case, the errors of intelligence analysts are best explained by deeply rooted cognitive bias rather than by motivated error. Unlike their political colleagues who were facing reelection, no obvious benefit accrued from a tranquil strategic environment.

Anthony Eden's estimation of the threat posed by Egypt's nationalization of the Suez Canal in 1956 illustrates the impact of cognitive predispositions on the overestimation of threat. The prime minister's formative experience was Britain's appeasement of Mussolini and Hitler in the 1930s, appeasement that resulted in war. Frequently, leaders tend to learn only superficially from history. Their beliefs are shaped by recent events, by events that they or their country experienced directly, by events that happened when they were first coming to political awareness, and by events that had major consequences (Jervis, 1976, pp. 177–204, 217–21, 262–70; Lebow, 1985a). Eden's experience preceding the Second World War met at least three of these criteria. Fifteen years later, when confronted with the Egyptian nationalization of the canal, Eden could only see President Nasir as yet another dictator. He did not consider the critical difference between Nasir in Egypt in 1956, and Mussolini in 1935 and Hitler in Germany in 1938. Rather, he saw what he expected to see, and what he expected to see was a threat of massive proportions.

Lack of Empathy in Contrasting Cognitive Contexts. Closely related to the overwhelming impact of beliefs is the effect of the lack of empathy on the misperception of threat. In this context, empathy refers to the capacity to understand others' perception of their world, their conception of their role in that world, and their definition of their interests. Leaders are frequently unable to empathize, in part because of a difference in cognitive contexts. When sender and recipient use quite different contexts to frame, communicate, or interpret signals, the opportunities for miscalculation and misjudgment multiply. As Robert Jervis (1985) argues, it is very difficult for one set of leaders to imagine how another sees them. This is so in part because the relevant evidence is often difficult to obtain, but, even more important, because leaders' beliefs about themselves are frequently so powerful that it is hard to conceive that others hold a different view (Fiske and Taylor, 1984; Lebow and Stein, 1987). Consequently, leaders are often deficient in their capacity to empathize. Awareness of how and why an adversary feels threatened, for example, is an important component of empathy, but political leaders often display no sensitivity to their adversary's sense of vulnerability while they dwell heavily on their own perception of threat.

This inability to empathize intrudes at both ends of the signalling process to confound the perception of threat. The leaders who issue the threat are frequently insufficiently sensitive to the way their adversary sees them and, consequently, overconfident that they can design and communicate clearly the appropriate threat. The target interprets the threat from a different cognitive context and deduces meaning that is unintended. International history is rich with examples of this kind of misperception.

Ernest May describes the failure of the U.S. attempt to coerce Spain over Cuba in 1898 (1961, p. 161). When President McKinley threatened "other and further action" in the "near future" in his annual message to Congress, Spanish leaders simply did not perceive the threat. The translation of the message circulated to members of the Spanish cabinet had extensive marginal notation, but the threat was not highlighted. On the contrary, since the statement praised the offer of autonomy to the rebels, the foreign minister considered the message "very satisfactory."

The threat was not poorly executed. Indeed, the message seemed clear enough to American leaders, but it was not perceived by Spanish leaders who approached Cuba from a wholly different political perspective. Because of this difference in cognitive context, Spanish leaders not only underestimated but also missed entirely the threat issued by the United States. The United States, of course, had no way of knowing that Spanish leaders had not "heard" their threat.

Richard Ned Lebow documents a similar case of underestimation of threat by India's leaders in 1961 (1981, pp. 216–22). Chinese soldiers surrounded and cut off several Indian outposts that had been set up in contested areas of Ladakh. After they demonstrated their capability to isolate Indian soldiers, the Chinese pulled their forces back, thinking that the threat was unmistakable but hoping that India would withdraw quietly because violence had been avoided. China's leaders seriously misjudged how Indian leaders were likely to interpret their action.

The Indian estimate of the Chinese action was dramatically different. They interpreted the withdrawal as a lack of resolve and as testimony to Chinese military inferiority. Consequently, they determined to occupy as much of the disputed territory as they could. India's leaders underestimated the Chinese threat in part because of the difference in cognitive contexts of the two sets of leaders. Prime Minister Jawaharlal Nehru, Krishna Menon, and their advisers believed that Peking was reluctant to attack India because it feared defeat. In fact, in large part because China was persuaded of its military superiority, its leaders believed that a show of force followed by military restraint on their part might encourage compromise by India. Prime Minister Nehru was also persuaded that China would not attack because it wanted to avoid being labeled the aggressor by the non-aligned states. The second assessment was particularly important in framing the context in which India's leaders evaluated Chinese actions. In large part because of the limits to empathy and the differences in cognitive contexts, the Chinese threat was so badly misinterpreted that it provoked rather than deterred further military action by India.

Similarly, the profound ideological differences between the United States and the Soviet Union have repeatedly impaired their capacity to empathize and have exaggerated their perception of threat. Because leaders of both superpowers are deficient in their capacity to empathize, to understand how the other sees them, both are prone to misinterpret benign actions as threatening. When, for example, the United States offered to extend aid to the Soviet Union to assist in the reconstruction of its economy after the war, Soviet leaders suspected that the United States was seeking a market to absorb the expected surplus of peacetime production (Gaddis, 1972, pp. 174–98). Ideological, political, and cultural differences reinforce this tendency to read the other's signals and actions as threatening and offensive.

Evidence from a variety of cases suggests that ideological, political, or cultural differences in cognitive contexts can easily constrain the capacity to empathize and can result in serious error in threat perception (Lebow and Stein, 1987). Whether threats are overestimated or minimized will be very much a function of the specifics of the differences, but the general proposition holds. Because adversaries often do not relate to one another in terms of a common frame of reference and do not empathize with each other, threats are easily misinterpreted.

The Heuristics of "Availability" and "Representativeness." In addition to these deeply rooted and fundamental impediments to threat perception, cognitive psychologists have identified a number of specific heuristics that can impair processes of perception and attribution. People are "cognitive misers": because of well-defined cognitive limits, their processing of information is selective (Anderson, 1982; Fiske and Taylor, 1984). Heuristics refer to short-cuts in the processes of information retrieval which leaders use to gain access to information stored within their organizing schemata and belief systems. Two of the most pervasive short-cuts are "availability" and "representativeness." Leaders tend to interpret threats in terms of what is easily available in their cognitive repertoire (Tversky and Kahneman, 1973). Often, what is most available to policymakers are their own intentions, plans, and experiences. Consequently, they tend to perceive the actions of others in their light.

Estimates of the German air threat generated by the British Air Ministry in the period preceding World War II illustrate the impact of availability on the misperception of threat (Jervis, 1985, p. 23). British officials argued that the best criteria for judging Germany's rate of expansion were those that governed the rate at which the Royal Air Force (RAF) could establish new units. Similarly, because the RAF emphasized strategic bombardment, they inferred that Germany planned to attack their cities. In both cases, British officials overestimated German capability in the air and the threat this posed.

Through almost exactly the same process of reasoning, Israel's military intelligence underestimated the likelihood of an Egyptian attack in 1973. Because Israel relied so heavily on its air force as its primary offensive instrument, military and political leaders were receptive to an intelligence evaluation that stressed the deterrent effectiveness of Israel's air force. An Egyptian attack, therefore, was considered unlikely before 1975, the earliest date by which Egypt could acquire and absorb the required aerial capability (Stein, 1985, p. 64). The availability of Israel's strategic planning led intelligence analysts to estimate Egyptian intention to attack in light of these plans. The result was a serious underestimation of threat. In both cases, leaders misperceived the threat in part because the most available referent was a self-image rather than an image of the other. This bias toward self-image as an available referent to evaluate others is likely to be greater when differences in cognitive contexts are greater. The one is likely to reinforce the other, with serious consequences for the perception of threat.

The bias of "representativeness" can also influence the perception of threat (Jervis, 1986b). Generally, people tend to exaggerate the similarity between one event and a class of events because they pay inadequate attention to base rate statistics, or the probability that the event is part of a general class independent of any specific information about the particular event (Ajzen,

1977; Bar-Hillel, 1977). We have already noted Anthony Eden's classification of President Gamel Ab'dul Nasir as yet another dictator. Although Mussolinis and Hitlers are exceedingly rare in the history of international politics, Eden quickly assumed that Nasir was representative of this class of leaders. In this case, it is very likely that both availability and representativeness worked together to compound the misperception of threat.

The "egocentric" bias. The "egocentric" bias refers to the predilection of people to see themselves as the central point of reference when they explain the actions of others (Ross and Sicoly, 1979; Fiske and Taylor, 1984; Jervis, 1976, pp. 343–55). When people exaggerate the causal significance of their own actions and discount the importance of other factors, they overestimate the linkages between themselves and the behavior of others. As a result, they tend to exaggerate threat for two closely related reasons: first, because they overestimate the extent to which another's behavior is targeted at them and, second, because they exaggerate the degree to which the behavior of others is the result of their prior actions.

Lebow, Stein, and Cohen (1989) nicely document the impact of the egocentric bias in their analysis of President Carter's perception of the Soviet threat after Afghanistan. Both dimensions of the bias worked to inflate Carter's estimate of the scope of the Soviet threat. He had come to office with a relatively benign perception of the Soviet Union and had made the improvement of America's relationship with the Soviet Union a cornerstone of his foreign policy. After the invasion, however, Carter rejected the hypothesis that the Soviet Union had engaged in defensive action of a beleaguered ally and saw the United States and the Western world as the target of the Soviet invasion. Carter's perception is consistent with people's tendency to exaggerate the extent to which they are the target of another's action. This tendency prompts leaders to interpret the behavior of others as threats to which they must respond.

Even more strikingly, Carter interpreted the Soviet invasion as a failure of American deterrence, even though in preceding years the United States had made no effort to deter Soviet action in Afghanistan. It is difficult to explain the self-inflicted estimate of failure and the escalated perception of Soviet threat without reference to the second dimension of the egocentric bias. Because American leaders exaggerated the extent to which Soviet behavior was the result of their own prior actions, even dovish members of the administration could conclude that the principal incentive for Soviet action had been the near certainty that the Soviet Union could "move with impunity." In reaching this conclusion, American policymakers discounted other explanations of Soviet action and placed themselves at the center of Soviet calculations. The interactive effect of these two dimensions of the egocentric bias was a dramatically heightened perception of Soviet threat and the corollary requirement of a firm American response.

Overconfidence. A closely related bias of overconfidence further complicates the signalling and perception of threat. People generally tend to be too confident of their capacity to make complex judgments and perform complicated mental operations (Fischoff, Slovic, and Lichtenstein, 1977). This bias can have dangerous consequences insofar as leaders tend to overestimate their ability to design and communicate appropriate threats and to assess the intentions of their adversary (Jervis, 1982).

In his analysis of American strategy in Vietnam, Wallace Theis (1980) demonstrates that leaders in Hanoi repeatedly misperceived threats that had been carefully designed and calibrated in Washington. American policymakers were confident, for example, that their adversary would be sensitive to fine differences in the deployment of American forces in the south. Leaders in North Vietnam, however, gave these kinds of factors no weight in their assessment of American intentions because they were unaware of their significance.

Leaders in the target state can also be overconfident in their perception of threat and insensitive to alternative explanations of action. During the Cuban missile crisis, there was widespread agreement that the Soviet Union had placed missiles in Cuba as part of a broadly based offensive strategy. No serious attention was given to the alternative hypothesis that the Soviet Union was motivated in large part by new information that the United States knew of its strategic vulnerability. On August 31, 1961, Deputy Secretary of Defense Roswell Gilpatric publicly spoke of American strategic superiority and the weakness of the Soviet intercontinental ballistics missile (ICBM) system. Soviet leaders thereby learned of the enhanced American intelligence capability to assess Soviet forces. Even more to the point, they knew that the United States knew of their strategic weakness. Yet, the following year, Kennedy and almost all his advisers dismissed the proposition that the Soviet Union was motivated even in part by weakness. As subsequent evidence and argument would show, theirs was an overconfident and exaggerated perception of the Soviet threat (Lebow, 1983, 1987). In this case, it is likely that the egocentric bias interacted with the propensity to overconfidence to shape the American perception of threat. In a skewed analysis, the United States saw itself as the primary determinant of Soviet action and, with little hesitation or doubt, expressed confidence in its assessment and excluded any other interpretation of its adversary's intentions.

The "Proportionality" Bias. Political psychologists have paid particular attention to the assumptions people tend to make about the appropriate relationship between means and ends. Generally, leaders expect their adversary to expend efforts proportionate to the ends they seek. Consequently, they make inferences about the intentions of others from the costs and consequences of the actions they initiate (Jervis, 1985, p. 15; Komorita, 1973; Lebow, Stein, and Cohen, 1988). When a state incurs high costs, others assume that important objectives were at stake for the leadership. Even if leaders consider the costs of an adversary's action to be low, but judge the immediate stakes to be lower still, they will perceive threat from this lack of proportion. As

Jervis (1985, p. 15) argues, the "how" is more important than the "what": leaders are likely to perceive a threat if an adversary demonstrates a high propensity to take risks or ignores accepted procedure. When an opponent infringes on an accepted norm of behavior, leaders infer that their adversary is no longer bound by conventional restraints and is, therefore, a serious threat (Cohen,1979, pp. 165, 177). Because they estimate the costs of "breaking the rules" as high, they consider the threat proportionately serious.

This bias toward proportionality inflates the perception of threat. Related in part to the bias toward overconfidence, it ignores the difficulty that people are often poor judges of the costs and consequences of an action they choose and that leaders may also differ in their concepts of cost. American officials judged the political and military costs of the Soviet invasion of Afghanistan to be extremely high—the disruption of detente, the loss of the SALT II treaty—and, consequently, reasoned that Soviet objectives were commensurate with these costs. As Lebow, Stein, and Cohen (1989) argue, only an extreme interpretation of Soviet intentions could justify the consequences the Soviet leadership incurred. Ironically, the costs were as high as they were in part because the punishment inflicted by American leaders was a function of their heightened perception of threat. American officials ignored this circularity in their reasoning. Moreover, it is striking that, despite their recent experience in Vietnam, no senior American leader advanced the proposition that Soviet leaders had misjudged the consequences of their intervention.

The "Fundamental Attribution Error." Psychologists who study cognitive processes of attribution examine how people characteristically construct explanations. In their research they have identified a fundamental error, people's tendency to exaggerate the importance of dispositional over situational factors when they explain the undesirable behavior of others and the corresponding tendency to emphasize situational rather than dispositional factors when they are explaining their own behavior (Jones and Nisbett, 1971; Kelley and Michela, 1980; Nisbett and Ross, 1980; Ross, 1977).

This error in attribution contributes significantly to the overestimation of threat. Like the egocentric bias, it transforms effect into intent. Soviet officials tend, for example, to attribute the high level of American defense spending to the dispositional factor of the contradictions of capitalism and its inherent opposition to the Soviet Union. Their own defense spending, they insist, is situationally determined; it is a reaction to American militarism (Milburn, Stewart, and Herrmann, 1982). The dramatic increase in the perception of the Soviet threat by officials in the Carter administration also illustrates the impact of this fundamental error. In explaining the Soviet intervention, American officials gave almost no weight to the situational factors that might have constrained the Soviet leadership, despite repeated efforts by Soviet officals to convey to Washington the scope of their dilemma (Garthoff, 1985, pp. 903, 905, 907). Rather, they looked almost exclusively to dispositional factors and estimated threatening intentions from Soviet action; misplaced causation contributed significantly to the misperception of threat. Moreover, in this case, the fundamental attribution error worked together with the egocentric and proportionality biases to compound the perception of Soviet threat.

Attribution of Greater Coherence and Centralization. Leaders frequently tend to attribute greater coherence to their adversary than the evidence warrants (Jervis, 1976, pp. 319–29; Levy, 1983). Leaders overestimate the control their adversaries have over their machinery of government and attribute intent to all their actions. This frequently misplaced attribution of centralized decision-making is consistent with the attempt to join discrepant information to existing images and beliefs.

This process often works to inflate the perception of threat. It is most apparent in the interpretation of defense spending by an adversary. Many analysts in the United States, for example, assess Soviet defense spending as the product of a centrally coordinated and coherent plan, even though they are aware of the bureaucratic pulling and hauling that characterize their own processes of defense allocation. In 1962, for example, senior American officials gave no thought to the possiblity that interservice rivalry may have been a factor in encouraging Nikita Khrushchev to risk the placement of missiles in Cuba, even though they themselves had just gone through intense bureaucratic struggles with the air force and navy over force missions and numbers of weapons (Ball, 1980). Soviet leaders similarly speak of the central role of the military-industrial complex in the United States in driving up levels of defense spending (MccGwire, 1987).

The cognitive biases that we have identified contributed in important ways to the misperception of threat by political leaders. Because they were pervasive and distorting, they frequently had harmful effects on strategy. Moreover, in many of these cases biases interacted with one another to aggravate misperception. Although the case evidence suggests that cognitive errors occur in clusters, existing psychological theory tends to treat these biases singly. Exploring the covariation among biases remains an important theoretical and research challenge both when biases compete with one another and when they reinforce each other to compound misperception.

The near ubiquity of cognitive biases and heuristics is an even more serious problem. Because they are generally characteristic of processes of attribution, estimation, and judgment, they do not appear to be related in any special way either to specific kinds of needs and interests or to types of political and strategic situations. We return to these difficulties and their implications for theory and policy after we examine the motivated misperception of threat.

Motivated Misperception of Threat

Explanations of motivated misperception locate error within the broader context of psychological fears and needs rather than expectations. They ask fundamental political as well as psychological questions: what needs are met by misperception? Whose interests are served? Motivated biases result from unacknowledged, subconscious needs and fears and from emotional stress which is generated by leaders' political and strategic interests as they see them. Because motivated errors can be situated within a broader political and strategic context, they may be easier to identify and classify.

Motivated errors provoke some of the same pathologies identified by cognitive psychologists. Although they flow from fears, needs, and interests, they become manifest in some of the same biases of inconsistency management, absence of empathy, egocentricity, overconfidence, proportionality, and pathologies of attribution. Indeed, the principal difference between the two psychological explanations is not so much in the biases they identify but rather in the source of the errors (Lebow, 1981, pp. 111–12). Psychologists who empathize motivation give attention to the impact of fears and needs, whereas cognitive psychologists look to processes of information management in an uncertain and complex environment. When motivated error culminates in pathologies of interpretation and judgment indistinguishable from cognitive biases, it too contributes to both the overestimation and minimization of threat.

International history is rich with examples of motivated underestimation of threat. Irving Janis and Leon Mann (1977, pp. 57–58, 107–33), in their analysis of decision-making, identify a pattern of "defensive avoidance" characterized by efforts to avoid, dismiss, and deny warnings that increase anxiety and fear. Although policymakers continue to think about the problem, they ward off anxiety by practicing selective attention and other forms of distorted information processing. When actually confronted with disturbing information, leaders will alter its implications through a process of wishful thinking. At the core of this repertoire of techniques of inconsistency management is the need to control and reduce fear (Janis, 1967; Lazarus, 1966). When the perception of threat simultaneously evokes fear and a feeling of helplessness, defensive avoidance and distortion become more acute.

Defensive avoidance contributed heavily to British officials' underestimation of the likelihood that Argentina was seriously contemplating a military challenge in the Falklands. British leaders could find no satisfactory policy option to deal with the growing threat of Argentinian military action. In part because they were reluctant to use military force, yet anxious to protect the islanders, they faced an intense and apparently irreconcilable conflict of values. Under these circumstances, as expected, they ignored repeated indications that Argentinian leaders were preparing to use force, discounted the scope of the Argentinian threat, and took refuge in defensive avoidance (Lebow, 1985b, pp. 180–202).

Similar dynamics were at work in the American underestimation of the threat in Iran. Gary Sick, a member of the National Security Council with responsibility for Iran during the Carter admininstration, writes: "At least equally important for the relative lack of attention paid to Iran during this critical period was the underlying realization that there were no attractive options available to Washington" (1985, p. 77). Sick argues that the specter of Vietnam loomed large, and neither the president nor his principal advisers were "philosophically prepared" to consider military intervention in a civil war in the Third World. Moreover, many of Carter's principal advisers in the State Department were strongly opposed to the Shah's repressive policies. Consequently, Sick concludes:

Since there were very few realistic policy options available, and since any substantial change in policy involved actions that were certain to be politically distasteful or worse, people were inclined to keep their thoughts to themselves. The combined effect was to stifle communication . . . and to encourage procrastination in the hope that the situation would resolve itself somehow (1985, p. 78).

Even when leaders are not frightened and hopeless, their needs can motivate error. A careful reading of studies of intelligence failures suggests a process of motivated underestimation (Betts, 1982; Handel, 1976). In the autumn of 1973, for example, Israel's leaders were preparing for a general election, and, in their campaign rhetoric, members of the governing coalition emphasized the calm along the borders and the improved strategic situation. In this kind of political climate, political leaders may have unconsciously discounted the growing evidence of Egyptian and Syrian military preparations and the conjointly inflated evidence that deterrence was secure. This tendency to wishful thinking and motivated denial of threatening information was reinforced by their satisfaction with the status quo. The policy implications that flowed from their analysis were attractive: no mobilization of civilian reserves unless Israel's leadership was absolutely convinced that Egypt was irrevocably committed to attack. Such a restrictive requirement for certainty reduced the attractiveness of any significant strategic response at the same time as leaders were motivated to dismiss evidence of threat (Stein, 1985). The result, predictably, was strategic and tactical surprise when Egyptian and Syrian forces attacked.

In his analysis of British intelligence during the 1930s, Wesley Wark (1985) finds a similar process at work. Intelligence analyses of German military strength did not shape policy, but policy shaped intelligence estimates. Under Neville Chamberlain, estimates of German capabilities increased, making a military confrontation with Germany less attractive. In 1939, when the scope of Hitler's ambitions became unmistakably apparent, estimates of relative German capabilities declined as British leaders prepared for war. Vested interest in a particular policy can best explain both the overestimation and the underestimation of the military threat posed by Hitler's Germany.

Psychologists who study cognitive and motivated error make a singular contribution to the explanation of the misperception of threat. At least in the first instance, they can explain both the remarkable degree of insensitivity which adversaries display to each other's signals and exaggerated perceptions of threat. Analysis of cognitive biases alone, however, cannot establish the likely direction of misperception or its probable occurrence; the direction of motivated errors is far easier to specify. Preliminary research indicates, moreover, that motivational biases are not random occurrences, but rather responses to underlying political and/or strategic conditions (Lebow and Stein, 1987). It is to these political and strategic conditions that we now turn.

The Strategic Roots of Misperception of Threat

Analysts traditionally have looked to the strategic environment as an important source of the distortion of threat. In particular, scholars have examined the impact of the "security dilemma" on the exaggeration of threat and the especially dangerous consequences that flow from the distorted perception which is more likely in this kind of strategic environment (Butterfield, 1951; Herz, 1950; Jervis, 1976, 1978; Snyder, 1985). The distinguishing characteristic of a security dilemma is that behavior perceived by adversaries as threatening and aggressive is initiated as a defensive response to an inhospitable strategic environment. What one set of leaders sees as defensive another sees as offensive. A "perceptual security dilemma" may develop, however, when strategic and psychological factors interact and strategic assessments are exaggerated or distorted by perceptual biases. In effect, leaders overrate the advantages of the offensive, the magnitude of unfavorable power shifts, and the hostility of their adversaries (Snyder, 1985).

In 1914, for example, leaders did confront elements of a security dilemma (Snyder, 1984; Van Evera, 1984). As French fortifications improved, German security required the vulnerability of Russian forces in Poland. Without this vulnerability, both Russia and France could mobilize to full strength and then attack jointly. Russian security, however, excluded precisely such a weakness: Russia could not tolerate a decisive German advantage in a short war and so planned a 40-percent increase in their standing forces by 1917. In this strategic situation, defensive preparation by Russia was an offensive threat to Germany. Conversely, a defensive strategy by Germany suggested immediate military action against Russia. Although offense was operationally more difficult than defense, Russia's slow mobilization created the incentive to develop offensive strategies to solve defensive problems. When offense and defense became virtually indistinguishable, threat perception escalated dramatically.

Although the strategic environment was inhospitable and dangerous, Germany's leaders exaggerated the threat and, as Jack Snyder (1985, p. 170) argues persuasively, reasoned inside out. They overestimated the hostility of their adversaries and, consequently, assumed the inevitability of a two-front war. The attractiveness of a preventive warfighting strategy then became overwhelming; indeed, after 1890, the General Staff gave no serious consideration to the possibility of a defensive strategy. German military planners overes-

timated the threat posed by their adversaries in ways that psychological theories expect and then argued that an offensive capability was the least
unsatisfactory option. Once they did so, Germany's neighbors confronted a
real security dilemma. Insofar as they could not distinguish between offense
and defense, their perception of the German threat escalated.

In 1914, the strategic environment conditioned and facilitated the overestimation of threat. The inhospitability of the strategic environment was
compounded by the motivated errors of the German military whose strong
commitment to an offensive military strategy is otherwise inexplicable. As
Janis and Mann (1977) would predict, these motivated errors occurred when
the German military felt itself up against a very difficult strategic situation
with no obvious solution. Predictably again, the result was catastrophe.[1]

Closely related to the impact of the international security dilemma on the
distortion of threat are unfavorable changes in the relative balance of power
(Cohen, 1979; Knorr, 1976). When the trends in the balance of military capabilities alter in favor of an adversary or leaders perceive an unfavorable
shift, the ensuing sense of vulnerability and fear promote an exaggerated
estimate of threat. In the autumn of 1986, for example, some senior military
officers in Israel estimated that Syria was preparing for imminent attack. Their
perception of threat was in part a function of Syrian military activity in southern Lebanon, but more broadly a response to their unfavorable estimate of
trends in the balance of military capabilities.

Vulnerability ensues not only from changes in relative capabilities, but also
from geostrategic conditions. Shallowness of space, unsettled borders, the
absence of strategic depth, repeated or protracted warfare, all can promote
a collective sense of vulnerability and an exaggerated perception of threat
(Knorr, 1976; Cohen, 1979). Analysts of Israel's foreign policy have suggested,
for example, that its acute perception of threat can only be understood in
the context of its strategic vulnerability and its repeated experience of attack
and war (Brecher, 1972; Yaniv, 1987).

Leaders can exercise considerable care in the interpretation of changes in
the relative strategic balance, mindful of the motivation to exaggerate threat
under these kinds of conditions. They can be especially vigilant if they are
aware that a "security dilemma" is at work, distorting and multiplying the
perception of threat. In this kind of strategic environment, policies must be
carefully designed to reduce spirals of mutual fear and reinforcing threat
(Jervis, 1976, pp. 58–113). Especially in this kind of environment, threat-based
strategies such as deterrence may not only be inappropriate, but also pro-
vocative and dangerous (Lebow and Stein, 1987).

The Political Roots of the Misperception of Threat

Leaders operate not only in the international system but in their domestic
political environment as well. Very often, leaders' perception of threat is

conditioned by their domestic political needs and interests and by the institutional nexus of policy. Graham Allison (1971) argues that "where you stand determines where you sit"; that is, that position in the institutional hierarchy determines predisposition and preference. Threat perception can similarly be seen as partly a function of institutionalized rivalry (Freedman, 1977; Prados, 1982). Snyder (1984) finds, for example, that the German military had a far more exaggerated perception of the threat posed by Germany's neighbors than did the civilian leadership. It is no coincidence that this acute perception of threat was accompanied by a strong commitment to an expensive offensive strategy. Perception and interest coincided.

In a well-known process, civilian and military officials responsible for defense often unwittingly exaggerate threat to increase the size of budgetary allocations. In his analysis of policymaking on Vietnam, Richard Betts (1977) finds that operational military analysts seeking to justify missions tended to overestimate threat, while autonomous intelligence analysts were considerably less alarmed. More recently, a comparison of the analyses of the Soviet threat by the Central Intelligence Agency (CIA) and the Pentagon has found distinct institutional differences (Gordon, 1986). The CIA has been consistently less pessimistic in its analysis of the Soviet military threat than has the Pentagon: it has disputed assertions by the Pentagon that the Soviet SS–19 missile has the accuracy to be an effective first-strike weapon; it has concluded that the United States previously exaggerated the yield of the Soviet underground tests of nuclear weapons and questioned allegations that the Soviet Union has violated the 1974 threshold test ban treaty; it has provided a more cautious reading of the pace of Soviet research on anti-missile systems; and it has disputed Pentagon estimates of Soviet military spending and concluded that Soviet defense spending has been constant for years.

Analysts attribute this difference to two closely related political processes. First, unlike the Defense Intelligence Agency, whose intelligence reports are commissioned by the Pentagon even though they circulate through the government, the CIA provides intelligence to a variety of government agencies and increasingly to Congress. Its analysts are therefore inherently less vulnerable to political pressure and less likely to shape their analysis unconsciously to conform to the expectations and preferences of a particular consumer. Second, Pentagon analysts may unwittingly exaggerate Soviet military capabilities in order to secure support for the budgetary requests submitted to Congress. This consistent difference in the pattern of threat perception appears to be related systematically to institutional interests.

The impact of the institutional context on leaders' perceptions is not simple and unidirectional. Leaders can also influence the form and content of information that flows through the hierarchy. Merely by making their expectations or preferences known, policymakers can encourage their subordinates to report or emphasize information supportive of those expectations and preferences. Perspectives confirmed and reconfirmed over time become more and more resistant to discrepant information. In this way, selective attention, denial, or any motivated error that results from the efforts of policymakers to cope with alarming information can be institutionalized. Again, the result is significant distortion in threat perception.

CONCLUSION AND RESEARCH AGENDA

The arguments and the evidence we have just reviewed are troubling. The arguments are troubling because the theory on which they are based is still primitive and inchoate; we have no integrated theory of misperception. The evidence is troubling because it suggests that the obstacles to accurate threat perception are so many and so pervasive. Indeed, it seems unlikely that leaders could avoid committing all the most important cognitive errors or that the political and strategic conditions that motivate misperception can be controlled. It might be more appropriate to ask not how, when, and why threats are misperceived, but, rather, how and when threats are accurately perceived.

A short but accurate answer is that we do not know. We do not know enough about the conditions that promote effective signalling and reasonably accurate perception of threat. Certainly, this is the critical question, both analytically and from a policy perspective. Policy and theory are closely related to one another, and the imperatives of both suggest several broad lines of research.

First, we need to know when and how threat is accurately perceived, and in what kinds of political and strategic environments. The first priority is to identify cases in history where leaders have perceived the threat that was issued with some degree of accuracy. It would be especially useful to identify cases where leaders were divided in their evaluation of threat (Barnhart, 1987). It would then be possible to hold the strategic, political, and institutional influences constant and to explore the impact of different cognitive and motivational processes on threat perception. With the benefit of hindsight, we could ask "what did leaders do right," "how did they do it," and "how did they differ systematically from those who were wrong?" How did Churchill and Chamberlain differ, for example, in their processes of threat assessment? Some analysts have speculated that Churchill was right for the wrong reasons. They theorize that he did not differ significantly from Chamberlain in the cognitive processes he used to evaluate the threat from Germany, but that he was lucky enough to begin with the "right" set of organizing beliefs.

This kind of controlled comparison is essential if we are to create a systematic body of knowledge about threat perception. Our analysis of cases of misperception at best permits us to identify both the immediate and the structural factors associated with distortion. It may well be, however, that some of these same factors are also present when perception is far more accurate. If this is so, then these factors may be necessary but unimportant components of a more general explanation of misperception. On the other hand, they may prove critical.

Second, we need to know a great deal more about the interaction of important psychological biases when leaders misperceive threat. Cognitive psychologists have identified a set of discrete heuristics and biases whose relationship to one another and to substantive and situational factors remains as yet unexplicated. The limited evidence we have reviewed indicates that at times these biases appear in patterned clusters rather than independently of one another. Our evidence suggests a number of propositions for further investigation. For example, it reveals that the bias toward self-image as an available referent to evaluate others is likely to be greater when differences in cognitive contexts are great and the propensity to empathy is low. The two seem to reinforce each other. We have also noted that the attribution of greater coherence and centralization to an adversary is consistent with the attempt to assimilate discrepant information to existing beliefs; it reinforces processes of inconsistency management. Analysis of Carter's perception of the Soviet threat also indicates that the bias toward proportionality interacted with his tendency to overconfidence, egocentricity, and fundamental errors of attribution to inflate his perception of threat. Finally the underestimation of the likelihood of an Egyptian attack by Israel's leaders in 1973 can be explained by a "theory-driven" process of judgment, by the heuristic of availability, and by the reinforcing impact of the bias toward self-image. In these two cases, heuristics and biases reinforced one another and were easily interpreted. When biases contradict each other, however, existing theory does not specify their relative importance, the likelihood that one will supersede the other, or the conditions under which each is likely to occur.

This first cut at the evidence suggests the necessity to encourage psychologists and political analysts to identify clusters of biases that are theoretically coherent and integrated and to examine the interactive effects of contradictory heuristics and biases. We also need to reread contemporary international history in order to isolate patterned misperception empirically. When did biases occur together, and what kind of impact did they have on the misperception of threat? What kinds of errors are characteristic of different kinds of biases? Are leaders insensitive to their adversary's values and interests, for example, because of an inability to empathize, because of the bias toward egocentricity, and/or because of the tendency to discount unpleasant information? An analysis of the interaction of the most important errors in theory and practice is a critical prerequisite of a better explanation of misperception.

Third, we must attempt to identify the political and strategic conditions that promote or diminish the occurrence of important cognitive and motivational biases. This will be difficult to do if the misperception of threat is largely the result of fundamental cognitive biases. Insofar as these errors are both characteristic and unrelated to specific situations, policy recommendations to minimize the impact of cognitive bias are more likely to be trivial or banal. The theory that we now have does not permit us to say a great deal that is useful to policymakers.

It is true that leaders would correct their errors if they were aware that their perceptions of threat were biased. Consequently, there is some value in sensitizing leaders to the pervasiveness of the most important kinds of errors. They can be urged to have greater empathy and to reconstruct the fundamental political beliefs of their adversary. They can be pressed to consider basic differences in cultural and ideological beliefs. They can be warned to guard against overconfidence and overgeneralization. The advice to leaders to be aware of these biases and to try to compensate for them may be correct, and leaders may even try to do so. They are not likely to be very successful, however, given the pervasiveness and deeply rooted nature of these kinds of cognitive errors. We cannot avoid the obvious conclusion that insofar as the misperception of threat is largely a function of fundamental cognitive biases, leaders can do little but resort to threat less frequently, with greater caution, and with greater awareness of the high risk of misperception by the target.

The evidence that we have reviewed is not entirely discouraging, however. On the contrary, it suggests that motivated error may occur with some frequency. In reading history, it is difficult at times to separate motivated and cognitive errors empirically because some of the processes can be similar and neither leaves direct behavioral traces. By searching for the political and strategic conditions that evoke fear and need, however, we can try to situate distorted threat perception within its broader political context and identify patterns of motivated biases. Our evidence suggests, for example, that domestic political crises and security dilemmas create a heightened sense of vulnerability. This sense of weakness increases the likelihood of motivated error and, in turn, of distorted threat perception. This kind of proposition must be the subject of further research across cases of both distorted and accurate perception of threat. If a relationship between strategic and political conditions and motivated error is substantiated, it would have implications not only for theory but also for policy. In deciding whether or not to use threat, leaders can be advised to pay special attention to the political and strategic environment of their adversaries and to their sense of vulnerability. A great deal of historical evidence suggests that when leaders feel themselves vulnerable, threats may provoke rather than deter (Jervis, 1976; Lebow, 1981; Lebow and Stein, 1987; Stein, 1987). Insofar as the political and strategic preconditions of vulnerability can be identified, leaders can be given at least a rough rule of thumb to distinguish those conditions that are especially likely to motivate misperception.

In the final analysis, there is no "technical fix" to the fundamental problems associated with the transmission and perception of threat. The use of threat is natural and ubiquitous, but problematic. It is problematic because of the deeply rooted cognitive and motivated errors that confound its transmission and perception. Tinkering with modes of signalling, channels of communication, or the format of the message is likely to have an impact only at the margin. Attempts to control bureaucratic rivalries or to manipulate domestic political environments are not likely to fare much better.

Far more important are the basic political and strategic factors that condition both the formulation and the impact of threat in an adversarial relationship. Threats, after all, are used to try to manage political and strategic problems. Psychological research can illuminate the fundamental obstacles to accurate perception of threat, but we must put politics back into the psychology of misperception. It is imperative that political scientists specify the international and domestic conditions that make cognitive and motivated error more likely and thereby exacerbate the misperception of threat with all its attendant costs and consequences.

NOTE

1. A school of German historians disputes this interpretation of German misperception of the Russian and French threat as motivated error. Rather, it argues that the structural contradictions of German society were powerful inducements to the deliberate exaggeration of threat (Fischer, 1975). Important industrial and economic groups benefited directly, they suggest, from the heightened perception of danger and the defense spending that followed. The political leadership alleviated the social tensions and sharp class conflict in Germany at the time, at least in part, by their emphasis on the growing external threat (Gordon, 1974). If this interpretation is correct, then Germany's overestimation of threat was not the result of misperception by its leaders, but rather a deliberate manipulation in response to alarming political as well as strategic factors.

REFERENCES

Abelson, Robert. 1973. The Structure of Belief Systems. Pp. 287–339, in Roger Schank and Kenneth Colby, eds. *Computer Models of Thought and Language*. San Francisco: W. H. Freeman.

Ajzen, Icek. 1977. Intuitive Theories of Events and the Effects of Base Rate Data on Prediction. *Journal of Personality and Social Psychology* 35:303–14.

Allison, Graham. 1971. *Essence of Decision: Explaining the Cuban Missile Crisis*. Boston: Little, Brown.

Anderson, J. R. 1982. *The Architecture of Cognition*. Cambridge, Mass.: Harvard University Press.

Ball, Desmond. 1980. *Politics and Force Levels: The Strategic Missile Program of the Kennedy Administration*. Berkeley and Los Angeles: University of California Press.

Barnhart, Michael A. 1987. *Japan Prepares for Total War: The Search for Economic Security 1919–1941*. Ithaca, N.Y.: Cornell University Press.

Bar-Hillel, Maya. 1977. *The Base-Rate Fallacy in Probability Judgments*. Eugene, Ore.: Decision Research.

Betts, Richard. 1977. *Soldiers, Statesman, and Cold War Crises*. Cambridge, Mass.: Harvard University Press.

———. 1982. *Surprise Attack*. Washington, D.C.: Brookings Institution.

Brecher, Michael. 1972. *The Foreign Policy System of Israel: Setting, Images, Process*. London: Oxford University Press.

Butterfield, Herbert. 1951. *History and Human Relations*. London: Collins.

Cohen, Raymond. 1979. *Threat Perception in International Crisis*. Madison: University of Wisconsin Press.

Edelman, Murray. 1977. *Political Language: Words That Succeed and Politics That Fail*. New York: Academic Press.

Fischer, Fritz. 1975. *War of Illusions: German Policies from 1911 to 1914*. Trans. Marian Jackson. New York: W. W. Norton.

Fischoff, Baruch, Paul Slovic, and Sarah Lichtenstein. 1977. Knowing with Certainty: The Appropriateness of Extreme Confidence. *Journal of Experimental Psychology: Human Perception and Performance* 3:522–64.

Fiske, Susan T., and Shelley E. Taylor. 1984. *Social Cognition*. Reading, Mass.: Addison-Wesley.

Freedman, Lawrence. 1977. *U.S. Intelligence and the Soviet Strategic Threat*. London: Macmillan.

Gaddis, John L. 1972. *The United States and the Origins of the Cold War, 1941–1947*. New York: Columbia University Press.

Garthoff, Raymond L. 1985. *Detente and Confrontation: American-Soviet Relations from Nixon to Reagan*. Washington D.C.: Brookings Institution.

Gordon, Michael R. 1974. Domestic Conflict and the Origins of the First World War: The British and the German Cases. *Journal of Modern History* 46 (June): 191–226.

———. 1986. C.I.A., Evaluating Soviet Threat, Often Is Not So Grim as Pentagon. *The New York Times*, July 16.

Handel, Michael. 1976. Perception, Deception, and Surprise: The Case of the Yom Kippur War. *Jerusalem Peace Papers* 19. Jerusalem: Leonard Davis Institute of International Relations.

Herz, John. 1950. Idealist Internationalism and the Security Dilemma. *World Politics* 2:158–80.

Janis, Irving. 1967. Effects of Fear Arousal on Attitude Change: Recent Developments in Theory and Experimental Research. In Leonard Berkowitz, ed., *Advances in Experimental Social Psychology* 3. New York: Academic Press.

———, and Leon Mann. 1977. *Decision Making: A Psychological Analysis of Conflict, Choice and Commitment*. New York: Free Press.

Jervis, Robert. 1976. *Perception and Misperception in International Politics*. Princeton, N.J.: Princeton University Press.

———. 1978. Cooperation under the Security Dilemma. *World Politics* 30:167–214.

———. 1982. Deterrence and Perception. *International Security* 7:3–32.

———. 1985. Perceiving and Coping with Threat. Pp. 13–33 in Robert Jervis, Richard Ned Lebow, and Janice Gross Stein, *Psychology and Deterrence*. Baltimore: Johns Hopkins University Press.

———. 1986a. War and Misperception. Paper presented to a conference on the Origins and Prevention of Major Wars. Durham, N.H.

————. 1986b. Representativeness in Foreign Policy Judgments. *Political Psychology* 7:483–506.

Jones, E. E., and R. E. Nisbett. 1971. The Actor and Observor: Divergent Perceptions of the Causes of Behavior. Pp. 79–94 in E. E. Jones, D. E. Kanouse, H. H. Kelley, R. E. Nisbett, S. Valins, and B. Weiner, eds., *Attribution: Perceiving the Causes of Behavior.* Morristown, N.J.: General Learning Press.

Kelley, Harold. 1972. *Causal Schemata and the Attribution Process.* Morristown, N.J.: General Learning Press.

————, and John Michela. 1980. Attribution Theory and Research. *Annual Review of Psychology* 31:457–501.

Knorr, Klaus. 1976. Threat Perception. Pp. 78–119 in Klaus Knorr, ed., *Historical Dimensions of the National Security Problem.* Lawrence: University Press of Kansas.

Komorita, Stuart S. 1973. Concession-Making and Conflict Resolution. *Journal of Conflict Resolution* 17:745–62.

Lau, Richard R., and David O. Sears. 1985. Social Cognition and Political Cognition. The Past, Present, and the Future. Pp. 347–66 in R. Lau and D. O. Sears, eds., *Political Cognition.* Hillsdale, N.J.: Lawrence Erlbaum.

Lazarus, Richard. 1966. *Psychological Stress and the Coping Process.* New York: McGraw-Hill.

Lebow, Richard Ned. 1981. *Between Peace and War: The Nature of International Crisis.* Baltimore: Johns Hopkins University Press.

————. 1983. The Cuban Missile Crisis: Reading the Lessons Correctly. *Political Science Quarterly* 98:431–58.

————. 1985a. Generational Learning and Conflict Management. *International Journal* 40:555–85.

————. 1985b. Miscalculation in the South Atlantic: The Origins of the Falklands War. Pp. 89–124 in Robert Jervis, Richard Ned Lebow, and Janice Gross Stein, *Psychology and Deterrence.* Baltimore: Johns Hopkins University Press.

————. 1987. Deterrence Failures Revisited. *International Security* 12:197–213

————, Janice Gross Stein, and David S. Cohen. 1989. Afghanistan as Inkblot: Assessing Cognitive and Motivational Explanations of Foreign Policy. Forthcoming.

————, and Janice Gross Stein. 1987. Beyond Deterrence. *Journal of Social Issues* 43:3–71.

Levy, Jack S. 1983. Misperception and the Causes of War: Theoretical Linkages and Analytical Problems. *World Politics* 36:76–99.

May, Ernest. 1961. *Imperial Democracy.* New York: Harcourt, Brace.

McGwire, Michael. 1987. *Military Objectives in Soviet Foreign Policy.* Washington, D.C.: Brookings Institution.

McClelland, Charles. 1975. Crisis and Threat in the International Setting: Some Relational Concepts. Threat Recognition and Analysis Project Technical Report 28. Los Angeles: University of Southern California, International Relations Research Institute.

Milburn, Thomas W., Philip D. Stewart, and Richard K. Herrmann. 1982. Perceiving the Other's Intentions, USA and USSR. In Charles Kegley and Pat McGowan, eds., *Foreign Policy USA, USSR.* Sage International Yearbook of Foreign Policy Studies. Beverly Hills, Calif.: Sage Publications.

Nisbett, R. E., and Lee Ross. 1980. *Human Inference: Strategies and Shortcomings of Social Judgment.* Englewood Cliffs, N.J.: Prentice-Hall.

Prados, John. 1982. *The Soviet Estimate: U.S. Intelligence Analysis and Russian Military Strength*. New York: Dial Press.

Reder, L. M., and J. R. Anderson. 1980. A Partial Resolution of the Paradox of Inference. The Role of Integrating Knowledge. *Cognitive Psychology* 12:447–72.

Ross, Lee. 1977. The Intuitive Psychologist and His Shortcomings: Distortions in the Attribution Process. Pp. 174–214 in L. Berkowitz, ed., *Advances in Experimental Social Psychology*, Vol. 10. New York: Academic Press.

Ross, Michael, and Fiore Sicoly. 1979. Egocentric Bias in Availability and Attribution. *Journal of Personality and Social Psychology* 37:322–26.

Schank, R. and R. Abelson. *Scripts, Plans, Goals, and Understanding: An Inquiry into Human Knowledge Structures*. Hillsdale, N.J.: Lawrence Erlbaum.

Sick, Gary. 1985. *All Fall Down*. New York: Penguin.

Snyder, Jack. 1984. Civil-Military Relations and the Cult of the Offensive, 1914 and 1984. *International Security* 9:58–107.

———. 1985. Perceptions of the Security Dilemma in 1914. Pp. 153–79 in Robert Jervis, Richard Ned Lebow, and Janice Gross Stein, *Psychology and Deterrence*. Baltimore: Johns Hopkins University Press.

Stein, Janice Gross. 1985. Calculation, Miscalculation, and Deterrence II: The View from Jerusalem. Pp. 60–88 in Robert Jervis, Richard Ned Lebow, and Janice Gross Stein, *Psychology and Deterrence*. Baltimore: Johns Hopkins University Press.

———. 1987. Extended Deterrence in the Middle East: American Strategy Reconsidered. *World Politics*, 39:326–352.

———, and Raymond Tanter. 1980. *Rational Decision Making: Israel's Security Choices, 1967*. Columbus: Ohio State University Press.

Theis, Wallace. 1980. *When Governments Collide*. Berkeley: University of California Press.

Thorndyke, Perry W., and Barbara Hayes-Roth. 1979. The Use of Schemata in the Acquisition and Transfer of Knowledge. *Cognitive Psychology* 11:82–105.

Tversky, Amos, and Daniel Kahneman. 1973. Availability: A Heuristic for Judging Frequency and Probability. *Cognitive Psychology* 5:207–32.

Van Evera, Stephen. 1984. The Cult of the Offensive and the Origins of the First World War. *International Security* 9:58–107.

Wark, Wesley. 1985. *The Ultimate Enemy: British Intelligence and Nazi Germany, 1933–1939*. Ithaca, N.Y.: Cornell University Press.

Yaniv, Avner. 1987. *Deterrence without the Bomb: The Politics of Israeli Strategy*. Lexington, Mass.: D. C. Heath.

3

On Estimating Adversary Capabilities

ROBERT L. BUTTERWORTH

During the Agadir crisis of 1911, the British Army's director of military operations personally misled the prime minister and the Committee of Imperial Defence with his estimate of British, French, and German military capabilities. He almost certainly did so on purpose, hoping to advance the prospects for gaining approval to develop an expeditionary force (May, 1984, pp. 12–17). In that event and so many others before and since, estimates of capabilities moulded defense postures and channeled security policies. Upon them rest decisions about deploying today's forces and building tomorrow's; their adequacy can make the difference between effective diplomacy and disastrous losses.

With so much at stake, estimates should be clear and compelling, but current methodology rarely meets this standard. "No one has ever developed a satisfactory, mutually agreed upon method for determining an army's wartime potential short of an actual war" (Dunnigan, 1983, p. 216). No abstract measure of capability makes unambiguous sense without considering the circumstances, the purpose, and the setting: Capable of what? How quickly? Against what opposition? As a result, apparently straightforward descriptive exercises often ignite searing conceptual battles. Whether SALT I (Strategic Arms Limitations Talks) was desirable, for example, depended in part on whether it is more important to control warheads (Kissinger's view in advancing the treaty) or throw-weight (which his opponents argued in opposing it; Kissinger, 1979, p. 1232–33; Nitze, 1976). Whether the United States needed an anti-ballistic missile (ABM) in 1971 depended in part on whether one ought to assume that the Soviet Union would be able to reprogram intercontinental ballistics missiles (ICBMs) to replace those that failed at launch. (Albert Wohlstetter thought so and concluded that without ABM the U.S. Minuteman force would soon be vulnerable to Soviet preemption. George W. Rathjens made no such assumption and found no need for additional protection for the Minuteman force; Rathjens and Wohlstetter, 1973, pp. 137–53.) And so on today: the United States does/does not need peacetime conscription, long-range intermediate nuclear forces in Europe, 600 warships.

Estimates depend on measures; different measures suit different circumstances; different circumstances are interesting to different views and theories. Hence, there are plenty of opportunities for estimates to go astray, missing the mark on factors that, in the event, prove critical. The measures themselves can be technically deficient or misused, the important circumstances may be missed, and the wrong theories may be advanced. Generally, these problems surface in three major estimative shortcomings: first, it is difficult to measure the capabilities of aggregated combined-arms forces; second, it is even more difficult to measure in advance the factors that have often decided operational outcomes; and third, it is nearly impossible to ensure that estimates are addressing the right subjects in the right ways.

ESTIMATING A FORCE'S ELEMENTS

Measuring Firepower

The firepower of a force unit, such as an army division, is sure to be an important element of its combat capability. Part of measuring firepower involves technical information obtained from engineering studies and testing programs, but they cannot measure weapons as the enemy actually fields them—in force units organized hierarchically in the service of a combined arms doctrine. To include the organizational aspects, firepower estimates usually involve two steps: determining the relative contribution of the different categories of weapons to the overall effectiveness of the unit, and then evaluating the number and quality of the specific weapons of each category that it has (Blaker and Hamilton, 1977; Karber, Whitley, Herman, and Komer, 1979, pp. 1–1 to 1–3). Differences of opinion about the relative importance of categories or aspects of weapons are reduced by referring to an empirical-"type" formation. For American analyses, this standard has usually been the "type" U.S. armored division of a particular date, and so the referent for aggregate force measurements have been known as an "armored division equivalent," or ADE. ("Type" division refers to a kind of unit as determined by formal doctrinal assignment and table of organization and equipment, or "TO&E," rather than by actual assignment, employment, manning levels, or inventories. The reference standard needs to be updated periodically as weapons modernization and doctrinal changes alter the TO&E.)

The first component of the ADE methodology, the category evaluations, primarily reflects firepower rankings: a tank scores higher than a sidearm, and a missile battery more than a tank. The categories themselves, and the weights they are accorded, reflect expert judgment informed by historical analyses, experience, and practical assumptions. An early scheme, for example, used these categories with approximately these weights: artillery, 90; tanks, 85; infantry fighting vehicles, 50; anti-tank guided missiles, 30; attack helicopters, 70; mortars, 30; armored personnel carriers, 20; and squad weapons (rifles, 1, and machine guns, 5). (There was also a category for air defense weapons with a direct fire capability.) Obviously, there could be appealing alternatives to these categories and especially their relative weightings, particularly when climate, terrain, tactical posture, and enemy activity can be specified more precisely.

The second step, scoring individual weapons, generally emphasizes firepower, mobility, and survivability. The "firepower" of a main battle tank, for example, might be measured by taking into account experiments conducted at test ranges using the tank's main gun against different types of targets, the fire-control system (including the range-finder and computer), the internal layout and organization of the tank, the gun stabilization and platform stability, the amount of ammunition carried, and the rate of fire. The tank's "survivability" might be measured in terms of the quality and quantity of its armor, its speed, its ability to dispense obscurants (such as smoke), its size, the ability to depress the main gun, and the crew's ability to sense the external environment. In some circumstances, survivability could also reflect unrefueled range, ground pressure, horsepower-to-weight ratio (for acceleration), height, and the mean time between failure (MTBF) for critical subsystems (Dunnigan, 1983, pp. 57–61). Other categories of weapons might achieve survivability in other ways. Artillery, for example, historically had little protective armor, depending instead on mobility for survival. With enough quickness and a "shoot and scoot" doctrine, the enemy artillery could not usually target the gun quickly enough to kill it. (Contemporary advances in counter-battery radars might be changing this calculation; see Dunnigan, 1983, pp. 80–83.)

Different models of weapons can then be scored on these evaluation factors by comparing them to the designated referent model. These scores can be aggregated to provide a numerical index of the weapon's overall effectiveness, relative to the benchmark. Scoring a division's overall firepower is then a straightforward matter of aggregating the number of weapons in each category, modifying the total by the effectiveness index of the particular models, and modifying that result, in turn, by the score computed to the relative importance of the weapon category. (Hence, the U.S. Army's methodology, since abandoned, was named WEI/WUV—Weapons Effectiveness Index/Weighted Unit Value. The "type" division used as reference, of course, will have a certain total number of points that defines the standard "ADE.")

Similar principles guide the measurement of air and naval forces, although more measures are required because their "weapons systems" have substantially more flexibility among platform, launcher, and warhead. While not every deck, tube, and round is fully interchangeable, the greater possibility for tailoring forces means that, except for platform characteristics, "type" measures might have little relevance to capabilities configured for specific circumstances. (There is a similar, but more manageable, problem of including munitions quality in the scoring of tanks or artillery.) For example, there can be useful type measures for aircraft on a strike mission, such as the gross take-off weight with which it can launch. This factor is relevant to combat potential, but so too is the composition of the load-out. (What sort of bombs—conventional high-explosive, cluster bomb units, or fuel-air explosives—and are they smart or dumb? What sort of air-to-surface missiles, and how do they acquire, track, and home on different targets?)

For estimating the potential combat capability of aircraft, therefore, both sets of characteristics must be evaluated, for intercept roles (defeating enemy aircraft on the wing) as well as for strike missions (attacking ground targets; see Dunnigan, 1983, pp. 98–120). In measuring the intercept roles, the aircraft's speed, maneuverability, weapons, and electronics would be important. For strike roles, the same properties are of interest, but their physical meanings and measurements are quite different. (For example, maneuverability for intercept roles generally requires engineering that is different from that for strike operations.) In both instances, other major determinants of combat capability include combat radius, ability to operate at night and in bad weather, and ability to "turn around" rapidly on the ground in order to generate a high number of sorties. Most of these factors, in turn, can be expressed as the result of other measurements (e.g., durability, maintainability, and MTBF for critical components).

The "mix-and-match" problem is even more severe for measuring naval forces. The notional load-out of a large American carrier, for example, consists of 90 aircraft of three general types. Most are strike aircraft, which can be armed with a variety of weapons for attacking naval or land targets. About one-quarter are usually fighters, equipped with weapons to intercept and defeat hostile aircraft. The remaining category, about one-fifth of the load-out, consists of various support aircraft, including reconnaissance, airborne warning and control, anti-submarine warfare, and tankers for aerial refueling. The carrier itself operates in association with other ships. Altogether they comprise the Carrier (Vehicle) Battle Group (CVBG), the primary force unit in the American fleet (at least for purposes of estimating force needs in major theatres), which consist of an aircraft carrier and several associated reconnaissance systems, surface warfare ships, submarines, and fixed- and rotary-wing aircraft. The cannon, bombs, missiles, torpedoes, depth charges, and so on are the aircraft's weapons. The aircraft themselves are the carrier's weapons, and the carrier and its associated escorts are the weapons of the CVBG. Force unit tailoring by selecting among all of these according to need and availability is much more common and in many ways easier than with ground forces.

As a result, the capabilities of naval forces are usually measured in terms of specific attributes of particular subsystems. Platforms can be described in terms of speed, range, size (displacement), offensive and defensive electronics suites, armoring, and damage control. Weapons can be described in terms of lethality against a designated target, effective range, rate of fire, and resistance to countermeasures. Recent descriptions of Soviet naval forces, for example, characterize them in terms of length, displacement, armament, propulsion, and date of initial operational capability; aircraft, missiles, mines, and anti-submarine warfare capabilities are accorded separate component descriptions (Department of Defense, 1987, pp. 80–89). With such information, scores can be developed for different types of naval formations as desired for a particular estimate.

Shortcomings: Aggregations, Application, and Intangibles

The approaches just described serve to measure and compare weapons of different categories, types, and models, and even, when there is a "type" force unit for common reference, the firepower of certain combat organizations. Lacking such a referent, an aggregate of weapons in an integrated command setting cannot be readily calibrated, and the static firepower measures currently available cannot adequately capture the complex interrelationships of the modern combined-arms force. The reason has to do largely with a type of synergy: an organized, balanced force is needed to deal with a range of possible threats, and its components, regardless of the relative importance of their effectiveness indices or category weights, generally provide mutual support. This holds true for basic force units within a single service (ground force divisions, for example) as well as for combined-arms forces (such as Soviet *front* or Western theatre commands). To estimate the capability of a force, a measure of the effects of just this sort of integration is needed.

Another problem is to determine what parts of the overall inventory should be counted. Should all weapons be included or only those in fighting units? Then what about those weapons that are kept as assets for higher level commands to add as needed to the firepower of their subordinate units? Count only the weapons that are working right now? What about those that are undergoing scheduled maintenance or repair or are missing a part— should they be counted if they are likely to be back in operation in one day? in a week? longer? And should the same rules concerning "time of availability" be used to determine which naval and air forces, which reserves and reinforcements, to count as well, for both sides? The North Atlantic Treaty Organization (NATO)—Warsaw Pact airpower comparisons in Secretary of Defense Caspar Weinberger's 1987 report to Congress, for example, show a Pact advantage of 1.7 to 1 in tactical airpower within the NATO Guidelines Area, which "leaves out several air armies that are controlled by the Soviet Supreme High Command, but which would be available for combat in a European war. It does not count 900 French and Spanish aircraft, since those nations do not participate in the integrated NATO military structure. It also excludes Soviet strategic interceptors, 4,000 Soviet trainer aircraft that would be available, and Soviet transport helicopters that can be configured for attack roles" (Correll, 1987, p. 40). Moreover, as arms control provisions have made abundantly clear, "determining what fits in which category can be equally complicated. U.S. and Soviet definitions of 'heavy' bombers and ICBMs have differed drastically. Dual-purpose systems, such as ground attack aircraft that double as air defense interceptors, produce similar counting problems. Large missiles, divisions, ships, and so on in any given class count the same as small ones. Old weapons count the same as new. Service troops count the same as combatants in many basic manpower comparisons" (Collins, 1980, p. 11).

Furthermore, it is difficult to assign these scores and determine the counting rules, let alone interpret the results, without having some view of the use that will be made of the force—how and where it is likely to fight against what enemy capabilities. Scoring methodologies most often concentrate on measuring forces with respect to the main enemy in the most important theatre—the ability of the superpowers "to engage one another in high-intensity combat in a European-type climate and terrain spectrum." It is quite evident, however, that weapons should be counted and scored differently for different climates and terrains; "a U.S. force modernized to combat Soviet clients in the Middle East would doubtless be very different than one modernized to fight the Soviet Union itself in Central Europe" (Regan and Vogt, 1987, pp. 1–10).

Similar problems apply, by the way, when the estimate rather than the force is to be put to use, such as happens in connection with monitoring arms control agreements. For the kinds of agreements that have characterized U.S.–Soviet negotiating efforts for the past two decades, the determination of numerical limits for production or deployment of various categories of weapons has been of central concern. As a result, a divergence can arise between the significance of a weapon to military operations and its significance as a treaty item. These matters are likely to require some fine judgments, particularly when questions of readiness are involved. Equipment used for training or preserved in long-term storage might pose no threat today or for the next year, but could perhaps be made into militarily useful assets during the anticipated lifetime of the agreement.

Current measures of capability fail in a third major way: They cannot be precisely or systematically applied to many factors that have been major determinants of military performance. As has often been argued in the current war between Iran and Iraq, for example, "numbers do not tell the whole story. The quality of military leadership, combat experience, training, and command and control also count" (Karsh, 1987, p. 15). Because "people factors," the fighting spirit and skill of the troops and their leadership, cannot be readily measured, they are often estimated by making reference to factors that are assumed to be causal correlates. Training that emphasizes indoctrination is often credited with heavily influencing the fighting quality of troops. It is generally considered to include the development and manipulation of appeals to pride, primary groups of friends, and fear of disobeying orders. Leadership, which is more elusive and less readily infused, is often expected to be of higher quality when military traditions and social attitudes are supportive.

Even exercises can at best show correlates, such as the presence of certain skills and some contributing factors, such as morale and generalized problem-solving abilities. These correlates, again, are not themselves the subjects of interest, and they are less directly predictors of combat performance than is, for example, the thickness of a tank's armor or the effective range of an artillery piece. What might be debilitating for some under certain circumstances could prove irrelevant or even stimulating to improved performance for others in different settings, whether it be Grant's reputed drinking in Lincoln's day or the much-discussed face-off in the European Center Region of the 1970s between the field effects of excess in vodka and those of cannabis. (Some indicators of morale do relate directly to combat potential, such as the incidence of "left hand wounds" in the British forces in Africa during World War I; see Farwell, 1986, p. 209, probably just one of the twentieth-century variants on the Roman problems with the Murci, as noted by Gibbon, 1980, p. 362.). Could it be that, with the peculiar chemistry of the "people factors," defense planning would improve with infusions of Japanese-style corporate socialization rituals (Hart and Lind, 1986, pp. 246–48)?

Shortcomings: Force Multipliers (or Dividers)

It is also difficult to estimate the "outputs" of force design philosophy. With scoring of the WEI/WUV type, different kinds of maneuver units can be compared in terms of their equipment schedules, but as yet there is nothing comparable for the functions known as combat support and combat service support (CS/CSS). Nonetheless, these functions, it is widely believed, contribute heavily to combat performance:

Without *engineer support*, enemy and natural obstacles become insurmountable. Rivers and minefields cannot economically be crossed. Fortifications become much less effective. With no *signal support*, communications become spotty at best and will most likely break down entirely under the stress of combat. With no *transportation support*, units run out of ammunition, fuel, food, and everything else within days. Without *military police*, the traffic problems soon become intolerable, prohibiting any movement. Combat troops must be detailed to take care of prisoners of war and perform other security duties. Without *maintenance support*, the equipment will probably be in no condition even to enter combat, much less continue for any length of time. Without *chemical troops*, enemy use of chemical or nuclear weapons will stop troops cold. Without *electronic-warfare troops*, the enemy will be able to eavesdrop on communications and disrupt them at will, without retaliation. Without *head-*

quarters, you will not be able to respond to enemy activity or initiate any effective action yourself (Dunnigan, 1983, p. 85).

Improving the measurements of these functions is important for improving resource management and efficiency. There is a particular additional interest in measuring CS/CSS contributions when assessing force balances, especially for Europe, because they dramatize the sharp differences between American and Soviet force design philosophies. Western, particularly U.S., divisions have a much heavier complement of CS/CSS troops and equipment than do their Soviet-style counterparts Given a division's worth of resources, the West spends relatively less on front-line combat "teeth."

The advantages claimed for the respective approaches tend to reflect the strategic situation and resources of each side. The Soviet Union, for example, is primarily a land power, situated with land lines of communication directly to the most important theatres of potential warfare, with poorly educated troops and officers. Soviet doctrine highlights offense and the importance of rapid advance, and emphasizes its determination to capitalize on number rather than quality. Accordingly, the Soviet force structure is much "leaner" and features a significantly higher ratio of "tooth to tail." Most of its units that are forward deployed in Germany, for example, are equipped with high-firepower weapons and are tailored for rapid advance. In all probability, they would be quickly used up in combat, but it is unanimously expected that reinforcement would be far easier for the Soviet side than for NATO. Little initiative is expected at local command levels; by Western standards, troop-leading procedures are relatively primitive. The Soviets would seek to maintain the effectiveness of the attack by following a "unit replacement" approach to casualties: maneuver units would continue to fight, without replacement of casualties, until the unit itself was used up (probably at about the 35 to 50 percent level of effectiveness).

These factors, it should be noted, are not immutable. The Soviets have made a vital and continuing effort to improve their capabilities in accord with their views of the requirements of future wars (Odom, 1983). Among their recent efforts there has surfaced a concern with improving leadership and initiative in field commanders: "The lack of sufficient intelligence or contradictory intelligence stresses and does not free the commander from his obligation to make a timely decision.... It is these original and daring decisions that permit surprise attacks on the enemy, catch him unaware and thus attain the best results in battle" (Grinkevich, 1986, pp. 91–92).

NATO differs strikingly from the Soviets with regard to available resources and strategic setting. A defensive posture offers the advantages of prepared positions, terrain channeling, and prearranged obstacles, mines, and demolitions. With more advanced economies and better educated troops and officers, NATO fields weapons that may be higher in aggregate lethality, notwithstanding their lower numbers, and it provides communications and headquarters staff to capitalize on local initiative and operational flexibility. With its advantages in mobilization during a war lasting at least several months, NATO's doctrine emphasizes establishing a defensive line and denying rapid advance to the enemy. This implies that NATO's in-place forces would have to be equipped well enough and be able to care for themselves until reinforcements could arrive. For NATO, this could take much longer than hoped, depending on the campaign at sea and against the airbases in Europe. Correspondingly, NATO maintains an "individual replacement" approach for unit casualties, both weapons and people, which can provide some benefit in training and morale. This approach also anticipates some advantage in numbers when facing relatively seasoned, and therefore worn-out, Soviet forces, and an advantage in experience when facing full-strength, but therefore relatively inexperienced Soviet forces.

To date, these differences in setting, resources, and force design philosophy have not been reducible to a single comparative measure. Nor have static analyses been able to address them usefully. Barry R. Posen, for example, tries to do so by manipulating the ADE scores. Noting the differences in inputs (implicitly the support costs) between the forces of the Pact and those of the West, Posen argues that NATO's military leaders must believe that such investments have at least comparable output benefits in terms of combat effectiveness. He then proceeds to award them a 50-percent increase in firepower (and uses that increase in his analysis to defend frontage! See Posen, 1984–1985, p. 69).

But support structure does not, of course, add to firepower. A tank, no matter how well commanded, maintained, and supplied, is still just one tank, and a division has just so many of them. Whether people and weapons perform close to their rated potential in actual operations is actually the motivation behind CS/CSS investments. Consequently, one might often better view "imperfect C^3I as a 'force divider,' rather than consider C^3I contributions as 'force multipliers' " (Myer, 1986, p. ES–2).

What is needed to solve these problems are sustained efforts to improve measures for scoring and comparing the quantitites and qualities of dissimilar forces, for assessing and depicting differences in the mix and rate of change of fielded forces, trends in performance growth, and the outputs of entire force-fielding systems (from statement of need, through design, validation, production, procurement, and introduction throughout the force). The performance potential of weapons equipment must be scored and then adjusted for intangibles, including personnel, C^3I, and logistics.

One such effort has been sponsored by the Defense Department's Office of Net Assessment (Regan and Vogt, 1987). This study computes an index for tactical airpower assets, for example, by scoring the key characteristics of the airframe itself: payload, range, basing modes and stand-off weapon range, maneuverability, and speed, many of which in turn result from other calculations and aggregations. The resulting index is then adjusted for the performance of the aircraft's combat support systems: target acquisition and guidance/fire control, susceptibility to countermeasures, weapon enhancements, navigation, and survivability. Next, an adjustment is made for factors reflecting obsolescence and productivity (sortie generation on a sustained basis). The resulting scores are then applied to the actual fielded force, taking into account the distribution of assets to tacair (tactical air) roles and inventory levels. Finally, that index in turn is adjusted for measures of such factors as C^3I systems effects, aircrew proficiency, logistics and maintenance, multi-role capability, and the tactical impact of inventory changes (i.e., the relative importance of numbers; for example, the effect is probably higher for air superiority combat than for strike missions; see Regan and Vogt, 1987, pp. 2–5).

To address the problem of indexing combined-arms forces, there are "adjustment coefficients...to enable summation of...values of different classes of conventional weapons to enable aggregate assessments of, say, air defense modernization or battlefield fire support modernization, thereby combining the potential of both surface and airborne weapon systems" (Regan and Vogt, 1987, pp. 1–12). The approach taken to develop a single overall figure of merit for total forces involves developing a baseline index for each of the baseline systems. That is, the performance indices for the baseline systems for scoring air defense weaponry (the HAWK missile), artillery (the M–109 SP howitzer), and armor (the M–60A1), for example, are themselves scored against an overall performance referent against equivalent target structures, thereby providing an intercomponent ratio that can be used to calculate an overall force index. The referent system chosen was that for the tactical airpower component, the F–4B Phantom and the assessed performance ratios "are intended to be indicative of the overall relative performance of the aircraft baseline system to the baseline systems of the other [force components] when the aircraft is performing in the tacair roles most similar to the ones in which the others perform" (Regan and Vogt, 1987, p. B–3).

With such improvements, static measures can better indicate trends in force modernization, comparative efficiencies in investment accounts, and gross disparities between competitors in major weapons. In some cases they can serve as secondary indicators of perceived capability. But the measures are not themselves the estimate; they leave out too much that is operationally significant. "Caution must be exercised to keep in mind the importance of balance and mix in force structure," for example (Regan and Vogt, 1987, p. B–3). More colloquially, the proverbial horseshoe nail that cost the battle is important to an operational force, even though it has no WEI/WUV score. Nor can the improved measures adequately depict the effects of time on the already hard-to-measure factors of aggregations, applications, intangibles, and support elements.

ESTIMATING THE FORCE IN OPERATION

As a result, static analyses usually need to lean heavily on military judgment and putative "rules of thumb" in order to address the richness of an actual operational context. But the judgment and the rules usually derive from battles and experiences that could not have looked much like war between U.S. and Soviet forces in NATO's Center Region. They are usually sprinkled into the analyses in ways that are too unsystematic and ad hoc to be used for disciplined comparisons. As Philip Karber suggests, "In the absence of established procedures [to measure the impact of . . . qualitative factors], military judgment must be used. However, judgment varies, and it is difficult to get agreement on the importance of any one of the qualitative factors influencing combat. Second, the WEI/WUV is often used to establish a theater balance of forces, and it is difficult to apply an analysis of specific operational or qualitative factors to an entire theater of operations. The theater level of analysis is simply too high to permit consideration of specific operational factors in any meaningful way" (Karber et al., 1979, pp. 1–2 to 1–3).

Static analyses of the European balance, for example, often fall back on comparing the Warsaw Pact and NATO in terms of gross aggregates, such as manpower, weaponry, maneuver units, and nominal force densities computed for a linear front. They then typically assume certain force levels available to each side, postulate certain a priori performance standards as requirements (for Blue *and* Red), calculate the results, and assert conclusions about policy for a wide range of circumstances. John J. Mearsheimer's (1983) arguments about conventional deterrence in Europe typify this kind of thinking. Choosing to examine what many consider the best case for NATO, that of full strategic warning, decision, and mobilization, he totals all the forces available to NATO for Center Region combat, compares them with some of the forces available to the Pact in the same area, and finds that NATO is not outnumbered by more than 2:1 in manpower, maneuver units, or major weaponry. Nor will it be, because, he asserts, NATO's reinforcement capabilities are adequate to keep pace with those of the Pact. Mearsheimer refers to a "widely believed" rule of thumb that offensives are successful only if they achieve superiority of at least 3:1 over the defense along a major axis of attack, and with arithmetic and geography he cannot find a way for the Pact to achieve that favorable ratio. Even when it appears that they can, as a practical matter they cannot. To avoid overcrowding, he feels that some will have to wait behind, out of the battle, while NATO crosses their "T." As a result, he argues, the Pact cannot count on a breakthrough to produce a lightning victory. This means that they lose, because the West has the definite advantage in a war of attrition. Consequently, according to Mearsheimer, NATO is successfully deterring the Soviets; Q.E.D. (see also Mearsheimer, 1984–985, p. 45).

The sketch simplifies three important operational complications.

1. The "front" can be very deep. In fact, the elasticity of force density over both space and time has been changing and growing ever more problematic with the fielding of new weapons with deeper reach, the growth of firepower in echelons above corps, and automated troop-leading procedures. The notion of defining force needs in terms of "covering your front" evokes images of trenches in World War I (static measures, perhaps, conjuring up views of a static war). On the modern European battlefield, threatened by Soviet Spetsnaz units, Operational Maneuver Groups, and Reconnaissance Strike Complexes, there also would be a need to "cover your six." This change has also caught the Soviets' attention:

The advent in the NATO armies of highly effective homing ammunition, airblast and cluster bombs, shells, and mines, multiple-launch rocket systems, combat helicopters, etc., has changed even further the principle of concentration of major efforts at key sectors. To begin with, combat can now be undertaken with considerably less personnel and materiel, and in shorter times, even in those sectors where troops are acting without nuclear weapons. Secondly, it is now possible to strike hostile positions througout their depth simultaneously. And this is the case for a new appraisal of the necessity to obtain the requisite manpower and equipment densities in the main direction, both when breaking through fortified lines and concentrating the main troop effort in defense, as well as for other approaches to defining criteria of combat formations dispersal to assure their higher survivability and reliable protection against powerful attacks (Vorobyov, 1987, p. 89).

2. Breakthrough can involve shock. The basic conceptualization of battle activity that can be accommodated by static measure approaches permits understanding breakthrough and maneuver only in terms of attrition. Posen's analysis is more helpful here, because he includes tactical airpower along with ground forces, assumes less of a mobilization-time ladder to get NATO out of its force-deficit hole, takes into account that there are ways for armies to concentrate forces with very high density, and looks at some empirical data in an effort to estimate attrition and exchange rates (Posen, 1984–1985). Nonetheless, his model still formulates breakthrough and maneuver as though they were similar to erupting pustules. The defensive skin, if unable to expand sufficiently, is ruptured, and some of the surrounding tissue is traumatized.

Actual breakthrough operations can be quite different. The event itself, its development, and the consequences of it might all be much more sudden, and they might have much more to do with shock effects in the command and control system, saturation of communications, or catastrophic breakdown in intelligence support than with aggregate sector balances and tactical exchange rates. It is nearly impossible to depict such effects with static measures; at best, they can try to represent the effects of damage (including shock and surprise) to the C^3I functions in terms of nodal attrition. That is, they model damage by taking pieces off the chess board, whereas to be more realistic operationally would require being able to model impaired decision-making by the chess player, certain spastic behaviors in the pieces themselves, erratic dysfunctions in communications between the chess player and his pieces and in his perceptions of the game, certain types of autonomous behavior by the pieces, and so forth (Marshall, 1984).

What is needed instead is an approach that can better take into account the critical questions of timing, in order to estimate relative capabilities in forcing advantageous tactical opportunities. An attacker, for example,

will almost always choose to mass. Massing allows an attacker to concentrate his combat capability in a narrow sector in an attempt to achieve a breakthrough. The sector of concentration is typically 6 to 10 kilometers wide, compared to a normal axis width of perhaps 60 kilometers.... the attacker's advantage is almost always transitory, since the defender will attempt to laterally move fires and reserves in a manner such as to thwart the massing. The real issue becomes one of how quickly this movement can be accomplished, and how well the sector being massed against can hold as forces move laterally (Bennett et al., 1987, p. 40).

The attacker's relative advantage also depends on the character of the defense and choices about whether to accept or decline battle. The type of defense will probably depend "upon operational choices, time, and the availability of engineering resources. Five different kinds of defensive postures [can be identified] in terms of increasing effectiveness: (1) a delaying defense, (2) a hasty defense, (3) a deliberate defense, (4) a prepared defense, and (5) a fortified defense" (Bennett et al., 1978, p. 41).

In addition, the possibilities of functionally multiplying the force ratio by achieving tactical advantage also need to be considered, including strategic maneuver (flanking) and surprise (which Dunnigan estimates as being capable of generating an equivalent force ratio reaching 5:1 in some cases; Dunnigan, 1983, p. 420). Sample attacker/defender force ratios that have been used as "threshold" values in earlier years include 5:1 for breakthrough, 3:1 for offensive, 1.7:1 for prepared defense, and 1.4:1 for hasty defense (Blaker and Hamilton, 1977, p. 60). Within this more detailed context, breakthrough should probably be considered, as recent Rand work suggests, "as a discrete event as part of a process involving several *phases of battle;* assault, breakthrough, exploitation, and pursuit.... attrition and rates of advance [are calculated] differently for the different phases" (Bennet et al. 1987, p. 41). These more refined models are particularly helpful when used together with the longstanding and continuing inquiries into the historical accuracy and present applicability of Lanchester-oriented analyses that emphasize force ratios (Merritt and Sprey, 1972; Goldich, 1986–1987).

3. The Soviets plan to win. Estimates based only on static measures often completely miss the real strategic problem at hand. In most cases, analysts relying on static measurements in estimating the adequacy of force balances must adopt a methodological posture of immutable omniscience, inasmuch as they must impute to both sides a view of the strategic situation, an analytic methodology, and a set of performance criteria which, if not met, must lead unquestionably to certain outcomes. In effect, they evaluate the West's position by assigning the cards and playing the Soviets' hand for them. Mearsheimer, for example, argues that if the Soviets cannot be sure of achieving a lightning victory then they will be deterred. It is most likely, however, that the performance criteria that will matter to the Soviets (or the West, for that matter) are (a) not simple ones to be applied in blanket fashion across all circumstances; (b) quite likely to be very different from those of the adversary and quite independent of the circumstances; and (c) included in vigorous programs to remedy whatever shortcomings they perceive, using Soviet goals and Soviet methodology, in the present and future military balance.

Concerning the importance of circumstance, consider Paul K. Davis' finding that "a single model of the Soviet Union can exhibit the following behaviors: In contexts in which NATO has invaded the Warsaw Pact and the Soviet Union sees itself in the ultimate showdown between the socialist and capitalist worlds (the scenario underlying most Soviet doctrinal writing), [it] will follow doctrinal tenets—and will even initiate nuclear war of that seems necessary. However, in contexts in which, for example, the war began with a Soviet conventional invasion after secret negotiations between the two Germanys, and in which the Soviet invasion was predicated upon an analysis that occupation of Western Germany could be accomplished quickly, conventionally, and with little risk of U.S. nuclear use, [it] might revert to a 'bargaining behavior' in preference to a pure 'warfighting behavior' should NATO prove cohesive and successful in thwarting the conventional campaign" (Davis, 1987, p. 26).

The other problems with these approaches—the assumption that Soviet calculations and assessments look like those of the West and the assumption that a strategic obstacle now is an obstacle forever—are considered more fully in the next section. Here it is sufficient to note that the use of static methodologies seems somehow to have encouraged an assumption of empirical stasis as well. Certainly, there was nothing wrong with Posen's view that "a survey of the history of armored warfare . . . suggests that the place to begin any assessment of the current NATO-Warsaw Pact military balance is the so-called 'breakthrough' battle. Armored attackers customarily have concentrated their best resources on narrow sectors of their enemy's front, hoping to achieve a degree of quantitative superiority that could cause a major rupture in the defense line. Such ruptures permit the deep exploitations" (Posen, 1984–1985, p. 49). The problem is that both he and Mearsheimer, having argued that breakthrough is unlikely under certain circumstances, conclude that NATO is on the right track in terms of investments (Posen) and posture (Mearsheimer).

Yet it now appears that the Soviets

believe that both sides possess enormous military capabilities that cannot be rapidly destroyed, even in nuclear conditions; thus, they foresee prolonged theater campaigns.

The operations may begin with a bitter struggle to seize the initiative, encompassing extreme destruction and mass casualties, and may spread to a multi-theater conflict. To achieve victory under these conditions, the Soviets believe that forces equipped with large quantitites of weaponry are required. These forces must be capable of attaining overwhelming superiority on the battlefield, coping with the expected heavy losses resulting from attrition, and ensuring a continuous supply of fresh forces and equipment for prolonged theater operations (Department of Defense, 1987, p. 64).

The need at hand is less to debate Soviet doctrine than to emphasize the importance of exploring operational issues, including the possibility of a responsive threat. Simple models for static analyses can help describe alternatives at high levels of aggregation. For particular questions of modernization, force structure, or doctrine, they may do too much violence. It is certain that they "*cannot be used to predict the outcome of specific engagements. Moreover, they should not be used alone to determine detailed acquisition strategies*" (Regan and Vogt, 1987, p. 1–4; emphasis in original).

Using Scenarios

To examine these questions, more extensive calculations are needed, and scenario-based analyses can often help. Static measures are used as inputs, but they are merged with models and approximations of operational functions. Then alternative developmental paths are examined and compared interactively under varying assumptions. Generally, this approach is appealing when more powerful analytic tools are yet unavailable or not sufficiently broad in applicability. Certainly the situation involved in estimating military capabilities is of this sort; no single theory or view of nuclear war, or of conventional war in Europe, seems sure to prove correct. As a result, estimates of capabilities must consider performance levels under alternative circumstances, which fully determined models using static measures cannot readily accommodate (Davis, 1987, pp. 25ff.). Scenario-based analyses seek to depict capabilities by identifying key tasks and resources across changing times and circumstances. The developmental sequence describes the phases of war, whereas the precise interactions of attack and response describe a particular scenario.

Systems analytic formulations of the strategic nuclear balance provide familiar illustrations (for example, Seiler, 1983, pp. 3–56, which is largely used here, and Rudwick, 1969, pp. 79–252). The key circumstances to specify (and vary) in these scenarios are the two conditions that fundamentally affect operational developments (Seiler, 1983, pp. 28–30). First is the static precombat balance of forces (total inventory or total active inventory? day-to-day or generated alert?), together with attack sequence decisions—crudely, who shoots first and how many bullets are there. Variations in this set of assumptions can be used to test the implications of being surprised about Soviet capabilities, such as covert generation, hidden assets, unanticipated allocation of "theatre" bombers, and of surprising the Soviets, perhaps by using central strategic systems in theatre operations.

The second basic condition involves specifying the developmental sequence ("time line") for the option or strategy being examined. For example, what if the Soviets shoot first but against strategic military targets only with minimal collateral damage? The adequacy of the U.S. retaliatory force, then and in general, will depend heavily on the pace and sequence of events. Time, in fact, proves to be critical to the whole range of potential and applied capabilities. The time that elapses before attacks are begun is tied, on the one hand, to the size and composition of the available inventory (alert level, time sustained in stressful postures, attrition to operational loads or enemy action), and on the other hand, to the ability to damage the enemy (the ability to know the precise location of enemy forces, and how well his intelligence and reconnaissance assets are functioning, which might, for example, call for attacking with bombers rather than re-entry vehicles). If the war is protracted, consideration of the problems posed by possible reconstitution and restrike activities by both sides will be required. Timing also affects logistics and power projection, throughout all phases of the war.

In addition, the time element heavily influences (though not necessarily in a simple or straightforward fashion) the probabilities for escalation and war termination. For example, "the decisions to launch a first strike should *not* be uniquely sensitive to the 'price of going second'... but should instead be sensitive to: (1) tactical warning of an opponent's first strike, (2) the *absolute* level of capability each side would have after the various attacks or exchanges—i.e., the absolute capability to execute various short-term and continuing operations against the other side's forces (and urban-industrial complex), (3) the assessment of the opponent's will and intentions, and (4) a number of command-control issues such as the capability to launch under attack, the assured survival of key leadership, the assured survival of communications necessary for retaliation, and the ability to maintain control over forces generally" (Davis, 1986, p. 26, emphasis in original; concerning war termination, see especially Ikle, 1971).

This scenario methodology cannot, of course, remedy deficiencies in information or insight. Scenario-based estimates of the nuclear balance are particularly sensitive to assumptions about U.S. knowledge of the location and characteristics of targets in the Soviet Union, and about the performance of Soviet weapons against American targets (Seiler, 1983, p. 13). Since there is no certainty about the quality and adequacy of intelligence in advance of a war or during it, there can be no certainty about choosing what to target for military purposes or whether the fielded force has the requisite destructive power. In addition, the operational nuclear environment is very unclear; weapons system reliability and communications are worrisome. Moreover, by now there is probably widespread agreement that the set of scenarios used in assessments of capabilities must be somewhat broader and more flexible than in the past. A few canonical scenarios may tend to inhibit proper consideration of true Soviet capabilities, while delimiting the span of required options for appropriate U.S. response. Increased flexibility in designing response potentials is not necessarily an avoidance of the specific; it may in fact call for more precision. Neither is flexibility a cover for uncertainty, for flexibility builds both actual and apparent potential for dealing with uncertainty. Current concepts of winning, victory, political gain in the face of military loss, acquisitive war goals, denial purposes, and similar descriptors suggest that focus on achieving deterrence can create a void in planning for cases where deterrence fails or falters (Foster and Walker, 1982, p. 81).

But the use of scenarios has clarified why these things are important. This approach still does not model real operations, but it can help assess vulnerabilities, show the importance of certain assumptions, check on the realism of certain planning factors, and stress the planning case—all to provide a basis for then acting to invest, reinforce, change doctrine, emphasize training, and redirect diplomacy. In this way scenario-based analyses are vital adjuncts to helping hedge against technological, political, and strategic surprise (Rudwick, 1969, 190–215). Furthermore, because they direct attention to specifying circumstances and interactions more explicitly, they are more likely to avoid prematurely "freezing" a particular definition of a problem (which the static analyses of the conventional balance in Europe have tended to do). In this way they can help guard against "future surprise." It should be kept in mind, after all, that such surprise can result not only from changes in the objective environment, but also from changes in the outlook of analysts and estimators. As Fred Ikle observes,

There was a time, for instance, when American strategists recommended civil defense measures to protect urban populations, when American arms control proposals argued that reductions in conventional forces should precede limitations on nuclear weapons, and when the official United States position belittled the risk of nuclear accidents and accidental war. Since then, all these positions have been reversed at least once and in some cases twice. During the same period, the Soviet government has turned upside down its position of demanding that reductions in nuclear armaments (if not their abolition) had to precede arms control measures designed to make mutual deterrence more "stable"; and Soviet spokesmen, who only a few years ago argued that active defenses against missiles should be increased rather than limited, now take the opposite view (p. 128).

The lesson is to avoid becoming fixated on one dominant scenario and seek instead a sufficient richness of qualitative and quantitative detail to address a range of plausible scenarios.

NEEDED: ESTIMATES OF THE ENEMY'S ESTIMATES

Scenario-based "dynamic" analyses can enrich estimates by including operational issues involving actual complex circumstances of combat, maneuver, and outcomes. They can be difficult to use for just the same reasons. It can be challenging, for example, to depict their results in a summary fashion that is still descriptive and meaningful (Seiler, 1983, pp. 31–39). A more subtle, subjective problem can also develop, in that the added richness and complexity can make it easier to forget Werner Heisenberg's warning that "since the measuring device has been constructed by the observer... we have to remember that what we observe is not nature in itself but nature exposed to our method of questioning."

A scenario-based analysis of the strategic balance, for example, would provide a particular view of the balance under certain conditions; that would not itself be a view of strategic deterrence. "While a favorable balance [of central strategic systems] may be a necessary condition for deterrence, it may or may not be sufficient" (Seiler, 1983, p. 54). The distinction is crucial. The balance can be understood as having an objective state that is epistemologically independent of how it is estimated by us or the Soviets. Deterrence, however, is an emergent property that might result from a great number of complex interactions, especially including Soviet estimates. They are quite likely to be very different from ours in their approaches to measurement and in their views of what should be measured. They might turn out to be better in certain respects, perhaps worse in others, but to ignore them is to foreswear meaningful efforts to influence Soviet behavior in peace, crisis, and war.

It is generally appreciated that these differences can determine whether a particular capability has a deterring effect. Less appreciated is that these differences speak directly to the very definition of capability—what would actually count in combat.

The Anglo-German competition in naval combatants illustrates this relationship. When Great Britain introduced the *Dreadnought* in 1905 in its naval competition with Germany, it did so from a position of superior technology. In antebellum calculations, British estimators would surely have given a substantial edge to their fleet; the new British ships, as Lord Fisher had directed, had been designed to emphasize speed above all. But particularly with the Battle of Jutland in May 1916 it became clear that British estimates were substantially in error: "The British Admiralty naturally focused on the German navy. Estimating its current strength [numbers] posed little difficulty.... The truly hard problems were to estimate the quality of the German navy as a fighting force and the strategy it would employ if war came.... It was not until well into the war itself (and in some cases after) that the Admiralty appreciated the superiority of German range finders, shells, mines, and torpedoes, not to mention the great advantage of the design of watertight subdivisions in heavy warships" (Kennedy, 1984, pp. 182–83).

A number of operational factors contributed to surprising the British, including an important element of "subjective technology" that affected British planning long before the war began:

Fisher and the other Royal Navy reformers were accustomed to the assumption that battles would be fought at 1,000 to 2,000 yards. Fisher hoped that his ideal capital ship (the *Invincible* type) would have a seven-knot speed advantage over ordinary fleets (25 knots to 18, plus the advantage of turbines in sustained sea-speed), and would thus overtake or pull away from another ship at 14,000 yards per hour. If 1,000 yards is the most lethal range and 3,000 yards out of effective range, a ship with this speed advantage could pull out of range or close the enemy in eight minutes. The resulting flexibility confers an enormous advantage. Even at 5,000 yards, the kind of range Fisher considered "long" when *Dreadnought* and *Invincible* were designed, most of this advantage remains. But if the maximum range is 14,000 yards it will take an hour to cover the same distance, at 21,000 yards an hour and a half—within which time a ship could sustain crippling damage (Fairbanks, 1987, pp. 10–11).

This case illustrates one major reason for working hard to estimate what the opponent thinks he is doing—to estimate his estimates. Capabilities might be defined differently by the adversary, and he might be right. (On the related critical issue of the ability of the Great Powers to adjust to such mistakes—a sort of "elasticity of estimate error"—and more generally on the matter of which aspects of military institutions proved to be important to wartime effectiveness, see the research efforts being organized by Millett and Murray, 1986.) An opponent's estimates can often be read, albeit imperfectly, in his force posture—weapons, force structure, readiness, and all the rest.

Most states do not build forces randomly, or just to be in fashion, or purely because of bureaucratic momentum. They build toward some mission, to meet some threat, in accordance with some doctrinal rationale—that is, with purpose. To speak of force development policy, then, is to speak of the rationale for developing specific kinds and sizes of forces. Why have tank divisions instead of infantry divisions? Why ICBM's, IRBM's, and ABM's? (Odom, 1985, p. 1).

Instances in which very different approaches are taken to very similar problems call for particularly close attention. The British started with technological superiority and emphasized speed. The Germans, initially less advantaged, took a different course and came out better off, even though both sides had the same set of variables and relationships with which to design ships. Today there are similarly notable, and worrisome, asymmetries. "The Soviet Union has generally been very advanced in working out new rationales for forces development. Its unclassified military literature is among the richest in the world, which is indicative of the existence of an even more extensive classified analysis. Even a casual familiarity with Soviet military force structure would convince a reader of Soviet military literature that there is a strong causal relationship between Soviet force development policy and actual Soviet force building" (Odom, 1985, p. 1).

For several years now the Soviets have taken a much more serious attitude than the West to the possibility of building meaningful defenses against nuclear attack. They have equipped and trained their forces in the Center Region and elsewhere for conventional military operations in environments contaminated with radioactivity, toxic chemicals, and germs. Their planning emphasizes the control of time across a wide spectrum of conflict scenarios that integrate a full range of escalatory potentials. In these and several other respects, Soviet views and practices differ sharply from American approaches (Trulock, 1986).

Taking seriously the effort to account for the opponent's posture, and trying to replicate and understand his estimates, might in some cases lead to preventing technological surprise (as in the British *Dreadnought* case). In other cases, it could provide indications about how to influence the adversary—not from the point of view of signalling intent so much as deploying the capabilities he finds to be the most attention-getting in terms of actual warfighting operations. (On this point and the general improverishment of strategic analysis at the hands of "crisis management," see Cohen, 1985–1986.) If it should turn out, for example, that the Soviets have a high opinion of the importance of F–16s to NATO's muscle in the Center Region, then it might be worth thinking about deploying a few extra squadrons of them to Germany during the next Berlin face-off—even if professional military opinion in the West finds the Soviet views to be exaggerated, and even if NATO's doctrine would call for deploying more air defense fighters first.

Once again, such insights into enemy estimates are telling in terms of Western capabilities, because estimates must consider, explicitly or otherwise, an application for the capability being estimated—a "for what?" and "under what circumstances?" set of calibrating parameters on the estimative process. American estimates have frequently had one overriding purpose: the deterrence of a deliberate strategic attack by the Soviet Union. Yet even when the United States seemed successful in accomplishing that objective, it was somehow incapable of deterring or defeating a host of other threats and attacks, such as Soviet military adventures in the Third World and terrorist assaults against its people and possessions. In fact, "it is usually not true that policies designed to deter a limited military attack will automatically deter any less violent threat. Often, open attack will not be 'the worst case,' merely the most obvious and unambiguous one, and for that reason in many ways the easiest, not the hardest, to deal with" (George and Smoke, 1974, pp. 78–79).

In the contemporary strategic environment, an estimate of deterrent capabilities cannot even stop when war begins. Shaping the probabilities for intrawar escalation and war termination remain important goals even (perhaps especially) once the shooting starts and they are important for peacetime planning (Kecskemeti, 1958; Ikle, 1971). While fighting or trying to end the war, as well as before it, "it is not America's general capacities that will help deter a specific threat but her capacity to deal with the particulars of that threat. The United States must possess practical, usable, and specific military options, and applying these options must be politically feasible" (George and Smoke, 1974, pp. 81–82). Albert Wohlstetter raised similar concerns about nuclear options in his classic "The Delicate Balance of Terror" (1959).

It is therefore critical to be able to estimate "the particulars of that threat," and that is a second major reason for trying very hard to estimate the opponent's estimates. Soviet force planning, for example, reveals a recurring pattern of activity that flows essentially from the traditional "cycle spelled out by Frunze.... First, military theorists identify the set of new technologies that are influencing warfare; next, they define the nature of future war; then they assess the adversaries' means and determine their own requirements for doctrine and forces as well as the implications for the state's economic and social policies" (Odom, 1987, p. 45). The most recent iteration of this process has led to

large changes in command and control, higher tempo for the theater offense, and much deeper operations much earlier than envisioned in the 1950s and 1960s.... Multifront operations on a frontage of over 500 kilometers aimed at moving 1200 kilometers within a month is a breathtaking concept when compared to 50 to 100 kilometers of offense as envisioned earlier. The concept of a long war, possibly of no use of nuclear weapons, of strategic defense, of coordinating offensive naval operations with theater campaigns—these are indications of doctrinal concepts and concomitant force builing goals that exceed anything we have imagined about Soviet military capabilities in the past (Odom, 1987, pp. 40–41).

And this is really the third major reason for concentrating efforts on understanding enemy estimates: Soviet and Western forces have had no significant combat against each other for over forty years. In 1914, "the British, like the other belligerents, fought a war which they had failed to imagine" (Kennedy, 1985, p. 204). For all the major powers, without exception, "pre-World War I estimates of military capabilities seem in hindsight to have been woefully wrong" (May, 1984, p. 507). Today the major powers "may be worse off than those before the First World War. They can count missiles, bombers, carriers, submarines, and armored divisions at least as precisely as governments before 1914 could count guns, horses, and dreadnoughts, but now, as then, no one can be confident what the totals signify" (May, 1985, p. 530).

As a result, intelligence and estimates are more important today than ever before. Thanks to military technology and the strategic competition, neither the stakes nor the uncertainty have ever been so high. "In reality, [today] even more than in 1914, certainly far more than in 1939, intelligence analysts, staff officers, and decision-makers have to rely on imagination rather than experience to assess capabilities" (May 1984, p. 530). Yet, as John Hines and

George Kraus observe, the imagination of American estimators has been frequently deficient in dangerous ways:

While there are many areas in which we could break out technologically and outflank the Soviets, we are in danger of losing our edge, if not the competition, because we have been outflanked in the area of strategic and operational thinking. Our focus on hardware development and hardware competition in the absence of any long-term comprehensive plan for employment not only inhibits our own strategy development, but also our ability to discern the strategies of an opponent who is unaccustomed to thinking about weapons and technological competition outside the full operational context in which they would be used (Hines and Kraus, 1986, p. 28).

Sustained and concerted attention to the estimates of others can help school the needed imagination, reduce the uncertainty in strategic planning, and constrict the possibility of technological surprise. For both psychological and operational reasons, there is no substitute for methodologies that can help ask how Birnam Wood might come to Dunsinane. As Frank Hubbard noted: "It's what a fellow thinks he knows that hurts him."

American estimates seem particularly susceptible to errors of the "thinks-he-knows" variety. Paradoxically, they are primarily inward-looking: they respond to questions, accept definitions, and use measurements that make sense within the American approach to war. Senators and congressmen perennially ask members of the Joint Chiefs whether they would rather have the Soviet force posture. Defense analysts repeatedly estimate whether American commanders would feel confident in assaulting NATO with the forces of the Warsaw Pact. Time and again forecasts are made projecting how long it will take for the Soviets to field systems analogous to those that the United States developed to address something that the United States found to be a problem. In other words, American estimates proceed by projecting American purposes onto the Soviet force posture. The results, mistakenly presented as estimates of Soviet capabilities, are actually evaluations of how well Soviet forces might be able to accomplish American objectives.

Missing here—and vitally important—are evaluations of adversary forces for adversary purposes. Serious efforts to replicate the opponent's estimates can help keep American estimates focused on efforts to understand the external strategic environment.

REFERENCES

Bennet, Bruce W., Carl M. Jones, Arthur M. Bullock, and Paul K. Davis. 1987. *Theater Warfare Modeling in the Rand Strategy Assessment System*. Santa Monica, Calif.: Rand. Draft report prepared for Office of Secretary of Defense/Office of Net Assessment, WD–2724–1-NA.

Blaker, James, and Andrew Hamilton. 1977. *Assessing the NATO/Warsaw Pact Military*

Balance. Congressional Budget Office. Washington, D.C.: U.S. Government Printing Office.

Cohen, Eliot A. 1985–1986. Why We Should Stop Studying the Cuban Missile Crisis. *National Interest* 2 (Winter):3–13.

Collins, John M. 1980. *U.S.-Soviet Military Balance: Concepts and Capabilties, 1960–1980*. New York: McGraw-Hill.

Correll, John T. 1987. Why NATO Needs a Conventional Defense. *Air Force* Magazine 70 (August):38–46.

Davis, Paul D. 1986. *A New Technique for the Study of Deterrence, Escalation Control, and War Termination*. Santa Monica, Calif.: Rand, P–7224.

Defense, Department of. 1987. *Soviet Military Power*. Washington, D.C.: U.S. Government Printing Office.

Dunnigan, James F. 1983. *How to Make War*. New York: Quill.

Fairbanks, Charles H., Jr. 1988. Choosing Among Technologies in the Anglo-German Naval Arms Competition, 1898–1915. In William Cogar, ed., *Naval History: Seventh Symposium of the U.S. Naval Academy*. Wilmington, Del.: Scholarly Resources. (forthcoming)

Farwell, Byron. 1986. *The Great War in Africa*. New York: W. W. Norton.

Foster, James L., and John K. Walker. 1982. *Concepts of Strategic War: A Basis of a New Approach to Strategic Assessment*. Santa Monica, Calif.: Rand. Prepared for Director, Defense Nuclear Agency, under Contract Number DNA–001–79–C–0034.

Gates, David. 1987. Area Defence Concepts: The West German Debate. *Survival* 29 (July/August):301–17.

George, Alexander L., and Richard Smoke. 1974. *Deterrence in American Foreign Policy: Theory and Practice*. New York: Columbia University Press.

Gibbon, Edward. 1980. *The Decline and Fall of the Roman Empire*. New York: Viking Penguin.

Goldich, Robert L. 1986–1987. The Strategic Importance of Mass. *The National Interest* 6 (Winter):66–74.

Grinkevich, D. 1987. The Time Factor in Battle. Excerpted in *Strategic Review* 15 (Spring):90–92.

Hart, Gary Warren, and William S. Lind. 1986. *America Can Win: The Case for Military Reform*. Bethesda, Md.: Adler and Adler.

Hines, John, and George Kraus. 1986. Soviet Strategies for Military Competition. *Parameters* (Autumn):26–31.

Ikle, Fred C. 1971. *Every War Must End*. New York: Columbia University Press.

Karber, Philip A., Grant Whitley, Mark Herman, and Douglas Komer. 1979. *Assessing the Correlation of Forces: France 1940*. McLean, Va.: BDM. Sponsored jointly by the Office of the Secretary of Defense, Director of Net Assessment, and the Defense Nuclear Agency under Contract Number DNA–001–78–C–0114.

Karsh, Efraim. 1987. The Iran-Iraq War: A Military Analysis. *Adelphi Papers* 220. London: International Institute for Strategic Studies.

Kecskemeti, Paul. 1958. *Strategic Surrender: The Politics of Victory and Defeat*. New York: Atheneum.

Kennedy, Paul M. 1984. Great Britain before 1914. Pp. 172–204 in Ernest R. May, ed. *Knowing One's Enemy*. Princeton, N.J.: Princeton University Press.

Kissinger, Henry A. 1979. *The White House Years*. Boston: Little, Brown.

Marshall, Andrew W. 1984. Problems in American Assessments in Strategic Deterrence. Lecture delivered at Fort Meade, Maryland.

May, Ernest R., ed. 1984. *Knowing One's Enemies*. Princeton, N.J.: Princeton University Press.

Mearsheimer, John J. 1983. *Conventional Deterrence*. Ithaca, N.Y.: Cornell University Press.

————. 1984–1985. Nuclear Weapons and Deterrence in Europe. *International Security* 9 (Winter):19–46.

Merritt, Jack N., and Pierre Sprey. 1972. Negative Marginal Returns in Weapons Acquisition. Pp. 484–85 in Richard G. Head and Ervin J. Rokke, eds., *American Defense Policy*. 3d ed. Baltimore: Johns Hopkins University Press.

Millet, Allan, and Williamson Murray, eds. 1986. On the Effectiveness of Military Institutions: Historical Case Studies from World War I, the Interwar Period, and World War II. Columbus: Mershon Center, Ohio State University. Manuscript.

Myer, Jonathan. 1986. *TASCFORM-C³I: A Developmental Methodology for Assessing Modernization of C³I Systems*. Arlington, Va: Analytic Sciences Corporation. Technical Report published under Contract Number MDA–903–85–C–0098 for the Assistant Secretary of Defense (C³I).

Nitze, Paul A. 1976. Assuring Strategic Stability in an Era of Detente. *Foreign Affairs* 54 (January):207–33.

Odom, William E. 1983. Trends in the Balance of Military Power Between East and West. Paper prepared for delivery at the 25th annual conference of the International Institute for Strategic Studies at the Chateau Laurier Hotel, Ottawa, Canada, September 8–11, 1983.

————. 1985. Soviet Force Posture: Dilemmas and Directions. *Problems of Communism* 34 (July-August): 1–14.

————. 1987. Past and Future Directions in Soviet Military Doctrine and Force Structure. Unpublished manuscript.

Posen, Barry R. 1984–1985. Measuring the European Conventional Balance. *International Security* 9 (Winter): 47–88.

Regan, Jonathan, and William J. Vogt. 1987. *The TASCFORM Methodology: A Technique for Assessing Comparative Force Modernization*. 2d ed. Arlington, Va.: Analytic Sciences Corporation. Prepared under Contract Number MDA–903–85–C–0098 for Director, Net Assessment, Office of the Secretary of Defense.

Rudwick, Bernard H. 1969. *Systems Analysis for Effective Planning: Principles and Cases*. New York: John Wiley and Son.

Seiler, George. 1983. *Strategic Nuclear Force Requirements and Issues*. Maxwell Air Force Base: Air University Press.

Trulock, Notra. 1986. The Role of Deception in Soviet Military Planning. Unpublished manuscript.

Vorobyov, Ivan. 1987. New Weapons Require Sound Tactics. Excerpted in *Strategic Review* 15 (Spring):88–90.

Weinberger, Caspar W. 1987. *Annual Report to the Congress: Fiscal Year 1988*. Washington, D.C.: U.S. Government Printing Office.

Wohlstetter, Albert. 1959. The Delicate Balance of Terror. *Foreign Affairs* 37 (January):211–45.

————, and George W. Rathjens. 1973. The ABM: Two Analyses. Pp. 137–53 in Eugene R. Rosi, ed., *American Defense and Detente*. New York: Dodd, Mead.

4

On the Economics of National Security

JUDITH REPPY

National security, properly defined, encompasses economic and social strength as well as military power. A healthy economy plays a dual role: it is both an end, as one of the values that the nation seeks to secure, and a means for achieving military strength. In particular, the military sector depends on the civilian side of the economy for soldiers and for the means to arm them.

Production of military goods and services, however, drains the civilian economy. There are exceptions to this statement, but for the most part military forces absorb resources that are then unavailable for consumption or investment. In wartime, with the survival of the state at risk, military needs take precedence, but in peacetime they must be balanced against other claims. The relevant analytic concept is the notion of opportunity cost, which defines the cost of military activities as the alternative set of civilian goods and services, including investment goods, that could have been produced using the same resources. At some level, expenditure for the military can weaken a nation rather than strengthen it because the economic costs outweigh whatever benefit is gained from the military forces. The point at which this occurs is a matter of intense political debate.

Thus, in thinking about resource use for national security, decision-makers must consider what resources are available for the military sector and how to mobilize them efficiently. They must also consider what the impact of this resource use may be on other government programs and on the performance of the economy as a whole, now and in the future. These issues—the trade-offs between the military and civilian sectors and the efficient use of resources within the military sector—are the major concerns of the field of defense economics. These questions are discussed in this chapter under three major headings: the mobilization of resources for the military sector; the trade-offs within the central government budget; and the broader question of the economic burden of military spending for the economy as a whole. The institutional context is initially that of the industrialized market economies, followed by brief discussions of the different considerations affecting defense spending in less developed countries and in planned economies.

MOBILIZING RESOURCES FOR THE MILITARY SECTOR

Broadly speaking, a state can command the resources it needs for its military forces through coercion, through market incentives, or through a combination of the two approaches. The problem of allocating resources to the military sector assumes a special character in wartime, when the urgency of the situation both demands and justifies the use of extraordinary state powers to nullify existing arrangements and channel men and goods to military uses. In peacetime, however, such measures are not politically feasible, at least in democratic nations.

As the nature of war has changed over time, the problem of mobilizing resources to serve the state has also changed (Howard, 1976; Milward, 1977, ch. 3). Whereas infantry once made up over 90 percent of an army, by World War II the number in combat jobs had shrunk to 40 percent in the armed forces of the United States (Binkin, 1986, ch. 2). A modern army relies on technologically complex weapons that, in turn, require specialized manpower and support facilities. The weapons must be continuously modernized in response to developments in other countries, and so the army must have close links to the most technologically advanced sectors of the economy. These characteristics reflect secular changes in the level of industrialization and the rate of technological change in the world economy, and in that sense they may be thought of as natural developments. But resources do not flow automatically to new uses, and the development of a modern military sector has involved substantial changes in institutions and procedures for acquiring command over the necessary men and materiel (Melman, 1970).

Acquisition by the state of the necessary resources raises issues of sufficiency, efficiency, and equity, issues that are well illustrated in the choice between conscription and an all-volunteer force (R. Cooper, 1977; Olvey, Golden, and Kelly, 1984, ch. 14). The state must draw on the civilian sector for an adequate supply of soldiers, and their availability and quality are crucial to force planning. Conscription provides the government with the legal means to insure a steady supply of new soldiers of the desired quality at a controllable cost. The main drawbacks of conscription are its unfairness in peacetime, when only a small fraction of the eligible age group need be drafted, and its economic cost in real terms.

A volunteer army has the advantage of enlisting only those who are willing to serve at the going wage, yielding a more efficient and equitable allocation of labor. But enlistment rates will fluctuate with the state of the economy, and those who choose to enlist may not be those who are most needed. The supply is affected by exogenous demographic changes: many nations today are having to rethink their military manpower use in the face of declining numbers of eighteen to twenty-four year olds. A volunteer army thus creates problems of planning and organization for the military services. The wage level necessary to recruit and retain high-quality soldiers is an accurate measure of their value to the economy, but the personnel costs must compete in the defense budget with other programmatic needs. Understandably, there is strong support for conscription, and most nations still rely on a draft to meet their manpower needs.

Although states may choose to use coercive powers to fulfill their military manpower requirements, they typically acquire their weapons from private contractors through the market or from some combination of state and private production. The alternatives range from domestic production of all weapons, through joint development with other nations, using various co-production and licensing schemes, to reliance on imported weapons and/or military assistance programs. The make-or-buy decision at the national level depends on economic factors, such as the size of the national arms procurement budget, the level of the national technology base, the importance attached to arms production as a tool of industrial policy, foreign exchange constraints, and the prospects for exports to other countries. It also depends on political factors, including alliance membership, historical patterns of arms procurement from former colonial powers, regional rivalries, fears over technology transfer, and the availability of military assistance programs (Pierre, 1982).

Only a few countries other than the two superpowers attempt to maintain a domestic productive capability for the full range of military hardware, and the cost of doing so has become increasingly prohibitive. Thus, in NATO, co-production of major new weapons has become common for the European partners, although the desire to standardize military hardware and to share development costs and gain wider markets is tempered by political concerns over jobs and preserving the national technology base (Reppy and Gummett, 1987). For countries such as Britain and France, arms exports are an important strategy for maintaining a large domestic arms industry and the jobs and technology base associated with that industry (Kolodziej, 1987a and 1987b, ch. 3). For countries that lack a technologically advanced industrial base, the only choices are production on the basis of technology licensed from abroad or imports of weapons.

Wherever it is technologically and economically feasible, governments generally prefer domestic production of weapons, if only to maximize the security of supply in case of war. Historically, weapons were typically produced by government munitions factories. Vestiges of an arsenal system still exist in many countries, even where the bulk of weapons development and production is carried out in the private sector. The shift to reliance on private contractors for both development and production of weapons is most complete in the United States, although, somewhat paradoxically, private firms operating in the defense market take on many of the characteristics of government enterprises (Peck and Scherer, 1962, ch. 5).

When dealing with private contractors, the government's problem is one of structuring an appropriate set of incentives to attract firms to work efficiently on the development and production of new weapons systems in the face of the considerable risks involved and given the contractors' alternative of producing for civilian markets. The difficulties of this task are compounded by the non-competitive structure of the defense market and by the asymmetry in information available about production cost and technical competence. In a competitive market, costs are minimized by the presence of alternative suppliers. In the defense market, there are only a few suppliers—sometimes only one—of a given weapon system, and in general the government has only imperfect information about the contractors' true costs.

In the United States, the defense industry is made up of a relatively small number of prime contractors (the top twenty-five prime contractors regularly receive nearly 50 percent of all prime contracts), plus thousands of smaller subcontractors and third-tier suppliers (Gansler, 1980). Many of the major defense contractors are also important producers in the civilian market, and their suppliers typically sell in both civilian and defense markets. Thus, although the defense industry is quite distinct, with its single customer and special procurement regulations, its members are connected at many points to civilian markets.

The classic treatment of weapons acquisition remains that of Merton J. Peck and Frederic Scherer (1962). Twenty-five years later most of their conclusions, based on their study of weapons programs of the 1950s, are still applicable. The incentives for firms to participate in defense contracting are the opportunity for profits and for technological gains. The drawbacks are the high level of risk, both technical and political, and the weight of government regulation, which can be a real barrier, especially to smaller companies. The U.S. government has succeeded in maintaining the participation of the defense contactors through contracts and accounting procedures that shift most of the risk to the government and allow, overall, a favorable rate of profit.

The government's goal of efficiency in defense procurement is more elusive. It is possible to specify an optimal contract structure under different assumptions about risk and information; recent analyses have focused on the problem of risk bearing and asymmetrical information, using a principal/agent approach (e.g., Weitzman, 1980). The difficulty, however, lies in the political realities of implementing the contract. The military requirements on which the proposal and contract were originally based are seldom stable for the whole development period. Contractors are able to exploit technical change orders and other contract provisions to renegotiate the terms of their contracts after the work is in progress, thus avoiding penalties for cost overruns (Fox, 1974, ch. 19). In the process the incentives for efficiency are lost.

The U.S. government has elaborate procedures for formal decision-making on new weapons and for oversight of their development. Beyond the formal arrangements, and probably far more important, is the informal network of alliances between contractors, military program officers, and congressional offices. This is the military-industrial complex (MIC), and it has been much analyzed (Rosen, 1973; Adams, 1982). It provides personal rewards to the participants in the form of job opportunities (the "revolving door") and a base of political support for the defense program. This network is effective in transferring information about military requirements and budgets to the contractors and in allowing contractors to propose informally new technological solutions, which then are translated into new contracts.

It is less effective in insuring a good match between operational needs and new weapons or, as noted above, efficiency in production. Popular accounts of mismanaged programs, cost overruns, and "gold-plating" abound (e.g., R. Kaufman, 1970; Fallows, 1981; Spinney, 1985). From a different perspective, defense analysts debate whether congressional and Defense Department procedures designed to increase oversight have succeeded only in lengthening the development cycle and increasing costs (Perry, 1980). From the point of view of the participants, however, the MIC is highly functional, and it has exhibited remarkable stability, despite the repeated efforts of reformers to eliminate the system of rewards that sustains it.

Similar cozy arrangements characterize the production of defense goods in other major weapons-producing countries (Ball and Leitenberg, 1983). Indeed, it may be argued that they are inevitable, given the fundamental market situation in which the anonymity of the classical competitive market is replaced by a close relationship between the program officer and an individual defense contractor. The incentives for the contractor to operate in the political arena of lobbying and influence peddling are strong, since the final decisions on budgets and programs are made in Congress or by a government bureaucracy rather than in a market with many buyers.

The broad conceptual framework for thinking about mobilization and management of resources for the military is not in contention (Weida and Gertcher, 1987). There are, however, a number of unresolved questions that depend on factual knowledge not yet available, as well as on underlying assumptions about economic behavior. One such question is whether the U.S. defense sector has the capability to increase production rapidly ("surge") in the case of an international crisis or conventional war. (In a nuclear war the question presumably would not arise.) Jacques Gansler (1980, ch. 5) has argued that bottlenecks in the supply of specialized parts and components would limit output, despite the presence of excess productive capacity in the large prime contractors. After the large increases in procurement and research and development spending during the Reagan military buildup, which did not encounter supply problems, it is more difficult to hold an alarmist view of U.S. surge capability (National Research Council, 1986). But the Reagan buildup was launched during a major and protracted economic recession, so that there was little competition from the civilian economy for productive capacity or manpower. In a more robust economic climate, the outcome might well have been different.

The question of surge capacity turns on the ability of the economic system to respond suddenly to expanded demands, that is, on the ease with which resources can be shifted between uses in the short run. New information on the direct and indirect demand for industry output by the Defense Department has been made available through the Defense Economic Impact Modeling System (DEIMS) (U.S. Department of Defense, 1985a). DEIMS was developed by the Department of Defense in part to answer the question, what will be the effect of an increase in defense spending on industry output? It is based on an input-output table of U.S. industries that are suppliers to the Department of Defense, combined with a very detailed breakdown of defense purchases and a standard econometric model of the U.S. economy.

Within the limits of the methodology, DEIMS offers detailed information about the composition of output implied by different levels of military spending and different mixes of programs, under given assumptions about the state of the rest of the economy. Similar, although less detailed, models exist for a number of other countries (Leontief and Duchin, 1983; Galigan 1984; Filip-Kohn, Krengel and Schumacher, 1980). They can be used to predict the changes in demands on the industrial sector of the economy from small increases or decreases in military spending. They do not, however, provide information about the flexibility of response of the economy over a longer time period. Nor do they tell us what the cost of mobilizing these resources for the military sector will be in terms of budgetary trade-offs or what the long-term consequences will be for the rest of the economy.

BUDGETARY TRADE-OFFS

The military requirement for manpower and weapons is only one of the numerous demands for public services that a government must meet. The provision of social welfare services, responsibility for regional development, and stimulation of economic growth are now also generally accepted as legitimate and desirable roles for government. The choice between military and nonmilitary spending incorporates value judgments on the importance of national security in relation to the other goals of society. It requires information about external threats and foreign policy goals and the likely effectiveness of military forces in meeting those threats and goals compared to the other instruments at the disposal of the government. But domestic needs and ways of meeting those needs must be taken into account as well.

The military claim for increased budgets is typically made in the name of national security, buttressed by threat analyses showing increased danger to the state from its external enemies. Advocates of other government programs make analogous claims, but those of defense carry special weight because of the importance of the security function to the survival of the state and because in most countries the defense sector has considerable domestic political power. The large size of the defense establishment and the mystique of military expertise work to its advantage in budgetary battles; it is difficult for civilians to challenge military requirements. In practice, then, the defense budget is relatively protected from budget costs, even though it is theoretically among the most "controllable" of government expenditures because it is not subject to the legal entitlements of social welfare programs.

The total government budget will be constrained by the level of revenues as well as whatever deficit is deemed politically acceptable (Crecine and Fischer, 1973). The trade-offs within the total come in the choice between defense spending and other government programs. William Domke, Richard Eichenberg, and Catherine Kelleher (1983) have studied the question of trade-offs between defense spending and welfare spending in four NATO nations for the period 1954–1974. They found no evidence for systematic trade-offs. Instead, the spending for the different functions appeared to be determined independently, mostly in response to domestic economic conditions. This result, however, was partially conditioned by their decision to omit the Korean War years from their study and by the apparent weakness of the fiscal constraint throughout the period, which was characterized by unusually high rates of economic growth.

For example, in the United States military expenditures fell as a percentage of federal government spending between 1955 and 1980, not because military spending was cut, but because domestic programs and the total size of the budget were growing more rapidly. From 1981 to 1986, however, there is clear evidence in the United States of a trade-off between sharply increased military spending and spending for nondefense federal programs, which shrank both relatively, as a fraction of federal spending, and absolutely, when calculated in constant dollars (U.S. Department of Defense, 1985b, pp. 115, 121).

Trade-offs occur between programs within the military budget as well as at the interagency level. Analysis of the Defense Department's budget is a useful exercise because of the relatively large fraction of the total budget that is appropriated in functional categories other than personnel (Kantor, 1979). The division of resources among competing programs should reveal the underlying policy choices, with the caveat that sometimes a small program may have a disproportionate significance because of its symbolic value—for example, in the decision to end the U.S. moratorium on the manufacture of chemical weapons—or because it represents the first step of a major initiative.

A rational government would allocate its spending to each program so as to equalize the marginal improvement to be expected per unit of expenditure in each category. It would apply this principle within the military budget as well as between broader government functions. Analysts differ in their descriptions of the process of allocation of the U.S. defense budget to individual programs. In principle, the systems analysis approach embedded in the Planning Programming Budgeting System (PPBS), which was introduced in the 1960s and is still in use, provides a method for choosing the most cost-effective solution for a military requirement from the set of all alternative solutions. Proponents of PPBS argue that it constitutes a framework for rational decisions (W. Kaufman, 1986).

Other observers believe that PPBS has never worked as advertised, that external fiscal constraints, rule of thumb, and organizational interests play an important role in determining the overall level and composition of the defense budget (Crecine and Fischer, 1973; Korb, 1977; Weida and Gertcher, 1987). For example, when defense spending is cut, spending for operations and maintenance is more likely to be affected than weapon developments or procurement. This is congruent with the organizational preferences of the military services, which prefer to protect new weapons programs as a guarantee of future force structure rather than spend on the more ephemeral activities of training and maintenance. From this perspective, military planning appears to be as much a response to fiscal constraints and organizational interests as to threat analysis.

The prescription for rational budget decisions is unrealistic on at least two points. There may be no consensus on goals or how they should be ranked. We lack information on the marginal effectiveness of allocating additional resources to individual programs, whether the trade-off is between broad government functions or within a particular function such as defense. We must conclude that budget analysis tells us more about the political strength of various groups within the government than about societal goals.

THE MILITARY BURDEN

Up to now we have been discussing the choices implicit in the government's use of resources for military activities. A different set of questions arises when we turn to the effects of that resource use on the rest of the economy. Here we must distinguish between short-run and long-run effects and between the highly aggregated level of analysis of macroeconomics and the disaggregated levels of sectoral and microeconomics.

In a market economy, the costs of military programs are measured by their budgetary costs. That is, if we put aside the distortions to prices that are introduced by the lack of true competition in the defense market, then the prices paid for weapons and manpower approximate the true opportunity costs of the resources used. But this simple static measure does not provide any insight as to the total impact of military programs on the economy over time. It is these total costs that should be of concern to policymakers as they weigh their decisions on military spending.

The economic burden of military spending is most commonly measured by the ratio of the defense budget to total gross national product (GNP) of the country in question, although variants of this measure may sometimes be more appropriate (Mosley, 1985, ch. 2). Behind the concept of the economic burden lies the notion that the output of goods and services, as measured by GNP, is a good measure of the carrying capacity of the economy, that is, its ability to sustain the drain of productive resources to the essentially nonproductive activities of the defense sector. The size of the burden is often interpreted as an index of the priority given to defense. The GNP-based measure of the burden of military spending has the further advantages that it is a ratio of two numbers expressed in the same currency and that the data needed to calculate it are readily available for most countries, so that international comparisons are easy to make. Such comparisons are used to make inferences about the relative bellicosity of states, about the fair distribution of the costs of alliances, and about changes in the importance of military spending over time.

This concept of burden, however, does not take one very far in analyzing the interactions between defense spending and the overall performance of an economy. We are most interested in the broad question, does military spending affect economic growth, and, if so, in what direction? The answer to this question, however, must be sought in a fairly detailed study of the effect of military spending on intervening variables such as investment or industrial structure. Without such detail, any evidence of a relationship between growth rates and military spending has little meaning, except for the trivial observation that military spending, as a component of GNP, tends to be correlated with increases in GNP. An explicit theory of the economy is needed, so that the impact of military spending can be traced through the complex relationships that characterize modern industrial economies. One consequence of this approach is obvious: the results of the analysis will depend on the economic theory used and how accurately it reflects the reality it purports to describe.

At the macroeconomic level, Keynesian theory suggests that increases in military spending will have a positive effect on output and employment in the short run, but that the long-term growth effects may be negative if military spending crowds out investment. The short-term stimulus is sharp because spending on procurement and construction, which are important components of defense spending, translates directly into increased demand for industrial output. In the long run, potential economic growth will be sacrificed if investments in productive capacity and civilian technology are, on balance, lower than they would have been without the increases in military spending. The strength of these effects and the effect on the rate of inflation depend on whether there is excess capacity in the economy or whether it is at full employment.

Empirical evidence for these hypothesized effects is contradictory. Early work by Bruce Russett (1970) showed a strong negative correlation between changes in military spending and changes in investment in the United States for the period 1939–1968, but that effect was largely owing to the big shifts in resource allocation during World War II. Kenneth Boulding's (1973) analysis of changes in the structure of the U.S. economy over a longer time period, 1929–1969, suggests that consumption, not investment, has "paid" for expanded government spending, including defense.

These studies used data from the United States only. In a series of papers Ron Smith and his colleagues (Smith, 1977, 1978, 1980; Smith and Georgiou, 1983) have systematically explored the relationship between military spending and a number of macroeconomic variables, using cross-sectional and time series data from OECD (Organization for Economic Cooperation and Development) countries in the postwar period and both correlation analysis and structural models. Smith finds a robust negative relationship between investment and military spending in the cross-sectional analysis, but the results from the time series data are less convincing. Moreover, the correlations are influenced by the extreme values of the Japanese case, in which very low rates of military spending have been associated with a strong economic performance. Without the Japanese data the relationships are less clear cut. As a general point, the simple correlations found in the cross-sectional data between military spending and other variables of interest are not evidence of causal relations, although they may be suggestive of such relationships.

With the exception of Boulding's work, these studies have not looked at the effect of other categories of government spending on the economy. It is not clear that defense is unique in its effects on the economy, only that it has been frequently studied. Econometric evidence for the United States suggests that changes in the defense budget will, in the short run, have the same kind of effect on the economy as changes in any other category of government spending for goods and services (Forest, 1983; Adams and Gold, 1987). This statement may not hold for other countries in which spending for the direct provision of social services, such as health services, looms large in the central government budget.

The most politically salient macroeconomic issue has been the relationship between defense spending and jobs. Unfortunately, much of the writing on the employment effects of military spending has been misleading (Mosley, 1985, pp. 89–92). The number of jobs created per dollar of military expenditure has been compared to those created by spending for relatively labor-intensive social services such as day care or hospitals. In fact, for the United States the employment effects of military spending and of government spending, taken as a whole, are essentially the same (Forest, 1983, p. 68; Blank and Rothschild, 1985, p. 690). There are differences in the occupational mix and in the goods and services produced, so the choice is not neutral from a societal point of view. It is incorrect, however, to claim that military spending "costs jobs."

Because military spending is typically the largest category of government spending for goods and services and one of the largest categories overall in the central government budget, it is a natural candidate for manipulation in the name of fiscal policy. It is somewhat ironic that the increases in military spending in the United States under the Reagan administration clearly stimulated output and employment in line with Keynesian theory of effective demand, despite the administration's commitment to the rhetoric of supply-side economics. In this and in other cases, increasing military spending proved the politically acceptable way to increase government demand.

Military spending is largely indistinguishable at the macroeconomic level from other forms of government spending in part because of the level of aggregation and in part because of the focus on short-run effects, where the short run is defined as the period of time to the next election. If one turns to the analysis of sectoral effects and long-term effects, then more interesting results emerge. To study them properly, detailed information about the defense industry and the composition of military spending over time is needed. The development of the DEIMS data base by the Department of Defense has substantially increased the amount of information available for the United States about the importance of military spending to individual industries. To the extent that technical coefficients are the same across countries, the results may be extrapolated to other countries. The DEIMS data base, however, reflects the situation of the early 1980s; earlier periods must be studied through case studies of individual industries (e.g., Tilton, 1971; Miller and Sawers, 1968; Kaldor, 1981, ch. 2; Flamm, 1987).

At the sectoral level, the pattern of military demand has been an important factor in the growth of certain industries, notably aircraft, electronics, and shipbuilding, in all nations with significant defense industries (Ball and Leitenberg, 1983). For example, in the United States military demand accounts for 50 percent or more of the output of the aircraft industry each year, and the government funds 75 percent of the industry's research and development (R&D), which is one of the highest as a percent of sales of any U.S. industry (AIAA, 1985, pp. 15, 114). The large domestic market and investment in new technology, both of which are heavily dependent on military spending, have formed the base from which U.S. manufacturers have dominated international markets for aircraft. Similarly, in France military demand for aircraft accounted for 70 percent of the industry's output in 1980, whereas in Britain the figure was 32 percent (Fontanel, Smith, and Willet, 1985, pp. 189–90). Although military demand is not such a large fraction of other broadly defined industries, it has stimulated growth in computers, electronics, and scientific instruments.

The regional impact of military spending is closely associated with the pattern of demand for various industries and the location of those industries. European countries that have regional and industrial policies are explicit in their use of military contracts to serve their policy goals. In the United States the post-World War II growth of the economies of California and the south-western region owes much to the concentration of defense contractors in those states, as well as to the concentration of military bases in the sunbelt states.

The most important question at the microeconomic level is the effect of military spending on technological change. New technologies—products and processes—are an important source of economic growth for the civilian sector. On the demand side, the military services are important customers for new technology. On the supply side, their spending for research and development (R&D) for new weapons is a substantial fraction of the total R&D performed in a number of industrialized states, including the United States, the Soviet Union, France, and Britain (SIPRI, 1986, ch. 15). In 1985 in the United States, government spending for military R&D reached 70 percent of total government-sponsored R&D and 31 percent of all R&D; including company spending by defense contractors would drive these figures higher.

This allocation of scientific resources to military activities carries a short-run opportunity cost for civilian research projects. In particular, military projects compete for scientific and technical personnel in specialized technologies, where there may be shortages of trained persons, even if general unemployment rates are high. There are important long-run implications as well, since R&D projects have their largest effect in the future, when the new technology they yield—if they are successful—enters the production process. The nations that invest heavily in military R&D may be losing out in opportunities in civilian markets. Japan is usually cited as the example of a nation that has succeeded by concentrating on civilian-based technology and products (Nelson, 1984).

Critics of military R&D spending assert that there are few benefits for the civilian economy since institutional barriers, for example, secrecy requirements, prevent the spread of new technology from the military to civilian sector (Kaldor, Sharp, and Walker, 1986; Reppy, 1985; Maddock, 1983). They emphasize the high opportunity costs of allocating such a large fraction of the nation's scientific resources to military projects when civilian technology is lagging.

Proponents of military R&D claim that there is substantial spin-off from military to civilian uses. In effect, they argue that there is a shared technology base, with relatively easy diffusion of new ideas and products between sectors. Examples of spin-off include jet engines, nuclear power, and early computer technology. Moreover, there are other examples, particularly in the field of electronics, where the military did not fund the early development of the new technology but played an important role as first customer in demonstrating its value in use (Tilton, 1971).

These are questions of fact, but they are extraordinarily difficult to settle by appeal to evidence. There are conceptual and practical difficulties in linking R&D programs to specific technological outcomes and in tracing the diffusion path of a new idea through the economy. Most of the evidence that we have on the effects of military R&D on economic performance are case studies, which do not permit generalization, or correlations of cross-sectional data on military R&D spending and indices of economic performance such as productivity or economic growth rates (DeGrasse, 1983). These correlations suffer from the same drawbacks as the correlation studies of macroeconomic effects, and again, the Japanese case is extreme.

The more speculative notion that military R&D influences not only differential rates of growth between industries, but also the technological lines of development within industrial sectors is even harder to test empirically. Since the proposition amounts to a claim that technology developed for military-related products has characteristics that are not appropriate for civilian products of the same industry, detailed information on product lines and their historical antecedents is needed. One study by Paolo Saviotti and A. Brown (1984) shows distinct technology trajectories over a long time period for military combat aircraft versus civilian passenger planes. Most of the evidence on this question, however, is anecdotal. A frequently cited example is the U.S. Department of Defense program for very high-speed integrated circuits (VHSIC), with its emphasis on nuclear-hardened electronic chips. This capability affects the manufacturing process and is unlikely to be of interest to commercial customers.

Recent work by Frank Lichtenberg has provided some econometric evidence of the effect of spending for military R&D on private R&D and productivity growth (Lichtenberg, 1984). He finds a substitution effect between government-funded and company-funded R&D in the United States, suggesting that federal R&D dollars displace private projects. This effect has serious implications for economic performance, since it has been shown that government-funded R&D does not contribute to productivity growth. Plausible reasons for this phenomenon are the concentration of government R&D in military products, which do not make the same contribution to productivity as new industrial processes, and the cost-plus environment of the defense market, which does not reward productivity improvements (Reppy, 1985).

The belief that military spending has had a negative impact on economic performance, especially in the United States and Britain, the two NATO countries that spend the largest proportion of their GNP on military R&D, has been buttressed in recent years by the strong performance of Japan and West Germany in international markets. To the extent that market power is an alternative to military power, the United States has lost ground since the early 1960s (U.S. Department of Labor, 1980). Again, however, the evidence for the role of military spending thus far is suggestive rather than conclusive. Many factors influence international trade performance besides R&D spending, so that simple correlations or other single-factor explanations are inadequate.

As a corollary to questions about the costs and benefits of increased military spending to the economy, we can ask, What would be the impact of reduced military spending? On the one hand, reduced government demand might be expected to result in a slackening of output and employment, unless it were offset by increased spending in other categories. Advocates of reduced military spending usually have their own list of alternative programs that they would like to see funded; this is the debate over budgetary priorities discussed above.

The real question, however, is not whether effective demand could be maintained, since clearly it could be, but what the adjustment process would be like at the sectoral level (Udis, 1973; Gordon and McFadden, 1984; President's Economic Adjustment Committee, 1985). This is, in another guise, the same question about the flexibility of a modern economy that was raised earlier with respect to the surge capability of the economy. U.S. experience with large-scale conversion from military to civilian production is limited to the periods immediately following World War II, the Korean War, and the Vietnam War. In each of these cases, the outcomes were affected more by the compensatory fiscal policies followed, or not followed, than by any detailed sectoral planning (Mosley, 1985, ch. 9).

It is difficult for firms accustomed to the specialized environment of the defense market to adjust to conditions in civilian markets, and there are many examples of defense contractors that tried to diversify into other products and markets, only to fail. Nevertheless, many supplier firms did leave the defense market in the years following Vietnam—so many that the alarm over surge capability was spawned. The adjustment process seemed no more traumatic than other shifts in the mix of products and firms. Indeed, it was largely masked by the upheavals caused by the OPEC (Organization of Petroleum Exporting Countries) oil price increases. The historical evidence supports the view that economic conversion, especially gradual economic conversion, would not cause serious economic problems, if compensating fiscal policy were implemented. The sectoral dislocations that would occur seem well within the capability of the economy to absorb.

DEFENSE SPENDING IN LESS DEVELOPED COUNTRIES

The question of the effect of military spending on economic growth has been just as hotly debated in less developed countries (LDCs) as in the industrialized nations (e.g., Benoit, 1973; Deger and Smith, 1983; Ball, 1988). The opportunity costs of devoting resources to military activities seem especially high for these countries, given that they are typically resource-constrained, especially in those resources of foreign exchange and technological know-how that are used heavily by the military sector. Some have argued, however, that the military sector can play a leading role in the modernization of the economy (Janowitz, 1964). Only two aspects of this debate will be discussed here: (1) the evidence for a relationship between military spending and the growth rate of GNP and (2) the choice between domestic arms production versus weapons imports in countries that lack a broad industrial base.

First, it must be emphasized that data reliability is a serious problem in these countries (Ball, 1988). Governments may not collect the data at all, or they may choose to conceal part of their military expenditures or arms imports. In addition, official foreign exchange rates may be unrealistic, complicating international comparisons. Thus, even more caution than usual must be applied to the interpretation of statistical findings.

Emile Benoit (1973) analyzed the relationship between the average military burden and the average growth rate of civilian output for 44 LDCs over the period 1950–1965. He found a positive correlation, a result that became statistically insignificant, however, when he included investment and foreign aid in a multiple regression analysis. Criticism of Benoit's work has centered on his methodology—particularly his narrow definition of foreign aid—and his interpretation of his findings (Ball, 1983). As noted above, simple correlation studies do not provide a basis for attributing causality. Other studies, using a more sophisticated methodology, have reached the opposite conclusion, namely, that military spending is associated with lower rates of economic growth in LDCs (Faini, Annez, and Taylor, 1984; Deger, 1986). Thus, no general conclusion can be drawn about the effect of military spending on economic growth in LDCs. This is not to argue that military spending has no effect on these economies, but only that the effect will vary according to initial conditions and the institutional arrangements of specific countries.

For the set of LDCs that have not successfully embarked on a path of industrialization, the make-or-buy decision with respect to military hardware has particular economic significance. Domestic production of military equipment is attractive because it increases national autonomy, may save foreign exchange, and serves as an element in a strategy of import-substituting industrialization. The political motive of increased autonomy is often decisive (Levite and Platias, 1983). But the economic costs are high, given the technological and capital requirements of modern weapons production and the narrow technology base of LDCs.

Nevertheless, some countries among the newly industrializing nations have succeeded in moving from dependence on arms imports, through domestic production on the basis of licensed technology, to the stage of indigenous development of new weapons, and even export to other countries. Brazil and Israel have had the most marked success, but other countries appear to be following the same path (Ross, 1984; Brzoska and Ohlson, 1986). One consequence of this new development has been increased competition in the arms trade, as former customers have become competitors.

DEFENSE SPENDING IN PLANNED ECONOMIES

The above discussion has been in the context of capitalist market economies in which private contractors supply most of the military goods and services.

In centrally planned economies, defense production, like the rest of industrial production, is controlled by the plan. Thus, the problem of attracting resources to the defense sector that must be solved in peacetime by Western governments through market incentives does not exist for the governments of the planned economies. Similarly, the macroeconomic effects of military spending do not arise in the planned economies in the same way that they do in capitalist economies because investment, employment, and output levels are determined by the central government.

This does not mean that planned economies have no economic problems associated with military spending: opportunity costs are inescapable in any system. They are short run, in terms of the trade-offs between military production and production for civilian needs, and long run, in terms of the effects of the displacement of investment and the absorption of technological resources by the military on economic growth. The practice of "taut" planning, which amounts to a policy of planned scarcities (Cohn, 1986, p. 8), exacerbates the opportunity costs of military spending in comparison to the situation for market economies, which have excess productive capacity much of the time. Even though resource use in a planned economy may appear inefficient, in that workers appear to be underemployed or engaged in unproductive tasks and capital to be underutilized, the economy is probably operating near its potential maximum, given its own set of institutions.

Other systemic differences between planned and market economies must also be considered. The plan replaces the market in the allocation of resources, but it creates its own perverse incentives with regard to product mix and technological change. The exigencies of fulfilling the plan cause enterprises to be slow in introducing new products or processes, which might disrupt production and endanger plan fulfillment. In order to reduce the vulnerability involved in depending on others for needed materials or parts, enterprises and ministries strive to be as self-sufficient as possible. The result is narrower specialization and a reduced flow of ideas among sectors.

Most of the evidence for the burden of military spending in a planned economy comes from studies of the Soviet Union (e.g., Becker, 1981). The difficulties in estimating Soviet military expenditures are well known (Holzman, 1980; Burton, 1983). Unfortunately, they are unavoidable owing to the secrecy practiced by the Soviet government. Indeed, since prices in a planned economy are not adequate measures of opportunity cost, more official Soviet information on its military spending would not solve the problem of accurately measuring the burden of military spending.

According to estimates made by the Central Intelligence Agency, the Soviet Union spends approximately 15 percent of its GNP on military activities, over twice the figure for the United States (U.S. Congress, Joint Economic Committee [JEC], 1986, p. 111). It allocates perhaps 50 percent of its R&D to the military (Holloway, 1984, p. 134). The 50 percent figure is particularly significant, given the technological backwardness of Soviet industry. Moreover, the military sector is able to command the highest quality resources in the most important industrial sectors such as machine building. The burden for the Soviet economy is clearly significant, but the Soviet leadership has been willing to sustain it.

The rate of economic growth in the Soviet Union has slackened over time, and in recent years the performance has been particularly disappointing. According to Western estimates, total factor productivity growth turned negative in the 1970s (U.S. Congress, JEC, 1986, p. 31). In the light of the poor economic performance, the drop in the rate of growth of military spending, which occurred in 1975 according to the latest CIA estimates, is not surprising. At first attributed to technical reasons, the plateau in Soviet military spending now appears to be the result of a deliberate policy decision in response to economic pressures and possibly changes in strategic planning (U.S. Congress, JEC, 1986, pp. 50–54, 101, 110; R. Kaufman, 1985).

Development and production of modern weapons has been the one sector of the economy in which the Soviet Union has competed successfully, at least in quantitative terms, with the West. Weapons production, however, draws on the resources needed to modernize the Soviet economy. This is the same trade-off as that faced by market economies, but it is exacerbated by the lower technological level of civilian industries in the Soviet Union and the higher institutional barriers to diffusion of new technology (Cohn, 1986).

A somewhat different picture emerges from the work of Julian Cooper, who has studied the production of civilian goods by military enterprises in the Soviet Union (1986). He finds evidence that the practice is much more extensive than had been realized and that it offers a conduit for the spread of superior military technology to the civilian sector. It is difficult to gauge the overall significance of the practice because we lack information on the importance of the civilian production in military enterprises relative to total civilian output. To the extent that the spin-off from military technology exists, it is a mitigating factor in the opportunity costs of military spending for the Soviet Union.

Most of the available evidence supports the view that the burden of military spending in the Soviet Union is very high, even higher than the simple ratio of spending to GNP would suggest. Opinions differ on whether it is in Western interests to drive that burden higher through competitive weapons programs or to seek to relieve the economic burdens on both sides through arms control agreements. Systemic differences between the Soviet Union and Western market economies prevent any simple conclusion as to which side can better bear the burden of an unrestrained arms race. Nonetheless, it should be noted that, whereas the economies of the West are stronger by all the usual measures of economic strength, the Soviet Union enjoys an advantage in its ability to command resources for the military sector and to sustain that allocation over a long time period.

AGENDA FOR FUTURE RESEARCH

This survey has demonstrated that, although much is known about the interactions between the military sector and the civilian economy, more remains to be learned. Unfortunately, the discussion of the issues of military spending and the economy has been most polemical, with many strong assertions but little evidence. For many of the issues, our current knowledge about military spending is not enough to settle the important questions at stake; new knowledge must be developed.

The field of defense economics is a branch of applied economics, but it has not received much attention from economists in recent years, outside of those working within the defense establishment. Instead, new scholarly research in the field has been performed by political scientists, and the questions studied have naturally been those with a large political component. This work has successfully elucidated the structure and operation of the military-industrial complex and the politics of the budget process. Less progress has been made on the important question of the impact of military spending on the economy over the long run, because the tools needed for such an inquiry are those of economics, not political science.

If the only problem were that economists have not paid sufficient attention to the questions associated with military spending, then the solution would be relatively simple. The deeper problem lies in the absence of a coherent theory of economics that could be applied to military spending. We can explain individual phenomena—for example, the opportunity cost of conscription—adequately, but there is no overarching theory that successfully ties together the various levels of analysis. Moreover, much of the standard economic analysis is irrelevant to the defense economy because its assumptions do not correspond to the institutions of the defense market. Research progress in the field of defense economics thus depends in part on advances in the larger field of economics.

Nevertheless, there is room for progress using existing tools of analysis to explain parts of the puzzle. At every level, better data on defense-specific effects would lead to better judgments about the overall impact of military spending. Economic data on employment, output, and productivity in which military and non-military categories are distinguished are almost nonexistent (Reppy, 1986). DEIMS represents a large step forward, but it is too closely tied to the budget forecasts of the Defense Department, and its predictions have yet to be tested against actual outcomes from U.S. defense spending. Such tests should be made and the results used in a systematic fashion to answer questions about the short-run macroeconomic and sectoral effects of military spending for the U.S. economy.

The most important—and difficult—unanswered question in the field of defense economics is that of the relationship between military technology and the civilian economy. As noted above, there are unresolved difficulties in analyzing the relationship between spending for military R&D, the resulting new technology, and the eventual incorporation of that technology into new products and processes. The construction of price indices that allow for technological change is only one of the problems faced by scholars working in this field (Saviotti and Bowman, 1984; Ziemer and Galbraith, 1983). We have relatively few empirical studies of diffusion of new technology, and still fewer that make the distinction between military-based technology and civilian technology, or that trace the spread of new technology from one sector to the other (Gummett and Reppy, 1988). Case studies of individual military innovations could be extremely useful in clarifying the stage of development at which diffusion to civilian uses is likely to occur and in answering the question of whether military technology is becoming more or less remote from civilian applications over time. Studies of innovations in the electronics and computer industries would be particularly interesting because of the large role which these technologies play in both civilian and military applications.

Case studies, however, cannot by themselves provide a convincing general answer to the question of the net impact of military spending on the economy. A more aggregated approach that links specific categories of military spending to indicators of economic performance is needed. Lichtenberg's work (1984) linking military R&D to changes in productivity is one example of this kind of approach. Cross-country comparisons of the relative performance of military and nonmilitary goods in international markets is another potential indicator of the overall impact of military spending on economic performance. Empirical research on these questions should avoid single-factor explanations, which fail to capture the complexities of the economic reality. Instead, the military-civilian distinction needs to be incorporated into full-fledged economic models to see if it adds explanatory power to the results.

Better information on the consequences of military spending for the economy would help decision-makers make the choice between military and other programs. Local and sectoral interests, which are differentially affected by specific government programs, will always be a source of some conflict over spending priorities. But a better understanding of the magnitude of the economic costs of military programs and their significance for long-term growth would allow the burden of decision-making for those programs to be focused where it belongs—on their military utility and on their implications for national and international security.

REFERENCES

Adams, Gordon. 1982. *The Politics of Defense Contracting: The Iron Triangle*. New Brunswick, N.J.: Transaction Books.

———, and David Gold. 1987. *Defense Spending and the Economy: Does the Defense Dollar Make a Difference?* Washington, D.C.: Brookings Institution.

Aerospace Industries Association of America (AIAA). 1985. *Aerospace Facts and Figures, 1985/86*. New York: Aviation Week and Space Technology.

Ball, Nicole. 1983. Defense and Development: A Critique of the Benoit Study. *Economic Development and Cultural Change* 31:507–24.

———. 1988. *Security and Economy in the Third World*. Princeton, N.J.: Princeton University Press.

———, and Milton Leitenberg, eds. 1983. *The Structure of the Defense Industry*. London: Croom Helm.

Becker, Abraham S. 1981. *The Burden of Soviet Defense: A Political-Economic Essay*. R–2752–AF. Santa Monica, Calif.: Rand Corp.

Benoit, Emile. 1973. *Defense and Economic Growth in Developing Countries*. Lexington, Mass: Lexington Books.

Binkin, Martin. 1986. *Military Technology and Defense Manpower*. Washington, D.C.: Brookings Institution.

Blank, Rebecca, and Emma Rothschild. 1985. The Effect of United States Spending on Employment and Output. *International Labour Review*, 124:677–97.

Boulding, Kenneth. 1973. The Impact of the Defense Industry on the Structure of the American Economy. Pp. 225–52 in Bernard Udis, ed., *The Economic Consequences of Reduced Military Spending*. Lexington, Mass.: Lexington Books.

Brzoska, Michael, and Thomas Ohlson, eds. 1986. *Arms Production in the Third World*. New York: Taylor and Francis.

Burton, Donald. 1983. Estimating Soviet Defense Spending. *Problems of Communism* 23 (2):85–93.

Cohn, Stanley. 1986. Economic Burden of Soviet Defense Expenditure: Constraints on investment Productivity. Pp. 14–23 in *The Economic Consequences of Military Spending in the United States and the Soviet Union*. Report of a conference held at Cornell University. Ithaca, N.Y.: Peace Studies Program, Cornell University.

Cooper, Julian. 1986. The Civilian Production of the Soviet Defense Industry. Pp. 31–50 in Ronald Amman and Julian Cooper, eds., *Technical Progress and Soviet Economic Development*. Oxford: Basil Blackwell.

Cooper, Richard V.L. 1977. *Military Manpower and the All-Volunteer Force*. R–1450–ARPA. Santa Monica, Calif.: Rand Corp.

Crecine, John, and Gregory Fischer. 1973. On Resource Allocation Processes in the U.S. Department of Defense. *Political Science Annual* 3:181–236.

Deger, Saadet. 1986. *Military Expenditure in the Third World Countries: The Economic Effects*. Boston: Routledge and Kegan Paul.

———, and Ron Smith. 1983. Military Expenditure and Growth in Less Developed Countries. *Journal of Conflict Resolution* 27:335–53.

DeGrasse, Robert, Jr. 1983. *Military Expansion, Economic Decline*. Armonk, N.Y.: M. E. Sharpe.

Domke, William R., Richard C. Eichenberg, and Catherine M. Kelleher. 1983. The Illusion of Choice: Defense and Welfare in Advanced Industrial Democracies, 1948–78. *American Political Science Review* 77:19–35.

Faini, Riccardo, Patricia Annez, and Lance Taylor. 1984. Defense Spending, Economic Structure and Growth: Evidence among Countries and Over Time. *Economic Development and Cultural Change* 32:487–98.

Fallows, James. 1981. *National Defense*. New York: Random House.

Filip-Köhn, R., R. Krengel, and D. Schumacher. 1980. *Macro-Economic Effects of Disarmament Policies on Sectoral Production and Employment in the Federal Republic of Germany*. Berlin: German Institute for Economic Research.

Flamm, Kenneth. 1987. *Targeting the Computer*. Washington, D.C.: Brookings Institution.

Fontanel, Jacques, Ron Smith, and Sue Willett. 1985. Les Industries d'armement de la France et du Royaume-Uni. Pp. 171–206 in *L'effort économique de défense. Arès*, nm. spécial.

Forest, Lawrence, Jr. 1983. *Defense Spending and the Economy*. Congressional Budget Office. Washington, D.C.: Government Printing Office.

Fox, J. Ronald. 1974. *Arming America: How the U.S. Buys Weapons*. Boston: Harvard University Press.

Galigan, Captain C. G. 1984. *The Economic Impact of Canadian Defense Expenditures FY1982/83 Update*. Kingston, Canada: Centre for Studies in Defense Resources Management, Royal Military College of Canada.

Gansler, Jacques. 1980. *The Defense Industry*. Cambridge, Mass.: MIT Press.

Gordon, Suzanne, and Dave McFadden, eds. 1984. *Economic Conversion*. Cambridge, Mass.: Ballinger.

Gummett, Philip, and Judith Reppy, eds. 1988. *The Relations between Defence and Civil Technologies*. Dordrecht: Kluwer.

Hartley, Keith. 1983. *NATO Arms Cooperation: A Study in Economics and Politics*. Boston: George Allen and Unwin.

Holloway, David. 1984. *The Soviet Union and the Arms Race*. 2nd ed. New Haven, Conn.: Yale University Press.

Holzman, Franklyn. 1980. Are the Soviets Really Outspending the U.S. on Defense? *International Security* 4 (4):86–104.

Howard, Michael. 1976. *War in European History*. New York: Oxford University Press.

Janowitz, Morris. 1964. *The Military in the Political Development of New Nations*. Chicago: University of Chicago Press.

Kaldor, Mary. 1981. *The Baroque Arsenal*. New York: Hill and Wang.

———, Margaret Sharp, and William Walker. 1986. Industrial Competitiveness and Britain's Defense. *Lloyds Bank Review*, no. 162:31–49.

Kantor, Arnold. *Defense Politics: A Budgetary Perspective*. Chicago: University of Chicago Press.

Kaufman, Richard. 1970. *The War Profiteers*. New York: Bobbs–Merrill.

———. 1985. Causes of the Slowdown in Soviet Defense. *Soviet Economy* 1 (1):9–31.

Kaufman, William. 1986. *A Reasonable Defense*. Washington, D.C.: Brookings Institution.

Kolodziej, Edward A. 1987a. Whither Modernization and Militarisation, Implications for International Security and Arms Control. Pp. 206–32 in Christian Schmidt and Frank Blackaby, eds., *Peace, Defence, and Economic Analysis*. London: Macmillan.

———. 1987b. *Making and Marketing Arms: The French Experience and Its Implications for the International System*. Princeton, N.J.: Princeton University Press.

Korb, Lawrence. 1977. The Budget Process in the Department of Defense, 1947–77: The Strengths and Weaknesses of Three Systems. *Public Administration Review* 37:334–46.

Leontief, Wassily, and Faye Duchin. 1983. *Military Spending: Facts and Figures, Worldwide Implications, and Future Outlook*. New York: Oxford University Press.

Levite, Ariel, and Athanassios Platias. 1983. *Evaluating Small States' Dependence on Arms Imports: An Alternative Perspective*. Occasional Paper No. 16, Peace Studies Program, Cornell University, Ithaca, N.Y.

Lichtenberg, Frank A. 1984. The Relationship Between Federal Contract R&D and Company R&D. *American Economic Review* 74 (2)73–78.

Maddock, Sir Ieuan. 1983. *Civil Exploitation of Military Technology*. Report of the Electronic EDO. National Economic Development Office, London.

Melman, Seymour. 1970. *Pentagon Capitalism*. New York: McGraw-Hill.

Miller, Ronald, and David Sawers. 1968. *The Technological Development of Modern Aviation*. London: Routledge, Kegan and Paul.

Milward, Alan S. 1977. *War, Economy and Society: 1939–45*. Berkeley: University of California Press.

Mosley, Hugh G. 1985. *The Arms Race: Economic and Social Consequences*. Lexington, Mass.: Lexington Books.

National Research Council. 1986. *The Impact of Defense Spending on Nondefense Engineering Labor Markets*. Report to the Panel on Engineering Labor Markets. Washington, D.C.: National Academy Press.

Nelson, Richard. 1984. *High Technologies Policies: A Five-Nation Comparison*. Washington, D.C.: American Enterprise Institute.

Olvey, Lee D., James R. Golden, and Robert C. Kelly. 1984. *The Economics of National Security*. Wayne, N.J.: Avery Publishing Group.

Peck, Merton J., and Frederic Scherer. 1962. *The Weapons Acquisition Process: An Economic Analysis*. Boston: Harvard University Press.

Perry, Robert. 1980. American Styles of Military R&D. Pp. 89–112 in F. A. Long and Judith Reppy, eds., *The Genesis of New Weapons*. New York: Pergamon.

Pierre, Andrew J. 1982. *The Global Politics of Arms Sales*. Princeton, N.J.: Princeton University Press.

President's Economic Adjustment Committee. 1985. *Economic Adjustment/Conversion*. Report prepared by the President's Economic Adjustment Committee and the Office of Economic Adjustment, OASD(MIL), Washington, D.C.

Reppy, Judith. 1985. Military R&D and the Civilian Economy. *Bulletin of the Atomic Scientists* 41 (9):10–14.

———. 1986. *Labour Use and Productivity in Military and Nonmilitary Related Industry*. Disarmament and Employment Programme Working Paper No. 2. Geneva: International Labour Office.

———, and Philip Gummett. 1987. Economic and Technological Issues in the NATO Alliance. Pp. 17–38 in Catherine Kelleher and Gale Maddox, eds., *Evolving European Defense Policies*. Lexington, Mass.: Lexington Books.

Rosen, Steven. 1973. *Testing the Theory of the Military-Industrial Complex*. Lexington, Mass.: Lexington Books.

Ross, Andrew. 1984. Security and Self-Reliance: Military Dependence and Conventional Arms Production in Developing Countries. Ph.D. diss., Cornell University, Ithaca, N.Y.

Russett, Bruce. 1970. *What Price Vigilance? The Burdens of National Defense*. New Haven, Conn.: Yale University Press.

Saviotti, Paolo, and A. Bowman. 1984. Indicators of Output of Technology. In Michael

Gibbons et al., eds., *Science and Technology Policy in the 1980s and Beyond*. London: Long.

Smith, Ron P. 1977. Military Expenditure and Capitalism. *Cambridge Journal of Economics* 1:61–76.

――――. 1978. Military Expenditure and Capitalism: A Reply. *Cambridge Journal of Economics* 2:299–304.

――――. 1980. Military Expenditure and Investment in OECD Countries. *Journal of Comparative Economics* 4:19–32.

――――, and George Georgiou. 1983. Assessing the Effect of Military Expenditure on OECD Economies: A Survey. *Arms Control* 4:3–15.

Spinney, Franklin. 1985. *Defense Facts of Life: The Plans/Reality Mismatch*. Boulder, Colo.: Westview Press.

Stockholm Institute of Peace Research. 1986. *SIPRI Yearbook 1986*. New York: Oxford University Press.

Tilton, John. 1971. *International Diffusion of Technology: The Case of Semiconductors*. Washington, D.C.: Brookings Institution.

Udis, Bernard, ed. 1973. *The Economic Consequences of Reduced Military Spending*. Lexington, Mass.: Lexington Books.

U.S. Congress. Joint Economic Committee (JEC). 1986. Allocation of Resources in the Soviet Union and China, 1985. Hearing. 99th Cong., 2nd Sess. Washington, D.C.: U.S. Government Printing Office.

U.S. Department of Defense. Office of Program Analysis and Evaluation. 1985a. *Defense Purchases: An Introduction to DEIMS*. Washington, D.C.

――――, Office of Assistance Secretary of Defense (Comptroller). 1985b. *National Defense Budget Estimates for FY 1986*. Washington, D.C.: Mimeo.

U.S. Department of Labor, Office of Foreign Economic Research. 1980. *Report of the President on U.S. Competitiveness*. Washington, D.C.: U.S. Government Printing Office.

U.S. National Science Foundation. 1984. *National Patterns of Science and Technology Resources*. NSF 84–311. Washington, D.C.: U.S. Government Printing Office.

Weida, William, and Frank Gertcher. 1987. *The Political Economy of National Defense*. Boulder, Colo.: Westview Press.

Weitzman, Martin L. 1980. Efficient Incentive Contracts. *Quarterly Journal of Economics* 94:719–30.

Ziemer, Richard, and Karl Galbraith. 1983. Deflation of Defense Purchases. In Murray Foss, ed., *The US National Income and Product Accounts*. Chicago: University of Chicago Press.

5

On Arms Acquisition and Transfers

ANDREW L. ROSS

Military power is perceived by policymakers and analysts alike to be a major prerequisite for national security. The implements of modern warfare are, in turn, viewed as a vital component of national military power. Consequently, weapons acquisition is necessarily a crucial and abiding concern of national security policymakers. Appropriate and adequate weaponry is a necessary, though insufficient, condition for the credibility of both deterrence and defense. The quantity and quality of available weaponry largely determine the effective range of available policy options during both times of war and times of peace.

Even though the acquisition of arms is typically justified as enhancing security against existing or potential threats, arms acquisition may actually erode rather than enhance security. The dilemmas resulting from a military buildup go well beyond the familiar problems analyzed by John Herz (1950, 1951, 1959) and Robert Jervis (1976, 1978) in their elucidations of the "security dilemma" and by Barry Buzan (1983) in his description of the "defence dilemma." Herz, Jervis, and Buzan are all concerned about the unintended and unforeseen consequences of acquiring arms. Yet it must be recognized that the *means* by which the implements of modern, industrialized warfare are acquired also impacts directly on security. Not all the means by which arms can be acquired serve a country's security interests equally well.

Various available arms acquisition options will be examined in this chapter. Of special concern is the relationship between specific acquisition strategies and a country's political and military autonomy. The maintenance of policy and behavioral autonomy—the minimization of external constraints on policy and behavior—is at the heart of national security. Yet policy and behavioral autonomy may be severely circumscribed if an optimal mix of acquisition strategies is not adopted. Particular acquisition options entail vulnerability to externally imposed restraints on state sovereignty, restraints that sharply limit the effective range of both domestic and foreign policy options.[1]

ARMS ACQUISITION: FORMS AND OPTIONS

Modern arms acquisition has its origins in the Industrial Revolution of the nineteenth century. Humanity's capacity for production and destruction increased immeasurably with the nineteenth-century rise and the twentieth-century consolidation of industrial economies and the concomitant industrialization of war. In the wake of this evolution, the commercialization of arms manufacturing, which had begun during the period of mercantilism, was greatly accelerated. During this period, private-sector military production displaced public-sector, predominantly arsenal-based, production, thereby injecting the politics of state–firm relations into the arms procurement process (McNeill, 1982).

Whether arms are acquired in response to perceived external (or internal) threats, or as a result of the politics of state–society relations evident in the functioning of the military-industrial complex or the pluralistic pulling and hauling of bureaucratic politics, the number of procurement options is finite. Since today's implements of destruction, whether produced by private or public-sector enterprises, are the products of modern industry and technology, industrial and technological capabilities are the primary determinants of the acquisition options available to particular countries.

Arms acquisition can take the form of independent, interdependent, or dependent acquisition—or some combination of these three basic forms. *Independent acquisition* is the self-reliant, autarkic acquisition of indigenously designed, developed, and manufactured weaponry. *Interdependent acquisition* involves cross-national, cooperative design, development, production, and procurement of weaponry. *Dependent acquisition* can take two, or a combination of two, forms: (1) procurement via import, whether from single or multiple sources; or (2) procurement via local production based on foreign technology—dependent production.

Although it is possible to identify analytically distinct forms of arms acquisition, for most countries these three forms tend to merge in practice. The arms import option associated with dependent acquisition, for instance, may be combined with elements of the self-reliance option associated with independent acquisition, resulting in a mixed local (perhaps initially dependent) production/import acquisition strategy. Or an essentially self-reliant actor may also engage in interdependent acquisition of a limited number of weapons or weapons systems. The three analytically distinct forms of acquisition, therefore, yield a multiplicity of acquisition options: three "pure" options—self-reliance, joint acquisition, and dependent (import and/or dependent production) acquisition—and a variety of "mixed" options.[2]

SELF-RELIANT ACQUISITION

Self-reliant, autarkic acquisition is the basic standard by which the other procurement options are measured. Only self-reliant acquisition based on the indigenous design, development, and production of military equipment presents no impediments to the maintenance of policy and behavioral autonomy.

Yet military self-sufficiency is beyond the possiblities of the vast majority of countries. Only a few countries have the requisite economic, primarily industrial and technological, capabilities. Klaus Knorr (1970, p. 68) argued that the larger the proportion of total national production accounted for by industrial production, the larger the share of total industrial production accounted for by capital goods production and the larger the proportion of consumer goods production accounted for by durable goods production, the greater the industrial potential for defense production. Of particular significance are the aerospace, electronics, energy, machine tools, shipbuilding, transportation, and ordnance and munitions industries (Knorr, 1970, pp. 62–65 and 68–73). Knorr (p. 62) stressed the increasingly crucial role of the electronics industry in the development of high tech weaponry. He also noted the importance of a highly skilled industrial labor force (p. 64) and how economies of scale are conducive to self-sufficiency (pp. 90–92).

In his discussion of the relationship between technology, research and development (R&D), and the potential for defense production, Knorr (pp. 74–75) argued that national scientific and technological progress enhances defense production potential by stimulating innovation through the adoption of new manufacturing methods and increased labor and resource productivity. Although R&D in defense-related industrial sectors does indirectly benefit military technology, military technology benefits little from nonmilitary R&D, according to Knorr. The greatest benefits from R&D efforts, of course, are derived when those efforts are applied directly to military technology (p. 79). The higher the proportion of the defense budget devoted to R&D, the more likely it is that a country will remain on the cutting edge of military technology and be capable of implementing a self-reliant acquisition strategy (pp. 79–80). A high level of investment in military R&D is especially important if strategy dictates the maintenance of national self-sufficiency in the production of technologically sophisticated weaponry (p. 81). The import of Knorr's analysis is clear: The option of across-the-board, self-reliant weapons acquisition can be successfully adopted only by countries with highly developed and diversified scientific and technological capabilities.

Richard Head (1974) complements Knorr's analysis of the relationship between national economic and technological capabilities and arms procurement. While acknowledging the significance of general economic capabilities, Head emphasized the rate of innovation, investment in R&D, and continual upgrading of R&D capabilities. He concluded that countries "with high overall R&D expenditures tend to spend the most for military R&D and tend to be leaders in weapons development" (p. 413). In addition, Head argued that the uncertainties surrounding the outcome, schedule, and costs of R&D programs, especially for the most sophisticated weapons programs, are such that it is improbable that countries without the most advanced technological capabilities have the capacity to become self-reliant (pp. 417–18).[3]

U.S.-Soviet Arms Acquisition

Soviet Acquisitions Process. Although European countries such as Britain, France, and Germany may have been self-sufficient in the past, the Soviet Union and the United States are the only countries that achieved self-sufficiency during the post-World War II period.[4] Soviet self-reliance is very much a postwar phenomenon. The Soviet Union did inherit Czarist Russia's relatively well-developed small arms, artillery, and naval shipbuilding capabilities. But defense production was a low priority during the years of the New Economic Policy (1921–1927) (Holloway, 1983a, p. 51). The development of the Soviet defense industry did not begin in earnest until the late 1920s and the adoption of the First Five–Year Plan (1928–1932). A primary objective of the Soviet drive to industrialize its economy under the First and then the Second Five-Year Plan (1933–1937) was to expand military production so that it could become militarily self-sufficient.

The Soviet strategy of militaristic industrialization dictated that defense production be assigned a higher priority than any other type of industrial production. The defense sector has consistently had top priority in the allocation of scarce material and human resources and has been able to commandeer needed resources from civilian industry (Holloway, 1983a, pp. 64–64, 1983b, p. 119). But while the defense sector was an integral part of the Soviet economy during the forced industrialization of the 1930s, the nature of the relationship between the military and civilian sectors of the economy changed dramatically after World War II: "Before the war the two had been intimately linked; after the war they grew apart, with the defence industry moving ahead rapidly in technology" (Holloway, 1983a, pp. 53–54). Having been able to acquire its own supply industries (its own metallurgical base and machine tool industry, for instance) under the priority system, the defense sector became vertically integrated and an autarkic enclave within the Soviet economy (Holloway, 1983b, p. 119). As a result of its enclave status and the priority system, the defense sector is more technologically advanced than civilian industrial sectors, even though, by most accounts, it continues to lag behind Western, especially American, defense industries (Holloway, 1983a, pp. 65–66, 1983b, pp. 135–140; Kaufman, 1985, pp. 182–1983).

The literature on Soviet military research, development, and production is beset with descriptive work on the role of organizational, and even individual, actors (Alexander, 1978–1979, pp. 6–24, 1982b, pp. 3–10; Holloway, 1983b, pp. 108–15; Hough, 1984; Woods, 1986, pp. 211–21); the nature of the weapons acquisition process (Alexander, 1974, pp. 427–33, 1978–79, pp. 31–39, 1982a, 1982b, p. 11–13; Aspaturian, 1972; Holloway, 1983b, pp. 140–45; Hough 1984); and sketchy case studies of weapons acquisition (Herold and Mahoney, 1974; Holloway, 1977). A multitude of state and party actors participate in an acquisition process marked by conservatism, bureaucratization, secrecy, and departmentalism (Alexander, 1978–1979, pp. 24–30). The products of the acquisition process reflect the nature of the process: "Soviet designers have shown a marked preference for simple designs; for the common use of subsystems and components in different weapons systems; and for incremental or evolutionary technological change" (Holloway, 1983b, p. 147).

Stan Woods (1986), in a notable but flawed attempt to show that the simplicity, standardization, and incrementalism that characterize Soviet weaponry is a result not of the acquisition process but of reasoned policy choices, noted instances of "creative improvisation" (the ZSU–23/4 anti-aircraft gun) and radical innovation (ICBMs and particle beam technology) in the acquisition process. Alexander (1978–1979, pp. 35–39), however, convincingly demonstrated that radical, innovative departures traditionally require the intervention of the Soviet Union's political leadership in the acquisition process. Yet Woods was correct in noting the functionalism of the Soviet acquisition process. He argued that (1) it facilitates the rapid introduction of new systems by reducing lead times for weapons development; (2) it is cost effective—development costs are reduced and production runs are stretched out, allowing for greater economies of scale and reduced unit costs; (3) it keeps R&D teams in being; (4) it produces standardized systems that are easier to produce, maintain, and operate; (5) it permits the acquisition of a greater quantity of systems; and, most importantly, (6) it produces systems that are militarily effective.

Today, the Soviet Union possesses a formidable, independent, full-scale military research, development, and production capability that has enabled it to achieve and maintain military self-sufficiency. However, foreign technology played a not insignificant role in the interwar period when German, British, and American military technology was acquired and absorbed (Scott and Scott, 1984; Holloway, 1983b). Holloway (1983a, p. 73) noted that, while it is difficult to determine precisely the importance of the role of foreign technology, it was probably greatest in the 1930s and mid–1940s. But it is not difficult to determine whether the role of foreign technology has increased or decreased. Although "Soviet reliance on foreign technology has on the whole tended to increase in the course of the past 20 years" (Davies, 1977, p. 65), it is clear that the role of foreign technology in the defense industry has been sharply reduced.

U.S. Acquisitions Process. While Soviet self-sufficiency is the result of a secular process of militaristic industrialization shaped by long-term planning,

American military self-reliance is the result of a more episodic, ad hoc process. Historically, the United States has alternated between periods of boom and bust, developing, producing, and procuring weapons during time of war and virtually dismantling its R&D, manufacturing, and acquisition apparatus during time of peace.

Prior to the current, modern period of weapons acquisition, the United States relied on the federal arsenal system for the development and production of military equipment. The public sector, in the form of army arsenals, naval shipyards, and the War Department's armories, rather than the private sector, was the primary source of American weaponry. Under the arsenal system, military technology tended to reflect rather than lead nonmilitary, civilian, or commercial technology (Reppy, 1983, p. 21). During the interwar period, however, technological advances, especially in the aircraft industry, began to erode the predominant role of the arsenal system in the acquisition process (Reppy, 1983, p. 22).

The transformation of state–society relations, which began during the interwar period as private-sector suppliers began to displace the public-sector arsenal system, was fully realized during World War II. As Peck and Scherer noted in their classic study of U.S. arms acquisition, "During World War II the bulk of weapons making in all fields shifted to private firms, and there it has stayed" (1962, p. 99). By the early 1980s, 70 percent of American military R&D and virtually 100 percent of all military production took place in the private sector (Reppy, 1983, p. 23).

The structure of the defense marketplace within which American arms acquisition takes place is characterized by a monopsonistic consumer, the state, and oligopolistic private sector corporate suppliers. Peck and Scherer (1962, pp. 55–64) argued that the arms acquisition process is distinguished by its nonmarket character. As Jacques S. Gansler (1980, pp. 29–31) observed, however, the state–firm relationship in the acquisition process is distinguished by the absence not of a market, but of a free, competitive market.

As a result of the monopsony power it exercises in the market, the state, or, more specifically, the Department of Defense (DOD), largely determines both the characteristics of the products developed and produced by corporate actors and the rules of the marketplace (Reppy, 1983; Gansler, 1980). The potent combination of the monopsony consumer power of the state, the oligopolistic characteristics of the supply side of the market, and the consequent features of the consumer–supplier market relationship serves to ensure, as Gansler (1980) and Reppy (1983) have demonstrated, a costly weapons acquisition process.

American defense R&D, in contrast to the evolutionary, incremental Soviet style of military R&D, is often characterized as innovative and radical in style (Long and Reppy, 1980, p. 14; Woods, 1986). When U.S. R&D is examined in the context of the characteristics of the American weapons acquisition process, it is apparent that the contrast between U.S. and Soviet military R&D is somewhat overblown. In addition to the well-known uncertainties resulting from the unpredictable outcomes, costs, and schedules inherent in defense R&D efforts (Hitch and McKean, 1960, pp. 247–49; Peck and Scherer, 1962, pp. 17–54), the nature of the U.S. acquisition process itself hampers innovation and radical progress. Gansler (1980, p. 105) argued that "the high visibility and accountability of the R&D decision-makers places them in a position in which they feel they must minimize the risk associated with a particular R&D program. Thus, there is a tendency to give the business to large, well-established firms, and to select conventional ideas for development." Furthermore, according to Gansler (p. 101), the large firms in which military R&D has become concentrated emphasize risk minimization (enhancing product peformance, for instance), rather than the pursuit of radical, innovative technological departures.

Much of the literature on the U.S. arms acquisition process was generated by an extended debate on the determinants of weapons acquisition. James Kurth (1973), in a highly regarded piece, distinguished between four unsatisfactory explanations—strategic, bureaucratic, democratic, and economic—and advanced two alternative explanations: the follow-on imperative and the bail-out imperative. Numerous, though unfortunately non-cumulative, case studies of the acquisition process drew on the bureaucratic politics and/or cybernetics approaches in vogue among political scientists during the late 1960s and 1970s (Armacost, 1969; Beard, 1976; Coulam, 1977; Davis, 1966–1967; Gray, 1979; Greenwood, 1975; Halperin and Kanter, 1973; Sapolsky, 1972). Advocates of the bureaucratic politics/cybernetics approaches attempted to discard what they viewed as the myth of a unitary, rational, monopsonistic state actor and to apply the concept of interest group pluralism to the study of the state. They disaggregated the state and emphasized the significance of organizational rivalries, bureaucratic pulling and hauling, and bargaining in the acquisition process. Graham T. Allison and Frederic A. Morris (1975, p. 126) boldly asserted that "the weapons in the American and Soviet force postures are *predominantly* the result of factors *internal* to each nation."

Adherents of yet another approach that stressed the role of the internal (as opposed to the external) forces driving the acquisition process pointed to the existence of a military-industrial complex (Adams, 1981; Carey, 1969; Cooling, 1977; Koistinen, 1980; Lens, 1970; Rosen, 1973; Sarkesian, 1972; Weidenbaum, 1974, pp. 39–150). The military-industrial complex (MIC) consists of the professional military and their civilian allies in the DOD, defense industrialists, and legislators with a vested electoral interest in military procurement. This "iron triangle" of interests, it is charged, exercises its influence in an attempt to assure an optimal level of funding for military development, production, and procurement programs. While the concept of the MIC offers valuable insights into the role of state-society relations in the arms acquisition process, its utility has been undermined by the polemical connotations that have come to be associated with the term *military-industrial complex*.

Several noteworthy attempts have been made to apply the concept of an MIC outside the American context. Edward Kolodziej (1987b) and Peter Wallensteen, Johan Galtung, and Carlos Portales (1985) successfully adopted a more flexible and informed version of the MIC approach, expanding it to the "military–industrial–scientific–technological complex" (MIST), without falling prey to earlier, more rigid versions of the approach, as Mary Kaldor (1986) did. Alex Mintz (1983, 1985a, 1985b) utilized the MIC approach in analyses of Israeli arms acquisition.

JOINT ACQUISITION

Joint weapons acquisition involves not only cross-national, collaborative research, development, manufacture, and procurement, but also, most importantly, agreement on the characteristics of the weapons that are the objective of joint acquisition. Such agreement is a precondition for the success of joint acquisition projects and may, as Richard G. Head (1974, p. 419) has suggested, presuppose shared perceptions of both the military threat and how it must be dealt with. As with self-reliant acquisition, joint acquisition necessarily involves both state and corporate actors. Joint acquisition, however, requires that those state and corporate actors be able, and willing, to engage in cooperative, multinational ventures.

The option of joint, interdependent acquisition has been adopted largely because of economic constraints. The high and rising costs of self-reliant acquisition has made joint acquisition appear more attractive than it might otherwise appear. Joint procurement permits the burden of R&D costs and the uncertainties of the weapons development process to be shared by project participants. Longer production runs for jointly procured systems yield lower unit costs. Therefore, "The major advantage of cooperative projects... is reduced national expenditure" (Head, 1974, p. 419). Yet, as Head (p. 419) noted, "This alternative is still expensive and requires a competent R&D base, which has generally limited cooperative projects to medium-sized states with advanced technological capabilities."

Although no country has relied exclusively on joint acquisition, West European countries have initiated a number of joint development, production, and procurement projects. These West European collaborative acquisition projects, both those that are exclusively West European and those undertaken in the broader NATO context, have been the focus of a not inconsiderable amount of attention (Dean, 1979; Feldman, 1984; Klepsch, 1979; Udis, 1978; Hartley, 1983; MacDonald, 1986; Taylor, 1982, 1984, 1986; Wells, 1985; Wallace, 1984; Wulf, 1986).

The goals of West European collaborative acquisition programs encompass political, military, economic, and technological objectives. Collaborative acquisition is intended to foster greater alliance and/or West European integration and cohesion; the standardization of military equipment; more efficient use of scarce national resources; the maintenance of competitive defense industrial capabilities; and the reduction, if not elimination, of European dependence on American military technology (Wulf, 1986, pp. 178–79). Economic and technological incentives, however, more than political and military incentives, motivate West European collaboration and determine the pattern of collaboration, particularly the emphasis on high technology projects (Dean, 1979).

Both the history and evolution of the intergovernmental organizational structure for collaborative acquisition have been intimately tied to NATO (Taylor, 1982, pp. 16–34). Yet according to Trevor Taylor (1982, p. 27), the fact that the institutional arrangements for cooperation existed primarily within the NATO framework until the formation of the exclusively West European Independent European Program Group (IEPG) in 1976 was purely incidental to the initiation and fruition of collaborative acquisition projects. Collaborative acquisition projects "by and large did not come about because of the pressure of NATO, nor did they increase the commonality or interoperability of weapons in the alliance. They were intended to develop and permit the survival of national arms industries in Europe" (Taylor, 1982, p. 27).

West European joint development, production, and procurement projects have spanned the spectrum of modern conventional weaponry and have involved the establishment of transnational defense firms. The most notable projects include the Anglo-French Jaguar fighter, Puma, Gazelle, and Lynx helicopters, and Martel missile; the French-West German Alpha Jet trainer, Transall transport aircraft, and HOT, Milan, and Roland missiles; and the British-West German–Italian Tornado multi-role combat aircraft. The HOT, Milan, and Roland missiles were produced by the Franco-German, French-based Euromissile (subsequently, the Euromissile Dynamics Group); Panavia was formed to manage joint production of the Tornado by Messerschmitt-Boelkow-Blohm, British Aircraft Corporation, and Aeritalia; and Turbo-Union Limited (TUL) was established to coordinate efforts on the Tornado engine project by Motoren-und Turbinen Union (MTU), Rolls-Royce, and FIAT. Despite the problems that have plagued these and other collaborative efforts, by the late 1970s approximately 15 percent of the British and French procurement budgets and 50 percent of the West German were for the acquisition of the products of collaborative projects (Taylor, 1982, p. 27).

Yet West European collaborative acquisition efforts remain constrained by powerful political, military, economic, and technological factors. These factors include nationalism and the consequent tendency toward unilateralism and a low level of national participation in collaborative projects; divergent national perceptions of operational military requirements; corporate competitiveness; and reluctance to compromise sovereign control of vital national scientific, technological, and industrial capabilities. Herbert Wulf (1986, p. 194) has concluded that "Armaments are only produced cooperatively when it is absolutely necessary, not when it is merely possible. This necessity arises when the financial strength or technological development of a particular country is insufficient for the independent implementation of a particular project."

DEPENDENT ACQUISITION

Dependent acquisition can take the form of either off-the-shelf import of foreign military equipment or the indigenous assembly/production of foreign-designed equipment (or some combination of the two).[5] The first form results in dependence on foreign military hardware, and the second in dependence on foreign military technology. Both forms lead to military dependency and the concomitant diminution of state sovereignty and loss of policy and behavioral autonomy. This most problematic of procurement options can best be examined in light of the Third World's experience.

Dependent arms acquisition by Third World countries can be understood in the historical context of the imperialist and post-imperialist military relations between North and South. Under colonialism the indigenous military establishments of Latin America, Africa, and Asia had been an integral component of the command structure of the imperial powers. Local military forces had been commanded, trained, financed, and equipped by the European colonial powers. Consequently, Third World countries were in a state of not only economic but also military underdevelopment at the dawn of political independence.

Confronted with external threats to their security and often even more threatening domestic conflict, possessing inadequately armed military forces, and lacking the scientific, technological, and industrial capability required for the local manufacture of essential military equipment, developing countries had little alternative but to import the hardware needed to equip their armed forces. The dependence of the developing countries of the Southern periphery on arms imports from the advanced industrial countries of the Northern core became the defining characteristic of post-colonial North-South military relations.

It was during the immediate post-independence period that single/predominant source acquisition, the first of two forms of the arms import option, was most in evidence. Although there were exceptions, developing countries tended to acquire arms from their former colonizers during the immediate post-colonial period. Having served with and been trained by core militaries, many Third World militaries were reluctant to sever the close ties established between the armed forces of the core and the periphery under colonialism. In this way the colonial military relationship was perpetuated in the post-colonial world. During the late 1950s and the 1960s, of course, the United

States and the Soviet Union, in their Cold War scramble for post-colonial empires, displaced the former European colonial powers as the major arms suppliers to the developing world. Thereafter, one of the two superpowers tended to play the role of single or predominant supplier.

The arms transfer policies of the advanced industrial countries fostered the Third World's dependence on Northern arsenals. Although commercial transfers have become increasingly important since the early 1970s, during the 1950s and 1960s developing countries were often able to acquire arms from what had become the two dominant suppliers, the United States and the Soviet Union, through grant aid or other financially attractive means. American arms transfers to the Third World during the 1950s and 1960s were primarily in the form of grant aid. The Soviet Union provided arms on extremely generous terms, offering 40 percent discounts, eight- to ten-year loans at the far below-market interest rate of merely 2.5 percent, and accepting payment in soft currencies and even commodities (Pierre, 1982, p. 78).

U.S. grant aid declined dramatically during the 1970s, and the Soviet Union toughened the terms of its arms sales—reducing the number and size of grants and often requiring payment in hard currencies (Pierre, 1982, pp. 46, 79). Nonetheless, by having provided arms through grants or at bargain basement prices, the two leading suppliers, purposely or not, had discouraged the pursuit of alternative arms acquisition strategies. Its low economic cost made military dependence appear relatively benign.

Most Third World countries, however, soon came to a full realization of the vulnerabilities and limitations inherent in dependence on foreign arms suppliers, especially dependence on a single or predominant external source of arms. The developing world's arms importers have been subjected to arms embargoes; interruptions in the flow of spare parts for imported hardware; the in-country presence of foreign personnel required to train local militaries in the maintenance, repair, and operation of imported systems; restrictions on the end use and resale of foreign equipment; and the attempts of suppliers to use the supply relationship to exert influence on their foreign and domestic policies.

Not surprisingly, developing countries have sought to counter the constraints inherent in dependence on a single or primary source of arms. The first of two counter-dependence strategies, and typically the first to be adopted, is to import arms from multiple sources. This initial counter-dependence strategy is a short-run, relatively low-cost option. Its objective is the distribution of dependence across a large number of suppliers so that no one supplier can effectively limit recipient political and military autonomy. The aim is to reduce not the fact but the impact of arms import dependence by spreading it around and distributing it across a larger number of suppliers (Kolodziej, 1987a, pp. 306–15; Neuman, 1986, pp. 38–60).

Despite the increasing popularity of multiple source import acquisition, there are major drawbacks to reliance on multiple suppliers as a counter-dependence strategy. Apart from the fact that dependence on imported military equipment is not actually reduced but is merely made to appear somewhat benign, multiple source acquisition often results in a polyglot assemblage of military equipment that poses significant training, logistical, and maintenance problems. Technicians and operators must learn to maintain, repair, and operate the aircraft, armored vehicles, missiles, and naval vessels not only of one foreign country, but of a large number of countries. Operational and technical capacities can be strained to the limit. Multiple source acquisition clearly means that the traditional goal of military standardization must be discarded.

Even though multiple source acquisition provides a degree of insulation from the effects of military dependence, any one supplier might still possess the ability to hinder military operations by withholding spare parts or withdrawing support and maintenance units for vital equipment, such as aircraft, that require frequent or near-continuous service. The operation of essential systems could be seriously curtailed, or even terminated, by such tactics. Clearly, multiple source acquisition is not a viable long-term counter-dependence strategy.

DEPENDENT PRODUCTION, IMPORT SUBSTITUTION, TECHNOLOGICAL DEPENDENCE, AND THE TRANSITION TO A MIXED ACQUISITION STRATEGY

The inherent inability of multiple source acquisition to insure military and political autonomy has prompted developing countries to turn to a second counter-dependence strategy: military import substitution (MIS). Substituting indigenously produced for imported weapons offers the prospect, albeit long term, of achieving a high degree of military self-reliance. By acquiring the capability to manufacture domestically a large proportion of the military equipment it requires, a developing country can begin to reduce, and in the long term perhaps eliminate altogether, the vulnerabilities inherent in dependence on arms imports, whether from single or multiple sources. Domestic production removes the constraints imposed by import dependence. When military equipment is acquired at home rather than from abroad, military planning and operations are no longer hampered by the possibility of arms embargoes, the withholding of spare parts, supplier efforts to use the supply relationship as leverage to exert influence, and the other circumscriptions of military dependence.

Military import substitution is a process that takes on different forms as it evolves through five distinct stages. During the first three of these stages, dependence on foreign military hardware is displaced by dependence on foreign military technology. The first stage involves simply the assembly of imported arms. Weaponry is still acquired from foreign suppliers, but is imported in the form of prefabricated components and is assembled in-country. The foreign supplier provides technical training and assists in erecting the facilities necessary for weapons assembly. Technical training includes not only assembly skills, but also the use of equipment needed to inspect, evaluate, and test the weapons being assembled. In the second stage, components are produced under license agreements with foreign suppliers. The complete weapon itself is still only assembled, but an increasing number of components are fabricated locally. It is in the third stage that MIS results in the actual production of complete weapons; foreign military equipment is manufactured under license. In the fourth stage, developing countries engaged in MIS utilize the technological skills and capabilities acquired in earlier stages to modify, redesign, or reproduce (through reverse engineering) foreign weapons systems. This is the first stage in which some element of indigenous research and development appears—in the form of either system redesign or reverse engineering. In the fifth stage, MIS finally results in the production of indigenously designed arms. Fifth-stage production can take two forms: (1) production based on local research and development but still incorporating foreign-produced or -designed components; or (2) production based entirely on indigenous, independent research and development.[6]

Large-scale military import substitution in the Third World is a relatively recent, but no longer analytically neglected, phenomenon (Ball, 1988; Brzoska and Ohlson, 1986; Katz, 1984, 1986; Neuman, 1984; Ross, 1981, 1984). Only four developing countries (Argentina, Brazil, Colombia, and India) were producing any of the four types of major conventional weapons—aircraft, armored vehicles, missiles, and naval vessels—in 1950 (Neuman, 1984, p. 172). By 1980, however, twenty-six developing countries were producing one or more of the major weapons systems. Of these twenty-six countries, fifteen were producing aircraft, six were manufacturing armored vehicles, nine were producing missiles, and twenty-four were building naval vessels. Six countries—Argentina, Brazil, India, Israel, South Korea, and South Africa—were producing each of the four types of weapons. By 1980, a total of eighteen developing countries had demonstrated the ability to manufacture either aircraft, armored vehicles, missiles, or naval vessels that were the products of domestic research and development programs. The tremendous increases in the number of Third World arms producers, the range of weapons produced, and the level of indigenous input are all the result of defense manufacturing and research and development programs initiated during the late 1960s and the 1970s (Ross, 1984, pp. 122–64).

That an increasing number of Third World countries have turned to domestic arms acquisition in an attempt to wean themselves from their dependence on external suppliers is beyond dispute. The success of military import substitution programs in actually reducing the level of external dependence and promoting military self-reliance and political-military autonomy has, however, triggered an as yet unresolved debate.

The growth of military manufacturing activities in the developing world has relied heavily on imported military technology. This technology has been acquired from the same sources that Third World countries have traditionally been dependent on for imported arms. The Third World's defense industries were constructed on a base of imported Northern military technology, and many of its products continue to incorporate imported technology in the form of either foreign components or components manufactured locally under licensing arrangements with Northern suppliers. Consequently, according to the conventional wisdom (Cahn and Kruzel, 1977, pp. 76–82; Clare, 1987; International Institute for Strategic Studies, 1977, p. 23; Lock and Wulf, 1979; Moodie, 1979a, 1979b, 1980; Neuman, 1980, 1984, 1986; Wulf, 1979, 1983), little has changed with the expansion of the Third World's defense production capabilities. According to this line of argument, military import substitution has not even led to the reduction, much less elimination, of dependence on imported arms. The declared goal of military self-reliance has not been, and will not be, attained. Instead, there has merely been a change in the form of dependence.

It may well be, however, that as military import substitution programs develop and mature, far more takes place than a mere change in the form of military dependence. The nature of military dependence undergoes a subtle but potentially profound transformation as developing countries turn from arms imports to arms production. Instead of importing only a finished product, developing countries have begun to import and assimilate the technological capability necessary to manufacture, and eventually develop, weapons domestically. Consequently, the Third World's defense manufacturers have been acquiring the means to alter the traditional North-South dependency relationship.

A static dependency relationship is inevitable when a country relies on foreign arms suppliers. But when arms production programs are initiated, and military production technology rather than arms are imported, a more dynamic relationship is established. Such a relationship has an inherent potential for the reduction, if not elimination, of military dependence. Promulgators of the conventional wisdom have failed to recognize the crucial difference between dependence on arms imports and dependence on technology imports. Dependence on arms imports engenders a static dependency relationship, whereas dependence on technology imports results in a dynamic relationship. The import of military technology has enabled a growing number of developing countries to build arms industries that may eventually provide the bulk of required military hardware, thereby greatly reducing the need for foreign hardware. As experience accumulates in the development and production of weapons, the world's newest defense manufacturers will also become increasingly less dependent on foreign military technology. J. Fred Bucy, of Texas Instruments, was right on the mark when he wrote in a 1976 Defense Science Report that "The release of technology is an irreversible decision. Once released, it can neither be taken back nor controlled. The receiver of know-how gains a competence which serves as a base for many subsequent gains" (quoted in Klare, 1984, p. 167). Dependence on foreign military technology can be overcome in the long term, just as technological dependence in other industrial sectors can be superseded (Dolan, Modelski, and Clark, 1983; Ernst, 1980; Street and James, 1979).

The manner in which Third World arms manufacturers have gone about MIS has insured the national autonomy of their defense industries. Even though foreign defense technology has played a major role in building up the Third World's defense industries, foreign defense firms have not. The emergence and growth of defense production in the Third World are not the result of Northern defense manufacturers shifting production operations to the South. Whether defense production is concentrated in the public sector, as in India, or the private sector, as in South Korea, or is spread across both sectors, as in Brazil, foreign defense firms have not been permitted to invest heavily in Third World arms industries. Foreign direct investment (FDI) in the defense sector has been strictly limited. Brazil, for instance, has sought to assure national control by restricting FDI in any given defense firm to 49 percent. Unlike many other industrial sectors in developing countries, therefore, the defense sector is not a penetrated sector.

Despite the success realized by countries such as Brazil, India, Israel, South Africa, and South Korea, not all of the Third World countries that have turned to military import substitution have eliminated, or will ever eliminate, the need for imported weapons and become self-sufficient. The need for external inputs remains. Argentina, for instance, even though it has long had an across-the-board production capability, still employed imported as well as locally manufactured weapons against the British in its attempt to wrest the Malvinas from Britain in 1982. Egypt, with its more recently acquired across-the-board production capability, still relies heavily on arms supplied by the United States and various West European suppliers. Other, less capable, producers, such as Chile, Indonesia, Mexico, Nigeria, Pakistan, Peru, the Philippines, Taiwan, or Thailand, are even further from the goal of military self-reliance. Even the most advanced producers have not yet completely eliminated the need for imported weapons. Israel still requires American supplies. Most of the technologically sophisticated weapons in the Indian arsenal are still imported. Even though South Korea produces some 70 percent of the military equipment which its armed forces have acquired in recent years, it still purchases American weapons and U.S. troops have not yet departed.

Those Third World arms manufacturers that exist in a high-threat, technologically sophisticated military environment have found it extremely difficult to throw off the shackles of military dependence. This is so even when, as in the cases of Israel, India, and South Korea, the resources devoted to military import substitution programs have been substantial. While Brazil, situated in a relatively benign security environment, greatly reduced the level of its dependence on imported arms in a short period of time, and South

Africa, confronted only by militarily weak adversaries, has become essentially self-reliant, Israel, India, and South Korea have found the process of reducing military dependence to be somewhat more arduous. Israel is located in what is arguably the most volatile region of the world and is confronted with adversaries that have been able to acquire some of the most advanced conventional weaponry available. The threat to Israel's security is immediate, constant, and nonreceding. India is confronted by two troublesome adversaries. One, China, has the world's largest military establishment. The other, Pakistan, has been armed with advanced American weaponry. And South Korea is confronted by an implacable foe: a North Korea that maintains a military establishment that is larger than South Korea's and that is supplied and supported by two major powers—the Soviet Union and China.

Although Israel, India, and South Korea have been able to reduce the level of their dependence on imported arms, it is inherently more difficult for them to become militarily self-reliant in the same sense that Brazil and South Africa have become self-reliant. Both South Africa and Brazil were able to utilize middle-level military technology in their quest for self-sufficiency. Given the nature of the threats they confront, however, Israel, India, and South Korea are compelled to acquire weaponry at the cutting edge of technology. In other words, the products of these three countries must be able to compete directly with those of the major arms suppliers—the two superpowers and the countries of Western Europe.

MIXED ACQUISITION POSTURES

Despite the numerous obstacles confronted in the attempt to nationalize arms procurement and reduce the level of dependence on arms imports, the manner in which Third World defense producers acquire arms increasingly resembles the manner in which many of the advanced industrial countries procure military equipment. The West European members of NATO, like the developing world's arms manufacturers, meet a portion of their military hardware requirements through import acquisition. For example, 30 percent of the defense contracts entered into by Italy in 1980 were for foreign military equipment (Rossi, 1983, p. 220). Over one-third of the military equipment purchased by Sweden during the 1970s was imported (Holmstrom and Olsson, 1983, pp. 147–48). Moreover, foreign (American) military technology played a crucial role in the post-World War II reconstruction of the defense industries of Western Europe's leading defense manufacturers—France, Britain, and West Germany—and Japan (Drifte, 1986). These and many other of the advanced industrial countries, again like Third World arms producers, continue to manufacture foreign military equipment under license and utilize foreign components in domestically designed equipment. According to Frederic Pearson (1986, p. 537), West Germany "has neither achieved nor even sought full military production autonomy. German industries often import key weapons components, including sophisticated aircraft engines and electronics." Therefore, the sources of military equipment for the Third World's arms producers and the advanced industrial countries are not very dissimilar.

As has become evident, those Third World countries that have attempted to nationalize arms procurement have joined the ranks of the numerous countries that have adopted mixed acquisition strategies incorporating elements of self-reliant, joint, and dependent acquisition. The inability of even the most advanced Third World defense manufacturers to produce 100 percent of their military requirements compels them to continue acquiring some proportion of their requirements from foreign suppliers. Therefore, Third World arms producers, like the vast majority of the Northern advanced industrial countries, manufacture what they can and import the rest.

A mixed posture that incorporates elements of self-reliant, joint, and dependent acquisition can assume a number of forms, ranging from limited production capabilities and extensive arms imports at one end of the continuum to extensive production capabilities and limited arms imports at the other end. Arms imports may be from a single/predominant source or multiple sources. However, countries that have made the effort to reduce their reliance on dependent acquisition are more likely to import arms from multiple sources than from a single or predominant source.

All things being equal, a country's political and military autonomy is to a large degree a function of where it is located on the continuum between self-reliant acquisition and dependent acquisition. Countries that have only limited production capabilities and a high import-to-production ratio are vulnerable and may well experience serious constraints on their political military autonomy, especially if they depend on a single or predominant supplier. Countries that have built up extensive indigenous production capabilities and have a low import-to-production ratio will be sensitive rather than vulnerable to disruptions in the supply of foreign arms and will have considerable policy and behavioral autonomy. The distribution of countries along the continuum between self-reliance and dependence is skewed toward the "negative" (limited production capabilities and a relatively high import-to-production radio) rather than the "positive" (extensive production capabilities and a relatively low import-to-production ratio) end of the continuum.

Of course, all things are not equal. As noted earlier, a high-threat, technologically sophisticated military environment complicates efforts to enhance self-reliance. The level of indigenous content must also be taken into account. The further a country has advanced through the five stages of production, and the greater, therefore, the level of local input, the more likely it is that import dependence will have been reduced and autonomy enhanced. It is quite possible, however, for a country to have developed an across-the-board production capability and be situated toward the negative end of the continuum. This situation is possible either because production is stalled at stage three with no local research and design input, or the security problems it confronts are of such magnitude that, even though the stage four and/or five production of aircraft, armored vehicles, missiles, and naval vessels is taking place, military supplies must still be acquired from abroad, especially during crises.

DIRECTIONS FOR FURTHER RESEARCH ON ARMS ACQUISITIONS

Clearly, weapons acquisition has not suffered from lack of analytical attention. Yet all is not well. Quantity is not to be equated with quality.

The primary deficiencies in the literature have less to do with the specific issues analysts have focused on than the approaches they have adopted. Bluntly stated, research on weapons acquisition, like research on international security in general, tends to lack genuine theoretical import. Too much of the literature is country-specific and noncumulative. The numerous, excruciatingly detailed case studies that have drawn on the bureaucratic politics approach have served to illustrate rather than develop the bureaucratic politics literature and, like the country-specific literature, are generally noncumulative. Much of the literature that does not consist of case studies or is not country-specific tends toward informed commentary rather than rigorous social scientific analysis. In addition, too much of the literature on the United States and the Soviet Union is narrowly policy-oriented and entangled in current, but passing, policy debates.

This rather dismal situation can be remedied. The case study approach, for instance, need not, and should not, be abandoned. The case study method is a valuable, and highly regarded, social science tool when properly utilized (Eckstein, 1975; Yin, 1984). Utilization of multiple case studies and the method of structured, focused comparison advocated by Alexander L. George (1979) and employed by George and Richard Smoke (1974) avoids the limitations inherent in the use of both case studies and the typical country-specific study. The structured, focused comparison of multiple cases would facilitate more rigorous, cumulative cross-national, and even country-specific, research on weapons acquisition postures and the weapons acquisition process. Cross-national research on weapons acquisition could also benefit from the methods and perspectives of quantitative international politics (QIP). The practitioners of QIP could perform an invaluable function by assembling a reliable, comprehensive, cross-national, time-series data base on arms acquisition.

Most importantly, however, work on arms acquisition should proceed in the context of broader theoretical work, whether it be work on the political economy of defense or international relations theory. Research on arms acquisitions falls squarely within the purview of the political economy of defense. This vital and expanding sub-field of international relations is concerned with the triangular interrelationship of politics, economics, and defense on both national and international levels. The insights generated by radical analyses of relations between weak and strong in the world system could also be brought to bear more fully on the international dimensions of arms acquisition. Finally, weapons acquisition could be examined from the perspective of the state-society approach pioneered, most recently, by Peter J. Katzenstein (1978). Weapons acquisition inevitably involves interaction between state and societal actors. While there is an implicit recognition of the role of state–society relations in arms acquisition in the military-industrial complex literature, that literature would certainly profit from the explicit utilization of the state–society research perspective.

NOTES

1. Although the following discussion of arms acquisition and national security draws selectively from literature on the international arms trade, that literature is not reviewed systematically here. Michael Brzoska, in his contribution to the second volume of this project, reviews contending perspectives on the arms trade, the evolving structure of the international arms trade, and the impact of the expanding number of suppliers.

2. There are actually four possible mixed options: self-reliant/joint acquisition; self-reliant/dependent acquisition; joint/dependent acquisition; and self-reliant/joint/dependent acquisition.

3. Bellany and Reppy, in their contribution to this volume, deal more broadly with defense science, technology, innovation, and R&D.

4. France has, admittedly, come relatively close. See Kolodziej, 1987a.

5. In preparing this and the subsequent section of this chapter, I have unabashedly and freely drawn on my earlier work in Ross, 1988 and 1986.

6. In actuality, of course, there is a continuum between these two forms of the fifth production stage.

REFERENCES

Adams, Gordon. 1981. *The Iron Triangle: The Politics of Defense Contracting*. New York: Council of Economic Priorities.

Alexander, Arthur J. 1974. Weapons Acquisition in the Soviet Union, the United States, and France. Pp. 427–44 in Frank B. Horton III, Anthony C. Rogerson, and Edward L. Warner III, eds., *Comparative Defense Policy*. Baltimore: Johns Hopkins University Press.

———. 1978–1979. *Decision-Making in Soviet Weapons Procurement*. Adelphi Papers Nos. 147 and 148. London: International Institute for Strategic Studies.

———. 1982a (April). *Patterns of Organizational Influence in Soviet Military Procurement*. Note N–1327-AF. Santa Monica, Calif.: Rand Corp.

———. 1982b (August). *Soviet Science and Weapons Acquisition*. Report R–2942-NAS. Santa Monica, Calif.: Rand Corp.

Allison, Graham T., and Frederic A. Morris. 1975. Armaments and Arms Control: Exploring the Determinants of Military Weapons. *Daedalus* 104:99–129.

Armacost, Michael H. 1969. *The Politics of Weapons Innovation: The Thor-Jupiter Controversy*. New York: Columbia University Press.

Aspaturian, Vernon V. 1972. The Soviet Military-Industrial Complex—Does It Exist? *Journal of International Affairs* 26:1–28.

Ball, Nicole. 1988. *Security and Economy in the Third World*. Princeton, N.J.: Princeton University Press.

Beard, Edmund. 1976. *Developing the ICBM: A Study in Bureaucratic Politics*. New York: Columbia University Press.

Brzoska, Michael, and Thomas Ohlson, eds. 1986. *Arms Production in the Third World*. London and Philadelphia: Taylor and Francis.

Buzan, Barry. 1983. *People, States, and Fear: The National Security Problem in International Relations*. Chapel Hill: University of North Carolina Press.

Cahn, Anne Hessing, and Joseph J. Kruzel. 1977. Arms Trade in the 1980s. Pp. 25–105 in Anne Hessing Cahn, Joseph J. Kruzel, Peter M. Dawkins, and Jacques Huntzinger, eds., *Controlling Future Arms Trade*. New York: McGraw-Hill.

Carey, Omer L., ed. 1969. *The Military-Industrial Complex and United States Foreign Policy*. Pullman: Washington State University Press.

Clare, Joseph F., Jr. 1987. Whither the Third World Arms Producers? Pp. 23–28 in United States Arms Control and Disarmament Agency, *World Military Expenditures and Arms Transfers 1986*. Washington, D.C.: U.S. ACDA, 1987.

Cooling, Benjamin Franklin, ed. 1977. *War, Business, and American Society: Historical Perspectives on the Military-Industrial Complex*. Port Washington, N.Y.: Kennikat Press.

Coulam, Robert F. 1977. *Illusions of Choice: The F–111 and the Problem of Weapons Acquisition Reform*. Princeton, N.J.: Princeton University Press.

Davies, R. W. 1977. The Technological Level of Soviet Industry: An Overview. Pp. 35–82 in Ronald Amann, Julian Cooper, and R. W. Davies, eds., with the assistance of Hugh Jenkins, *The Technological Level of Soviet Industry*. New Haven, Conn.: Yale University Press.

Davis, Vincent. 1966–1967. *The Politics of Innovation: Patterns in Navy Cases*. Monograph Series in World Affairs, Vol. 4, No. 3. Denver: Social Science Foundation and Graduate School of International Studies, University of Denver.

Dean, Robert W. 1979. The Future of Collaborative Weapons Acquisition. *Survival* 21:155–63.

Dolan, Charles F., George Modelski, and Cal Clark, eds. 1983. *North-South Relations: Studies of Dependency Reversal*. New York: Praeger.

Drifte, Reinhard. 1986. *Arms Production in Japan: The Military Applications of Civilian Technology*. Boulder, Colo.: Westview Press.

Eckstein, Harry. 1975. Case Study and Theory in Political Science. Pp. 79–137 in Fred I. Greenstein and Nelson W. Polsby, eds., *Handbook of Political Science*, Vol. 7, *Strategies of Inquiry*. Reading, Mass.: Addison-Wesley.

Ernst, Dieter, ed. 1980. *The New International Division of Labour, Technology and Underdevelopment: Consequences for the Third World*. Frankfurt: Campus Verlag GmbH.

Feldman, Jan. 1984. Collaborative Production of Defense Equipment Within NATO. *Journal of Strategic Studies* 7:282–300.

Gansler, Jacques S. 1980. *The Defense Industry*. Cambridge, Mass.: MIT Press.

George, Alexander L. 1979. Case Studies and Theory Development: The Method of Structured, Focused Comparison. Pp. 43–68 in Paul Gordon Lauren, ed., *Diplomacy: New Approaches in History, Theory, and Policy*. New York: Free Press.

————, and Richard Smoke. 1974. *Deterrence in American Foreign Policy: Theory and Practice*. New York: Columbia University Press.

Gray, Robert C. 1979. Learning from History: Case Studies of the Weapons Acquisition Process. *World Politics* 31:457–70.

Greenwood, Ted. 1975. *Making the MIRV: A Study of Defense Decision Making*. Cambrige, Mass.: Ballinger.

Halperin, Morton H., and Arnold Kanter, eds. 1973. *Readings in American Foreign Policy: A Bureaucratic Perspective*. Boston: Little, Brown.

Hartley, Keith. 1983. *NATO Arms Co-operation: A Study in Economics and Politics*. London: George Allen and Unwin.

Head, Richard G. 1974. The Weapons Acquisition Process: Alternative National Strategies. Pp. 412–25 in Frank B. Horton III, Anthony C. Rogerson, and Edward L. Warner III, eds. *Comparative Defense Policy*. Baltimore: Johns Hopkins University Press.

Herold, Robert C., and Shane E. Mahoney. 1974. Military Hardware Procurement: Some Comparative Observations on Soviet and American Policy Processes. *Comparative Politics* 6:571–99.

Herz, John. 1950. Idealist Internationalism and the Security Dilemma. *World Politics* 2:157–80.

————. 1951. *Political Realism and Political Idealism*. Chicago: University of Chicago Press.

————. 1959. *International Politics in the Atomic Age*. New York: Columbia University Press.

Hitch, Charles J., and Roland N. McKean. 1960. *The Economics of Defense in the Nuclear Age*. Cambridge, Mass.: Harvard University Press.

Holloway, David. 1977. Military Technology. Pp. 407–89 in Ronald Amann, Julian Cooper, and R. W. Davies, eds., with the assistance of Hugh Jenkins, *The Technological Level of Soviet Industry*. New Haven, Conn.: Yale University Press.

————. 1983a. The Soviet Union. Pp. 50–80 in Nicole Ball and Milton Leitenberg, eds., *The Structure of the Defense Industry*. New York: St. Martin's Press.

————. 1983b. *The Soviet Union and the Arms Race*. New Haven, Conn.: Yale University Press.

Holmström, Per, and Ulf Olsson. 1983. Sweden. Pp. 140–80 in Nicole Ball and Milton Leitenberg, eds., *The Structure of the Defense Industry: An International Survey*. New York: St. Martin's Press.

Hough, Jerry F. 1984. The Historical Legacy in Soviet Weapons Development. Pp. 87–115 in Jiri Valenta and William C. Potter, eds., *Soviet Decisionmaking for National Security*. London: George Allen and Unwin.

International Institute for Strategic Studies. 1977. *Strategic Survey*. London: International Institute for Strategic Studies.

Jervis, Robert. 1976. *Perception and Misperception in International Politics*. Princeton, N.J.: Princeton University Press.

————. 1978. Cooperation under the Security Dilemma. *World Politics* 30:167–214.

Kaldor, Mary. 1986. The Weapons Succession Process. *World Politics* 38:577–95.

Katz, James Everett, ed. 1984. *Arms Production in Developing Countries: An Analysis of Decision Making*. Lexington, Mass.: D. C. Heath.

————, ed. 1986. *The Implications of Third World Military Industrialization: Sowing the Serpents' Teeth*. Lexington, Mass.: D. C. Heath.

Katzenstein, Peter J., ed. 1978. *Between Power and Plenty: Foreign Economic Policies of Advanced Industrial States*. Madison: University of Wisconsin Press.

Kaufman, Richard F. 1985. Causes of the Slowdown in Soviet Defense. *Survival* 27:179–92.

Klare, Michael T. 1984. *American Arms Supermarket*. Austin: University of Texas Press.

Klepsch, Egon. 1979. *Future Arms Procurement: USA–Europe Arms Procurement*. London and New York: Brassey's and Crane, Russak.

Koistinen, Paul A.C. 1980. *The Military-Industrial Complex: A Historical Perspective*. New York: Praeger.

Knorr, Klaus. 1970. *Military Power and Potential*. Lexington, Mass.: D. C. Heath.

Kolodziej, Edward A. 1987a. *Making and Marketing Arms: The French Experience and Its Implications for the International System*. Princeton, N.J.: Princeton University Press.

———. 1987b. Whither Modernisation and Militarisation, Implications for International Security and Arms Control. Pp. 206–32 in Christian Schmidt and Frank Blackaby, eds., *Peace, Defence, and Economic Analysis*. London: Macmillan.

Kurth, James R. 1973. Why We Buy the Weapons We Do. *Foreign Policy* 11:33–56.

Lens, Sidney. 1970. *The Military-Industrial Complex*. Philadelphia and Kansas City: Pilgrim Press and the National Catholic Reporter.

Lock, Peter, and Herbert Wulf. 1979. The Economic Consequences of the Transfer of Military-Oriented Technology. Pp. 210–31 in Mary Kaldor and Asbjorn Eide, eds., *The World Military Order: The Impact of Military Technology on the Third World*. London: Macmillan.

Long, Franklin A., and Judith Reppy. 1980. Decision Making in Military R&D: An Introductory Overview. Pp. 3–18 in Franklin A. Long and Judith Reppy, eds., *The Genesis of New Weapons: Decision Making for Military R&D*. New York: Pergamon Press.

MacDonald, K. C. 1986. Collaboration in Procurement Versus National Interest. Pp. 167–79 in The Royal United Services Institute for Defence Studies, ed., *Defence Yearbook 1986*. London: Brassey's Defence Publishers.

McNeill, William H. 1982. *The Pursuit of Power: Technology, Armed Force, and Society Since A.D. 10*. Chicago: University of Chicago Press.

Mintz, Alex. 1983. The Military Industrial Complex: The Israeli Case. *Journal of Strategic Studies*. 6:103–127.

———. 1985a. The Military-Industrial Complex: American Concepts and Israeli Realities. *Journal of Conflict Resolution* 29:623–39.

———. 1985b. Military-Industrial Linkages in Israel. *Armed Forces & Society*. 12:9–27.

Munoz, Heraldo, ed. 1981. *From Dependency to Development: Strategies to Overcome Underdevelopment and Inequality*. Boulder, Colo.: Westview Press.

Moodie, Michael. 1979a. *Sovereignty, Security, and Arms*. The Washington Papers, Vol. 7, No. 67. Beverly Hills, Calif.: Sage Publications.

———. 1979b. Defense Industries in the Third World. Pp. 294–312 in Stephanie G. Neuman and Robert E. Harkavy, eds., *Arms Transfers in the Modern World*. New York: Praeger.

———. 1980. Vulcan's New Forge: Defense Production in Less Developed Countries. *Arms Control Today* 10:1–2, 6–8.

Neuman, Stephanie G. 1980. Arms Transfers, Indigenous Defence Production and

Dependency: The Case of Iran. Pp. 13–150 in Hossein Amirsadeghi, ed., *The Security of the Persian Gulf*. London: Croom Helm.

———. 1984. International Stratification and Third World Military Industries. *International Organization* 38:167–97.

———. 1986. *Military Assistance in Recent Wars: The Dominance of the Superpowers*. The Washington Papers/122. New York: Praeger, for the Center for Strategic and International Studies, Georgetown University.

Pearson, Frederic S. 1986. "Necessary Evil": Perspectives on West German Arms Transfer Policies. *Armed Forces & Society* 12:525–52.

Peck, Merton J., and Frederic M. Scherer. 1962. *The Weapons Acquisition Process: An Economic Analysis*. Boston: Division of Research, Graduate School of Business Administration, Harvard University.

Pierre, Andrew J. 1982. *The Global Politics of Arms Sales*. Princeton, N.J.: Princeton University Press.

Reppy, Judith. 1983. The United States. Pp. 21–49 in Nicole Ball and Milton Leitenberg, eds., *The Structure of the Defense Industry: An International Survey*. New York: St. Martin's Press.

Rosen, Steven, ed. 1973. *Testing the Theory of the Military-Industrial Complex*. Lexington, Mass.: D. C. Heath.

Ross, Andrew L. 1981. *Arms Production in Developing Countries: The Continuing Proliferation of Conventional Weapons*. N–1615-AF. Santa Monica, Calif.: Rand Corp.

———. 1984. Security and Self-Reliance: Military Dependence and Conventional Arms Production in Developing Countries. Ph.D. diss., Ithaca, N.Y.: Department of Government, Cornell University.

———. 1986. World Order and Third World Arms Production. Pp. 277–92 in James Everett Katz, ed., *The Implications of Third World Military Industrialization: Sowing the Serpents' Teeth*. Lexington, Mass.: D. C. Heath.

———. 1988. Arms Acquisition and National Security: The Irony of Military Strength. In Edward Azar and Chung-in Moon, eds. *National Security in the Third World: Internal and External Threats*. Aldershot: Elgar.

Rossi, Sergio A. 1983. Italy. Pp. 214–56 in Nicole Ball and Milton Leitenberg, eds., *The Structure of the Defense Industry: An International Survey*. New York: St. Martin's Press.

Sapolsky, Harvey M. 1972. *The Polaris System Development: Bureaucratic and Programmatic Success in Government*. Cambridge, Mass.: Harvard University Press.

Sarkesian, Sam, ed. 1972. *The Military-Industrial Complex: A Reassessment*. Beverly Hills, Calif.: Sage Publications.

Scott, Harriet Fast, and William F. Scott. 1984. *The Armed Forces of the USSR*, 3rd ed. Boulder, Colo.: Westview Press.

Street, James H., and Dilmus D. James, eds. 1979. *Technological Progress in Latin America: The Prospects for Overcoming Dependency*. Boulder, Colo.: Westview Press.

Taylor, Trevor. 1982. *Defence, Technology and International Integration*. New York: St. Martin's Press.

———. 1984. *European Defence Cooperation*. Chatham House Papers No. 24. London: Routledge and Kegan Paul, for the Royal Institute of International Affairs.

———. 1986. European Arms Cooperation. Pp. 181–201 in the Royal United Services

Institute for Defence Studies, ed., *Defence Yearbook 1986*. London: Brassey's Defence Publishers.

Udis, Bernard. 1978. *From Guns to Butter: Technology Organizations and Reduced Military Spending in Western Europe*. Cambridge, Mass.: Ballinger.

Wallace, William. 1984. European Defence Co-operation: The Reopening Debate. *Survival* 26:251–61.

Wallensteen, Peter, Johan Galtung, and Carlos Portales, eds. 1985. *Global Militarization*. Boulder, Colo.: Westview Press.

Weidenbaum, Murray L. 1974. *The Economics of Peacetime Defense*. New York: Praeger.

Wells, Samuel F., Jr. 1985. The United States and European Defence Co-operation. *Survival* 27:158–68.

Woods, Stan. 1986. Weapons Acquisition in the Soviet Union. Pp. 203–41 in Roman Kolkowicz and Ellen Propper Mickiewicz, eds., *The Soviet Calculus of Nuclear War*. Lexington, Mass.: D. C. Heath.

Wulf, Herbert. 1979. Dependent Militarism in the Periphery and Possible Alternative Concepts. Pp. 246–63 in Stephanie G. Neuman and Robert E. Harkavy, eds. *Arms Transfers in the Modern World*. New York: Praeger.

———. 1983. Developing Countries. Pp. 310–43 in Nicole Ball and Milton Leitenberg, eds., *The Structure of the Defense Industry: An International Survey*. New York: St. Martin's Press.

———. 1986. West European Cooperation and Competition in Arms Procurement: Experiments, Problems, Prospects. *Arms Control* 7:177–196.

Yin, Robert K. 1984. *Case Study Research: Design and Methods*. Beverly Hills, Calif.: Sage Publications.

6

On Science, Technology, and Military Power

IAN BELLANY

The link between the acquisition and application of scientific and engineering knowledge, on the one hand, and the power of the state, on the other, is nowhere denied. The experiences of the Second World War seemed to illustrate the direct relevance of national scientific and engineering capabilities to military power. The relationship between national scientific and technological innovation and economic growth, and hence economic power, while not well understood, is universally perceived to be a real one. The connection between national scientific and engineering achievements—from Nobel prizes to moon landings—and national prestige translates scientific knowledge into power over opinion. "To the degree that political power is sought and is perceived to depend on the use of knowledge," as Harold D. Lasswell has observed, "knowledge will be sought and applied" (Lasswell and Lerner, 1974).

To put things slightly differently, the acquisition and employment of scientific and engineering knowledge, whose intensity can be measured approximately by the number of qualified scientists and engineers employed within the state at any one time, is a strategic resource and industry. (The word "scientist" as used in this chapter includes engineers; science subsumes engineering except where the narrower meaning is plainly intended.)

Commentators in the West on the first Soviet nuclear test explosion in 1949 fell into two categories. One—the suprised category—had based their assessment of Soviet capability on the old strategic indices. At the beginning of World War II, steel production in the Soviet Union was 50 percent higher than Britain's, and its power production was about equal to that of the British. By the end of the war, Soviet steel production had dropped to the same level as that of Britain, and power production remained on a par (Milward, 1977).

The other category, the unsurprised, had taken more notice of the newer index of the size of the Soviet scientific manpower base. In fact, the Soviets had entered the war at a scientific manpower level well above that of the other major European powers (Britain was well below the level) and more closely comparable to that of the United States (Derek Price, 1964).

In other words, the perception that scientific manpower was a new scientific resource took some time to become firmly entrenched. In the United States it took the Soviet Sputnik launch to drive the message home. In Britain realization was not especially slow. J. D. Bernal's *The Social Function of Science*, an essentially Marxian analysis of the contribution which planned (centrally planned) science could make to what we have described here as state power, was published in 1939.[1] However, the British and U.S. governments in World War II only fitfully acted as if they believed science was a strategic resource to be nurtured and fostered through central planning or otherwise.

The successful, chiefly American, wartime program to produce the first weapons based on nuclear fission did a great deal to quell resistance to the notion that scientific endeavor could be organized and managed to achieve a particular goal. Scientists themselves often expressed the fear that organization would stifle individual creativity but the fear proved to be unfounded. Of course, 95 percent of the creativity involved in the Manhattan Project had to do with applying existing knowledge of the basic physics and chemistry involved. Only 5 percent involved basic science, and therefore not all doubters were immediately convinced. However, today "big science"—to use Derek J. de Solla Price's famous description—is everywhere. On both frontiers of pure physics—the inner frontier of the very small, the atomic and the subatomic, and the outer frontier of the very large and the study of the cosmos—experimental forays are carried out almost exclusively by large teams of scientists whose apparatus is so costly as to be within the reach of only the richest states or groups of states.

But it would be wrong to credit the war with the shift toward big science when the trend toward bigger science had begun long before. The percentage of scientific papers published in *Chemical Abstracts* with multiple authors—the result of team work, in other words—was only about 15 percent in 1900. By 1940 the figure had risen to 35 percent, and by 1980 the figure was probably about 100 percent (Derek Price, 1963).

The argument about whether the pursuit of scientific knowledge could be planned, organized, and managed without killing the goose that laid the golden eggs of scientific discovery and progress is no longer a black and white one. The interesting questions now are more complex and have to do with the balance between science and government. The limits of permissible disproportion between the two are quite easy to set. The comparative failure of the Soviet Union to capitalize on its enormous and growing stock of scientific manpower since its flurry of military and prestige successes in the 1950s and 1960s points to the dangers of too much planning and state direction of science. At the other end of the scale, there is the difficult fact that science cannot escape government altogether. Because basic scientific research can, as big science, be expensive, and because its nature is such that its findings cannot be appropriated by the funder of the work, if government did not pay the bills, it is hard to see who would.

There is no doubt, however, that national investment in the pursuit of scientific knowledge is correlated with national power. In 1980, six countries led the world in annual expenditure on research and development (a reasonable if imperfect measure of investment in the pursuit of scientific knowledge): Britain, France, Japan, the United States, the USSR, and West Germany (SIPRI, 1986; U.S. Congress, Office of Technology Assessment, 1985). The total number of scientists and engineers employed in these countries for the year 1979 were estimated to be (in thousands) 88, 73, 282, 620, 1300, and 122, respectively.

The power correlation is not exact, of course. Britain and France have an acknowledged strength along the prestige dimension and to a lesser extent along the military. West Germany has strength along the economic dimension, and Japan even more so. Japan also has great prestige, scoring its greatest achievements in engineering rather than in the purer sciences that qualify for Nobel prizes. The United States and the Soviet Union are strong along all three dimensions of power, although few would dispute the United States' clear bilateral superiority in the economic and prestige areas. Nor do many disagree that the United States has the military edge, in spite of the fact that its investment in the acquisition and application of scientific knowledge is apparently inferior to that of the Soviet Union.

The correlation between the size of the scientific personnel base and military power, from the global point of view, is not of particularly recent origin. The powerful symbolism of the Manhattan Project is again responsible for giving a contrary impression: that it inaugurated both big science and big defense, big defense being the large (by historical standards) peacetime annual defense budgets of the United States and other countries that have been a fixture since 1945. The truth of the matter is a little more complicated. Just as big science was already well on its way by 1939, so was big defense.

Derek Price's (1963) chief contribution to the understanding of the nature of scientific activity is his demonstration that science, in at least one sense, has always been "big." The global number of scientists, for as far back as can be measured and certainly since the mid-nineteenth century, has been growing at a steady exponential rate. In other words, the number of scientists continues to double with a steady rhythm—every ten to fifteen years or so. Hence, the famous aphorism that of all the scientists who ever lived, over 80 percent are alive today, and its corollary, that the situation was exactly the same at any time in the past—the contemporary number of scientists always exceeding the gathered up number of their deceased predecessors.

Somewhat surprisingly, one can make almost the same kind of statement about the growth of military power, or at least about the growth of military spending. Calculation based on figures for annual global military expenditure (omitting the World War years) (SIPRI, 1976) between 1908 and 1975 show an exponential rate of growth in real terms (inflation-adjusted) corresponding remarkably closely to the rate of growth in the global number of scientists. The doubling period for military expenditure is between thirteen and fourteen years. It too is a process that goes back to the nineteenth century, for at least twenty years. Global military expenditure (in real terms) in 1895 was approximately half of that of 1908, and that of 1882 was half that of 1895 (Choucri and North, 1975).

Neither scientists nor military expenditure appear spontaneously; governments are entirely responsible for military expenditures and increasingly so for scientists.

The United States launched a number of central government initiatives in the nineteenth and early twentieth centuries in order to stimulate scientific activity in the country. Lincoln created the National Academy of Sciences during the Civil War; Congress established the Army Corps of Engineers at West Point in 1902; and Wilson authorized the organization of the National Research Council during the First World War. But the most consequential of the early initiatives was the Morrill Act of 1862 and the establishment of the land grant colleges. These intitutions reflected de Tocqueville's observation of twenty years earlier that "scarcely anyone in the United States devotes himself to the essentially theoretical and abstract portion of human knowledge," in that the applied sciences of agriculture and engineering were the chief beneficiaries. Nonetheless, they did lead directly and indirectly to the creation of the engineering profession in the United States (Office of Technology Assessment, 1985).

After the Second World War, and after the Soviet detonation of a fission device, the National Science Foundation was created in 1950 with a mandate to improve national potential in scientific research and education. After the Sputnik launch, the National Defense Education Act of 1958 provided central funds (matched by funds from the states) for improving education, chiefly in the area of the sciences.

The Defense Department has made continual claims on the scientific manpower of the United States and, from time to time, has also acted to replenish the national pool of scientists. The proportion of total national (government and private) spending on research and development (total "real" national expenditure on research and development is in turn roughly proportional to the number of scientists in employment) taken up by the Department of Defense declined from roughly 50 percent in the mid–1950s to about 30 percent in 1984, reaching a low of 25 percent in the late 1970s. This saucer-shaped trend parallels quite closely the trajectory followed by the fraction of gross national product (GNP) taken up by defense as a whole over the same period. Non-defense government expenditure on R&D as a proportion of all R&D expenditure has over the same period taken on a dome shape, so that the proportion of government R&D spending going to defense fell from 90 percent in the mid–1950s to 50 percent in the late 1970s and went up again to 67 percent by the mid–1980s (SIPRI, 1986; Sapolsky, 1977; Office of Technology Assessment, 1985).

The contribution which the defense budget makes directly to producing scientists is roughly in proportion to the amount of defense R&D spending that is spent within universities and other educational institutions.

In recent times, this contribution has been comparatively small. In 1985, the DOD was responsible for 67 percent of all government R&D spending but for only 13.5 percent of all governmental support for basic research, the kind of work that tends to be carried out in educational institutions. This contribution declined as a result of the Mansfield amendment to the FY 1970 military procurement authorization. The amendment, with its echoes of de Tocqueville and the Morrill Act, redirected the DOD to spend less on pure research and more on applied research. Even though the amendment was modified and weakened the following year, the DOD, together to some extent with other science funding agencies of government, cut its spending on basic research. Government spending on mathematics—the most basic of the sciences—took on the familiar saucer shape, with a flat low point in the mid–1970s. It recovered to its 1970 level only in 1985 as a result of a rise in National Science Foundation spending (David, 1985). Even so, in 1983, the DOD still funded 42 percent of all basic research in mathematics (down from 62 percent in 1968).

Shortages in scientific personnel, particularly in university teachers of mathematics, engineering, and computer science, arose in the United States by the late 1980s (David, 1985; U.S. Congress, Office of Technology Assessment, 1985). It is not unreasonable to suspect that the period of austerity in government funding on basic research is implicated in this personnel shortfall in scientific areas. Even so, this is a small criticism to set against the United States' considerable achievement in deploying its scientific resources, at least since 1957. The United States has maintained at least an edge on the Soviet Union along the military axis of power and has outstripped it along the economic and prestige axes.

Why has the United States been more successful in this area than the USSR, where science would seem to be synonymous with state planning in the manner advocated by Bernal? According to Don K. Price (1974), the reason is the United States' decentralized policy on science. Science is "protected" from politics, for instance, in that the military professionals act as an independent buffer between science and the politician's wish (on occasions) to try to exploit scientific advances too soon. Seen from this perspective, the fact that the Department of Defense was still funding 42 percent of all basic research in mathematics in the United States in 1983 reveals how the military protects science from swings in political mood (as symbolized by the Mansfield amendment) toward favoring applied over basic research. Certainly, when science is not protected from politics extraordinary things can happen. The nightmarish attempts to create a Nazi science in pre-war Germany and a Stalinist science in the USSR in the post-war period are object lessons.

Don Price's internal quadripartite balance of power between the "four estates" of science, politics, administrators, and professionals, of course, admits that where science can need protection from politics, politics can also need protection from science. Unchecked, science is quite capable of pressing its claims too far.

In Britain a large portion of the country's scientific resources are applied to the commercial exploitation of nuclear energy from fission and fusion. As a result, in 1986 Britain had a record of no export of a power reactor for over twenty years and a scheduled new generation of domestic nuclear power plant to be based on American designs. In the military sphere, the British began work on the so-called Chevaline program to modify the reentry system of its Polaris A3 missiles in the early 1970s. Modified missiles began to enter service in the mid–1980s. The aim of the program was to give warheads a better chance of penetrating the Soviet Galosh-based ABM system. The ABM system was severely limited by treaty in 1972, and the cost of the Chevaline amounts to about 15 percent of the expected cost of the entire new Trident D5 flotilla, due to replace the four Polaris vessels from the early 1990s. This makes Chevaline another example of politics not getting protection from science.

Although similar instances of science having its own way in the United States are not totally unknown (and we will be touching on this question in the next section of this chapter), Don Price's balancing process seems to work better in the United States than in Britain. The reason is not clear. The British system is not greatly dissimilar, although the sometime nationalization of ownership of companies in the energy and defense sectors has had a centralizing effect in Great Britain. An important factor may simply be size. One of the great economies of scale attending scientific research arises from the fact that it is a risky endeavor. A single failure can make a small scientific establishment look bad: in a large establishment, it is likely to be offset by corresponding research successes elsewhere. Similarly, in the interplay between science and politics, a large system tolerates imbalances better than a small one. If the United States' space shuttle program is an instance of science not having been protected from politics and too much, as a result, having been attempted too soon, at least there are the older military-derived space launchers in reserve. Had the French Ariane space launcher, say, gone similarly wrong, there would have been no second line of defense.

Britain's comparative failure to make science pay along the economic and military axes of power may be a result then of its having only one scientist to every seven employed in the United States. Its better success rate along the prestige axis remains explicable because prestige of the sort that comes from the work of outstanding, rather than rank-and-file, scientists (and this certainly subsumes Nobel prize winners) actually shows diseconomies of scale (Derek Price, 1963). The 7 to 1 ratio of all scientists between the United States and Britain comes down, according to Derek Price's square root rule of thumb, to nearer only 2 1/2 to 1 in the case of outstanding scientists.

As we move along the spectrum, we see that the Soviet Union represents an extreme case of centralization. And in the Soviet Union there are several post-war practical instances of science not getting protection from politics. The SS–6 ICBM, the Galosh ABM system, the Mya–4 (Bison) bomber, and the first generation of Soviet multiple warhead payloads (MRV and MIRV)—all are examples of the premature deployment of technically unsatisfactory systems that should never have left the proving grounds. In the civil sector, the Tu–144 supersonic transport is another instance (Holloway, 1983). Interestingly, the picture over time seems to be suggestive of change. The SS–20 intermediate range ballistic missile, first deployed by the Soviets in 1977, is hardly an illustration of science needing protection from politics. Rather, it demonstrates the reverse: politics needing protection from science. Though an engineering and technical success, it made doubtful strategic or political sense since it added little to the Soviet nuclear arsenal while arousing widespread fears in the United States and Europe.

SCIENCE AND THE CENTRAL BALANCE

So far, we have established a link between the power of states and their scientific resources, and we have made connections between science and military power in particular, presenting new evidence that the connection is of considerably longer standing than is sometimes imagined. But we have said nothing about why such a connection should exist. Today it is easy to say why, and the answer has two parts: (1) the nature of the central military relationship between the United States and the Soviet Union and (2) the nature of modern society.

The military relationship between superpowers is characterized by both competition and cooperation. (Cooperation can be either explicit, when it is called arms control, or tacit.) The proportion of one to the other at any one time is likely to fluctuate, with neither ever being entirely absent. Moreover, with regard to a mature two-state power balance relationship, cooperation tends to be concentrated chiefly on quantitative aspects of the military strength of each—numbers of missiles and bombers, for instance—whereas competition will concentrate on qualitative aspects of military strength, that is, innovations and improvements in weapon types. Empirically, there may be little disposition to disagree with this description. Since 1972, at least, superpower competition in missile and bomber *numbers* has kept broadly within and below the numerical guidelines and ceilings laid down as part of the SALT I treaty of that year. That is, there has been virtually no competition in quantities. Qualitative competition has been a different story, with MIRV warheads and cruise missiles entering deployment virtually unchecked. Since 1983, there has been a strong surge of American interest in acquiring radically new weapons with which to defend itself against ballistic missile attack.

The generalization can be carried a little further still. In two out of three U.S. armed services, most of the 42-percent increase (in constant dollars) in the United States' defense budget between 1980 and 1985 has gone into more sophisticated equipment rather than more of it. The exception is the navy where the priorities have been the other way around.

The competitive urge has been stronger in the kinds of weapons acquired as opposed to their number because, as a result, there is more promise of getting a worthwhile advantage over the other side. Simply adding extra weapons of existing types is something that is both readily detected by the other side *and easily reacted to or compensated for.* The advantage gained will be short-lived and possibly even negative in that the preexisting balance of forces is soon reestablished but with new expense having been incurred. Going for new weapons, on the other hand, may give a more lasting advantage, because the other side needs to call on its resources of ingenuity as well as its production line capacity in order to make an effective response.

The parallel with companies in an oligopolistic competition is very close (Bellany, 1982, 1985). In the duopoly case, the two companies concerned can, and occasionally will, compete on something quantitative, like the price of their product. Normally they will not compete, for experience will have taught them that one price cut simply begets a counter cut, and neither company is better off. It is much more likely that they will compete qualitatively, on, say, advertising, because an effective response to a good promotional campaign can be difficult. As a result, the successful advertiser may obtain an advantage over its rival in terms of a sustained improvement in its market share.

Quantitative arms control is easier than qualitative control partly, of course, for reasons of verification. The chief reason is that quantitative arms control proposals, in a mature bipolar relationship, are normally pushing at an open door, whereas qualitative arms proposals are asking for cooperative behavior in the very sector where the competitive urge is strongest.

This simple model then explains the importance of science because it is science and engineering that make qualitative changes in weaponry possible. Moreover, qualitative changes are the only kind worth pursuing in a mature, strategic nuclear relationship such as has existed between the United States and the Soviet Union since, at least, the early 1970s.

Although the above might be termed the external reason why science is important, there is also an internal reason. Where a society is uncomfortable with large defense budgets, it is generally less uncomfortable if the large defense budget is spent on advanced weapons and weapons systems, and on a comparatively small number of personnel to man them, than on basic weapons and a comparatively large number of personnel. Predictably, it is the navy, with its decision to focus on size rather than sophistication in the post–1980 defense buildup, that is experiencing the most embarrassment as a result of the demographic turndown in the size of the enlistment base, putting pressure on the voluntary enlistment system.

Of course, large armies mean conscription, and they are also apt to mean large casualties. The toleration level for both—outside a situation of national emergency—seems to be declining even in those European countries with long traditions of universal military service. Comparisons have been made between the number of casualties the United States was prepared to accept in the First World War (about 1500 combat deaths a week) and the 200 combat deaths a week that were found intolerable in Vietnam (Sapolsky, 1977). There are reports that the Soviet Union found it difficult to tolerate the casualty rate it had been experiencing in Afghanistan. The Soviets' apparent sensitivity to casualties in the Afghan campaign and Moscow's decision to withdraw militarily from Afghanistan may be a straw in the wind and an indicator of change in Soviet society.

Even so, the asymmetries between Soviet and American society need not be stressed here. It is reasonable to suppose that the internal factor causing the United States to emphasize qualitative over quantitative additions to military strength will operate more weakly in the Soviet Union. There are two connected reasons why this might be so, and both have to do with differences in the political and economic structures of the two countries. In the United States, as in France and somewhat more ambiguously in Britain, large investments in military research and development seem to be compatible with innovation, leading to creation of wealth in the economy as a whole. Indeed, there may be certain non-defense side benefits from this kind of activity. The Soviet case seems to be different, with the insulation of the military-industrial sector from the civil sectors of the economy.[2] By contrast, where most Western states see no non-defense side benefits in large conscription-based forces, for the Soviet Union conscription still has a nation-building function.

It would be wrong to assume automatically that the Soviet political system has never felt uncomfortable with the idea of a large standing army or that the Soviet economy can indefinitely afford large conventional forces of a kind that is sufficiently well trained to operate sophisticated weaponry. After all, the Soviet defense establishment, like the American, seems to have a vertical technological unity. Sophisticated strategic weaponry could, in theory, sit side by side with basic weapons for the conventional forces, but in practice this is not what happens. The cutting edge of military innovation is at the strategic level, but the fruits of innovation are more or less quickly passed downward.

From the power perspective with which this chapter began, power seeking through military innovation per se is neither condemnable nor condonable: it is in the nature of international politics. What can be held up for examination are those cases in which a military innovation proceeds to the stage of deployment and no worthwhile margin of power accrues. In the language of

Don Price's four estates model, we would say that this situation occurs either when politics presses science too far or when science presses politics too far.

When politics dominates science, the result is the premature deployment of new weaponry, before technical shortcomings or production snags have been taken care of. When premature deployment occurs, the other side is gratuitously alerted to the existence of the new weapon and will normally have more than enough time to develop a counter of its own.

It is easier to think of instances of politics dominating science in the Soviet Union than in the United States, at least as regards nuclear weapons. The cases of the SS–6 ICBM and the Galosh ABM system have already been mentioned. The United States' responses to these innovations—the advanced ICBM and SLBM (Sea Launched Ballistic Missile) programs of the Eisenhower and Kennedy years and the multiple warhead and penetration aid programs, respectively, led the Soviet Union to be hoisted with its own petard. That is, the SS–6 and the Galosh created only short-lived power margins for the Soviets. This edge quickly turned markedly negative as the United States reacted to these new weapons with weapons of its own which had huge advantages over the Soviet systems.

When science presses politics too far, the result is a new weapon that may be successful enough technically but possesses dubious political virtues. The United States' modern cruise missile, whatever its military utility, obscures the distinction between a conventional and nuclear weapon delivery system. The cruise missile may have destroyed for good the usefulness of the delivery vehicle or launcher as a proxy measure of nuclear capability. Once the Soviets acquire a similar capability of their own, which will allow them to threaten the highly populated U.S. coastal areas with sea-based cruise missiles, a political question mark may be set alongside the technical accomplishments of range, accuracy, and miniturization embodied in the system.

Earlier, we had another example of politics ultimately failing to check science: the finely gradated series of technical shifts in the United States from an ICBM and SLBM force with single warheads, to single warheads and decoys and other penetration aids, to multiple warheads with penetration aids (MRV), and finally to multiple independently targeted re-entry vehicles or warheads (MIRV) with penetration aids. This was part of the price that had to be paid for science ultimately being permitted to pursue its own logic in MIRVing, the subsequent hue and cry in the United States over the size of the upper limit to how many separately targetable warheads the much heavier Soviet ICBM force could be made to carry when the Soviet rocket forces adopted the same technology.

In much the same way, with regard to conventional forces, imbalances between science and politics would again be of two kinds. When science needed protection from politics, we would expect to see weapons suitable to their operational circumstances, but unreliable or ineffective in operation.

Where politics needed protection from science, on the other hand, this would show up in weapons that worked well but were inappropriate to their operational circumstances. The differences between the science–politics balance within the United States and the Soviet Union, as regards the procurement of conventional weapons, are possibly more interesting than the similarities. During the present century, the balance in the United States has undergone a shift. The armed forces, required to economize on manpower, are going to be more open to technological innovation than their predecessors were. By and large, the United States' armed forces are going to be more open than their Soviet counterparts.

It would be surprising if the four estates model were to prove as interesting or as important in the conventional sphere as in the strategic nuclear arena. The reason is simply that science looms larger in the nuclear than in the conventional sphere. This can be seen by looking, for instance, at the British or United States' defense budgets. In both cases, the proportion of the budget devoted to nuclear activities is rather small. Conversely, the proportion of the defense R&D budget devoted to nuclear activities is rather high.[3] This is not to say that the model has nothing to say about the R&D and procurement of conventional weapons. Indeed, it is to be hoped that this chapter has already said enough to disprove that notion. But it does suggest that its explanatory role outside the nuclear area will be a subsidiary one, required to sit no more than coequally alongside considerations of interservice rivalries, arms export strategies, and government–armed services–industry relations. For this reason, the balance of this chapter is geared to the nuclear end, while saying enough, perhaps, about its application to conventional forces to act as an encouragement to future work.

WORK TO BE DONE

The employment here of Don Price's four estates model of the systemically beneficial decentralization of power as between scientists, administrators, professionals, and politicians does not do the model full justice. Nonetheless, enough may have been said to persuade the reader of its virtues, perhaps even of the virtues of the "science of science" approach of this chapter, for solving the puzzling problems involved in harnessing defense science to political purpose. By science of science is meant the body of work carried out by historians and sociologists into the relationship between science and society, in the broadest sense. Don Price's work is a particularly accessible and fruitful example. Derek Price's research is just as fruitful, if a little less accessible in view of his quantitative methodology, though no less typical of the genre for that reason.

The work of these two modern pioneers immediately suggests one kind of useful, new, albeit non-defense specific step forward. This would be to compile numerical indices of the degree of decentralization of the four estates and to chart the rise and fall of these indices over time.

The most obvious and simplest index of importance is the proportion of science expenditure (spending on research and development) funded by individual government departments. Any tendency for these proportions to change in the direction of greater inequality would signal an increase in centralization.[4] Unfortunately, compiling such indices is not as easy as it sounds. The definition of science expenditure is not straightforward. Even the distinction between government departments is not always easy to make. In the United States, the difference between the Defense Department and the Department of Energy, as funders of work on nuclear physics, for instance, may be more academic than real. While these definitional difficulties can no doubt be overcome, the instances of science needing protection from politics or politics needing protection from science in the United States, though important, have not been so gross, one suspects, as to allow easy correlations to be made with movement over time in the science concentration index.

A comparative inquiry involving Britain, where to all appearances the imbalances have been grosser and where the same science concentration index can be used, might be more immediately productive. Other, more defense-focused comparative studies of Britain and the United States could be equally revealing.

Certainly, similar, independent explanations have been advanced for the United States' development of MIRV and modern cruise missiles, and the British Chevaline program. The possibility has been raised (Shapley, 1980) that the ending of the Apollo program meant that the United States' scientific estate turned toward other outlets (i.e., development of MIRV and cruise technologies). In Britain, without something to follow on from the Polaris A3 warhead and reentry vehicle program, it is said that research teams working on nuclear warhead and related technologies would have been dispersed (Freedman, 1980). Chevaline became an outlet for the energies of scientists faced with the end of a major program (Polaris) and a long interval before the probable start of the next one.

What remains unclear, of course, and a matter for further study, is why these particular weapon programs rather than others received the scientists' attention. Here again the historians and sociologists of science have something to contribute. Thomas P. Hughes (1983) is the originator of the "reverse salient" concept of scientific advance. According to Hughes, a technological system improves in a manner analogous to the movement forward of a military front line. Any part of the system whose progress is slower than the rest creates a reverse salient in the line. When that happens scientists focus their attention and innovative activity on the reverse salient. Thus, if we were trying to discover why scientists focus on the development of the modern cruise missile, we would begin by noting that in the improvement of medium-range missiles a reverse salient had arisen in respect of the capacity of missiles to deliver conventional warheads as cheaply and accurately as aircraft (over typical tactical aircraft ranges). Ballistic missiles were (and remain) too expensive to hold out much promise here, but cruise missiles became a different matter when light and cheap jet engines and compact and cheap electronics became available. To use the new technology for the delivery of nuclear warheads as well preempted the appearance of a new reverse salient—a tactical range missile that could be used only for the delivery of conventional munitions.[5]

MIRV may have attracted the interest of scientists in an analagous way. Intercontinental-range missiles had failed to keep up with the long-range bomber in the important respect that their payload had to be dedicated to a single target. MIRV corrected this reverse salient. But this interpretation probably does not tell the whole story. Another element was present in the transition from the single warhead to the multiple warhead, that is, MRV, (a halfway house in the development of the MIRV). This is sometimes referred to as "technological sweetness," which scientists are supposed to find irresistible. It has something to do with the "elegance" of what is being proposed, and is not unlike the appeal to mathematicians of some proofs over others that may be equally correct but lacking in this aesthetic quality. What was elegant about the MRV was the conversion of part of the missile payload that had been used (or designated) previously for carrying penetration aids, that is, dummy warheads, to the carrying of real warheads, as lighter (higher yield-to-weight ratio) nuclear warheads emerged from the testing program. No amount of ingenuity by the defender could then allow him to discriminate between the real and the dummy. Moreover, some real warheads could be given dummy-like features.

The usefulness of the reverse salient concept is not restricted to looking backwards. For instance, a search made for possible reverse salients at the present time in the line of offensive strategic nuclear weapons would reveal a number of candidates. One of these would be the lack of "stand-off" capability on the part of the intercontinental-range missile compared to the bomber. In other words, the scientists' interest in seeing ICBMs and SLBMs equipped with warheads that are themselves miniature cruise missiles (or something very similar) is to be anticipated if the reverse salient characterization of innovation is accurate.[6]

Historians and sociologists of science have, of course, developed other explanations of innovation. The notion of a technological "trajectory" (Dosi, 1982), owing something to Thomas Kuhn's seminal idea of a paradigm, sees innovation as a process of progressive refinement of some original item of equipment. British work on the Chevaline reentry system, which refined the original Polaris A3 MRV within the political guidelines laid down by the British government (which had ruled out the MIRV option), certainly seems to have more to do with technological trajectories rather than repairing reverse sa-lients.[7] The starting point of this particular trajectory is usually seen as the German V–2 missile.

Historians and sociologists of science have explored the different expla-nations of innovation and the linkages between them (MacKenzie and Wajc-man, 1985), although the notion of the pull exerted by technological "sweetness" has not received the formal scrutiny it perhaps deserves. But where this literature is deficient is in its treatment of defense science. The attention it receives is disproportionately small and of mixed quality relative to the proportion of all scientific activity that is defense-related (about 25 percent in Western Europe and the United States).

To return to the four estates model, one general reason why the process of checks and balances between the four components may fail is the existence of obstructions to the flow of information. Where sections of the four estates are cut off from relevant information, they cease to participate effectively in the balancing process. There are two principal causes of obstruction: (1) a very general one which refers to the lack of scientific expertise on the part of politicians and government officials; and (2) a more defense-specific cause which is a result of the official secrecy attached to most defense projects.

The lack of scientific expertise on the part of non-scientists and its remedy in the shape of scientific advice to politicians is a longstanding issue that has already received the attention of several investigators, including Don Price himself (Snow, 1962; Don Price, 1962, 1965; York and Greb, 1982). Donald MacKenzie, the sociologist of science, introduces a concept that highlights the importance of scientific advice.[8] He describes a "ditch" of skepticism about the reliability of any well-established science-based enterprise, which is encountered halfway between those professionally close to the enterprise (the scientists) and the purely lay person. Persons who are neither lay nor scientific (Don Price's politicians, professionals, and administrators) tend to place too much faith in the enterprise. Politicians' normal antennae are usually good enough to alert them to the skepticism of the lay public, but without scientific advice it is difficult to see them learning about the skepticism of the scientists.

The scientific advice problem is commonly perceived to fall under two headings: the difficulty of ensuring that politicians get a range of scientific advice; and the question of how to ensure that politicians get not only scientific advice, but also advice *about* science.

Arranging for politicians to receive a range of scientific advice seems to be harder at the level of the chief executive than that of the legislature. Chief executives seem to be vulnerable to the crony factor when it comes to sci-entific advice. For example, Winston Churchill, during the Second World War, would listen to no one on scientific questions but the Oxford physicist Lord Cherwell.[9] Perhaps the most serious single consequence of this fact was an excessive diversion of British wartime resources into the aerial bombing of German civilian targets.

The other problem heading—advice about science—boils down to a question about the backgrounds of scientific advisers. An adviser with experience in the administration of scientific programs in addition to a scientific qualification would be more likely to know something about the sociology of the scientific profession than someone who was simply a distinguished scientist.

One way of moving forward on these old questions would be to examine the backgrounds of persons appointed to scientific advisory positions over the entire post-Second World War period. Specifically, we can investigate whether they were attached to chief executives, government departments, or legislatures, and classify them according to background. In addition, the backgrounds of chief executives themselves, of their principal political advisers (including cabinet members), and of chairmen of the appropriate congressional committee (or in Britain, parliamentary committees) can be scrutinized to determine to what extent these individuals had any scientific training.

Derek Price's original observations (1963) about the rapid doubling rate of the population of scientists led him to forecast that we would soon see people with science training achieving high political office. The immediate impression, if we think of Jimmy Carter and Margaret Thatcher, is that the prediction was a good one. But it would be interesting to put this observation to the more formal and wider ranging test outlined above, and to look at trends over time and at differences as between the United States and Britain. This would not answer the questions posed about scientific advice, but it would enable them to be asked in a more precise fashion.

The other obstacle to the smooth flow of information between the four estates is secrecy. Where there is secrecy the extent of concentration of power across the four estates is increased. Actors who are not privy to the secrets involved are effectively excluded from the checks and balances system. When this happens, there will be increased incidences in which science does not get protection from politics and politics does not get protection from science. Different scientific activities vary in the extent to which secrecy is a characteristic. Applying the four estates model to space science or medical science, which are open compared to defense science, suggests that we should expect a better balance between science and politics in these two areas (other things being equal). In all science, the more secretive British system should, other things being equal, evidence more instances of science and politics out of balance than the comparatively more open U.S system.

Taking a cross-section through defense science, some aspects of defense science are intrinsically more given to secrecy than others. The degree of secrecy that attaches to all aspects of intelligence gathering is normally very great. In the post-war period, the importance of scientific techniques to intelligence gathering has risen rapidly. As a result, we should not regard as complete those modern studies of the phenomenon of "intelligence failure" that overlook the imbalance between science and politics as a possible contributory cause. Somewhat analogously, the trend in the verification of arms control agreements has also been toward reliance on scientific techniques, as in national *technical* means. The system of checks and balances between the four estates within the context of verification will be most at risk in those areas of arms control in which verification technology overlaps extensively with intelligence-gathering technology, as in the SALT I and SALT II agreements. Where the overlap is small, as, for instance, in the nuclear non-proliferation treaty, the risk is accordingly reduced.

Within defense science, the tendency to be secretive about weaponry fluctuates over time. Whether warranted or not, it will reach a peak of intensity in wartime; it will be high too in periods of Cold War. Whether the degree of secrecy required to engage effectively in qualitative military competition, with an opponent in "normal" times is sufficiently high to interfere with the working of the checks and balances process between science and politics is a legitimate topic for further study.

NOTES

1. J. D. Bernal, *The Social Function of Science* (London: Routledge, 1939).

2. This is a simplification of a complex situation. There is a sense in which the Soviet economic structure as a whole is not well integrated, with individual sectors setting up their "own" suppliers. The defense sector is no exception. See David Holloway, *The Soviet Union and the Arms Race* (New Haven, Conn.: Yale University Press, 1983), p. 119.

3. This task is not quite as easy as it sounds. In the case of Britain, the strategic nuclear part of the defense budget amounts to about 5 percent. The nuclear part of defense R&D, on the other hand, is somewhere between 20 and 52 percent, depending on the method of calculation. See Philip Gummett, "Problems for UK Military R&D" in Ian Bellany and Tim Huxley, eds., *New Conventional Weapons and Western Defence* (London: Cass, 1987).

4. One way of doing this would be to use a Lorenz chart. The percentage of R&D spent forms the y axis, and the percentage of government departments accounting for that proportion of expenditure forms the x axis. A straight-line relationship would denote perfect equality, and a reverse L shape, perfect inequality.

5. The interesting missile here is the SLCM, Tomahawk cruise missile; the ALCM (air-launched cruise missile) is not assumed to be dual-capable. The full story of its development would give weight to the fact that a precursor existed in the form of the shorter range and originally conventionally armed-Harpoon, a U.S. Navy cruise missile. 138 The conventional SLCM, whose dimensions are precisely the same as those of its nuclear armed twin, is fitting, in one of its marks, with a Harpoon warhead. Official studies have been made of the possibility of fitting the Harpoon with a nuclear capability. See T. B. Cochran, et al., *Nuclear Weapons Databook: Vol. 1, U.S. Nuclear Forces and Capabilities* (Cambridge, Mass.: Ballinger Publishing Co., 1984), pp. 172, 192. For an official naval comment on the conventional SLCM, which unwittingly gives

credence to the "reverse salient" concept, see *Hearings before the Committee on Armed Services, United States Senate, 99th Congress, 1st Session, on S.674; Part 7, Strategic and Theater Nuclear Forces* (Washington, D.C.: U.S. Government Printing Office, 1985), p. 3863.

6. This is one way, of course, of looking at work on the so-called MARV, or maneuvreable reentry vehicle. The reader is invited to identify other reverse salients. For instance, missiles may have fallen behind bombers in their ability to avoid radar detection. Thus, the application of "stealth" technology to missile warheads can be anticipated.

7. Chevaline is meant to improve the capacity of the Polaris payload to penetrate late mid-course and terminal anti-missile defenses. It does so by creating a greater spatial separation between individual warheads than was possible under the A3 design, thus forcing the defender to intercept each warhead (and, the attacker hopes, each dummy warhead too) individually. The spatial separation is created in such a way, however, that the package of warheads carried by any one launcher homes in on a single target. It can only be assumed that the additional technical difficulty involved in converting Chevaline into a true MIRV would be slight.

8. Donald MacKenzie, oral presentation to Science Policy Study Group Workshop, London, June 1987.

9. C. P. Snow, *Science and Government* (New York: Mentor Books, 1962).

REFERENCES

Bellany, Ian. 1981. An Analogy for Arms Control. *International Security* 6:3.
———, et al. 1985. Non-proliferation of Nuclear Weapons: Commentary from a Public Goods Perspective. *The Nuclear Non-Proliferation Treaty*. London: Cass and Co.
Choucri, Nazli, and Robert C. North. 1975. *Nations in Conflict: National Growth and International Violence*, San Francisco: W. H. Freeman.
David, Edward E., Jr. 1985. The Federal Support of Mathematics. *Scientific American* 1252:5.
Dosi, Giovanni. 1982. Technology Paradigms and Technological Trajectories: A Suggested Interpretation of the Determinants of Technical Change. *Research Policy* 11.
Freedman, Lawrence. 1980. *Britain and Nuclear Weapons*. London: Macmillan for the Royal Institute of International Affairs.
Holloway, David. 1983. *The Soviet Union and the Arms Race*. New Haven, Conn.: Yale University Press.
Hughes, Thomas P. 1983. *Networks of Power: Electrification in Western Society, 1880–1930*. Baltimore: Johns Hopkins University Press.
Lassell, Harold D., and Daniel Lerner. 1974. Preface. In Albert H. Teich, ed., *Scientists and Public Affairs*. Cambridge, Mass: MIT Pres.
Mackenzie, Donald, and Judy Wajcman. 1985. *The Social Shaping of Technology*. Philadelphia: Open University Press.
Milward, Alan S. 1977. *War, Economy, and Society 1939–45*. London: Allen Lane Penguin Books.
Price, Derek J. de Solla. 1963. *Little Science, Big Science*. New York: Columbia University Press.

————. 1964. The Science of Science. In Maurice Goldsmith and Allan Mackay, eds., *The Science of Science: Society in a Technological Age*. London: Souvenir Press.

Price, Don K. 1962. *Government and Science*. New York: Oxford University Press, Galaxy Book.

————. 1965. *The Scientific Estate*. Cambridge: Belknap Press of Harvard University Press.

————. 1974. Money and Influence: The Links of Science to Public Policy. *Daedalus* 103:3.

Sapolsky, Harvey M. 1977. Science, Technology and Military Policy. In Ida Spiegel-Rosing and Derek J. de Solla Price, eds., *Science Technology and Society: A Cross Disciplinary Perspective*. London: Sage Publications.

Shapley, Deborah. 1980. Arms Control as a Regulator of Military Technology. *Daedalus* 109:145–157..

SIPRI. 1976. *Yearbook of World Armaments and Disarmament*. Cambridge, Mass.: MIT Press, London: Almqvist and Wiksell International, Stockholm.

————. 1986. *Yearbook of World Armaments and Disarmament* Oxford: Oxford University Press.

Snow, C. P. 1962. *Science and Government*. New York: Mentor Books.

U.S. Congress. 1985. Office of Technology Assessment. *Information Technology R&D: Critical Trends and Issues*. OTA-CIT–268. Washington, D.C.

York, Herbert, and Allen Greb. 1982. Scientists as Advisers to Governments. In J. Rotblat, ed., *Scientists, the Arms Race, and Disarmament*. London: Taylor and Francis.

7

On Basing

ROBERT E. HARKAVY

The superpowers' competition for external basing access—usable both for conventional power projection and as an element of the strategic nuclear equation—is one of the key elements of their global power struggle. Nevertheless, it has received only scant attention from national security scholars, at least in a comprehensive way.

This competition has been evidenced, for instance, in a number of the most salient events of the recent past. Reports of the U.S. air raid on Libya in 1986 in response to Libya's support for terrorism stressed the importance of France's refusal of overflight rights to the United States. Afterward, Britain's Thatcher government would encounter severe domestic criticism for allowing American use of British bases as launching points for the raid. The fall of the Marcos government in the Philippines prompted anxieties in the United States about retention of critical air and naval facilities. In response the Pentagon sought fall-back positions in nearby nations and in the island groupings of the Central Pacific. News that the United States was again utilizing intelligence facilities in Pakistan—in close proximity to the southern rim of the USSR—fueled speculation about a deal connected to Islamabad's assistance to the United States in channeling aid to the Afghan rebels fighting the Soviets. Meanwhile, New Zealand's refusal to allow continued visits by nuclear-armed U.S. naval vessels sparked a political crisis between the two nations. The crisis involved the possibility of American economic retaliation which might also spill over into U.S.-Australian relations, themselves made uneasy by a long-festering debate over U.S. bases there. U.S. basing access appeared increasingly precarious—or at least increasingly more costly—in a variety of other places where long-lived alliance ties had frayed over time: Greece, Turkey, Portugal, Spain, among them.

The United States was not entirely alone in this regard. The USSR, under some pressure from various manifestations of the Reagan Doctrine, was casting anxious glances at Mozambique's (and perhaps Angola's) flirtation with the West which, if pursued to the point of political realignment, could threaten Soviet access to important bases. And looking to the future, analysts in the U.S. national security bureaucracy (and presumably their Soviet counterparts as well) were already attempting to gauge the looming possible basing implications of space-based defenses. Either or both sides might require externally based ground-based lasers or other critical installations if the race for dominance of space should become more serious (*London Daily Telegraph*, 1984).

HISTORICAL BACKGROUND: A REVIEW OF TWENTIETH-CENTURY PRACTICE

There is nothing altogether new about the use by one military power of access to another's soil. There is, indeed, a long history of basing access and its associated diplomacy. Thucydides wrote of basing issues (in Sicily) which arose during the Peloponnesian wars (Thucydides, translated by Rex Warner, 1954, p. 447). Closer to the present, the successive maritime empires—regional to global—of Venice, Portugal, Spain, Holland, and Britain relied on external naval bases. They both reflected and determined maritime supremacy (Boxer, 1965, 1969; Kennedy, 1976). It was not surprising then that bases like Gibraltar or Dakar were the objects of imperial rivalries.

American and Russian strategic doctrines are sensitive to the need for bases. As early as the turn of the last century, Admiral Alfred Mahan developed an elaborate theory of national supremacy as a consequence of naval dominance and the control of a worldwide network of bases. For Mahan, coaling stations to service and fuel a nation's fleet of naval vessels and commercial shipping were the foundation stones of national survival and wealth. If coaling stations are now no longer needed, the underlying logic of Mahan's thinking informs the reasoning of advocates of a Rapid Deployment Force, a 600-ship navy, and a global defensive nuclear system—military systems that critically depend on foreign installations for their operation . Admiral Mahan viewed the combination of undivided sea control and preeminent basing access as crucial to the rise and fall of imperial naval power. Ironically, the supersession of sailing vessels by those powered by steam increased the dependence of major powers on bases, that is, coaling stations (Mahan, 1898; Rosinski, 1977). The British exploited the openings of both the Napoleonic wars and World War I by picking off rivals' overseas assets; such were the easy fruits of maritime dominance.

Admiral Sergei G. Gorschkov's writings (Gorschkov, 1979) reflect traditional Great Russian dismay at earlier naval weakness—specifically, the absence of a global basing network that might have circumvented reliance on British bases and hence altered the embarrassing outcome of the war with Japan in 1905. The United States emerged from World War II determined not to repeat its earlier, almost cavalier, ignoring of the importance of external bases. It learned the importance; for both offensive and defensive purposes; of the facilities acquired from the United Kingdom in the Lend-Lease/destroyer deal in 1940 as well as Japan's effective use of mid-Pacific bases at the outset of World War II. (Weller, 1944; Patch, 1951).

The modern period, which here is somewhat arbitrarily defined as the period since the close of World War I—has seen three more or less identifiable phases of global access diplomacy, albeit somewhat telescoped and hence not altogether discrete (Harkavy, 1982).

The colonial period, from 1919 through World War II.

The early post-war period, characterized by a tighter bipolar, ideologically based alliance structure.

The present period, characterized by a greater multipolarity, ideological diffusion, proliferation of independent sovereignties, and the changing basis of North-South relations.

The interwar period—as an extension of the pre-World War I global system—saw most of what is now referred to as the Third World remain under colonial control. Thus, basing networks, in a relative sense, were mostly a function of the scope of rival empires. Britain had by far the largest global basing and military deployment structure, followed in turn by France, Spain, Portugal, the Netherlands, Italy, Japan, and the United States. The USSR and Germany had virtually none. There was curiously little congruence, as there certainly is today, between the relative military power of the major states and the extent of basing access.

Furthermore, as the interwar period was characterized by shifting, relatively impermanent alliances (less clearly ideologically based than would be the case later), there was no pre-World War II equivalent to the highly structured and durable NATO and Warsaw pacts. There was also little if any stationing of forces by major powers on their allies' soil, which applied to naval and air bases as well as to ground force deployments. Some German utilization of Italian and Spanish bases in the late 1930s and contemporaneous Japanese access to Siamese (Thai) facilities were among the few exceptions. These patterns constituted an extension of what had been normal practice for centuries. It is the recent period that constitutes an anomaly, an important point not easily or often discerned by the casual observer. Also lacking by comparison with the present period was a nexus of arms sales to granting of basing access. At any rate, the arms trade of that period was still conducted on a "free market" basis; that is, it was removed from governmental licensing restrictions (Harkavy, 1975). Otherwise stated, earlier arms sales were not a major instrument for acquiring basing access. Nowadays, that relationship has become a hallmark of contemporary diplomacy.

The Western powers retained most of their pre-war colonial holdings in the early post-war period. These possessions were gradually reduced and eliminated over the next thirty years. But of greater significance, the West— underwritten by massive U.S. military and economic aid—was able to fashion an elaborate system of formal security alliances around the Eurasian rimland. These alliances—as primarily embodied in the NATO, ANZUS, CENTO, SEATO and Rio pacts, and supplemented by Washington's security ties with Japan, South Korea, and Taiwan (Paul, 1973)—provided the West an elaborate basing structure. It is within that framework that American conventional and nuclear strategy is cast and U.S. diplomacy is conducted.

During this early Cold War period, which preceded the partial unraveling of Pax Americana beginning in the 1960s, a convergence of security interests was assumed between the United States, and most of its allies and clients. Access was usually freely granted and was not normally the subject of hard negotiations over *quid pro quo* (U.S. compensation for bases), or of "status of forces," that is, contingent restriction of access.

The Soviets, meanwhile, with a few early exceptions (China, Finland, Albania) were constrained within their contiguous heartland empire and had little in the way of external access (Remnek, 1979, p. 359). Such developments were to await not only the upcoming political upheavals in the Third World, but also the Soviets' construction of a blue-water navy and long-range air transport capability. These capabilities generated new basing requirements while providing the power projection capability needed to sustain and (if necessary) defend a global basing structure.

The more recent period has seen gradual but cumulatively profound changes, resulting in a qualitatively different pattern of access and its associated diplomacy. The Soviets' leapfrogging of the old containment ring has eventuated in their acquisition of facilities in numerous Third World locales: Cuba, Peru, Angola, Mozambique, Libya, Syria, Algeria, India, Vietnam, Cambodia (Kampuchea), among others. Basing is now fully a two-bloc game and is wholly enmeshed in the big powers' competition for global influence. The old colonial empires have almost completely vanished, and many ex-colonial nations have not allowed a continued Western presence. (Some, indeed, now host a Soviet presence.) As a result, numerous former points of access have been lost to the West.

Increasingly, the United States has found it difficult to persuade many of its often reluctant clients that their security interests are convergent with its own. The result in many cases has been a move toward decoupling, resulting variously in full denial of access, the imposition of more restrictive terms of access, or, in combination, the imposition of higher costs in the form of rent, increased security assistance and economic aid, and political *quid pro quo* arrangements (Cottrell and Moorer, 1977).

Decoupling and growing perceptions of a decline and even divergence in security interests between basing states and the United States (access in exchange for protection and/or extended deterrence) have altered the diplomacy of access. That access must now be bargained for and bought. The balance of leverage between base holders and base seekers is more symmetrical today than in the past. Primarily, the instrument of arms supplies (or more broadly, security assistance) has become the foremost unit of exchange (Harkavy, 1979). Many U.S. clients—the Philippines, Spain, Portugal, Greece, Turkey, Morocco, and Somalia, among others—have sought and obtained large annual military and economic assistance packages. These compensations constitute a form of rent, in some instances totaling nearly $1 billion per year. Sometimes, too, the qualitative aspects of arms supplies (sophistication of aircraft, missiles, etc., and their lethal accessories) form the basis for bargaining. The same has been true regarding the Soviet overseas military presence, as suggested by the disparate experience of Moscow's arms relations with Egypt, Libya, Algeria, and Vietnam, among others (Dismukes and McConnell, 1979).

Generally, as elaborated below, basing access correlates with a close arms supply client relationship, featuring a sole or predominant major power role. Conversely, the now fairly large number of LDCs that acquire arms from both sides of the Cold War bloc divide tend, in most cases, to be free of a superpower presence, at least as pertains to major facilities. Shifts in arms transfer client relationships across the ideological divide usually result in concomitant shifts in access patterns. Witness the recent *volte face* in Egypt, Sudan, Somalia, and China (away from the USSR) and Ethiopia and Vietnam (away from the United States)!

Profound technological as well as political changes have altered contemporary patterns of foreign basing access. Several major changes stand out here. First, the longer ranges of aircraft and ships—along with the advent of aerial refueling—have greatly reduced the earlier requirements for more extensive chains of access needed, for instance, in aerial resupply of arms or troops during war. This trend has been reinforced by the now far smaller number of ships and aircraft of all types in all countries—more combat capability packed into fewer systems. In the 1930s, even some medium-range powers such as Argentina or Romania fielded 1,000 or more combat aircraft and far more surface vessels than now. The result: fewer bases all around, both at home and abroad.

The contrast can be seen rather starkly using a comparison of large-scale U.S. airlifts to the Middle East, respectively, in 1941–1942 and in 1973. In the earlier period, the United States, in mounting an airlift (also in ferrying fighter aircraft) to beleaguered British forces in the Middle East, had to use an elaborate chain of air staging bases stretching from Florida via Cuba, Puerto Rico, Barbados, Trinidad, British Guiana, Northeast Brazil (Recife, Natal), Fernando de Noronha, Takoradi (now in Ghana), Lagos, Kano (now in Nigeria), Khartoum, and on to Egypt. A shorter, though still elaborate, staging network was utilized to ferry aircraft to the United Kingdom via Newfoundland, Labrador, Greenland, Iceland, and Northern Ireland. By contrast, in

1973 the United States needed only Portugal's Lajes Air Force Base in the Azores Islands (supported by U.S. aircraft carriers) to mount a massive arms airlift to Israel. Afterward, still newer technological advances (C–141 aircraft "stretch" program, enhanced refueling capability) has enabled the United States, if required, to mount a similar airlift from Dover, Delaware, to Tel Aviv without the use of any intermediate stops.

Similar trends have been evidenced regarding naval bases necessary to support a global maritime presence. In the 1930s, the British Royal Navy utilized numerous main operating bases to establish a presence across the whole of the Indian Ocean and Western Pacific littorals (Cole, 1956). Today, with smaller fleets (but some nuclear-powered ships, better at-sea refueling, and other provisioning) the same approximate mission (albeit minus that of colonial control) is performed with a small number of U.S. bases. Yokosuka, Guam, Subic Bay, and Diego Garcia support an extensive U.S. naval deployment all the way from the Central Pacific to the Southwest Asia/Persian Gulf area.

But that is not the whole story. Whereas the sheer quantitative requirements for traditional air and naval bases have declined, there has been an enormous increase in requirements for numerous new "technical" basing facilities. Many of these requirements are not very visible or widely publicized, but are crucial to a modern, global military establishment. That trend has been gradual but ineluctable. Before World War II, there were some such "technical" requirements: radio receivers, transmitters, relays, and so on; terminals and relays for underwater cables; and some rudimentary radar and communications intercept facilities (Kennedy, 1971). But in combination, these functions were of limited importance vis-à-vis those of naval and aircraft main bases.

Now, the number and functions of such new basing requirements have expanded dramatically: signal intelligence (SIGINT), space tracking (telescopes, radars, laser sources), satellite control and data relay, ground terminals for underwater sonar cables (anti-submarine warfare), early warning radars (for missiles, bombers), seismological detection of nuclear explosions and downwind detection of air samples (nuclear explosion monitoring), navigation and positioning aids for aircraft and submarines, communications all along the spectrum from ELF (extra-low frequency) to UHF (ultra-high frequency), and a vast array of research, testing, and environmental activities (Carroll, 1966; Arkin and Fieldhouse, 1985). These new requirements have coincided with the expansion of modern military activity fully to three dimensions: surface (land and sea), the underwater, and outer space. Indeed, these newer technical facilities—alone or in combination—often deal with the interrelationships of military activities extending across all of these domains. Anti-submarine detection can involve satellites; navigation satellites assist mid-flight corrections for missiles launched from underwater, and so forth. Communications traverse all these media as part of integrated networks (Harkavy, 1988; Richelson and Ball, 1985).

DEFINITIONS

A certain amount of semantic confusion surrounds a number of terms and concepts now used to describe the subject which, by common convention, long fell under the heading of "basing" or "overseas bases." Indeed, earlier book titles used these terms without any self-consciousness about definitional ambiguity. As is so often the case, what is involved is not merely a matter of alternative or optional scholarly usage, but some subtle political and ideological issues as well, including the degree and types of foreign access, the political or economic terms of such access, and the extent to which it is temporary or permanent.

One frequently (and interchangeably) sees the terms *base, facility,* and *installation.* The last-named usually assumes the character of a strictly technical term, devoid of political/ideological content. It refers to one finite physical operation with one function. The terms *base* and/or *facility* appear to be a bit broader in scope but, although often used interchangeably, have come to connote a politically distinct set of circumstances (Hagerty, 1977). *Base*— a much more frequently used term for centuries up to the recent past—has come to define a situation in which the user nation (ie., foreign presence) has unrestricted access and freedom to operate. *Facility*, meanwhile, has come to be the preferred term where the host nation exerts sovereignty and where the user nation's access is contingent, restricted, and subject to ad hoc decisions about use in given situations.

By these definitions, European access to installations in former colonial holdings would have defined a base. This meaning was similarly applicable to those situations in which states were significantly unequal in power and leverage and in which "status of forces agreements" granted more or less open-ended access and use to the foreign presence. U.S. basing access in the period immediately after World War II illustrates this narrow understanding of base access. What used to be called basing now really refers to our prior definition of facility, since in an era of lapsed colonialism and diffused global sovereignty, there are virtually no more bases, only facilities. That is nominally true, but most writers continue to use the former term, if only after a formal demurrer regarding definitions (Harkavy, 1982; Hagerty, 1977).

One might prefer the use of a still broader term, *foreign military presence.* Everything that falls under the headings of bases and facilities would thereby be included. So too would large military formations (combat units, etc.) and military advisory groups, and headquarters operations that may be spread around office buildings in a host city's downtown.

Still broader is the notion of *military access* (sometimes coterminously referred to as *strategic access* but meant to connote a broader purview than would apply merely to strategic nuclear forces). This concept subsumes not only permanent or durable basing facilities, but also such disparate activities as naval ship port visits (Watson, 1982; Watson and Watson, 1986), regular or occasional access for fishing fleets or oceanographic vessels (some with "gray area" military purposes), overhead use of airspace (aircraft overflights) (Dadant, 1978), ad hoc military aircraft staging (sometimes involving use of commercial airports), human intelligence activities (HUMINT), whether fully clandestine or not, smaller military advisory groups, and so on. Clearly, the dividing line between this concept and those previously discussed is often indistinct, involving blurred, gray areas. For instance, more than occasional use of a port for warship visits can come, at some point, to define a facility, though a formal definition of the facility might require permanent stationing on land of shore personnel engaged in maintenance, repair, or reprovisioning. Likewise, frequent and more or less regular use of access to airports becomes, at some point, a *staging base*, or rather, a commercial *staging facility*.

EMERGING MACRO-POLITICAL TRENDS AND BASES

The preceding review of historical developments leads next to a discussion of emerging macro-political trends which, in a fundamental way, may now and in the near future impact on basing access. Such an analysis merges the somewhat distinct but overlapping endeavors of futurology (hence, the terminology of macro-political trends projected into the future) and of international systems analysis (identification of basic variables useful for describing *any* historical epoch). Systems analysis, considered by many scholars to be the most promising road to a general theory of international relations, might be used to "explain" why the United States has experienced a long-term, seemingly ineluctable, reduction in its access to bases over the past several decades, although its needs have never been greater. Or one might cautiously try to "predict" whether those trends are likely to be redirected, extrapolated, or reversed.

Ranging from the relatively abstract to the mundane, the following are some of the issue areas that appear most relevant to an analysis of emerging macro-political trends, as they would in turn impact on basing politics.

- Broad changes in the global political "climate" for big-power basing, involving a complex web of essentially subjective, psychological factors revolving about issues of sovereignty, national dignity/humiliation, and so on.
- Shifting conditions of international economics, involving north-south, east-west, intra-OECD dimensions: trade, investment, raw materials.
- Changing global political structure, involving such factors as polarity (bipolarity versus trends toward multipolarity), the continued role of ideology in determining alignments, propensities toward or against neutralism on the part not only of LDCs but also of nations now firmly within the Western or Eastern military blocs.
- The future of arms control, centrally involving SALT/START, test bans, and outer space, as it applies to basing; also potentially involving arms transfers, nuclear

weapons-free zones, nuclear non-proliferation, and perhaps conventional arms control in Central Europe.

• The remnant "decolonialization" of the Third World, that is, how many and what additional new nations might be created from presently remaining non-independent island groups.

• Trends in intra-Third World warfare: how many wars, what types (conventional or unconventional), extent of big-power involvement, and so on.

• Trends in conventional weapons developments, and the relationship to arms transfers and warfare in the Third World.

• Changes in the extent of nuclear proliferation, that is, a possible large-scale expansion of the number of nuclear armed states.

A comprehensive analysis of the myriad interrelationships among the above areas would, of necessity, be beyond the scope of this chapter. Some illustrative points, however, are offered here.

Regarding the "climate" for big-power access, it is clear that recent years have witnessed an increasingly less permissive environment for foreign access (Harkavy, 1982; Cottrell and Moorer, 1977). A foreign presence is, for obvious reasons, welcome almost nowhere, except where it can be construed as contributing directly and visibly to protection. Almost everywhere, both in the Third World and within the U.S. orbit of Western democracies, governments are subject to pressures regarding a foreign presence. Even the so-called special Anglo-American relation has been placed under stress (Campbell, 1986). Bruised dignities and compromised sovereignties are involved here, often at the level of rivalry over wages paid local personnel. In Western countries, and in U.S. clients in the Third World, Soviet propaganda and diplomacy are calculated to unhinge U.S. basing access (Cottrell, 1963). The United States in turn engages in various activities, such as at present in Nicaragua, to deny Soviet access to facilities. Bases are very visible political targets.

Furthermore, there is now a lot of "lateral" pressure among Third World countries involving superpower basing presences, echoed in U.N. resolutions—for instance, in such manifestations as the Iraqi Charter of 1980 which called on all Third World countries to eliminate foreign bases (Weinland, 1981). Some of these pressures are global and some are regional: discussions among Indian Ocean littoral countries about demilitarization of that region—in reality, specifically directed against the U.S. base at Diego Garcia; intra-Arab pressures linking U.S. bases in Oman, Morocco, and so on, to the Israeli issue. The United States seems, relatively speaking, to be especially vulnerable to these pressures for all of the usually cited reasons, that is, the legacy of Western colonialism, the failures of U.S. public diplomacy, anti-Americanism, and the facts of political control in most Soviet client states which preclude open opposition to a foreign presence. The moves toward "closure" of the seas and overland airspace as evidenced by the Law of the Sea regime further illustrate this pattern which generally involves an attempt by smaller countries to limit the major powers' freedom to operate at sea and in overhead airspace.

In addition, recent years have witnessed the spread of anti-nuclear and environmental movements throughout the Western world and elsewhere. The recent U.S. problems in New Zealand well illustrate how such factors can constrain U.S. basing access even in connection with an old ally, and one rather remote from the Cold War front lines. Pressures have been felt in the United Kingdom and Canada as well—for instance, involving the stationing of U.S. cruise missiles in the United Kingdom and testing of cruise missiles in Canada's airspace.

Generally, the psychological environment for foreign military access— particularly that involving nuclear weapons or even nuclear-powered vessels—will likely become even less permissive. Presumably, that trend could in some circumstances be reversed by increased global tensions , which at least in some places made a U.S. protective presence more desirable. That in turn could depend on perceptions of U.S. strength and resolve, though paradoxically, that same strength can induce resentment. Otherwise, it is also possible that in the future, Soviet basing access will suffer from the same pressures as now apply more seriously to the United States. Soviet problems in Egypt—which are clearly related to issues of national pride and independence—could be the forerunners of a more general phenomenon.

It is, of course, also difficult to predict just what macroeconomic trends, possible economic crises or cataclysms, or shifts in the global economic power balance will unfold in the near to distant future, and their impact on basing access. The uncertainties are no more obvious than in the light of various recent surprises and reversals: the oil glut replacing the oil shortage, the fluctuating strength of the U.S. dollar, or debt problems in Latin America and elsewhere among developing countries. In general, the overall balance of leverage between developed and developing nations is at stake.

Any number of possible broad changes in the international system could affect basing structure and involve dramatic shifts in political alignments. Though it is unlikely, Western Europe and the United States could split, perhaps dramatically. (This could, of course, involve partial split-offs.) Germany's *Ostpolitik* could be pushed much further, perhaps even to a "second Rapallo." The People's Republic of China (PRC) could become more closely aligned with the United States; contrariwise, one might envision a revival of the Sino-Soviet alliance. Historically, long-term, stable, ideologically based alliances have been more conducive to basing access, and multipolar global systems with more rapidly shifting alignments less so (Harkavy, 1982). There now seems to be an overall trend toward alliance decoupling. If so, access will presumably become more precarious and problematic, certainly more costly to the base-seeking state. Alliances based on "pragmatic" rather than ideological grounds are probably less conducive to access, because the basis for them will likely be more ephemeral.

The overall future of arms control is, at this writing, very unclear, both generally and with respect to specific arms control domains. It is also presumably subject to volatile short-run as well as long-run political shifts within the United States and USSR. The 1988 U.S. presidential election could have a variable impact. Whether the now seemingly frozen "SALT structure" will survive is unclear, as are the futures of test ban treaties and possibly those pertaining to anti-satellite weapons. Developments in any of these domains could affect basing requirements in response to changing (i.e., allowed) weapons deployments; ground and/or space-based laser weapons, cruise missile deployments, missile launching facilities, C^3I installations connected to ballistic missile defense, numbers of externally based nuclear-armed submarines, seismological stations, and communications. Certain arms control arrangements, such as those pertaining to shorter and intermediate-range nuclear missiles in Europe, will also affect basing requirements and associated diplomacy. One result of the latter may be the movement of U.S. nuclear deterrent capabilities out to sea, involving increased deployments of cruise missiles on submarines and surface ships.

The post-war decolonialization process is nearly complete, save a few remnant, nagging issues such as Namibia. But there may be further pressures in international forums which could involve Diego Garcia, Ascension, the Falklands, Bermuda, Greenland, the various quasi-independent states now emerging from U.S. trusteeships in the Central Pacific, the Canary Islands, Mayotte, and Gibraltar, to cite a few salient situations. Some of these do involve important Western basing assets (note Ascension's crucial importance in the Falklands war as well as for space tracking and tanker refueling). Given their strategic location, the Central Pacific islands could well become an important focus of superpower contention at some point in connection with growing Soviet naval power in the Far East, as that region becomes the strongest node of the international economy. The overall climate of North-South relations could have an ultimate bearing on the disposition or use of some of these small strategic prizes.

With regard to Third World warfare, it is important to note that some of these wars, particularly because of the diplomacy of big-power arms resupply, have had a large impact on basing access. Enhanced Soviet access to Vietnam was apparently part of the price of Soviet aid to Vietnam during its war with China in 1979. Soviet access to Syria has been enlarged as a result of the crisis in Lebanon, among other things, involving the basing of submarines at Tartus. U.S. access to Argentina has now been curtailed because of Washington's tilt toward the United Kingdom in the Falklands crisis. And, of course, there is the matter of Soviet bases in Afghanistan and conceivably in Central America. Soviet and U.S. bases were reversed after the Horn war of 1977–1978. The potential for Soviet access to Grenada was forestalled by an American invasion.

Arms transfer diplomacy—related to the foregoing—will be important, both generally and with reference to specific cases, to the future of basing diplomacy. Arms have become the principal medium of exchange of basing diplomacy. In few cases indeed has significant basing access been granted to either superpower without a significant arms transfer relationship, though the reverse of this proposition does not necessarily hold; that is, arms transfers do not always or automatically translate into access (Harkavy, 1982). Overall leverage is critical. Current analyses of the presently evolving trends in arms transfers tend to coalesce around some of the following points, all of which are germane to the future of basing access diplomacy.

- The overall volume of transfers to the Third World may now be receding, owing mainly to OPEC's decline (note the huge proportion of arms transfers recently accounted for by oil states), and also to the debt problems of other states. Otherwise, the near "saturation" of some arms markets and the vastly increased unit costs of modern weapons such as high performance aircraft and main battle tanks have been important factors (U.S. Arms Control and Disarmament Agency, annual; Harkavy and Neuman, 1987).

- The United States seems to be overtaking the USSR as an arms supplier, as measured by new orders, reversing the trend of recent years. This has resulted in part from the relaxation of self-imposed U.S. restraints as earlier embodied in Presidential Directive 13. It may also have resulted from the successes of U.S. arms in Lebanon and the corresponding Soviet debacle, that is, a perception in the Third World that U.S. arms technology is ascendant.

- Superpowers may increasingly be able to tilt some local arms balances with infusions of qualitatively more advanced systems, that is, ECM (Electronic Counter Measures), ECCM (Electronic Counter-Counter Measures), precision bombing technology, FLIR (Forward Looking Infra-Red), etc. If so (if that is one lesson of Lebanon), it may result in greater big-power leverage in bargaining for bases via arms sales, that is, the quality and sophistication of those sales may be paramount. Conversely, the Iran-Iraq war points to the problem of "absorption" as often overriding that of technology.

- More and more LDCs—as well as some developed ones—are demanding technology transfer, that is, assistance to indigenous arms production programs. As the case of the recent U.S.-Turkey agreement may indicate, this too may become part of the arsenal of leverage available to a major power seeking basing access.

The future impact of nuclear proliferation on basing diplomacy appears somewhat indeterminate. Indeed, even experts widely disagree about how many additions to the nuclear club there may be by the year 2000 or 2005 (Dunn, 1982). What, for instance, would be the impact—on basing—of the addition of some or all among the following to the nuclear club: South Africa, Taiwan, South Korea, Pakistan, Iraq, India, Argentina, or Brazil? Many "theoretical" treatments of nuclear proliferation project an overall "decoupling" of alliance systems, a kind of disaggregation, as superpowers are predicted as attempting to distance themselves from nuclear clients which, in a variety of circumstances, could trigger escalation toward a superpower nuclear exchange (Dunn and Kahn, 1975). But one might as easily argue that access might be enhanced in some cases involving big-power defensive or deterrent assistance to clients threatened with newly "nuclearized" neighbors (Jones, 1984).

TYPES OF BASES

The following ten categories describe the full spectrum of the types of facilities utilized nowadays by the major powers. They essentially define the scope of the subject. Excluded are fugitive and temporal relations such as port visits, aircraft overflights, and small-scale military advisory groups. These contact points as well as the structured relations listed below might be captured by the notion of "foreign military presence."

* Airfield—or any other site concerned with the operation of aircraft for military purposes.
* Naval—port or any other site concerned with the operation of ships for military purposes, such as repair dockyards and mid-ocean mooring buoys.
* Terrestrial—any site concerned with the conduct of land warfare, such as army bases, exercise areas, fortifications, or fixed artillery.
* Missile—sites concerned primarily with the maintenance and launching of missiles, or fixed artillery sites.
* Space—sites concerned with the operation or monitoring of military satellites other than communication satellites.
* Communications and control—sites concerned with military communications or the control of military systems.
* Intelligence and command—sites concerned with the gathering of intelligence information by non-satellite means, and sites exercising command over military systems.
* Environmental monitoring—sites carrying out monitoring of environmental factors of military importance, such as military meteorological stations.
* Research and testing—sites associated with military research and with developmental testing of military systems.
* Logistic—sites not obviously assignable to airfield, naval, or terrestrial, and concerned with the production, storage, and transport of military material, with the administration of military forces, and the housing, medical treatment, and maintenance of military personnel.

What is subsumed under most of these categories is rather obvious. Airfields provided by other nations can be used for the permanent stationing of fighter aircraft, bombers, tankers, naval ASW craft, and reconnaissance planes. They also serve as transit or staging bases for transport aircraft carrying men or materiel or for ferrying short-legged aircraft. The United States, for instance, bases fighter-bombers in Japan, South Korea, Turkey, the United Kingdom, Germany, the Netherlands, Spain, Iceland, and the Philippines; tankers in Spain, Iceland, and the United Kingdom; U–2 reconnaissance planes in the United Kingdom and Cyprus; and P-3 Orion anti-submarine warfare (ASW) aircraft in the Philippines, Azores, and some fifteen to twenty other countries. The Soviets have comparable deployments of combat aircraft in Vietnam, South Yemen, and Ethiopia, among others (Department of Defense, 1987).

With regard to naval access, one can point not only to the main U.S. fleet hubs and repair facilities in Japan and the Philippines, among others, but also to the large number of countries that allow port visits, minor repairs, or provisioning. The USSR has important naval access in Syria, Angola, Ethiopia, and Vietnam, among others, even while continuing to make more extensive (relative to the United States) use of mooring buoys and fleet rendezvous areas in international waters (Petersen, 1979).

Concerning terrestrial deployments—concentrations of army forces—most of what is important in the present period concerns the large U.S. deployments in Western Europe (primarily Germany) and Asia (Korea, Japan, Okinawa); and the Soviet counterparts in Eastern Europe and Mongolia. Otherwise, there is also the extensive Cuban presence in Africa (Angola, Ethiopia) and in Central America (Nicaragua and formerly in Grenada).

Both the United States and the USSR field extensive short, medium, and intermediate surface-to-surface missile capabilities in Europe (Lance, Pershing, cruise missile versus SS–20s, Scuds, Scaleboards, etc), the longer-ranged elements of which are scheduled to be dismantled under the U.S.-Soviet theater nuclear weapons accord. Earlier, the United States had Jupiters and Thors in the United Kingdom, Italy, and Turkey, and Matador and Mace missiles in Taiwan and Okinawa, respectively. The USSR tried to install nuclear-armed missiles in Cuba. Furthermore, both sides field large numbers of surface-to-air missiles (SAMS) in association with their respective land–army formations in Europe and Asia. Soviet personnel are also involved with the operation of long-range SAM–5 missiles in Libya and Syria.

Overseas facilities in connection with the growing militarization of space are becoming increasingly important for the United States and USSR and, to a lesser degree, for the United Kingdom and France. Involved here are missile tracking and control facilities and facilities associated with a variety of methods for tracking the satellites of other nations by optical instruments, lasers, and the like (Arkin and Fieldhouse, 1985). While the USSR utilizes some land-based facilities for these purposes, it continues to rely very heavily on sea-based satellite tracking facilities that are less prone to the political vicissitudes of access diplomacy (U.S. Senate, Committee on Commerce, Science, and Transportation, 1982; Watson and Watson, 1986).

Under communications, the major powers utilize global networks all across the frequency spectrum—from ELF used to communicate with submarines to systems relying on higher frequencies that are more usable for land-to-land and aircraft communications (Ford, 1955; Blair, 1985). The relevant technologies are changing rapidly and, with them, the requirements for access. In some areas, satellites are superseding ground and sea-based facilities. Fears about the potential vulnerability of satellites at the outset of major war also dictate reversed reliance on ground facilities. Meanwhile, intelligence facilities can take a variety of forms: SIGINT listening posts, SOSUS (sound surveillance systems) with land-based terminals for ASW hydrophone networks, and seismic arrays for ascertaining and locating underground nuclear explosions (Richelson, 1985, 1986; Richelson and Ball, 1985).

Viewed from another (more "functional") angle, the categories listed earlier in this chapter may be aggregated into two basic types of purposes for overseas bases: (1) conventional power projection and (2) nuclear deterrence or warfighting. A mere glance at these categories further reveals that many facilities may be dual-purpose in connection with these functions, just as facilities in virtually all of these categories will relate to both of them to some degree.

Waging and deterring conventional warfare involves, of course, far broader considerations than that of basing access. A comparison of rival superpower capabilities would involve earmarked ground forces, long-range airlift and-sealift capabilities, as well as overseas naval and aircraft orders of battle applicable to specific regions or locales. Net assessments of such capabilities have, of course, been common in recent years in relation to various possible scenarios involving the Persian Gulf, Iran, and the Arabian Peninsula area. They also apply to Northeast Asia and the Caribbean.

Basing access—permanent, temporary, ad hoc, or contingent—is still a major part of this equation, both as pertains to possible direct involvement by superpowers in Third World conflicts (either against a Third World nation or a rival major power), or to warfare involving allies, clients, or surrogates. This can be seen on several levels, most particularly regarding (1) forward basing of aircraft in proximity to possible areas of conflict, and (2) the use of transports for carrying arms in resupply operations.

The United States, for instance, forward-bases fighter attack aircraft in a number of locales in connection with combat contingencies. It has large-scale deployments (F–16, 15, 14, A–10, etc.) in Germany, the United Kingdom (A–10, F–111), Belgium, Spain, the Netherlands, and Iceland for general war contingencies involving NATO. Deployments of F–16s at several airbases in Eastern Turkey can be used against a possible Soviet thrust through Iran toward the Persian Gulf. Similarly, combat aircraft are stationed in Japan, Okinawa, South Korea, and the Philippines to deal with general war contingencies, a new Korean war, or a renewed outbreak somewhere in Southeast Asia. The ranges of these combat aircraft have been significantly extended by backup tanker refueling capability stationed nearby. Tankers are permanently stationed in the United Kingdom, Spain, the Philippines, Okinawa, Diego

Garcia, Iceland, Guam, Canada, and Greenland, but can be rotated to other
bases as well. More recently, the U.S. overseas deployments have included
airborne warning and control aircraft (AWACs) stationed in the United Kingdom, Iceland, and Germany, and several types of electronic warfare aircraft
co-located with other types of combat aircraft.

The Soviets have some forward-based combat aircraft outside the USSR
proper. There are, of course, large-scale deployments throughout the Warsaw
Pact area in Eastern Europe (2,000 tactical aircraft), and in Mongolia there
are deployments against China. In recent years, there have also been forward
deployments in Vietnam (Tu–95 Bears, Tu–16 Badgers), and at several bases
in Afghanistan in connection with the ongoing conflict there. In addition, the
USSR has utilized several main bases overseas for reconnaissance and ASW
aircraft (Tu–95D, IL–38)—in Angola, Ethiopia, South Yemen, Cuba, Syria, and
perhaps Libya. Aside from constituting one aspect of continuous Cold War
deterrence and presence, these forces would be crucial to interdiction both
of surface naval forces and submarines in the event of a general or a limited
war.

In addition to the superpowers, both the United Kingdom and France have
some modest deployments of combat aircraft overseas. The Royal Air Force
(RAF) maintains aircraft or helicopters on the Falkland Islands, Ascension,
Belize, Brunei, Cyprus, Gibraltar, and Hong Kong, as well as tankers on
Ascension en route between the United Kingdom and the Falklands. France
has forward-based combat aircraft and tactical transports in Djibouti, Central
African Republic, Chad, Gabon, Ivory Coast, and Senegal. These deployments
are, in many cases, clearly related to ongoing or potential points of conflict.

The staging of men and materiel plays a key role in big-power interventions
in the Third World and in the arms resupply of clients in combat. Both
superpowers plan carefully in terms of long-range staging routes or networks
in connection with intervention or resupply contingencies. The United States
devotes considerable attention to a logistics chain running through the Mediterranean to Southwest Asia and on to the Persian Gulf. Involved are staging
points and tanker refueling bases in the Azores, Spain, Morocco, Cyprus,
Turkey, Egypt, and perhaps Saudi Arabia. A "back" route through Hawaii,
Guam, the Philippines, Australia, Thailand, Diego Garcia, Kenya, and Oman
is part of this chain. Trans-Pacific routes, as well as those between the United
States and southern Africa and on to the Indian Ocean, are also deemed vital.
By comparison, the USSR focuses on north-south staging routes running
across the Mediterranean or through Southwest Asia, and southward through
Africa toward Angola and Mozambique. Another east-west route connects
clients and allies on an arc from Libya via Syria, India, and on to Vietnam.

Several recent Third World wars have underlined the importance of staging
routes for moving arms, advisory personnel, and surrogate forces. The 1973
Middle Eastern conflict highlighted U.S. dependence on access to airbases in
the Azores and for tankers in Spain. For the USSR, overflight permissions from

Turkey and Yugoslavia were critical. The Soviets utilized staging bases and the airspace of numerous North and West African states in supplying its friends in the Angolan conflict in 1975–1977; in a parallel situation, Cuba's movement of forces relied on several African (and perhaps Caribbean) staging points. The Soviet resupply of Ethiopian forces in 1977 highlighted the importance of access to South Yemen (perhaps, too, unauthorized overflights over Iraq and Pakistan); India was critical to the resupply of Vietnam in its war with China in 1979. As noted earlier, however, longer range aircraft and more numerous tankers on both sides appear to have reduced the necessity for access to staging bases, as well as allowing for easier circumnavigation of restricted airspace, regardless of how costly they have been in terms of time, payload, and crew fatigue, a point underscored by the U.S. raid on Libya.

Naval forces—fleets—are, of course, still vital elements of overseas power projection. They variously involve amphibious operations, utilization of carrier aircraft, offshore bombardment, and interdiction of rivals' naval forces. Bases are vital to such forces, for homeporting of station fleets, refueling, crew rotation, and maintenance. Traditional writings—which form the inspiration for the current U.S. maritime strategy—stress the indivisibility of sea control and the importance of early-on preemption of rivals' fleets at war's outset (Rosinski, 1977; Mearsheimer, 1986; Watkins, 1986).

The United States still maintains the largest global naval presence (as measured by ship-days in various oceans), and the most extensive basing structure, despite some gradual reduction of these assets in the past decade. The main external basing ports for U.S. fleets are at Yokosuka and Sasebo (Japan), Subic Bay (Philippines), Diego Garcia, Bahrein, Naples (Italy), Souda Bay (Crete), and Rota (Spain). Fourteen carrier battle groups are at heart of U.S. naval power projection capability, augmented by several refurbished battleships mounting sea-launched cruise missiles. A smaller Soviet overseas surface naval capability, still lacking large carriers and associated airpower, is hinged on bases at Camranh Bay (Vietnam), Dahlak Archipelago (Ethiopia), Aden (South Yemen), Latakia (Syria), and Luanda (Angola) (Department of Defense, 1985). The base at Luanda supports a small West African flotilla. The Ethiopian base provides drydocking and missile storage for Soviet surface forces in the western Indian Ocean.

Still other aspects of power projection are embodied in the subjective areas of coercive diplomacy and "presence" (showing the flag), essentially peacetime phenomena, but those closely related to alignment policies, support for client states, conventional deterrence, and the politics of prestige. As analyzed in detail by two Brookings volumes, respectively devoted to the rival superpowers, both sides have utilized air and naval forces in numerous instances of coercive diplomacy. Note, for instance, U.S. support of Jordan in 1970 and Soviet support for its client in the Seychelles (Kaplan and Blechman, 1978; Kaplan, 1981). These activities will, of course, rely on nearby support facilities.

The potential for such interventions is often measured by ship steaming distances from overseas bases (Institute for Foreign Policy Analysis, 1977). Meanwhile, "presence" is often measured by "ship-days" in various large bodies of water. Year-to-year measures of that sort have been used to monitor the growth of Soviet naval power in areas such as the Western Pacific, Indian Ocean, Caribbean, and Mediterranean (Watson, 1982). Even without an elaborate basing structure, the USSR has long maintained a high-profile presence in some maritime regions by dint of extensive use of support ships in lieu of land-based facilities and the corresponding utilization of mooring buoys outside of 12-mile limits. The locations of these buoys have been noted in the open literature (Petersen, 1979).

NUCLEAR DETERRENCE/WARFIGHTING AND OVERSEAS FACILITIES

To a surprising degree, the strategic nuclear deployments of both the United States and the USSR rely considerably on access to overseas facilities, a dependency that might increase in the case of a major crisis or a protracted, conventional war. Earlier in the postwar period, of course, the United States relied heavily on overseas bases for its B–47 bomber "Reflex" force (primarily in the United Kingdom, Spain, and Morocco) (Goodie, 1965; Klass, 1971); for deployments of Thor and Jupiter missiles in Italy, Turkey, and the United Kingdom; and for Matador missiles on Taiwan. Nuclear-capable submarines were also dependent on external facilities—Guam, Rota (Spain), and Holy Loch (Scotland).

Nowadays, U.S. land-based strategic missiles and B–52 bomber forces are based in the United States. Earlier dependence on submarine bases has been lessened (Rota and Guam are being phased out) in the era of longer range sea-based Trident submarines armed with D–5 missiles capable of being launched at distances of 8,000 km. Nevertheless, a variety of external facilities remain important for the U.S. nuclear deterrent posture. The B–52 bomber fleet still relies on a variety of tanker refueling bases in places like Greenland and Iceland for its optimal effectiveness as well as on numerous dispersal and post-attack recovery facilities. The U.S. deploys numerous FBS (forward-based systems), that is, nuclear-capable aircraft that can reach into the USSR from Turkey, the United Kingdom, and South Korea, although they are not listed as "strategic."

Submarines intended to attack Soviet nuclear forces make use of forward bases in the Philippines and in Sardinia. The various radar picket lines (BMEWs, DEW/North Warning, Pinetree) essential to anti-missile and bomber warning utilize access to the United Kingdom, Greenland, and Canada. There are also fighter interceptors in Iceland. Ships carrying SLCMs (sea-launched cruise missiles) make refueling stops at numerous ports and can also be resupplied by aircraft using foreign airbases.

Overseas weather stations give meteorological support to bombers. Precise positioning and navigation of submarines is (or has been) afforded by several systems requiring external access—Omega, Loran-C, Loran-A, and ground stations related to the NAVSTAR satellite global-positioning system.

ASW, which is crucial to nuclear deterrence, relies on a number of types of bases overseas. Numerous facilities are available for P–3C aircraft engaged in routine surveillance. They are also capable of carrying forward-based nuclear depth charges which are readily available for quick shipment overseas. SOSUS grids of underwater hydrophones, linked to shore-based data processing facilities, rely on access to numerous U.S. allies and clients: the United Kingdom, Iceland, Azores, Norway, Japan, et al. Satellite tracking and control facilities (GEODSS, Baker Nunn telescopes, radars, etc.) require access in numerous places. Also needed are airbases for satellite film recovery and early warning satellites' down-link relays (Australia, Germany). A vast proliferation of overseas communications facilities is related to the U.S. nuclear structure, ranging across the frequency spectrum. Submarines, for instance, rely on VLF (very low frequency) facilities, and bomber and ground systems on communications at a higher frequency (Arkin and Fieldhouse, 1985). The navy relies on external airbases for its TACAMO aircraft which are used as communications relays to submerged submarines. The air force needs bases for its ELINT craft, as well as for U–2 and SR–71 high altitude reconnaissance. The United States also deploys a global network of seismic arrays to detect nuclear explosions, in connection with ("horizontal") nuclear proliferation activities and with (hypothetical) war scenarios involving the actual use of atomic weapons (Richelson and Ball, 1985).

The Soviet Union, though far more reliant on ships for space tracking and communications, also uses numerous overseas facilities for components of its nuclear strategic power. Airports in Cuba are perceived as potential recovery bases for Backfire bombers. Access to airfields around all major oceans (Cuba, Vietnam, Angola, etc.) could be vital to ASW operations. Naval bases are also important for ASW operations, as well as for storage of submarine missile reloads. For the USSR as well as for the United States, key client states provide communications, intelligence, and space-tracking facilities. This is particularly important in connection with the Soviets' worldwide communications network hinged on the Molniya satellites (Richelson, 1986).

In recent years, there has been increased discussion of the possibility of the superpowers' mutual interdiction of bases as part of the escalation ladder leading from protracted conventional war to some level of nuclear exchange. Often, this possiblility is viewed as part of the tit-for-tat exchange pattern that might also involve various possible horizontal escalation steps. This could involve a variety of efforts by either superpower to degrade the other's nuclear strategic posture amid a conventional war to enhance deterrence and escalation dominance. If, for instance, the USSR was stymied in a ground assault against Western Europe (and perhaps also amid mutual efforts at anti-satellite interdiction), one escalatory option might be destruction of key U.S. C³I facilities overseas: SOSUS, satellite control and data down-links, communications, and so on, in such diverse places as Japan, the Philippines, Guam, Alaska, Iceland, or Greenland. The United States could respond in kind against a less elaborate Soviet overseas network, but one that derives redundancy from extensive use of shipboard facilities. Such exchanges might also be initiated or continued at a higher level on the nuclear "ladder," that is, after tactical or even theatre nuclear exchanges within Europe or on the ground in the Far East.

RELATIONSHIP TO THEORETICAL ASPECTS OF INTERNATIONAL RELATIONS

The subject of basing access intersects with a number of critical *areas of international relations* theory, a term that is loosely construed and perhaps better defined as "areas of conceptualization." As such, the subject may be seen to have broad significance and interest beyond the mundane mechanics of military technology. Specifically, one may relate basing competition to the traditional corpus of geopolitical theory: broad competing conceptions of grand strategy, that is, maritime versus continental strategies; international systems analysis; conceptualization of national interest or "strategic interests"; and definitions of balance of power and measurements of national power.

The relationship to traditional geopolitical theory is rather obvious. Its core involves fundamental questions about the relationship of landpower and seapower, that is, whether dominance of the heartland translates into global hegemony or, conversely, whether seapower encircling Eurasia can contain, if not defeat, a heartland-based power (Cohen, 1963; Parker, 1985). Seapower advocates or theorists, such as the noted Mahan, further insisted on the indivisibility of global maritime power. They saw it as virtually an all or nothing proposition, surely under wartime conditions if not beforehand (Mahan, 1898). That thesis emerged by inference from the progression of the serial maritime empires (Portugal, the Netherlands, Britain), each of which deployed truly global basing systems to support far-flung station fleets (Boxer, 1965, 1969). Although these basing systems were the results of victorious wars, they also served as springboards for increased advantage over rivals as the result of follow-on conflicts. One notes that Britain seized most French overseas possessions during the Napoleonic wars and repeated the pattern against Germany in 1914 (Kennedy, 1976). Of late, these historical events have been echoed by the new U.S. maritime strategy (and its hoped-for focus on "horizontal escalation") (Dunn and Staudenmaier, 1984; Gray, 1988; Mearsheimer, 1986; Watkins, 1986); the Soviet thrust for a global maritime presence during the Gorschkov era (Gorschkov, 1979); and the more recent, allegedly reactive, Soviet partial withdrawal from global ambitions so as to protect strategic underseas assets in the "bastions" (Fukuyama, 1987; Kolodziej and Kanet, 1988).

In this context, one might also cite the work of George Modelski (1980) on "oceanic empires" with its post-Vietnam emphasis (directed at U.S. foreign policy) on *points d'appui* (bases) and on the avoidance of getting "bogged down" in land wars of attrition. From a somewhat distinct ideological perspective, that also echoes the maritime strategy associated with the early Reagan administration (Watkins, 1986; Mearsheimer, 1986).

But whereas earlier geopolitical theories tended to deal primarily with the dimensions of land and sea (surface), more recent theories have had to account for the expansion of the purview of military geography to outer space and to the underseas. The interwar period also saw a brief vogue of airpower theories that focused on trans-Arctic routes and that were inspired by the assumption of the anticipated primacy of strategic bombing (Jones, 1955). Paralleling these developments, basing access has acquired the nature of a complex multidimensional game involving space, the underseas, and the land and water surfaces. If, in Cohen's (1963) memorable phrase, geopolitical theories deal with the "world that matters,"—critical terrain in whatever realm—it might now appear that the global basing aspects of the control of outer space may increasingly come to define new expressions of geopolitical theory.

Systems analysis—dealing with what was once alternatively defined by Stanley Hoffmann (1960) as a sociology of international relations—can also be connected to basing access and power projection, as noted in the earlier historical review of the subject. For one thing, the relative extent of big-power basing systems (qualified by the problem of maritime versus continental power) constitutes one measure of polarity. Today superpower basing networks seem to underline the tenacity of bipolarity. But to the extent that alliances have been unraveling of late—translating into the decoupling of basing access as illustrated by the case of New Zealand—that may highlight the earlier distinction drawn by Morton Kaplan (1957) between "tight" and "loose" bipolar systems. The earlier dominance of British and French basing systems warns us that global access and national power may not always be closely related. The partial bifurcation of military and economic power (note the cases of the USSR, OPEC, and Japan) further muddies the application of systems analysis to access problems or, conversely, to more accurate descriptions of global systems.

Recent extensive scholarly discussions of the Reagan Doctrine and endless revisionist analyses of the U.S. postwar containment doctrine have underscored the ambiguous nature of national interests—specifically, "core" or primary interests, those things that are most worth defending (Wildavsky, 1983; Deibel and Gaddis, 1987). In the past, such arguments have ranged across the importance of specific regions to the production of sinews of war; matters of cultural and political affinity; or sources of raw materials. Basing access has also been central to such definitions, in connection with chokepoints, sea lines of communications, and vital air transit points. Changing global military geography and the shifting importance of resource locations have rendered the relationship of some basing points to core interests a somewhat ephemeral matter.

In the context of modern military technology and associated geography, however, one point stands out, as illustrated by numerous recent events. Strategic value is often not correlated with the size of land mass. Many small islands and nations have become critical terrain (Kemp, 1977). Grenada provides one example, as do Cyprus, Mauritius, Diego Garcia, Ascension, Djibouti, and Belau. (Diego and Ascension, for instance, are critical to the U.S. global tanker refueling structure.) American policy toward Chile appeared to shift when the Pentagon apparently began thinking of basing F–15 anti-satellite systems (ASAT) aircraft on Easter Island in the Pacific. The United States and the USSR are now locked in a virtual bidding war for support of fisheries in the Southwest Pacific, a region that is clearly of interest to Soviet maritime strategists. Star Wars may yet reveal heretofore undreamed of new points of primary strategic interests for either or both superpowers.

The quest for basing access as it relates to national interests has also impinged on one of the key problems discussed by Hans Morgenthau and others who are partisans of a "power/realist" approach to international politics (Keohane, 1987). They essentially defined morality in terms of prudence, further defined as the adjustment of ambitions to the practical limitations of power. These questions have been echoed in recent arguments over the necessary extent of a U.S. global presence. Some think in terms of layered redundancy to deal with as large a range of contingencies as possible. Others prefer first to define the limits of what is worth defending and then to construct an appropriate basing or access system to suit these aims (U.S. Senate, Committee on Foreign Relations, 1979).

Some scholars, in a broadly theoretical vein, have attempted to identify the changing historical basis for the "ends" of global politics, that is, what is or has been at stake. Samuel Huntington (1971) has traced an historical progression from gold (mercantilism) to territory to industrial growth. Those are, of course, in all instances "objective" ends, howsoever arguable in a relative sense. Many arguments over access and "presence" are couched in the distinction between military necessity and prestige, for it is often conceded that prestige feeds back into military necessity. Broadly speaking, that raises interesting questions about the "ends" of contemporary international politics, to the extent victory or conquest may be rendered unlikely by the facts of a nuclear stand-off.

SUMMARY

By the late 1980s, the future outlines of basing diplomacy appeared a bit unclear. Generally speaking, there seemed a clear trend toward decoupling. American access to nuclear-related facilities appeared to be under increasing pressure in a variety of places, as did its access in connection with conventional military operations in the Third World. Some analysts perceived Soviet interest in forward power projection to be waning, particularly as Soviet overseas clients seemed increasingly to be perceived as drains on the Soviet economy. But the relentless march of technology—in areas such as space, communications, seismology, sonar, and geodesy—had produced ever-new needs for extended access. There seemed to be a push on both sides for dispersal and redundancy of military assets, so as to reduce vulnerability to preemptive (conventional or nuclear) strikes. On balance, it appeared that, for both superpowers, basing requirements were as crucial as ever, even as the political climate for access became ever less permissive. It had become a crucial aspect of the contemporary military competition.

REFERENCES

Arkin, William M., and Richard W. Fieldhouse. 1985. *Nuclear Battlefields: Global Links in the Arms Race*. Cambridge, Mass.: Ballinger.

Blair, Bruce. 1985. *Strategic Command and Control*. Washington, D.C.: Brookings Institution.

Boxer, C. R. 1965. *The Dutch Seaborne Empire: 1600–1800*. New York: Alfred A. Knopf.

———. 1969. *The Portuguese Seaborne Empire: 1414–1825*. New York: Alfred A. Knopf.

Campbell, Duncan. 1986. *The Unsinkable Aircraft Carrier*. London: Paladin.

Carroll, John M. 1966. *Secrets of Electronic Espionage*. New York: E. P. Dutton.

Cohen, Saul. 1963. *Geography and Politics in a World Divided*. New York: Random House.

Cole, D. H. 1956. *Imperial Military Geography*, 12th ed. London: Sifton Praed.

Cottrell, Alvin. 1963. Soviet Views of U.S. Overseas Bases. *Orbis* 7 (1):77–95.

———, and Thomas H. Moorer. 1977. *U.S. Overseas Bases: Problems of Projecting American Military Power Abroad*. Washington, D.C.: Georgetown University, CSIS, Paper No. 47.

Dadant, P. M. 1978. *Shrinking International Airspace as a Problem for Future Air Movements—A Briefing*. Santa Monica, Calif.: Rand Corp. Report R–2178–AF.

Deibel, Terry L., and John Lewis Gaddis, eds. 1987. *Containment: Concept and Policy*. Washington, D.C.: National Defense University Press.

Department of Defense. 1987. *Soviet Military Power: 1987*. Washington, D.C.: U.S. Government Printing Office.

Dismukes, Bradford, and James McConnell, eds. 1979. *Soviet Naval Diplomacy*. New York: Pergamon.

Dunn, Keith A., and William O. Staudenmaier. 1984. *Strategic Implications of the Continental-Maritime Debate*. Washington, D.C.: Georgetown University, CSIS, and Praeger.

Dunn, Lewis. 1982. *Controlling the Bomb: Nuclear Proliferation in the 1980s*. New Haven, Conn.: Yale University Press.

———, and Herman Kahn. 1975. *Trends in Nuclear Proliferation, 1975–1995*. Croton-on-Hudson, N.Y.: Hudson Institute.

Ford, Daniel. 1985. *The Button*. New York: Simon and Schuster.

Fukuyama, Francis. 1988. Soviet Military Power in the Middle East: Or, Whatever Became of Power Projection? Pp. 159–82. In Jacob Goldberg, Mark Heller, and Steven Spiegel, eds. *Soviet-American Competition in the Middle East*. Lexington, Mass.: D. C. Heath.

Goodie, Clifford B. 1965. *Strategic Air Command*. New York: Simon and Schuster.

Gorschkov, Sergei G. 1979. *The Sea Power of the State*. Annapolis, Md.: U.S. Naval Institute Press.

Gray, Colin S. 1986. *Maritime Strategy, Geopolitics and the Defense of the West*. New York: National Strategy Information Center.

Hagerty, Herbert G. 1977. *Forward Deployment in the 1970s and 1980s*. Washington, D.C.: National Defense University. National Security Affairs Monograph 77–2.

Harkavy, Robert E. 1975. *The Arms Trade and International Systems*. Cambridge, Mass.: Ballinger.

———. 1979. Pp. 131–51 in Stephanie G. Neuman and Robert E. Harkavy, eds., *Arms Transfers in the Modern World*. New York: Praeger.

———. 1982. *Great Power Competition for Overseas Bases*. New York: Pergamon.

———. 1988, forthcoming. *Bases Abroad*. London: Oxford University Press, for the Stockholm International Peace Research Institute (SIPRI).

———, and Stephanie Neuman. 1987. U.S. Arms Transfer and Control Policies: The Middle East. Pp. 17–48 in Steven Spiegel, Mark Heller, and Jacob Goldberg, eds., *The Soviet-American Competition in the Middle East*. Lexington, Mass.: D. C. Heath.

Hoffmann, Stanley. 1960. *Contemporary Theory in International Relations*. Englewood Cliffs, N.J.: Prentice-Hall.

Huntington, Samuel. 1971. Arms Races: Prerequisites and Results. Pp. 269–377 in Robert Art and Kenneth Waltz, eds., *The Use of Force*. Boston: Little, Brown.

Institute for Foreign Policy Analysis. 1977. Environments for U.S. Naval Strategy in the Pacific-Indian Ocean Area, 1985–1995. Cambridge, Mass.: Unpublished report.

Jones, Rodney. 1984. *Small Nuclear Forces*. Washington Papers No. 103. New York: Praeger.

Jones, Stephen. 1955. Global Strategic Views. *The Geographical Review* 15 (4):492–508.

Kaplan, Morton. 1957. *System and Process in International Politics*. New York: John Wiley and Sons.

Kaplan, Stephen S. 1981. *Diplomacy of Power*. Washington, D.C.: Brookings Institution.

———, and Barry M. Blechman, eds. 1978. *Force without War: U.S. Armed Forces as a Political Instrument*. Washington, D.C.: Brookings Institution.

Kemp, Geoffrey. 1977. The New Strategic Map. *Survival* 19 (2):50–59.

Kennedy, Paul. 1971. Imperial Cable Communications and Strategy, 1870–1914. *The English Historical Review* 86 (141):728–52.

———. 1976. *The Rise and Fall of British Naval Mastery*. New York: Scribner's.

Keohane, Robert O. 1987. Theory of World Politics: Structural Realism and Beyond. Pp. 126–67 in Paul R. Viotti and Mark V. Kauppi, eds., *International Relations Theory*. New York: Macmillan.

Klass, Philip. 1971. *Secret Sentries in Space*. New York: Random House.

Kolodziej, Edward A., and Roger E. Kanet, eds. 1988. *Limits of Soviet Power in the*

Developing World: Thermidor in the Revolutionary Struggle. Baltimore, Md.: Johns Hopkins University Press.

London *Daily Telegraph*. July 10, 1984. Space Wars Bases Likely in Europe.

Mahan, Alfred Thayer. 1898. *The Influence of Seapower Upon History, 1660–1783*. Boston: Little, Brown.

Mearsheimer, John. 1986. A Strategic Misstep. *International Security* 2 (2):3–57.

Modelski, George. 1980. The Theory of Long Cycles and U.S. Strategic Policy. Pp. 3–19 in Robert Harkavy and Edward Kolodziej, eds., *American Security Policy and Policy-Making*. Lexington, Mass.: D. C. Heath.

New York Times. 1986. In Battle of Wits, Submarines Evade Advanced Efforts at Detection. April 1: C1.

Parker, Geoffrey. 1985. *Western Geopolitical Thought in the Twentieth Century*. New York: St. Martin's Press.

Patch, Buel W. 1951. Overseas Bases. *Editorial Research Report* 2 (2).

Paul, Roland. 1973. *American Military Commitments Abroad*. New Brunswick, N.J.: Rutgers University Press.

Petersen, Charles. 1979. Trends in Soviet Naval Operations. Pp. 37–87 in Bradford Dismukes and James McConnell, eds. *Soviet Naval Diplomacy*. New York: Pergamon.

Remnek, Richard. 1979. The Politics of Soviet Access to Naval Support Facilities in the Mediterranean. Pp. 357–403 in Bradford Dismukes and James McConnell, eds., *Soviet Naval Diplomacy*. New York: Pergamon.

Richelson, Jeffrey. 1985. *The U.S. Intelligence Community*. Cambridge, Mass.: Ballinger.

———. 1986. *Sword and Shield*. Cambridge, Mass.: Ballinger.

———, and Desmond Ball. 1985. *The Ties That Bind*. Boston: Allen and Unwin.

Rosinski, Herbert. 1977. *The Development of Naval Thought*. Newport, R.I.: Naval War College Press.

Thucydides (translated by Rex Warner). 1954. *The Peloponnesian War*. Baltimore: Penguin Books.

U.S. Arms Control and Disarmament Agency. Annual. *World Military Expenditures and Arms Transfers*. Washington, D.C.: U.S. Government Printing Office.

U.S. Senate, Committee on Commerce, Science and Transportation. 1982. *Soviet Space Programs, 1976–1980:*. Washington, D.C.: U.S. Government Printing Office.

U.S. Senate, Committee on Foreign Relations, prepared by Congressional Research Service, Library of Congress. 1979. *United States Foreign Policy Objectives and Overseas Military Installations*. Washington, D.C.: 1979.

Watkins, James D. 1986. *The Maritime Strategy*. U.S. Naval Institute Proceedings. (January 1986, supplement.)

Watson, Bruce W. 1982. *Red Navy at Sea: Soviet Naval Operations on the High Seas, 1956–1980*. Boulder, Colo.: Westview Press.

———, and Susan Watson, eds. 1986. *The Soviet Navy*. Boulder, Colo.: Westview Press.

Weinland, Robert G. 1981. Superpower Access to Support Facilities in the Third World: Effects and Their Causes. Unpublished paper, presented at International Studies Association meeting, Philadelphia, March 18–21, 1981.

Weller, George A. 1944. *Bases Overseas: An American Trusteeship in Power*. New York: Harcourt, Brace.

Wildavsky, Aaron, ed. 1983. *Beyond Containment: Alternative American Policies Toward the Soviet Union*. San Francisco, Calif.: Institute for Contemporary Studies.

8

On Public Support

RICHARD C. EICHENBERG

The political events of the 1980s have made public opinion a central focus of the study of national security. In Western Europe, public alienation from security policies was revealed in both polls and protests. In fact, many observers came to believe that the domestic foundation of Western security policy had crumbled under opposition to the neutron bomb and to NATO's decision in 1979 to modernize its intermediate nuclear forces (INF). In the United States, the eruption of the Nuclear Freeze Movement and the increasing intervention of the Congress in the arms control process produced similar observations. In an article that has become a classic, Michael Howard argued that the traditional task of *deterrence* had been transformed. Given the quantity and destructiveness of nuclear weapons, Western governments would now be compelled to provide *reassurance*, "to persuade one's own people, and those of one's allies, that the benefits of military action, or preparation for it, will outweigh the costs" (1983, p. 317).

For strategists and political scientists, the growing attention to domestic consensus represents one of those happy marriages of scholarly interest and policy relevance, for studies of the linkage between domestic politics and international policy have long been part of the research agenda. In addition, as public anxiety increased during the early 1980s, there was a rush of new scholarship designed to investigate the extent and origin of the public's concerns. This chapter reviews that research, with particular reference to two sets of questions that frame the connection between domestic consensus and military strategy.

1. *Description.* Because domestic concerns erupted very suddenly, the most important task is to sort out the degree of change and continuity in recent opinions of security issues. Has the security consensus eroded completely, or has change been confined to specific issues? Indeed, is it possible that change is more apparent than real,

the result perhaps of overinterpreting single opinion surveys or overemphasizing the opinions of minorities?

2. *Explanation*. The official and popular reaction to the domestic turmoil of the 1980s was largely ad hoc and tied to specific events and public opinion polls. The assumption seemed to be that the public's concern was a short-term affair, to be explained by such slogans as "pacifism," "neutralism," or "anti-Americanism." What was lacking was an attempt to synthesize theory and hypotheses from the fields of international relations, comparative politics, and strategic studies in a broader explanation of domestic attitudes. Why should opinion on security issues change? Why should consensus erode? Could popular attitudes be explained by long-term forces in international politics, or was the uproar largely a short-term affair? Theoretically, what pattern of domestic cleavage should characterize opinions of security issues? Were these cleavages stable? And why?

The following pages review and evaluate the state of theory and research on these questions. Because recent research has not interpreted domestic consensus in terms of broader theory, we begin with a review of plausible theoretical *explanations* of factors that might undermine domestic consensus on issues of national security. Following this review, a number of recent *descriptive* surveys of change and cleavage in public opinions are examined in order to evaluate the most relevent hypotheses. The concluding section summarizes the discussion and raises some questions for future research.

THEORY: THE DEBATABILITY OF FORCE

Many observers interpreted the emergence of domestic anxiety and protest during the 1980s as a sudden eruption. Yet a review of theoretical work in international and comparative politics, as well as strategic studies, might have suggested that the increasing contentiousness of security politics was a natural result of the changes that had occurred in the global and domestic environments of post-World War II policy.

Change in the International System

In the field of international relations, the major theoretical works of the 1970s were directed at describing and analyzing changes in the nature of the international system. As such they did not directly address questions of domestic consensus. Yet elements of these theories have important implications for domestic consensus. For example, Robert Keohane and Joseph Nye (1979) based their analysis of complex interdependence in part on the *relative decline* in the utility of military force. The emergence of strategic parity in the early 1970s introduced caution into military planning. The Vietnam experience had already raised a bitter and sweeping debate about the domestic acceptability of the use of force abroad. Moreover, some of the most pressing problems of the 1970s—economic, resource, and ecological interdependence—produced competition for attention and resources, and they could hardly be solved using military force (Keohane and Nye, 1977, p. 27–29; Bergsten, Keohane, and Nye, 1975, pp. 6–9).

Of course, the theory of complex interdependence was much debated. Keohane and Nye were criticized for both exaggerating and understating the utility of military force (Baldwin, 1979; Art, 1980). In fact, the nature of international politics and the utility of force were becoming more debatable in the wake of Vietnam and in the face of competing priorities, domestic as well as international. As Edward Kolodziej observed, "If military power has never been more pervasive, its utility has never been more questionable" (1980, p. 35).

For the European democracies, the utility of force seemed even more questionable and thus debatable (Kelleher, 1987). Perhaps the superpowers could continue to invest in the race to maintain a sort of dynamic parity, but for European states such a competition would be prohibitively expensive. In any case, it was in Europe that the stalemate effect of nuclear weapons seemed most obvious. Moreover, the detente and *Ostpolitik* of the 1970s reduced the perception of threat, and the economic problems of the decade placed a serious strain on resources. In such an environment, was it any surprise that the defense budget—both the symbol of national security and a challenge to domestic welfare—would come under fire?

The emergence of U.S.–Soviet parity contributed to the contentiousness of security policy in another way by focusing attention once again on the American commitment to the security of Western Europe. Uncertainty about American commitments in the post-Vietnam period of parity was soon matched by discussions of declining American strength and leadership in the economic realm (Kolodziej, 1981). To be sure, there were also scholars who argued that the American commitment had been largely unaffected by changes in the nuclear balance (Quester, 1981; Schilling, 1983). Nonetheless, the very existence of the debate indicated an unsettledness and a search for new approaches to security.

In summary, although the peace movements and opinion polls of the early 1980s appeared to be a sudden and surprising development, a review of the literature in international relations casts them in a more familiar light. Scholars and policymakers had been arguing for over a decade about the impact of interdependence, strategic parity, and the putative decline of American power on policy and alliance cohesion. Should it be any surprise that this "noisy, even cacophonous debate" (Freedman, 1981, p. 344) found its expression in public opinion as well?

Social Change and National Security

Nor would a review of scholarship on the *domestic* politics of security suggest that societal cleavage was all that novel. Scholars of an historical bent could point to a persistent conflict in the security politics of democratic societies: between the liberal, "idealist" vision of security achieved through trade, negotiation, or international law, and the "realist" vision of security achieved through a balance of power. As both Michael Howard and Stanley Hoffmann observe, the liberal ideal has emerged persistently in the history of western societies. Although the arguments have varied with circumstances, the idealist vision is usually based on an explicit critique of balance-of-power policies: they are the problem rather than the solution. The way to real security and peace is not to treat the symptoms with deterrence but to solve the underlying conflict through negotiation, trade, or law. Indeed, for Hoffmann, this idealist vision is an essential *part* of the liberal democratic tradition (Hoffmann, 1973, 1985; Howard, 1978; Gilbert, 1961). Of course, the idealist strain in democratic societies has been submerged periodically. Yet the vision may have grown in recent decades, fueled by the social changes experienced by democratic societies since the end of the Second World War.

The most important of these changes were the culmination of democratization and the expansion of the welfare state. As both Edward Morse (1974) and Harold and Margaret Sprout (1968) argued, these were related processes with important implications for security politics. Before the Second World War, the welfare state remained fragmented and small in most Western societies. The full emergence of universal suffrage and the sense of solidarity produced by the war brought with them demands for universal income and social security that would ultimately place pressure on the traditional priority of national security.

The growth in domestic priorities could also interact with changes underway in the international system. In an age of strategic parity, detente, and arms control, why spend more for military force when its utility was in such dispute? As Morse argued with respect to French politics: "In such circumstances, the classic guns or butter issue is inevitably posed in politics" (1974, p. 202; for a contrasting view, see Kolodziej, 1987).

These developments in domestic politics were complicated by a second set of social changes underway in the advanced democracies: the process of generational replacement that could produce a new cohort of citizens with values and priorities in conflict with traditional security policies. Ronald Inglehart argued that a "silent" but steady revolution was underway in the industrial democracies. Younger citizens who had matured politically during its secure and prosperous years of the 1960s and early 1970s had developed "post-material" values that emphasized quality of life and self-fulfillment rather than the material and security concerns of earlier age cohorts (Inglehart, 1977, 1984a; see also Szabo, 1983). In addition, this younger generation had not benefited from the prodigious expansion in access to higher education that had accompanied the post-war social reform. Together with a secure and prosperous environment, increased levels of education could help lessen the threat felt by the younger generation because higher education fostered a cosmopolitan world view (Inglehart, 1977, pp. 11, 76).

Inglehart's research has been much debated (Boltken and Jagodzinski, 1985; Inglehart, 1985a), but several conclusions seem clear. First, Inglehart and others have presented convincing evidence that the *value* changes predicted by his theory are in fact present. There is now growing evidence that these changes are not the result of a "life-cycle" effect attributable to temporary youthful idealism (Inglehart, 1982, 1985b; Dalton, 1977, 1987; see also Jennings, 1987). Second, Inglehart's ideas should be read in conjunction with the international theory of the 1970s. The socialization environment of the successor generation was dominated by the Vietnam War and the emergence of strategic parity and arms control—previously the issues that had provoked debate about the utility of force. Finally, the significance of higher education for the process of generational change should be emphasized, for the higher educated are more likely to hold firm policy views *and* more likely to articulate them. Taken in combination, these observations suggest not only that generational change might produce an erosion of the consensus underlying the "old" policies of deterrence and military balance. They also suggest that debate on these issues would become more informed and more intense.

In summary, although the apparent lack of consensus on issues of security policy in the early 1980s surprised many observers, the theoretical ideas of political scientists might have predicted them. Changes in the global system and in domestic societies had not necessarily rendered military force less useful in any absolute military sense, but they had prompted greater debate about its political utility.

Short-term Factors

Each of the theoretical perspectives discussed above involve long-term, secular changes that may have contributed to an erosion of domestic support for security policy. Short-term forces may also be at work. First, it seems obvious that public concern might be a simple reaction to recent events and decisions. In Western Europe, the INF decision raised for the first time in many years the prospect of a new dimension to the arms race in Europe. In the United States, the buildup of defense forces under Presidents Carter and Reagan combined with specific decisions—such as the MX missile system—to bring the arms race very close to the public's consciousness, much as the ABM debate of the late 1960s had done. Second, the deployment decisions were taken in an atmosphere of extreme international tension that had caused a dramatic rise in the public's fear of war. Beginning with the hostage situation in Iran and continuing with the INF decision in late 1979 and the Polish crisis in 1980 and 1981, the crisis atmosphere was palpable. Perhaps the public outcry of the early 1980s should therefore be understood as a short-term reaction to the tension and apparent loss of control in global events, and not as the culmination of a long-term trend (Joffe, 1987; Eichenberg, 1988).

A third short-term explanation might be called the "Reagan factor." Admittedly, President Carter had already adopted a strident tone in East-West relations late in his term, but that tone became vituperative and even bellicose in the early years of the Reagan presidency. For both Europeans and Americans, the early Reagan administration signaled the final end of detente at precisely the time that global conditions had deteriorated. One British expert explained negative evaluations of American policy in this way: "the source of growing anti-Americanism in Britain does not appear to be an unalterable generational shift of culture, but a more or less accurate perception of the current defense strategies and international posture of the Reagan administration....There remains a large reserve of diffuse goodwill...which a change in foreign policy or president can easily replenish" (Crewe, 1987, p. 56).

Finally, the early 1980s saw a deep economic recession—a time not just of scarcity of resources and budgetary conflict, but also of broader gloom about the prospects for recovery and adaptation to a new, "high tech" global division of labor. Certainly, this gloom would affect debates about the need to add to the defense budget, but perhaps it had a broader significance as well, deepening the alienation and fear that had already been ignited by international crises and the prospect of an arms race (Russett and DeLuca, 1983, pp. 180–81).

In summary, although a review of theoretical work suggests some factors that could contribute to a long-term decline in the domestic security consensus, short-term factors should not be ignored. Of course, it is difficult to sort out the relative impact of these two sets of factors, but it is crucial to try. Long-term factors are deeply rooted and change only slowly. To the extent that they have conditioned the public's perception of security, they are unlikely to be reversed. In contrast, short-term events may have only a passing impact, and in any event they are likely to provide governments with opportunities for intelligent adjustment.

CONTINUITY AND CHANGE IN PUBLIC OPINION

The degree of consensus in public opinion can be judged in two ways. The first is to examine the overall population percentages: is the general public deeply divided, or is there a preponderance of opinion in one direction or another? How much has the overall division of opinion changed over time? The second method is to examine patterns of domestic cleavage at particular points in time. Does the population divide in systematic ways in their opinions of security issues? Are these patterns of cleavage stable?

This and the following section examine these questions by reviewing recent research on European and American public opinion. Emphasis is placed on summarizing and interpreting recent research findings (Shaffer, 1982; Capitanchik and Eichenberg, 1983; Russett and DeLuca, 1983; Eichenberg, 1985, 1988; Flynn and Rattinger, 1985; Flynn, Moreton and Treverton, 1985; Graham and Kramer, 1986; Graham, 1987; Rochon, 1988; Domke, Eichenberg, and Kelleher, 1987; Holsti and Rosenau, 1986; Wittkopf, 1986, 1987; Ziegler, 1987a, 1987b). With regard to both the opinions of the *overall public* and the pattern of *cleavage* within the public, we will summarize the degree of continuity and change in public opinion and evaluate the theoretical perspectives discussed above.

Continuity

In both Europe and the United States, the most striking continuity is in the solid support for continued membership in the NATO Alliance. Despite the strategic quarrels of the 1960s; the turbulence of the 1970s caused by the Vietnam War, Watergate, and economic crisis; and the bitter defense debates of the late 1970s and early 1980; the level of support for NATO has remained above 60 percent in all countries except (unsurprisingly) France. Indeed, except for a brief dip during the INF controversy in 1981 and 1982, support for NATO actually *increased* in most countries during the 1980s (Domke, Eichenberg, and Kelleher, 1987, Table 1; Eichenberg, 1988, Table 4.1; Rielly, 1987).

These percentages represent a degree of consensus rarely found in opinion surveys on any domestic or foreign policy issue. Nonetheless, an important question remains. Is support for NATO merely symbolic, a reflection perhaps of more general political sympathies and not of support for security policies per se? For several reasons, the attachment to NATO appears to have genuine political significance. In the first place, we should recall that the Alliance itself did not become a political issue during the controversy over INF. The attachment to the Alliance was not "cost-free" in domestic debates. Furthermore, we will see below that the dominant Alliance partner was seriously questioned, both by the public and by elites; yet support for the Alliance with the United States emerged quite strongly.

Perhaps the reason for the consensus on NATO membership should be sought in structural factors rather than in short-term controversy. In the United States, the continuing commitment to Europe in the face of some bitter transatlantic quarrels is probably due to a more general hardening of attitudes in East-West relations and the resulting support for Alliance policies that balance the major adversary. In Europe, however great the discontent with the policies of the United States (or with European NATO partners), there is also a shortage of alternatives. As Anton DePorte has persistently argued (1979, 1983), the endurance of NATO rests on a perceived need to deter Soviet influence or aggression. Failing a truly united Europe and a solution to the German problem, NATO will remain the probable choice. In DePorte's words:

"The Alliance endures not because it is perfect, but because it serves the interests of its members better than the feasible alternatives" (1979, pp. 243–44).

Public opinion surveys bear out DePorte's reasoning. In the United States, there was indeed public resentment about lack of European support on such issues as the suppression of Solidarity or the bombing of Libya. Yet the polls also show a continuing commitment to defend Europe against the Soviets (Schneider, 1985, pp. 339, 354; Rielly, 1987). In Western Europe, there has obviously been discontent with the United States and even some support for "neutralism" when that option is offered in the abstract. But when neutralist or other alternatives are presented in survey questions as a concrete alternative to NATO, the option of Alliance remains the preferred choice of Europeans (Domke, Eichenberg, and Kelleher, 1987, Table 2).

Continuity is also evident in attitudes toward defense spending. With the exception of American and British opinions in 1981 and 1982, recent years have seen little public support for increasing defense spending. Even in Britain and the United States, the public's willingness to increase defense spending collapsed completely after a brief spurt of support in the early 1980s. In every Western country, the dominant view is that defense spending should be held stable. Moreover, in every Western country including the United States, there is little sentiment to increase defense spending if it has to be financed through a cut in domestic programs or an increase in taxes.

Opinions on nuclear weapons and arms control issues also show considerable continuities. This observation may seem paradoxical in light of the intensity and visibility of recent public protest against nuclear weapons in both Europe and the United States. Nonetheless, although there are surprisingly few opinion time series on nuclear weapons issues, the available evidence does suggest continuity with the past.

One continuity appears to be ironic: Western publics are understandably repulsed by the prospect of being the victims of nuclear war, but they have also been willing to submerge this revulsion to support nuclear deterrence. As early as the 1950s, public opinion in Western Europe had developed what might be called a "no first use" philosophy; in surveys from 1955 through 1982, considerable percentages of Europeans believed that nuclear weapons should *never* be used in a war, while substantial percentages believed they should only be used in response to an opponent's "first use" (Adler and Spencer, 1985, Tables 1 and 2; Eichenberg, 1983, p. 155). In a comprehensive survey of American public opinion, the Public Agenda Foundation found much the same result. Indeed, a substantial percentage of Americans believe that it is already official American policy *not* to use nuclear weapons first (Belsky and Doble, 1984, pp. 24, 63).

Nonetheless, Europeans and Americans also accept nuclear deterrence. This observation has become commonplace as concerns American public opinion. As William Schneider observes, public opinion in the United States shows a distinct duality: Americans want to maintain strength to deter the

Soviet Union, but they also endorse arms control and stop short of endorsing threats to *use* nuclear weapons as part of the deterrent. Thus, it is really no surprise that large numbers of Americans supported the Reagan defense program at precisely the same time that other polls showed a very strong desire for arms control and a rejection of the use of nuclear weapons (Schneider, 1985, pp. 340–52; see also Nincic, 1987).

The same duality characterizes European opinion. Despite the rejection of first use and the intensity of concern about the neutron weapon and the INF deployment, absolute rejection of nuclear deterrence was not widespread. The most obvious examples are found in France and Britain where, despite substantial public skepticism about the INF deployment, support for the independent, national nuclear deterrents remains high (Crewe, 1985, pp. 32–39; Fritsch-Bournazel, 1985, p. 84; Rochon, 1988, ch. 2; Eichenberg, 1988, ch. 3). Even in the Netherlands, a country that was deeply divided on the INF issue, substantial percentages continued to support nuclear deterrence, however grudgingly (Eichenberg, 1983, p. 151).

Despite the variety of surveys (and responses) that accompanied the INF debate, European doubts about the deployment seemed to be conditional rather than absolute. For example, opposition to the INF deployment was much smaller when the survey question mentioned either Soviet deployments or arms control negotiations. Like the "first use" questions discussed above, questions about "new " nuclear weapons generally evoked revulsion. But when deterrence was invoked by mentioning Soviet deployments, opposition declined. A similar result was achieved when NATO obligations were mentioned and especially when deployment *with negotiation* was described to survey respondents (Shaffer, 1982, Tables 42 and 43; Rattinger, 1986; Eichenberg, 1988, Table 3.5).

Thus, it would be incorrect to say that there is no domestic consensus on the subject of nuclear deterrence. On the contrary, public opinion in both Europe and the United States generally supports deterrence in spite of their revulsion of nuclear weapons. Rather, public opinion on both sides of the Atlantic indicates that the consensus underlying nuclear deterrence is conditional. Certainly, the prospect of *using* nuclear weapons tends to frighten the public and to erode support for nuclear strategy. Second, the public seems to be saying that deterrence must be accompanied by political efforts to manage nuclear weapons. In summary, public opinion in both Europe and America confirms Schneider's "two-track" characterization; neither the Europeans nor Americans favor "strength over peace or peace over strength. They favor a 'two track' policy that engages both values" (1985, p. 340; see also Nincic, 1987).

Change

If the state of domestic consensus on Alliance, defense spending, and nuclear issues shows continuity with the past, there are two sets of issues on which change is evident. First, in Western Europe, the general image of the United States has clearly eroded. There is also abundant evidence that Europeans' confidence in the coherence and wisdom of American foreign policy has declined. Second, in both the United States and Europe, perceptions of the East-West power situation have changed noticeably. Although it is not the case that citizens feel less secure as a result, it does appear that the widespread perception of U.S.–Soviet parity has introduced a new element of contention into domestic security debates.

The decline in the general American image has been precipitous. After a sharp decline in the "favorable" ratings of the United States that accompanied the Vietnam War and the Watergate scandal, the image of the United States had gradually returned to the levels of the early 1970s. However, beginning in 1980, a very sharp erosion set in (Crespi, 1982; Crewe, 1987). Confidence in the wisdom of American foreign policy actually turned negative, despite continuing adherence to Alliance with the United States. In addition, Europeans apparently drew a distinction between the "security community" of the military alliance and the broader question of economic and political collaboration. For example, in a sophisticated analysis of European public opinion, Andrew Ziegler found that "Atlanticism" on the security dimension was definitely orthogonal to collaboration on other matters (1987a). On matters related to European defense, Europeans remained Atlanticists. On economic and political matters, they resembled the "partial partners" described by Kolodziej (1981).

Thus, to the extent that there was a decline in consensus during the 1980s, it seems fair to characterize it more as an erosion in the transatlantic consensus than in the internal consensus of individual countries. Moreover, although the evidence is circumstantial, it appears that the decline in confidence in the United States was a consequence of the hardline tone of American foreign policy that had been initiated by President Carter and intensified by President Reagan. Of course, the European complaints about President Reagan are now familiar: the slow start on arms control talks with the Soviet Union that conflicted with Europe's attachment to the negotiating process; the famous "slip" on fighting a nuclear war in Europe; the escalation to military confrontation in Central America, when many in Europe saw the region's problems as political; and the bitter debates on East-West sanctions in the aftermath of martial law in Poland.

In addition to these transatlantic quarrels, it also seems clear that some degree of domestic contention on issues of deterrence and arms control has become a permanent part of Western security politics. On the related questions of the state of the military balance and its consequences for Western security, there has been an evolution toward divisiveness. On one issue there can be no doubt: in both Europe and the United States, the 1960s and 1970s saw an erosion in the perceived strength of the United States and NATO relative to the Soviet Union and the Warsaw Pact. Perceptions varied among countries, but by the early 1980s, opinion in all NATO countries was increasingly divided around two views: that parity in East-West strength existed, or that the Soviet Union and its allies had achieved superiority (Russett and Deluca, 1983; Crespi, 1982; Schneider, 1985).

These views mirrored a similar division among strategic experts and politicians, a division that also focused on the *implications* of any shift in the East-West military balance. On this question there is less historical evidence of public perceptions, but the evidence that does exist suggests that the public did *not* conclude that their security had declined. In West Germany, for example, there has been very little change in the degree of confidence in NATO's ability to repel attack, despite substantial changes in perceptions of the power situation. In most European countries, a plurality continues to place faith in the willingness of the United States to defend Western Europe— even if it exposes the United States to attack. Even more striking, it does not appear that changes in perceptions of American power affect confidence in the American commitment to Europe. In the late 1970s, perceptions of U.S. power were eroding, yet confidence in the United States increased. Conversely, in the 1980s, perceptions of American power improved, yet confidence declined. Finally, in both the United States and Europe, public opinion is quite comfortable with parity: it is a majority or plurality preference on both sides of the Atlantic (Eichenberg, 1988, ch. 2; Schneider, 1985, pp. 328–30).

Although changing perceptions of power did not bring a sea-change in perceptions of security, they did greatly complicate the task of domestic consensus. One relationship was clear in European attitudes: those citizens who saw parity in military power were also most confident of their security. Indeed, they were more confident in their security than those (in the minority) who saw the West as *superior*. Since the overall population was increasingly divided between the perception of parity and the perception of Soviet superiority, the stage had been set for contentious debates about the requirements of security policy.

In this context, the divisions revealed by European peace movements and the American freeze movements are comprehensible. Although citizens—like their governments—had perceived an increase in Soviet military power, a substantial percentage perceived essential parity, and in any case there was not a drastic erosion of confidence in security. Like strategists themselves, citizens were increasingly polarized in their views. The theorists had debated these issues throughout the 1970s, but citizen concerns had not been mobilized, for the 1970s had been an era of detente and arms control. Once that period ended in the crisis atmosphere of the early 1980s, the debate about the extent and consequences of change in the military balance gained full steam.

DOMESTIC CLEAVAGE IN PUBLIC OPINION

Historical trends in Western public opinion are fairly well documented, but the same cannot be said for our knowledge of domestic cleavage. To be sure, public opinion in the United States has been richly described. Several scholars and organizations have repeatedly conducted surveys devoted entirely to foreign and security policy. In Western Europe, however, the data are less uniform. Although hundreds of individual surveys have been published during the past several years, it is difficult to generalize on the basis of this material. One reason is that most European survey results are published in simple bivariate percentages. For example, opinions of nuclear weapons or the use of military force may be published according to the age group or party affiliation of the respondents, but there is rarely a breakdown *within* these categories. We may know what young people *or* Social Democrats think, but it is difficult to establish what young Social Democrats think. Second, most breakdowns are presented for isolated questions or single countries, and they are rarely available for more than one year. Third, survey agencies frequently change the wording of their questions or use different questions in different countries. All of these failings make it difficult to generalize about the similarity of cleavage patterns across issues, countries, or time periods. The single largest gap in our knowledge of European opinion thus stems from the lack of repeated comparative surveys that could be directly reanalyzed.

Nonetheless, the last several years have witnessed several efforts to compile and analyze available breakdowns of public opinions on security issues, and within the limits noted above, they converge in their conclusions. Since studies of American and European opinion diverge in intellectual approach as well as data available, they are treated separately in this section.

Western Europe

As noted above, recent years have brought much attention to the opinions of the European "successor generation" of young people who grew to political maturity during the prosperous and secure years of the 1960s and 1970s. Because of their secure environment and their attachment to "higher level" values of self-fulfillment (and because of their disproportionate presence in protest demonstrations), theorists and officials alike saw the younger cohorts as major source of erosion in the domestic security consensus (Inglehart, 1984b; Pym, 1982).

Initial studies of the age distribution of security attitudes confirmed this reasoning. In the broadest examination of the views of the younger generation, Stephen Szabo concluded that younger Europeans tended to be more critical of the United States; less supportive of defense spending; less attached to the NATO Alliance; and less supportive of armed force as an instrument of national policy (1983, pp. 170–73). Subsequent studies have found much the same result. On issues from defense spending to nuclear weapons and arms control, the young are generally less enthusiastic about national security policy (Russett and DeLuca, 1983, p. 187; Flynn and Rattinger, 1985, pp. 377–78; Eichenberg, 1988).

Yet a generational theory based on age alone must also be qualified. In the first place, there is evidence that age differences are not stable. The distance between generations appears sensitive to "period effects" that move the opinions of different age groups closer together and back again. For example, during the rise and decline of international tensions between 1979 and 1983, Eichenberg found that the "generation gap" in opinions of defense spending closed considerably before widening once again (1988, ch. 5). Although generational differences have not been traced over time for other issues, these findings call into question the proposition that age alone produces a fundamentally different disposition to reaction to security issues.

A second source of doubt is straightforward: while there are indeed age differences on some issues (or in some years), there are also issues on which age differences are minor or nonexistent. For example, in surveys conducted during the West German election campaign of 1980 (just after the INF decision and the Soviet invasion of Afghanistan), there were sharp age differences on some questions, such as the symbols of national security and arms control, but not on the issues of *Ostpolitik* (Forschungsgruppe Wahlen, 1980). Szabo (1984a) documents sharp age differences on the INF question, while Richard C. Eichenberg (1985) shows that in some years age differences on other nuclear issues were minor. Other studies show similar variations in the strength of the correlation between age and security attitudes (Rattinger, 1986; Joffe, 1987). Given the welter of separate percentages published over the past five years, it is not possible to ascertain whether these variations are systematic. Perhaps age differences are most salient for certain types of issues (such as threat perceptions or images of the United States and the Soviet Union), and not for others (such as defense spending or support for the Atlantic Alliance).

All of these questions suggest that the correlation between age and security attitudes, such as it is, must compete with other explanations of cleavage in security opinions. In addition, close study of generational theories indicates that an exclusive focus on age differences may be misleading. In fact, very few generational theories are unicausal. Among those who have studied the issue most systematically, there is agreement that the generational phenomenon arises from the combined effects of cohort experience (age) and educational attainment (Adler, 1983; Inglehart, 1977, pp. 4, 9–10; Szabo, 1983, 1984b). For these authors, generational change in security attitudes is a combined result of three societal trends: (1) the *value changes* that result from the prosperity and security of the post-war generation; (2) the *cognitive* effects of expanded access to higher education—especially the development of a cosmopolitan and "less threatened" world view; and (3) the *socialization* effects of conditions and debates during the period of education (the Vietnam War, detente, and arms control). Although these effects are difficult to separate, clearly the theory suggests an *interactive effect* of age and educational achievement.

This hypothesis is supported by the evidence. Cross-national comparisons (Szabo, 1983, pp. 171–72; Flynn and Rattinger, 1985, pp. 377–78; and Eichenberg, 1988) show much evidence of a young, university-educated generation that is usually more skeptical of post-war security policies than are their elders. That evidence is buttressed by similar findings in studies of single countries or single issues (Mueller and Risse-Kappen, 1987; Winn, 1983; Szabo, 1984a).

Nonetheless, as was the case with the correlation with age alone, the correlation of security attitudes with age *and* education is not robust. For example, on the issue of alternatives to the NATO Alliance—raised frequently in the context of the supposed "neutralism" of the successor generation— there are marginal differences according to age and education (Domke, Eichenberg, and Kelleher, 1987, Table 2), despite the fact that there are differences in responses to a more abstract "neutralism" question (Szabo, 1983, p. 172). On other issues (defense spending, views of the United States and of the military balance), age–education differences vary. In some years and on some issues, there is a distinct successor generation effect, while in others there is little correlation (United States Information Agency [USIA], 1980; Forschungsgruppe Wahlen, 1980; Winn, 1983; Mueller and Risse-Kappen, 1987). Thus, although there is stronger evidence of a distinct, successor generation based on the combined effects of age and education, it is not consistent across issues, time, or countries. Finally, there is some fragmented evidence that the effect of education on security attitudes is not confined to the young: on some issues in some years, the *older* educated are also distinct in their views. For example, in the 1980 USIA survey cited above, the older educated opposed "out-of-area" military operations more than did the younger educated. There are also other examples of distinctive attitudes among the older educated (Winn, 1983; Eichenberg, 1988, ch. 5).

Although the evidence is hardly solid, these results suggest that either higher education is the real causal variable or that education is masking other influences on opinions. The latter hypothesis is plausible. When the opinions of the older generation are examined closely (Eichenberg, 1988, ch. 5), it turns out that the skeptics among the older educated are largely partisans of left and center-left parties. That is, older, educated partisans of Socialist, Labor, and Liberal parties at times exhibit attitudes similar to those of the younger, educated successor generation.

This finding reinforces a consistent finding of secondary analyses: the deepest, most stable, and most cross-nationally uniform correlation in public opinion on security issues is with the partisan attachment of the respondent (Flynn and Rattinger, 1985, p. 378; Szabo, 1984a, 1987; Rattinger, 1986; Ziegler,

1987b). In secondary analyses, this cleavage far exceeds the average distance among age or educational groups (Rattinger, 1986). Analysis of primary survey materials confirms that significant partisan polarization is present *within* all age and educational groups, although the young, educated "successor generation" in some countries does remain the most hostile to traditional security policies *and* the most polarized along partisan lines—a pattern that also characterizes younger elites (Eichenberg, 1988, ch. 6; Dalton, 1987).

To summarize, the weight of the evidence resembles the glacier process described by Inglehart (1984a, pp. 25–26). There is evidence that opinions on security issues have been inherited to some extent from traditional party attachments or party positions. These are visible among all social groupings of all ages. Yet the successor generation does stand out, both in its more critical views and in the more severe partisan polarization within this younger group. The major question that remains is *why* these correlations are so strong. We will return to this question after reviewing the cleavage structure of public opinion in the United States.

The United States

The study of cleavage in European public opinion has been strong on hypotheses and weak on data to test those hypotheses. That is, a number of theoretical expectations from the fields of international and comparative politics would suggest why security attitudes should be correlated with specific independent variables. However, with few exceptions, evaluation of these ideas has been restricted to the task of collating and comparing a myriad of secondary survey results. Lacking comparative opinion surveys on a variety of security issues that could be subject to primary analysis, researchers have attempted to generalize by comparing breakdowns to many single questions.

Research on American opinion has been quite different. A number of large scale surveys have been designed specifically to allow the study of both public and elite opinions on a large number of issues. Chief among these are the surveys of the Chicago Council on Foreign Relations (Reilly, 1975, 1979, 1983, 1987), but there are other valuable surveys as well (Holsti and Rosenau, 1984, 1986; Russett and Hanson, 1975). These and other surveys, available from archives, allow for reanalysis, replication, and far more cumulation than has been possible in the study of European opinion.

Perhaps because the data are so rich, students of American opinion have generally not started with hypotheses relating independent variables to security opinions. Rather, the primary focus has been the exploration of the underlying structure of opinions—the dependent variables. Using a variety of clustering techniques, these scholars have sought to discover the extent to which a number of individual opinions are interrelated in larger attitude clusters. Although there have been both theoretical and methodological disputes about the number of clusters that characterize American attitudes and about the labels that should be assigned to these clusters, these studies have produced a great deal of substantive convergence.

For example, in virtually every study of the Chicago Council surveys, researchers have concluded that a major restructuring has taken place in American public opinion. According to one prominent analyst of these studies (Schneider, 1985), American opinions have experienced three distinct phases. The first, lasting until the post–World War II period, encompassed the familiar isolationist/internationalist cleavage: the primary distinction among Americans was the relative willingness to accept a global role for the United States. The second phase, evoked by the Cold War, produced a consensus in favor of containment and internationalism: Americans accepted both the need to contain the Soviet Union and the need to commit the United States to alliances in pursuit of the containment strategy (Schneider, 1985, pp. 359–60).

The third phase was brought on by the Vietnam War. Although some had thought that the effect of Vietnam was to reawaken the isolationist/internationalist split in the United States, research shows that the actual effect was more complex. Isolationists per se remain a minority. Certainly, there is still a rather unilateralist sector (labeled non-internationalist by Schneider) that believes in the need for global involvement to contain the Soviets but prefers a "go it alone" approach. But the major cleavage that developed in the post-Vietnam era was a split among internationalists themselves. In the words of Michael Mandelbaum and William Schneider, the American public became increasingly split between "liberal internationalists" who emphasized economic interdependence, arms control, and the use of international organizations, and "conservative internationalists" who emphasized the Soviet threat, military containment, and the global defense of liberal economic values (Mandelbaum and Schneider, 1979, pp. 40–44). This division of the American public (and leadership) into non-internationalist, liberal internationalist, and conservative internationalist has been variously labeled by other scholars (see especially Wittkopf, 1986, 1987). Nonetheless, the political substance of the cleavage is similar in all studies, and its presence in both public and elite opinion has been documented into the 1980s (Maggiotto and Wittkopf, 1981; Wittkopf and Maggiotto, 1983; Schneider, 1985, 1986; Holsti and Rosenau, 1984, 1986).

According to Schneider, the dynamics of American security politics are governed by this cleavage. Since there are far fewer non-internationalists among leaders and activists, they tend to divide into a competition for allies, who must be sought not only among sympathetic members of the public but among the non-internationalist public as well. Yet the non-internationalist public has ambivalent sentiments. To be sure, they are sensitive to Soviet power and to the need to defend American interests (a sentiment they share with conservative internationalists), but in the wake of Vietnam they have also become wary of overseas commitments (a sentiment they share with liberal internationalists). To this must be added the consistent finding that, despite its distrust of the Soviet Union, a large majority of Americans support the notion of at least attempting to control weapons. Thus, it is not surprising that American security policy undergoes swings from militancy to conciliation (for a potential coalition exists for both). It is also no surprise that the public seems to exhibit a contradictory profile: concerned about Soviet power, yet overwhelmingly in favor of a nuclear freeze; concerned about potential Soviet influence in Central America, yet unwilling to commit American aid or forces there. Depending on short-term conditions, either the liberal or conservative internationalists might prove capable of tapping one or the other sentiment of the non-internationalists in the public (Schneider, 1985, pp. 357–59; for a brilliant analysis of the 1976 U.S. presidential election in these terms, see Mandelbaum and Schneider, 1979).

Despite the fact that these divisions in American public opinion have evolved in reaction to quite specific circumstances, the correlates of American opinion are actually quite similar to patterns in Europe. Although American party affiliation does not have the link to ideology that it has in Europe, ideology itself is by far the strongest correlate of liberal and conservative internationalism. As in Europe, education and (to a lesser extent) age are strong but secondary influences. One of the most surprising and consistent findings of this body of research is that the presumed generational effects of the Vietnam War have not materialized in either elite or public opinion (Holsti and Rosenau, 1980, 1986; Wells, 1986)

THE DOMESTIC POLITICS OF SECURITY: A SYNTHESIS

As in Europe, the primary correlates of American opinion are found in the ideology, educational level, and age of the citizen. American and European opinions also exhibit similar trends in the movement of overall popular sentiments. Despite acrimonious debates on a number of issues, the populations of the United States and Western Europe have remained committed to deterrence and to the Atlantic Alliance, and both show a decided preference for a "dual" policy of deterrence *and* negotiation. Thus, despite a number of transatlantic differences over the past several years, the weight of the evidence suggests that the basic political conflict is much the same on both sides of the Atlantic.

Why should this be the case? Despite the obvious differences in interest and circumstance, the fundamental issue facing the Western democracies is really quite similar: the role of military force in national security policy. Of course, in the United States, this issue was highlighted above all by the Vietnam War, but the emergence of strategic parity and the pull of domestic problems have also played a role. In any case, as the studies cited above suggest, the American public is divided less by the traditional question of whether to seek security through international involvement than by the question of *how* that security should be pursued. The crucial distinction between liberal and conservative internationalists is the degree to which they accept use of military force in the pursuit of national security.

European opinion is similar, although it has evolved in reaction to different traditions and national interests. Certainly, Vietnam and strategic parity increase the debatability of force, but for Europeans this debate is nothing new. As noted in the opening sections of this chapter, ideological conflict on the question of military force has a long tradition in Europe. Indeed, the new "liberal/conservative" cleavage that has arisen in the United States is quite familiar to Europeans. The distinction between "idealism" and "realism," however well worn, seems useful and appropriate. After all, what has always separated these two schools of thought is their contrasting views of the utility of military force. For idealists, security is to be sought primarily in negotiation and the reconciliation of conflicting interests. Indeed, idealism is rooted in an explicit critique of the policies of power balance. For realists, a balance of military power has always been primary, and the reconciliation of conflicting interests has been seen as a distant goal, if not a utopia. In recent decades, while all sides of the political spectrum in Europe have come to agree that a dual policy of strength *and* negotiation is the appropriate approach to security, in emphasis the left and the right are still noticeably different.

This interpretation would explain the somewhat surprising strength of the correlation in Europe between ideology and security views. Recent interpretations have emphasized the distinctly critical views of younger or educated Europeans. Yet older Europeans are also familiar with debates on security issues that divided polities along party lines. The "breakdown of consensus" on security issues is often equated with the security controversies of the 1980s, but there were heated debates much earlier. The peace movements of the 1950s are well known (Boutwell, 1983; Parkin, 1968). Less frequently noted are the increasing debates of the late 1960s which arose from the demands of the democratic left for a detente "pillar" to go along with NATO's policy of deterrence (Eichenberg, 1988, ch. 6). This ideological division was managed through NATO's adoption of the Harmel Doctrine in 1967. Henceforth, NATO was committed to both military strength *and* arms control negotiation with the Soviet Union and the Warsaw Pact.

In this context, the views of the "successor" generation, generally considered "new" to security politics, can instead be interpreted as an extension or intensification of a very old debate. In both Europe and the United States, the young educated stand out as the most critical of security policies, although even this group is itself severely divided along ideological lines. This does not seem surprising. In addition to the relative prosperity and security enjoyed by this generation, their "security environment" was far more conditioned by detente and arms control than were earlier generations. What is more, they grew to maturity during a time of explicit resurrection of traditional questions: does additional force bring additional security? If not, are negotiation and detente not rational, both politically and economically?

In summary, it may be argued that the recent anxiety and polarization in

Western public opinion are a manifestation of deep-seated historical divisions, stimulated by short-term events and magnified by long-term global and domestic changes that have rendered national security more debatable than before. This interpretation has implications for the questions posed at the outset of this chapter. One question has to do with the distinction between long-term and short-term factors. Clearly, certain long-term forces will make consensus on security issues more difficult. The effect of parity is the most significant, for it is precisely this issue that divides opinions of the marginal utility of force. For the left, which has always emphasized the irrelevance or futility of force, the nuclear stalemate reinforces and intensifies traditional views. For the right, less convinced of the potential for political settlements, additional force is necessary to preserve deterrence. Moreover, this basic division will be complicated by other long-term trends, especially the growth of the welfare state (which sensitizes distributive debates and the "guns/butter" trade-off) and the secular growth in access to higher education (which expands the attentive, active public and intensifies attachment to policy views).

But if there are long-term trends that complicate the building of consensus on security policy, there is also evidence that short-term forces, some of them manageable, may be the crucial determinant of how severe this consensus problem becomes. A simple example is found in the issue of defense spending. As we have seen, public opinion is rarely enthusiastic about defense spending. Yet, when economic growth allowed both guns *and* butter, Western governments increased defense budgets throughout the 1960s and 1970s without incurring the wrath—or even the notice—of domestic audiences. Thus, should the economic problems of recent years prove to be a short-term phenomenon, past patterns suggest that incremental increases to defense budgets will be possible.

Paradoxically, the evidence also suggests that there is a potential consensus on the controversial questions of nuclear deterrence and arms control. In both the United States and Europe, there remains a substantial consensus on the need for deterrence and alliance. What stimulated the anxiety and protest of the 1980s was a perceived imbalance in Western security policy, a perception that was intensified by the severe crisis atmosphere of the period. Once negotiations resumed and East–West relations took on the form of a more restrained competition, both protests and polls registered a relaxation. Like politics in general, consensus on security policy is found in the center. In the field of security, centrist policies are those that meet both the left's desire for negotiation and the right's desire for strength. Governments have achieved this balance in the past. There seems to be no reason why they should not also do so in the future.

THE RESEARCH AGENDA

There remains considerable room for additional research that would define or challenge this interpretation. Treatments of the domestic politics of security in Western Europe remain theoretically strong but weak on the data necessary to fully examine competing hypotheses. What might be called the "political sociology" of security in Europe is relatively well developed in historical writings that trace the evolution of class and ideological divisions on issues of national security, as well as in the more recent theoretical and empirical literature of comparative politics. There is also a challenging literature treating the impact of generational change, the impact of education, and the increasing intrusion of welfare politics. Yet examination of these hypotheses has been hindered by the lack of comprehensive, comparative opinion surveys that would allow an exploration of attitude clusters, as has been done in the United States. The argument here is that such an analysis would reveal a similar set of clusters related to fundamental attitudes toward military force, but at present the hypothesis cannot be tested directly.

In the United States, there has been a great deal of convergence and cumulation in the identification of opinion clusters, but less theoretical work has been done on explaining them (Ferguson, 1986; Kegley, 1986). The strong division of opinion around issues of military force, clusters that are correlated with ideology, does indeed suggest that Vietnam created deep fissures in American politics. Yet the fissure may be older than that. In fact, the split between idealists and realists is as old as the United States itself. It found its first expression (imported from Europe) in colonial America, where the Enlightenment critique of the balance of power found a strong echo. In the words of Felix Gilbert, "American foreign policy was idealistic and internationalist no less than isolationist" (1961, p. 72). Nor did the Cold War totally eliminate ideological division on military issues. For example, Samuel P. Huntington's study of the military profession highlights the ideological nature of differing societal views of the military (1957, especially ch. 6). Finally, idealism and internationalism have emerged periodically as a guiding motif of American foreign policy, most notably in the ideas of Presidents Wilson and Carter.

Despite this regularity, very little work has been done on the political sociology of national security in American politics. Perhaps one reason is the persistent notion that the United States remained isolated for much of the past two centuries. A second is the assumption that the Cold War erased ideological conflict on issues of military force. Third, no doubt there is a normative view that ideological conflict is bad for security policy. Finally, research on the issue is hindered by lack of historical data. Nonetheless, students of American public opinion are in a much better position to explore the historical roots of these divisions. Although there are no older surveys that match the comprehensiveness of the Chicago Council studies, there *are* a number of questions on election and other surveys that would at least allow a historical comparison of correlations whose place in recent clusters is well documented. Of course, such studies would also require better theory along the lines of the "political sociology" tradition of European studies.

Future studies would also benefit from a broader basis of comparison. Two additional areas of research should be integrated into future studies of strategy and domestic consensus. The first is studies of consensus in non-Western political systems, democratic and otherwise. There is, for example, a rich study of public opinion in Israel (Arian, Herman, and Talmud, 1987). In addition, although public opinion studies are limited, issues of domestic consensus in the Soviet Union and Eastern Europe are of obvious—and increasing—importance.

A second task for future research is to integrate past and present studies of the interaction between elite and public opinion. There are several studies of this issue for the 1960s (Deutsch et al., 1967; Lerner and Gorden, 1969), but systematic comparisons of more recent public and elite opinions have only begun (Eberwein and Siegmann, 1985; Eichenberg, 1988, ch. 6). In addition, students of American politics and comparative politics have recently developed a rich literature on the "elite-public" question (Page and Shapiro, 1983; Page, Shapiro, and Dempsey, 1987; Shapiro and Page, forthcoming; Dalton, 1985, 1987).

This latter group of studies made the consistent argument that public opinion on security issues behaves in a "ration" way (see especially Shapiro and Page, forthcoming; Nincic, 1987). The more common image of public opinion on security issues is that it is ill informed, inconsistent, and easily changed. The studies reviewed here challenge this argument. Public opinion moves in systematic ways over time, and individual opinions are systematically correlated with political and other characteristics of citizens. Citizen views are also well represented by elites (Dalton, 1987). These findings are obviously crucial, not just for security policy, but also for normative and empirical theories of democratic government.

REFERENCES

Adler, Kenneth. 1983. The Successor Generation: Why, Who and How. Pp. 4–16 in Stephen F. Szabo, ed., *The Successor Generation: International Perspectives of Postwar Europeans*. London: Butterworths.

———, and Charles S. Spender. 1985. European Public Opinion on Nuclear Arms: An Historical View. Selected data presented to the Convention of the International Studies Association, Washington, D.C.

Arian, Asher, Tamar Herman, and Ilan Talmud. 1987. *National Security Policy and Public Opinion in Israel: The Guardian of Israel*. Boulder, Colo.: Westview Press.

Art, Robert. 1980. To What Ends Military Power? *International Security* 4:3–35.

Baldwin, David. 1979. Power Analysis and World Politics. *World Politics* 31:161–94.

Belsky, Lisa, and John Doble. 1984. *Technical Appendix to Voter Options on Nuclear Arms Policy: A Briefing Book for the 1984 Elections*. New York: Public Agenda Foundation.

Bergsten, C. Fred, Robert Keohane, and Joseph Nye, Jr. 1975. International Economics and International Politics: A Framework for Analysis. Pp. 3–36 in C. Fred Bergsten and Lawrence B. Krause, eds., *World Politics and International Economics*. Washington, D.C.: Brookings Institution.

Boltken, Ferdinand, and Wolfgang Jagodzinski. 1985. In an Environment of Insecurity: Postmaterialism in the European Community. *Comparative Political Studies* 17:453–84.

Boutwell, Jeffrey. 1983. Politics and the Peace Movement in West Germany. *International Security* 7:72–92.

Capitanchik, David, and Richard C. Eichenberg. 1983. *Defence and Public Opinion*. Boston and London: Routledge and Kegan Paul.

Crespi, Leo. 1982. U.S. Standing in European Public Opinion: Some Long-Term Trends. Washington, D.C.: Office of Research, United States Information Agency.

Crewe, Ivor. 1987. Why the British Don't Like Us Anymore. *Public Opinion* 9:51–56.

———. 1985. Britain: Two and a Half Cheers for the Atlantic Alliance. Pp. 11–68 in Gregory Flynn and Hans Rattinger, eds., *The Public and Atlantic Defense*. Totowa, N.J.: Rowman and Allanheld.

Dalton, Russell. 1987. Generational Change in Elite Political Beliefs: The Growth of Ideological Polarization. *Journal of Politics* 49:476–97.

———. 1985. Political Parties and Political Representation: Party Supporters and Party Elites in Nine Nations. *Comparative Political Studies* 18:267–99.

———. 1977. Was There a Revolution? A Note on the Generational Versus Life Cycle Explanations of Value Differences. *Comparative Political Studies* 9:459–73.

DePorte, Anton. 1983. NATO of the Future: Less Is More. *The Fletcher Forum* 7:1–26.

———. 1979. *Europe between the Superpowers: The Enduring Balance*. New Haven, Conn.: Yale University Press.

Deutsch, Karl, et al. 1967. *France, Germany and the Western Alliance*. New York: Scribner's.

Domke, William, Richard C. Eichenberg, and Catherine M. Kelleher. 1987. Consensus Lost? Domestic Politics and the "Crisis" in NATO. *World Politics* 39:382–407.

Eberwein, Wolf-Dieter, and Heinrich Siegmann. 1985. *Bedrohung oder Selbstgefahrdung? Die Einstellungen sicherheitspolitischer Fuhrungsschichten aus Funf Landern zur Sicherheitspolitik*. West Berlin: International Institute for Comparative Social Research, Science Center Berlin.

Eichenberg, Richard C. 1988. *Society and Security in Western Europe: A Study of Public Opinion in Four Countries*. London: Macmillan.

———. 1985. Public Opinion and National Security in Western Europe. Pp. 226–48 in Linda Brady and Joyce Kaufman, eds., *NATO in the 1980s*. New York: Praeger.

———. 1983. The Myth of "Hollanditis." *International Security* 8:143–59.

Ferguson, Thomas. 1986. The Right Consensus? Holsti and Rosenau's New Foreign Policy Belief Surveys. *International Studies Quarterly* 30:411–24.

Flynn, Gregory, and Hans Rattinger, eds. 1985. *The Public and Atlantic Defense*. Totowa, N.J.: Rowman and Allanheld.

———, Edwina Moreton, and Gregory Traverton. 1985. *Public Images of Western Security*. Paris: Atlantic Institute for International Affairs.

Forschungsgruppe, Wahlen, E. V. 1980. *German Election Study, 1980*. Ann Arbor, Mich.: Inter-University Consortium for Political and Social Research.

Freedman, Lawrence. 1981. *The Evolution of Nuclear Strategy*. New York: St. Martin's Press.

Fritsch-Bournazel, Renate. 1985. France: Attachment to a Nonbinding Relationship. Pp. 69–100 in Gregory Flynn and Hans Rattinger, eds., *The Public and Atlantic Defense*. Totowa, N.J.: Rowman and Allanheld.

Gilbert, Felix. 1961. *To the Farewell Address: Ideas of Early American Foreign Policy*. Princeton, N.J.: Princeton University Press.

Graham, Thomas. 1987. Future Fission? Extended Deterrence and American Public Opinion. Cambridge, Mass.: Center for Science and International Affairs, Harvard University.

———, and Bernard M. Kramer. 1986. The Polls: ABM and Star Wars: Attitudes Toward Nuclear Defense, 1945–1985. *Public Opinion Quarterly* 50:125–34.

Hoffmann, Stanley. 1985. Realism and Its Discontents. *The Atlantic* (November:131–36).

———. 1973. The Acceptability of Military Force. Pp. 2–13 in Adelphi Paper No. 102, *Force in Modern Societies*. London: International Institute for Strategic Studies.

Holsti, Ole R., and James N. Rosenau. 1986. Consensus Lost, Consensus Regained?: Foreign Policy Beliefs of American Leaders. *International Studies Quarterly* 30:375–410.

———. 1984. American Leadership in World Affairs: Vietnam and the Breakdown of Consensus. Boston and London: Allen and Unwin.

———. 1980. Does Where You Stand Depend on Where You Were Born? The Impact of Generation on Post-Vietnam Foreign Policy Beliefs. *Public Opinion Quarterly* 44:1–22.

Howard, Michael. 1983. Reassurance and Deterrence. *Foreign Affairs* 61:309–20.

———. 1978. *War and the Liberal Conscience*. New Brunswick, N.J.: Rutgers University Press.

Huntington, Samuel P. 1957. *The Soldier and the State: The Theory and Politics of Civil-Military Relations*. Cambridge, Mass.: Harvard University Press.

Inglehart, Ronald. 1985a. New Perspectives on Value Change: Responses to Lafferty and Knutsen, Savage, and Boltken and Jagodzinski. *Comparative Political Studies* 17:485–532.

———. 1985b. Aggregate Stability and Individual Level Flux in Mass Belief Systems. *American Political Science Review* 79:97–116.

———. 1984a. The Changing Structure of Political Cleavages in Western Society. Pp. 25–69 in Russell Dalton, Scott Flanagan, and Paul Beck, eds., *Electoral Change in Advanced Industrial Democracies*. Princeton, N.J.: Princeton University Press.

———. 1984b. Generational Change and the Future of the Atlantic Alliance. *PS* 17:525–35.

———. 1982. Postmaterialism in an Environment of Insecurity. *American Political Science Review* 75:880–900.

———. 1977. *The Silent Revolution: Changing Values and Political Styles among Western Publics*. Princeton, N.J.: Princeton University Press.

Jennings, Kent. 1987. Residues of a Movement: The Aging of the American Protest Generation. *American Political Science Review* 81:367–82.

Joffe, Josef. 1987. Peace and Populism: Why the European Anti-Nuclear Movement Failed. *International Security* 11:3–41.

Kegley, Charles W. 1986. Assumptions and Dilemmas in the Study of Americans' Foreign Policy Beliefs: A Caveat. *International Studies Quarterly* 30:447–72.

Kelleher, Catherine McArdle. 1987. Nation-State and National Security in Western Europe. Pp. 3–13 in Kelleher and Gale Mattox, eds., *Evolving European Defense Policies*. Lexington, Mass.: Lexington Books.

Keohane, Robert, and Joseph Nye, Jr. 1977. *Power and Interdependence*. Boston: Little, Brown.

Kolodziej, Edward. 1987. *Making and Marketing Arms: The French Experience and Its Implications for the International System*. Princeton, N.J.: Princeton University Press.

———. 1981. Europe: The Partial Partner. *International Security* 5:104–31.

———. 1980. Living with the Long Cycle. Pp. xx–yy in Edward Harkavy and Edward Kolodziej, eds., *American Security Policy and Policy-Making: The Dilemmas of Using and Controlling Military Force*. Lexington, Mass.: Lexington Books.

Lerner, Daniel, and Morton Gorden. 1969. *Euratlantica: Changing Perspectives of European Elites*. Cambridge, Mass.: MIT Press.

Maggiotto, Michael, and Eugene R. Wittkopf. 1981. American Public Attitudes Toward Foreign Policy. *International Studies Quarterly* 25:601–32.

Mandelbaum, Michael, and William Schneider. 1979. The New Internationalisms: Public Opinion and American Foreign Policy. Pp. 34–90 in Kenneth Oye, Donald Rothchild, and Robert Lieber, eds., *Eagle Entangled: U.S. Foreign Policy in A Complex World*. New York: Longman.

Morse, Edward. 1974. *Foreign Policy and Interdependence in Gaullist France*. Princeton, N.J.: Princeton University Press.

Mueller, Harold, and Thomas Risse-Kappan. 1987. Origins of Estrangement: The Peace Movement and the Changed Image of America in West Germany. *International Security* 12:52–88.

Nincic, Miroslav. 1987. America's Soviet Policy and the "Politics of Opposites." Department of Political Science, New York University.

Page, Benjamin I., and Robert Y. Shapiro. 1983. Effects of Public Opinion on Policy. *American Political Science Review* 77:175–90.

———, Robert Y. Shapiro, and Glenn Dempsey. 1987. What Moves Public Opinion? *American Political Science Review* 81:23–43.

Parkin, Frank. 1968. *Middle-Class Radicalism: The Social Bases of the British Campaign for Nuclear Disarmament*. Manchester: Manchester University Press.

Pym, Francis. 1982. Defense in Democracies. *International Security* 7:40–44.

Quester, George. 1981. The Superpowers and the Atlantic Alliance. *Daedalus* 110:23–40.

Rattinger, Hans. 1986. National Security and the Missile Controversy in the West German Public. Paper presented to the Annual Meeting of the American Political Science Association, Washington, D.C.

Rielly, John E. 1987. *American Public Opinion and U.S. Foreign Policy 1987*. Chicago: Chicago Council on Foreign Relations.

———. 1983. *American Public Opinion and U.S. Foreign Policy 1983*. Chicago: Chicago Council on Foreign Relations.

————. 1979. *American Public Opinion and U.S. Foreign Policy 1979*. Chicago: Chicago Council on Foreign Relations.

————. 1975. *American Public Opinion and U.S. Foreign Policy 1975*. Chicago: Chicago Council on Foreign Relations.

Rochon, Thomas. 1988. *The Politics of the Peace Movement in Western Europe*. Princeton, N.J.: Princeton University Press.

Russett, Bruce, and Donald DeLuca. 1983. Theater Nuclear Forces: Public Opinion in Western Europe. *Political Science Quarterly* 98:179–96.

————, and Elizabeth C. Hanson. 1975. *Interest and Ideology: The Foreign Policy Beliefs of American Businessmen*. San Francisco: Freeman and Sons.

Schilling, Warner. 1983. U.S. Strategic Nuclear Concepts in the 1970s: The Search for Sufficiently Equivalent Countervailing Parity. *International Security* 6:3–26.

Schneider, William. 1986. "Rambo" and Reality: Having It Both Ways. Pp. 41–74 in Kenneth Oye, Robert Lieber, and Donald Rothchild, eds., *Eagle Resurgent? The Reagan Era in American Foreign Policy*. Boston: Little, Brown.

————. 1985. Peace and Strength: American Public Opinion on National Security. Pp. 321–64 in Gregory Flynn and Hans Rattinger, eds., *The Public and Atlantic Defense*. Totowa, N.J.: Rowman and Allanheld.

Shaffer, Stephen. 1982. *West European Public Opinion on Key Security Issues: 1981– 1982*. Washington, D.C.: Office of Research, United States Information Agency.

Shapiro, Robert Y., and Benjamin I. Page. Forthcoming. Foreign Policy and the Rational Public. *Journal of Conflict Resolution*.

Sprout, Harold, and Margaret Sprout. 1968. The Dilemma of Declining Resources and Rising Demands. *World Politics* 20:660–93.

Szabo, Stephen. 1987. The Federal Republic of Germany: Public Opinion and Defense. Pp. 185–202 in Catherine M. Kelleher and Gail Mattox, eds., *Evolving European Defense Policies*. Lexington, Mass.: D. C. Heath.

————. 1984a. The West German Security Debate: The Search for Alternative Strategies. Paper presented to the Convention of the International Studies Association, Atlanta, Georgia.

————. 1984b. Brandt's Children: The West German Successor Generation. *The Washington Quarterly* 7:50–59.

————, ed., 1983. *The Successor Generation: International Perspectives of Postwar Europeans*. London: Butterworth.

United States Information Agency. 1980. *Multi-regional Security Survey 1980*. Washington, D.C.: Machine-readable Division, National Archives and Records Service.

Wells, Robert. 1986. The Vietnam War and Generational Differences in Foreign Policy Attitudes. Pp. 99–125 in Margaret P. Karns, ed., *Persistent Patterns and Emergent Structures in a Waning Century*. New York: Praeger.

Winn, Gregory F. T. 1983. Westpolitik: Germany and the Atlantic Alliance. *Atlantic Community Quarterly* 21:140–50.

Wittkopf, Eugene. 1987. Elites and Masses: Another Look at Attitudes toward America's World Role. *International Studies Quarterly* 31:131–60.

————. 1986. On the Foreign Policy Beliefs of the American People. *International Studies Quarterly* 30:425–46.

————, and Michael Maggiotto. 1983. The Two Faces of Internationalism: Public Attitudes toward American Foreign Policy in the 1970s—and Beyond? *Social Science Quarterly* 64:288–304.

Ziegler, Andrew. 1987a. The Structure of West European Attitudes Toward Atlantic Cooperation: Implications for the Western Alliance. *British Journal of Political Science* (July):457–77.

———. 1987b. Public Attitudes in Europe Toward Atlantic Cooperation: A Comparative Analysis. Paper prepared for presentation at the Convention of the International Studies Association, Washington, D.C.

9

On Force Posture

JOHN RAINIER

Designing a nation's military force posture is more than the straightforward, rational process implied by official statements such as the Annual Report to the Congress by the U.S. secretary of defense. Force posture design is not merely an exercise in determining the military capabilities required to safeguard national interest in the face of perceived external or internal threats. It is also an exercise on domestic and bureaucratic politics.

Like all military policy, force posture design has what Samuel Huntington has described as a "Janus-like quality." It combines aspects of two worlds: international and domestic politics. In the international system a state employs military forces to balance power, fight wars, and maintain alliances as part of its competition with other states. Concurrently, its government presides over a domestic political struggle concerning the allocation of scarce resources between interest groups, institutions, and social classes that seek conflicting interests and goals. Significant military policy decisions—such as those involved in force posture design—affect and are affected by both worlds. States must continually reconcile perceived strategic imperatives with their finite economic and technological resources in a domestic environment of competing political claims and objectives (Huntington, 1961).

Force posture design—the process of selecting and developing an appropriate mixture of military capabilities to address threats to national interests—forms the critical link between the state's foreign and domestic policies. Although this vitally important function seems to merit a deliberate, rational approach, its practice by modern states often appears to be inherently non-rational. Tensions stemming from the two worlds it joins push force posture design away from a purely objective calculation derived from a comparison of threats and military capabilities (which one could call "rational") toward a subjective (or "non-rational") process that is heavily influenced by the divergent perceptions and competing demands on scarce national resources of policymakers, members of interest groups, citizens, and force posture designers themselves. In short, while official statements present force planning as a rational process, influences that intrude on force planning inject a host of competing demands that alter the force structure in ways that conflict with the expected outcomes of rational modeling.

Because resource constraints cause force planners to design for a few primary contingencies, the force posture chosen by a state is seldom suitable to address the specific international problems it encounters. This tendency to design for a limited number of contingencies leads to a situation similar to that faced by a carpenter who has only two screwdrivers to turn a wide variety of screws: the force posture must be stretched to fit unforeseen contingencies. For example, in 1982, the United States deployed a Marine Amphibious Unit in Beirut to "restore Lebanese sovereignty and to insure Israeli security" (U.S. Congress, Senate Foreign Relations Committee, 1982, p. 3). While Marine forces are designed for rapid insertion and support from ships offshore, they are ill-equipped to solve foreign civil wars. The president's three-part strategy called for forcing the withdrawal of all foreign troops, restoring Lebanese government sovereignty and the strength of the Lebanese armed forces, and reestablishing a Lebanese national consensus based on a reconstructed economy. By 1984, the purpose assigned the Marine's changed from simply maintaining minimal order to lending legitimacy to the Lebanese government, a mission "foreign to their nature and capabilities" (U.S. Congress, Senate Foreign Relations Committee, 1984, pp. 51–52). In a blow to U.S. prestige and regional interests, the president was forced to withdraw the Marines who had suffered more than 250 casualties without having had any appreciable impact on settling the Lebanese conflict. The Marine force was ill suited to the military strategy and political aims for which it was used. Nor were there other military forces readily available to cope with the complexity of Lebanese and Middle East politics.

To illustrate the problems involved in force posture design, this chapter focuses on the U.S. experience. The American example is used as a guide to analyze force posture planning elsewhere, notwithstanding differences in size, scale, and national political institutions. Where relevant, illustrations will be suggested to compare and contrast with the insights drawn from the U.S. case.

THE CONCEPT OF FORCE POSTURE DESIGN

The term *force posture* refers either to an output of the force planning process or to an input of strategic and foreign policy. As an output, this term describes the total capability of a state's current military forces (Hammond, 1974). In this sense, force posture is the sum of all military capabilities created to safeguard national interests. These interests are translated into force posture requirements through the following sequence:

1. National interests →
2. Foreign policy objectives →
3. National security objectives
   (Minus) allies' contributions →
4. Force posture requirements →
5. Force posture →

Force posture as an input may be viewed as an array of coercive policy instruments available to policymakers to use in attempting to create an international environment congenial to a state's aims and interests. As the discussion below suggests, a mismatch often occurs between the forces needed to meet a nation's strategic and foreign policy needs of the moment and those that are available under conditions of scarce resources and competing notions of national interest. For example, the conventional modernization program that produced the M–1 tank and the Bradley Fighting Vehicle improved the ability of the U.S. armed forces to fight a war in Central Europe (which has not erupted) but has not contributed to their ability to fight lower intensity conflicts in Lebanon or Grenada (which have). A gap arises, therefore, between lines 3 and 4 of the schemata sketched above, that is, between national security objectives and force posture requirements. Similarly, the Reagan administration expenditures of $1.6 trillion for defense have produced an impressive amount of end-items and trained personnel, but still fall short in critical areas, such as air- and sealift to deliver these forces where they might be needed around the globe (Weinberger, 1987, Part IIIE). Another gap emerges between lines 4 and 5, that is, between force requirements and actual force posture.

Force posture design refers to the architectural process conducted by a state's national defense authorities which leads to the establisment of force posture requirements. In other words, it is the process through which force planners determine what military capabilities are required to carry out tasks designated by political leaders (lines 3 through 5 of the sequences listed above). The resulting force posture "requirements" comprise a desired force posture that both guides and justifies defense spending. One must differentiate force posture design decisions from those associated with strategy or procurement. How they differ may become clearer from the analysis below.

PPBS: A RATIONAL APPROACH TO FORCE POSTURE DESIGN

As a starting point for analyzing force posture design, one can examine U.S. practice, which was instituted by Secretary of Defense Robert McNamara in the 1960s. McNamara saw a need for the secretary of defense to become an active manager of all aspects of U.S. force posture design in order to insure that this process and its weapon system outputs would be responsive to foreign policy and military strategic needs. The Planning-Programming-Budgeting System (PPBS) was created in order to systematically relate force posture design to budgeting decisions. This approach was adapted from the business world where top management defines explicit criteria to evaluate the firm's activities, in this case the military programs arising from the individual armed services. These criteria also provided the conceptual basis for the development of quantitative measures and indices by which to compare rival armed service claims and to determine whether programs were being effectively and efficiently administered (Enthoven and Smith, 1969, chs. 1–2).

McNamara's version of PPBS involved the following elements: combined consideration of costs and military requirements (which he called cost-effectiveness), explicit evaluation of force posture alternatives to accomplish the same military missions, detailed documentation for both the secretary and the Congress, active employment of a systems analysis staff section reporting directly to him, and multi-year budgeting in the form of a Five-Year Defense Program to guide the military services (Enthoven and Smith, 1969, ch. 2). PPBS still guides U.S. force posture design. Although the names of specific reports and presidential decision memoranda have changed with presidential administrations, PPBS methods have become institutionalized as a means of presenting Pentagon force posture decisions to the Congress. Its criteria dominate U.S. defense planning down to the lowest levels (U.S. Congress, House Armed Services Committee Hearings, 1985, pp. 108–15).

While at first glance PPBS appears too technical and budget-oriented to play a valuable role in military policymaking, one must understand PPBS in order to understand U.S. force posture design. Lawrence Korb's explanation of PPBS shows how the Department of Defense actually designs the nation's force posture while it is developing the defense budget for a specific year (Korb, 1980).

During the Planning phase, the secretary of defense reviews inputs from the Joint Chiefs of Staff (JCS) concerning projected threats and U.S. military commitments, and from the National Security Council concerning current military policies. The secretary integrates those inputs with a budgetary target sent to him by the Office of Management and the Budget into a document called the Planning Guidance which he issues to the armed services. This guidance outlines the rationale underlying the projected defense policy. For example, the secretary "tells the Army how many sets of unit equipment it must preposition in Europe and provides a timetable for meeting the objective" (Korb, 1980, pp. 181–83). The Planning phase ends at a meeting between the president, the secretary of defense, and the Joint Chiefs of Staff where the force posture for the budget year is evaluated as to how responsive it is to policy guidance and how well it addresses expected threats.

During the Programming phase, the armed services and agencies within the department submit Program Objective Memoranda (POM) in which they request specific numbers of men and equipment (e.g., designation of reinforcements and amounts of prepositioned equipment for Europe) to support the consolidated Planning Guidance. At this point, programs "are reviewed for consistency and cost-effectiveness by the military and civilian hierarchy within [the Department]" (Korb, 1980, p. 183). The JCS analyzes these POMs and provides its corporate military judgment on whether the sum of the POMs will add up to a "balanced and effective military force" (Korb, 1980, p. 183). The secretary of defense concludes the Programming phase by deciding those issues that he must change in order to link the programs to the defense policy he has outlined (Weinberger, 1987, Part IE).

The Budgeting phase involves formal submission by the military departments of three budgets for the coming year: a basic budget commensurate with the POM, a minimum budget (5 percent less), and an enhanced budget (5 percent more). For example, the Army budget would request a specific amount to be spent for buying new prepositioned equipment for Europe. The services establish priorities between their programs in terms of "their contribution to achieving defense objectives" (Korb, 1980, p. 184). The president's views on these priorities are clarified in the budget which he submits to Congress (Weinberger, 1987).

This brief description of U.S. force posture design demonstrates an attempt by U.S. military planners to link force levels and weapons programs to perceived threats and to budget force capabilities within an integrated plan over five-year cycles—an ostensibly rational approach. U.S. force posture decisions are expressed in the idiom of systems analysts. To demonstrate the rationality of programs in the proposed defense budget, the secretary's Annual Report to the Congress frequently describes force posture design in a sequence similar to that listed above (Weinberger, 1987, p. 15). However, actual force posture design is neither as straightforward nor as rational as its practitioners would lead one to believe. Because force posture design sets a basis for defense budgets that consume vast amounts of resources (e.g., the U.S. defense budget for FY 1987 was approximately $282 billion), that process is bounded and influenced by many political, economic, and bureaucratic constraints.

THE NON-RATIONALITY OF U.S. FORCE POSTURE DESIGN IN PRACTICE

By examining selected major U.S. force posture decisions since 1945, one can evaluate how well decision-makers have fulfilled the ideal criteria embodied in the PPBS system. Since World War II, U.S. force posture has reflected its leaders' efforts to build and sustain the nation's dominant role in the international system. Post-war U.S. force posture design has involved two approaches—one to implement the containment policy of the Cold War from the late 1940s until the late 1960s, and the second to prepare for limited wars, an approach that has been used since the turning point of the Vietnam War. Since World War II, the guidance to U.S. force planners (lines 1 through 3 of the sequence provided earlier) has fluctuated concerning the number and kinds of wars they should prepare U.S. forces to fight. These changes in guidance, partly caused by frequent changes of civilian leaders, have made U.S. force posture design a fundamentally politicized process since 1945. Not surprisingly, it has evidenced the characteristic instabilities of the larger domestic and foreign political environments of which it is a part.

Like other world powers before it, the United States has experienced drastic changes in its role in the international system based on changes in its power (in all dimensions ranging from economic to military) relative to other actors in the system. Studies of U.S. force posture design, for example, William Kaufmann's (1982) analysis of conventional force planning during the period 1950–1980, demonstrate that many "non-rational" factors affect U.S. force planning, despite the rational appearances of annual reports to the Congress. U.S. force planning illustrates both the tensions faced by a great power in the modern international system and the inherent mismatch between force planning and military strategy.

U.S. force planning in the late 1940s was interwoven with the beginning of the Cold War. Planners were guided by what Secretary of Defense James Forrestal called the "four outstanding military facts of the world" at that time: (1) the predominance of Soviet land power in Eurasia; (2) the predominance of American sea power; (3) the U.S. monopoly on atomic weapons; and (4) America's enormous productive capacity (Huntington, 1961, p. 31). These "facts" were the key elements of the planning environment within which the United States organized the Department of Defense and developed the containment policy which signified the beginning of the Cold War. American strategy rested on four assumptions: (1) that the world was divided into two coalitions directed by the superpowers; (2) that American material strength, particularly military power, was adequate and applicable to organize a world order and meet the Communist challenge; (3) that U.S. and international security interests were indivisible; and (4) that the domestic consensus to support this role would last (Kolodziej, 1980, pp. 22–30).

U.S. force planning was oriented toward preparing for a long-term war against a coalition led by a single opponent, the Soviet Union. In that sense, American strategy was similar to the one used to defeat the Axis powers during World War II. Ironically, at the same time they began to implement the containment strategy, President Truman and the Congress responded to the domestic urge to turn inward by curtailing the FY 1948 defense budget (Kolodziej, 1966, Part II). The changing face of the international system in the early 1950s shocked American leaders into revising their estimate of the Soviet threat upward. As an outgrowth of the successful Soviet atomic test, NSC–68, and the Korean War, the Joint Chiefs of Staff divided the world into eleven regions and estimated U.S. force posture requirements to address contingencies in each region. The prohibitive cost of simultaneously addressing all of these threats moved U.S. planners to scale down force posture requirements to the following: 27 Army and Marine Corps divisions, 408 warships, and 41 Air Force and Marine Corps fighter attack-wings (Kaufmann, 1982, p. 2).

Throughout the 1950s, the Eisenhower administration emphasized a strategy of Massive Retaliation. In order to build economic strength, Eisenhower curtailed conventional spending through the New Look which substituted the nuclear threat and airpower for land power (Taylor, 1960, chs. 1–3). When he introduced the Flexible Response doctrine in 1962, Kennedy directed the JCS to conduct a second conventional force study, which called for 55 divisions, 82 fighter-attack wings, and 600 ships. Because these requirements exceeded the amounts that Kennedy and the Congress were willing to spend, the Kennedy administration emphasized the unlikelihood of fighting in all theatres at once (Kaufmann, 1982, pp. 4–6). McNamara established formal guidance that U.S. forces should be prepared to fight "two-and-one-half wars" simultaneously. This guidance revolved around the following assumptions:

(1) No more than two major conventional wars and one lesser contingency would arise simultaneously;

(2) Conventional planning was oriented toward defending the most demanding theaters—Europe, Korea, and Cuba;

(3) Allied forces were taken as a given with U.S. forces making up the deficit;

(4) Defense would be conducted in forward areas;

(5) Planners designed forces to fight the initial, defensive phase of a war (lasting three to six months) and assumed that mobilization would supplement active forces in longer wars;

(6) War supplies should be stockpiled for six months;

(7) The National Guard and Reserves would provide a significant portion of land and air forces (nine divisions and twelve fighter-attack wings);

(8) Reserves should be prioritized for early call-up;

(9) Forces should have the versatility to fight in more than one theater against more than one opponent;

(10) Reserves would supplement active forces in the event of simultaneous multiple contingencies. (Kaufmann, 1982, pp. 8–9)

The turning point in the Vietnam War signalled the need for the United States to scale back its international commitments and design its forces to fight limited wars. This change was formally acknowledged in the Nixon Doctrine which called for a partnership relationship with allies who shouldered a fair share of defense burdens (Nixon, 1970, p. 3822). Concurrently, the Nixon administration revised force planning guidance to a "one-and-one-half war" strategy. This meant the U.S. force posture design was oriented toward being prepared to simultaneously fight one major contingency in Europe or Asia and a lesser contingency elsewhere. This shift in emphasis was based on the following assumptions:

(1) Strategic and theater nuclear forces would deter an attack on U.S. allies;

(2) Enemy forces were unlikely to be able to coordinate two simultaneous major attacks; and

(3) U.S. force planning should emphasize heavier preparation for the most significant theater—Europe—because weakness there would invite attacks (Nixon, 1970, pp. 3839–40).

Since 1970, U.S. force planning to fight limited wars has been based on the "one-and-one-half war" assumptions, but vestiges of the "two-and-one-half war" approach remain. Those assumptions, made early in the Cold War, are no longer valid. U.S. presidents and force planners face new realities: the number of threats, allies, and adversaries have increased dramatically; there is a growing disparity between America's absolute power and its ability to influence international events; American interests are becoming more region-alized despite the globalization of U.S. contacts; and the domestic consensus favoring a major commitment of American military power overseas has eroded (Kolodziej, 1980, pp. 31–40). These changing realities have further increased the complexity of the U.S. force posture design process. American design planners can no longer rely on a nuclear monopoly, air superiority, control of the seas, or weapons technology advantages.

Based on his review of U.S. conventional force planning in the post-war era, William Kaufmann identifies three requirements for the U.S. conventional force posture:

(1) Substantial reduction in overseas deployment of U.S. forces;

(2) Establishment of a large strategic reserve in the continental United States equipped and trained to deal with multiple contingencies and theaters; and

(3) Provision of enough air- and sealift to rapidly deploy these reserves to deal with requirements overseas. (Kaufmann, 1982, pp. v-vi)

Kaufmann argues that the United States failed to achieve these requirements during the period 1950–1980. Overseas commitments were not significantly reduced. For example, President Carter shelved a plan to withdraw a division from Korea, and repeated proposals to decrease U.S. deployments in Europe have been abandoned in the face of allied pressures. U.S. reserve forces were supplied outmoded equipment and were not trained to respond to foresee-able contingencies. Strategic lift was not provided, partly because of rivalry between the armed forces and their indifference. The Navy has placed higher priority on aircraft carriers, submarines, and surface combat vessels; the Air

Force has sought strategic missiles, bombers, and tactical fighters; and the Army has emphasized mechanized forces. Because it falls between the interests of the individual armed services and costs a great deal, the strategic lift that is essential to project military power is always last in priority (Huntington, 1961; Luttwak, 1985, pp. 240–44; U.S. Congress, House Committee on Merchant Marine and Fisheries, 1981). This example concretely demonstrates American divergence from rational force planning in the face of multiple threats which the armed services perceive differently.

The turbulence and drain in resources caused by the Vietnam War also contributed to the U.S. failure to fulfill these requirements. During the 1965–1975 period, half of each defense budget was spent on that war. Disagreement over American involvement in Vietnam undermined support for military expenditures across the board. Subsequent presidents have increased overseas commitments, thereby spreading military capabilities over more strategic objectives and deepening the gap between resources and policy goals (Kaufmann, 1982). For example, President Carter's creation of the Rapid Deployment Force to support his doctrine in the Persian Gulf expanded commitments which he had previously said needed to be reduced. Given the calls for balanced budgets such as the Gramm–Rudman–Hollings Act and the congressional unwillingness to sustain the Reagan administration's defense buildup (evidenced by pending reductions in the military officer corps directed by Congress), one can expect more pressure on Pentagon planners. U.S. defense budgets will probably shrink in real terms during the next decade, and force planners will be challenged when they offer initiatives requiring new allocations of resources (Weinberger, 1987).

From the post-war American experience, one can make two further observations about force planning. American planners face a tension between planning forces to fight immediately and forces that can be expanded to fight a sustained conflict. The first kind of force is attractive when a state fears strategic surprise, possesses little strategic depth, or must win quickly because it cannot sustain a war of attrition. The situation of Israel illustrates these cases. Elements of this thinking are also present in the superpowers' strategic force planning. A large, combat-ready force is both expensive and difficult to sustain. The alternative approach is officer-heavy. The officers in an expansible armed force spend most of their time on procurement issues and peacetime bureaucratic battles with the other services and the Congress. Although it is cheaper to buy or maintain such a force, it is not very effective in a come-as-you-are battle, for example, Grenada.

One can also see how strategy affects force posture. If one plans to fight one type of war against a single opponent in one theatre (e.g., mechanized warfare against the Warsaw Pact in Central Europe), the state's force posture will be skewed away from readiness to fight unexpected wars. The impact of Massive Retaliation on force planning in the 1950s is an excellent example. If, however, the state prepares to fight multiple opponents in multiple theaters at different levels of intensity, a very different force posture is used. An example is the recent creation of the Light Infantry Division to fight lower intensity wars in places like Central America.

CONSTRAINTS ON U.S. FORCE POSTURE DESIGN

International Politics

U.S. force posture design responds to three international imperatives: those originating from U.S.–Soviet conflict; from alliance commitments; and from Third World threats (e.g., Libya). Stratic competition with the Soviets is also affected by arms control negotiations and accords that constrain American force planning. U.S. membership in alliances like NATO raises burden-sharing issues. These issues introduce strains within the alliance and hamper force planning as a consequence of the greater complexity and unreliability of allied cooperation (line 3 in the sequence described earlier). Third-party threats can confuse planning to fight against the primary foe and exacerbate alliance cohesion problems (e.g., threats by Iran or Libya which confuse coalition members).

Arms control accords (and the effort to reach them) can influence U.S. strategic force planning and capabilities. The United States must determine what balance it will strike in mutual restraint (both qualitatively and quantitatively) with the Soviet Union. Distrust may be so pervasive that arms control negotiations may have little impact on planning. For example, because of mutual superpower distrust, the SALT I treaty set nuclear force "limits" so high that the 1972 treaty occasioned an arms race without strictly violating the letter of the initial accord (Brown, 1983). When even these expansive limits proved too confining, they were abandoned (in 1986) to permit the modernization of U.S. strategic forces. Similarly, the Soviet Union has stretched the limits of the SALT II treaty which was never ratified but was tacitly observed until the mid-1980s.

The cases of the MX missile and Strategic Defense Initiative (SDI) demonstrate another aspect of the interplay between arms control and force posture design. In a sense, these weapons have become "bargaining chips" which the United States is developing in order to gain leverage in strategic arms control negotiations with the Soviet Union. Negotiations at the Reykjavik Summit in 1986 revolved around the U.S. potential to develop SDI. Offers by both sides to cut offensive systems were linked to expectations about SDI (Mandelbaum and Talbott, 1986). The potential development of SDI has fundamentally altered U.S. strategic force planning (Bundy, et al., 1984). Deterrence built on a combination of offense and defense complicates force planning by increasing the number of contingencies that must be addressed. Spending priorities must also be redefined as the superpowers emphasize strategic defense rather than offense. (For an overview, see *Daedalus*, 1985.)

U.S. membership in NATO further complicates force planning by bringing burden-sharing issues such as the division of military labor and resource support to be assumed by allies. NATO is a "defense club" that provides non-excludable benefits to all member states (Hartley, 1983, ch. 2). Citizens and opposing politicians are quick to criticize the U.S. government for not requiring allied "free riders," for example, Denmark, to pay a "fair share" to defend the "club." U.S. force planners are constrained by Congress which limits forward deployment in Europe to 320,000 troops. Disagreements with allies about political issues, such as whether to impose economic sanctions against Libya, detract from military coordination with other NATO members (Golden, 1983, chs. 2–3).

Alliance membership also causes the United States to consider multinational weapons production programs which further complicate its force planning. Economists criticize the inherent inefficiency of relying solely on U.S. firms to produce weapons and favor approaches, like the NATO Rationalization Standardization and Integration Program (RSI), which foster multilateral development and production. If one focuses purely on economic efficiency, joint production of weapons such as the Multiple Launch Rocket System makes more sense than preserving special relationships with a few U.S. firms. Carried to an extreme, such thinking would force the U.S. government to promote efficiency by shopping competitively among firms of all member nations, abolishing barriers to weapons imports, providing sensitive information on national security matters to foreign firms, and extending competitive bidding to all stages of production (Hartley, 1983, ch. 10). Although such methods may be more rational economically, they would make force posture design less responsive to strategic imperatives that counsel rational control over weapons production. (See Kolodziej, 1987; Ross, vol. 1, ch. 5).

Each alliance has special political-military arrangements that challenge alliance-wide force posture designs. For example, within the context of NATO, U.S. force planners must determine how to treat French conventional forces and logistic facilities that would be critical to NATO's success in a war against the Warsaw Pact (Hackett, 1978). In addition, since U.S. strategic weapons are available to support NATO allies, the wartime role that British and French nuclear forces would play is not clearly defined. While both the Greeks and the Turks are responsible for defending a portion of NATO's Southern Region, their rivalry over Cyprus and mineral rights in the Aegean Sea has frequently forced cancellation of major NATO exercises in that region, further complicating U.S. force planning (since the NATO Southern Region Commander also commands the U.S. Sixth Fleet). Like arms control negotiations, these alliance issues deflect American force planning from the rational model described above.

Domestic Politics

The checks and balances embedded in the U.S. Constitution constrain the executive branch in planning national defense. The determination of the essential elements of military policymaking—force levels and specific weapon systems as well as the allocation of time, and human and material resources required to execute military plans—is divided between the executive and legislative branches. Inevitably, the demands of national strategic planning must compete with other claims on resources arising from both branches of the government. These conflicting pressures must be mediated through the competition between the Congress and the president to control force level and resource allocation decisions. Because they lead a representative democracy, U.S. presidents must sustain a broad consensus behind defense policies while making timely and adequate preparations for armed conflict. Since the Congress annually appropriates funds for weapon systems and for the size of the armed forces, U.S. force planners face a greater burden of proof than their counterparts in the Soviet Union who are normally given first priority by their state's authoritarian system (Kolodziej, 1966, Part I). Congressional appropriations for controversial programs (such as the MX missile) often hinge on votes by individual congressmen who are motivated by a desire to improve their chances for reelection. The outcome on a major force development program may be linked to local political issues, such as whether a particular firm may get a contract, rather than to national security interests. For example, during procurement debates for the Cheyenne helicopter in the 1960s and 1970s, several congressmen demonstrated constituency-serving behavior in supporting or opposing the Lockheed proposal (Liske and Rundquist, 1974, Part II). Congressional oversight clearly causes planners to worry about domestic political support when they are designing for the U.S. force posture.

Economics

The consensus on what resources can be made available to U.S. force planners has shifted frequently since 1945. Before 1950, the U.S. defense budget was limited by an implicit ceiling of $15 billion (approximately $100 billion in 1987 dollars). The constraint led to cancellation of many service programs, induced a reduction in troop strength, and contributed to the poor showing of U.S. forces in the early stages of the Korean War (Schilling et al., 1962). Eisenhower's New Look strategy was based on the notion that restraining defense spending would improve the economic well-being of the nation without damaging national security. His programs brought about a reduction of two Army divisions, a decrease in the Navy by fifty ships, and a reduction of 300,000 men in the active-duty forces (Huntington, 1961, pp. 64–113; Kolodziej, 1966, chs. 5–6). Conversely, during the Kennedy administration, defense budgets were increased in an effort to stimulate the economy while fulfilling the new Flexible Response strategy. Kennedy emphasized counterinsurgency programs in the Army and maintenance of nuclear superiority through the purchase of strategic missiles and bombers (Kolodziej, 1966, ch. 7).

Bureaucratic Problems

Edward Luttwak, an outspoken critic of the current U.S. defense management structure, has accused the Pentagon of relying on a "fatally flawed" management approach based on the U.S. experience in World War II. He specifically attacks the Pentagon's organizational structure as being oversized and unnecessarily complex. He traces this complexity to the use of three levels of higher management within the Department of Defense to supervise most issues: the uniformed command within one of the armed services, the service secretary's staff, and the office of the secretary of defense. This structure creates "formidable barrier[s] to innovation" which often overcomplicate decision-making and "always delay and sometimes prevent innovation totally" (Luttwak, 1985, pp. 89–92). The influence of these factors is demonstrated by the long delay between the decision to purchase a weapon and its fielding. The procurement process takes long enough that American military forces seldom receive the full benefit of scientific advancement (Fallows, 1981; Luttwak, 1985; Spinney, 1985). Thus, force planners must factor a time lag of several years into consideration of how many new weapons will affect military capabilities.

Although rivalry between the U.S. armed services has existed since the late eighteenth century, critiques by Maxwell Taylor and Edward Luttwak suggest that in the last forty years this tendency has become acute for U.S. force planners. Parochial interests, for example, support for the 600-ship Navy, were placed ahead of U.S. national interests (Taylor, 1961; Luttwak, 1985). Development of new weapons, such as the cruise missile which can be used by all of the armed services for a wide variety of contingencies, has further aggravated traditional interservice rivalries.

The Department of Defense decision-making structure promotes conflict among the services. According to Maxwell Taylor, the division of responsibilities among the service secretaries in the 1950s often induced the Joint Chiefs of Staff to split their votes on issues that cut to the heart of differences between the Army, Air Force, and Navy-Marine Corps positions on how wars should be fought. At that time the Army stressed overseas deployments, the need to adopt a Flexible Response strategy, and preparation for a long war like World War II. The Army called for establishment of a unified readiness command in the continental United States to control reinforcement of overseas areas. The Navy advocated using carrier task forces and Polaris submarines as part of the strategic deterrent. The Air Force wanted more strategic missiles and bombers to prepare for a general nuclear war. These rivalries detracted from joint development of the U.S. armed forces during the period when the current unified and specified command structure was established by the 1958 Defense Reorganization Act (Taylor, 1960, ch. 6). In his review of Pentagon planning in recent decades, Luttwak indicates that service rivalries have increased rather than decreased over time. Today the clash between Army plans to build attack helicopters, Navy plans for a 600-ship fleet, and Air Force plans to build MX missiles during an era of shrinking defense budgets means that service rivalries will continue to shape U.S. force posture in ways that are not always clearly related to national strategic needs (Luttwak, 1985).

Intraservice rivalries also detract from rational force posture design. Rivalry exists within the U.S. Army as well as between the Army and other services. Recent articles written by Army generals evidence widespread skepticism about the Light Infantry Division, which was added to the force posture in the mid–1980s. Internal rivalries are fostered by the Army's current force posture: there are seven different types among the eighteen active Army divisions (Bahnsen, 1985; Damon and Krisler, 1985). Belief in the worth of one's own unit drives a member of a Heavy Division to question the value of Airborne, Airmobile, and Light Divisions (and vice versa). Military advice offered to civilian supervisors is colored by these views. Hence, these rivalries affect many aspects of force posture design.

Some specific examples illustrate how these rivalries detract from U.S. force posture planning. Cruise missiles can be deployed on air, land, or sea with conventional or nuclear warheads. Service rivalries complicate efforts to rationally deploy this efficient, cheap weapon and therefore hamper rational force posture design. Cruise missiles can carry both conventional and nuclear warheads to a range of 1550 miles to strike a variety of targets ranging from radars to short-range ballistic missiles or naval vessels. This multiple capability complicates strategic planning by both friendly and opposing military experts (Coffey, 1980). U.S. force planners must prepare for contingencies around the globe, but they tend to focus their efforts on preparing for the least likely, but most important, contingency—a war in Europe.

Technological Dependency

Some analysts criticize U.S. military planners for relying too heavily on sophisticated weapons. Amplifying arguments first presented by Chuck Spinney at the Pentagon, James Fallows argues that Pentagon planners often try to build a "magic weapon" that will make victory automatic. He charges that U.S. force planners prepare exclusively for future battles in which technology will help American soldiers overcome enemy numbers. This approach has led to the development of weapons like the F–15 fighter aircraft which employs the latest in avionics at a cost that constrains procurement. These complex weapon systems cost from two to ten times as much as the systems they replace and are extremely difficult to keep operational. Fallows cites studies which show that, while in individual combat these systems are advantageous, in battles where four or these aircraft "fight" against four less sophisticated aircraft, the sophisticated weapons do not improve combat performance (Fallows, 1981, chs. 2–3). Spinney traces the costs of relying on complex systems: when all maintenance and spare parts costs are taken into account, the F–15 costs twice as much as the F–4E which it replaced (Spinney, 1985, p. 87).

Information

Given their imperfect knowledge, U.S. force posture designers have difficulty allocating for the future. Uncertainty about how threats and friendly capabilities will change increases the complexity of their task. Force planners must choose between funding research that may lead to superior weapons or funding current forces that can be used immediately. For example, they must choose between buying an MX missile with today's costs, technology, and political consequences, or a Midgetman missile in the next decade with a different set of costs, capabilities, and arms control and security consequences. Their uncertainty is further complicated by the possibility that strategic offensive weapons may be coupled with the SDI. They have no way of accurately forecasting the proper mix of weapons that will be needed for future conflicts.

Because it has chosen a complex force posture, the United States must also choose between investing in military infrastructure such as logistical facilities or deploying additional combat forces. For example, in recent years the U.S. Army decided to field the seventeenth and eighteenth active-duty divisions within the same end-strength that had supported sixteen divisions for the previous decade. This decision meant that programs to improve base facilities for existing units had to be delayed. Dollars invested in facilities, such as buildings and ranges would have offset procurement of weapons or pay for more volunteer soldiers (Bahnsen, 1985).

CONCLUSIONS

This analysis of force posture design leads to two tentative conclusions. First, while force posture design is often described as a rational, deliberate process of matching military capabilities to external threats, in practice that process deviates from this norm owing to numerous political, economic, bureaucratic, technological, and informational constraints. Despite the Pentagon's emphasis on the PPBS approach, force planning for both the Cold War and limited wars has been heavily influenced by what might be termed non-rational factors; for example, Eisenhower's emphasis on nuclear weapons and airpower in the New Look to save money. When the Pentagon did attempt to rationalize force posture requirements, American leaders found ways to avoid purchasing the forces stipulated by the JCS. As William Kaufmann argues, leaders have also failed to curtail commitments, build versatile reserves, or buy the strategic air- and sealift necessary to support post-war conventional strategy. Over the past forty years, the U.S. force planning process has become far more complex. U.S. forces have been primarily oriented toward fighting a major conflict in Europe or Northeast Asia and are not easily transformed to fight limited wars elsewhere. Pentagon planners cannot rely on a nuclear monopoly or air superiority in preparing for those limited wars.

Although this chapter has focused on the U.S. case, one can assume that other states confront similar force planning constraints. The Soviet Union must also balance conventional and strategic planning considerations. Alliance considerations constrain the Federal Republic of Germany even more than they do the United States. Many developing states have neither the resources to buy nor personnel who can use sophisticated weapons. For example, India and Pakistan are constrained by scarce resources from deploying advanced weapons. Chinese military reforms are aimed at improving the technical ability of the peasants who are the backbone of the People's Liberation Army so that they can use modern weapons.

The second conclusion with regard to force design is that the constraints examined seem to reinforce each other and prompt planners to make trade-offs, for example, developing a new weapon because technology offers it or as a bargaining chip in competition with an untrusted adversary. Domestic political battles focus economic constraints and confuse both allies and adversaries.

AGENDA FOR FURTHER RESEARCH

Although this chapter has investigated U.S. force planning, one can offer an agenda for expanding this analysis to cover force posture design in other states. An expansion of this research could amplify the study of international issues associated with adversary and allied relationships. Such an expanded study could include the effects of other factors (political system, level of economic development, culture, etc.) on force posture design. At the very least, a broader project could lead to better qualification of the model of force posture design offered here.

The limited focus of this chapter and the lack of research materials available on force posture design in other states offer one direction in which the scope of this work might be expanded. Generalizations advanced here should be deepened and expanded through a detailed evaluation of specific nation-state force postures, following the example of Barry Blechman and Stephen Kaplan's study of the use of force in the postwar era (Blechman and Kaplan, 1978). Such studies could clarify the relationship betwen a state's level of economic development and its force posture design; between military planning and the type of political system (pluralistic or authoritarian) which the state uses; and between culture and force posture design. With enough variety in the states studied, one could draw firmer conclusions about how and why an underdeveloped Latin American state governed by a military junta creates a different force posture than that which is designed by a highly developed European democracy. Both the role played by elites in determining the state's force posture and the influence of individual perceptions on force planning merit further research.

The multilateral aspects of force posture design—those related to arms control negotiations and alliances—might also be analyzed further. Although both arms control and burden-sharing have been analyzed extensively, neither has been explicitly studied with respect to its interaction with force posture design. Multilateral decision-making within an alliance such as NATO clearly affects the force posture design conducted by member states and their adversaries. The development of "bargaining chips" such as the MX missile or SDI has been studied in the context of the arms control process, but not as it influences and is influenced by force posture design.

This chapter has illustrated the Janus-like quality of force posture design as a process of reconciling competing external and internal imperatives. Attempts to rationalize force planning appear to be futile in the face of the international and domestic constraints that influence this process. While it forms a crucial link between a state's foreign and domestic policies, force planning is hard to separate from other military processes. There is still much to learn about the impact of political, economic, bureaucratic, and technological constraints on the process of planning force postures.

REFERENCES

Bahnsen, John. November 1985. The Kaleidoscopic U.S. Army. *Armed Forces Journal International*, pp .78–88.

Blechman, Barry, and Stephen Kaplan. 1978. *Force Without War*. Washington, D.C.: Brookings Institution.

Brown, Harold. 1983. *Thinking About National Security: Defense and Foreign Policy in a Dangerous World*. Boulder, Colo.: Westview Press.

Bundy, McGeorge, George Kennan, Robert McNamara, and Gerard Smith. 1984. The President's Choice: Star Wars or Arms. *Foreign Affairs* 63:264–78.

Coffey, Joseph. 1980. Arms, Arms Control, and Alliance Relationships: The Case of the Cruise Missile. Pp. 69–84 in Edward A. Kolodziej and Robert E. Harkavy, eds., *American Security Policy and Policy-making*. Lexington, Mass.: D.C. Heath.

Daedulus. 1985. Weapons in Space. American Academy of Arts and Sciences, Cambridge, Mass.

Damon, Major General Sam, and Brigadier General Ben Krisler. May 1985. Army of Excellence? A Time to Take Stock. *Armed Forces Journal International*, pp. 86–94.

Enthoven, Alan, and K. Wayne Smith. 1969. *How Much is Enough?* New York: Harper Colophon Books.

Fallows, James. 1981. *National Defense*. New York: Random House.

Federal Republic of Germany, Ministry of Defense. 1985. *White Paper, 1985*. Bonn: Federal Republic of Germany, Government Printing Office.

Golden, James. 1983. *The Dynamics of Change in NATO: A Burden-sharing Perspective*. New York: Praeger.

Hackett, General Sir John. 1978. *The Third World War, August 1985*. New York: Berkley Books.

Hammond, Paul Y. 1974. The Cross-National Comparison of Force Postures. Pp. 298–309 in Frank B. Horton III, Anthony C. Rogerson, and Edward L. Warner III, eds., *Comparative Defense Policy*. Baltimore: Johns Hopkins University Press.

Hartley, Keith. 1983. *NATO Arms Co-operation: A Study in Economics and Politics*. London: George Allen and Unwin.

Huntington, Samuel P. 1961. *The Common Defense: Strategic Programs in National Politics*. New York: Columbia University Press.

Kaufmann, William. 1964. *The McNamara Strategy*. New York: Harper and Row.

———. 1982. *Planning Conventional Forces, 1950–1980*. Washington, D.C.: Brookings Institution.

Kolodziej, Edward A. 1966. *The Uncommon Defense and Congress, 1945–1963*. Columbus: Ohio State University Press.

———. 1980. New Assumptions to Guide the Use and Control of Military Force. Pp. 21–43 in Edward A. Kolodziej and Robert R. Harkavy, eds. *American Security Policy and Policymaking*. Lexington, Mass.: D.C. Heath.

———. 1987. *Making and Marketing Arms: The French Experience and the Implications for the International System*. Princeton, N.J.: Princeton University Press.

Korb, Lawrence J. 1980. The Process and Problems of Linking Policy and Force Posture through the Defense Budget Process. Pp. 181–92 in Edward A. Kolodziej and Robert R. Harkavy, eds., *American Security Policy and Policymaking*. Lexington, Mass.: D.C. Heath.

Kronenberg, Philip, ed. 1981. *Planning U.S. Security*. Washington, D.C.: National Security Affairs Institute.

Liske, Craig, and Barry Rundquist, 1974. *The Politics of Weapons Procurement: The Role of Congress*. Denver: University of Colorado.

Luttwak, Edward. 1985. *The Pentagon and the Art of War*. New York: Simon and Schuster.

Mandelbaum, Michael, and Strobe Talbott. 1986. Reykyavik and Beyond. *Foreign Affairs* 65:215–35.

Neuman, Stephanie, ed. 1984. *Defense Planning in Less-Industrialized States: The Middle East and South Asia*. Lexington, Mass.: Lexington Books.

Nixon, Richard. 1970. U.S. Foreign Policy for the 1970s: A New Strategy for Peace reprinted in U.S. Congress, House. February 18, 1970. *Congressional Record*. 91st Congress, 2nd sess., pp. 3821–43. Washington, D.C.: U.S. Government Printing Office.

Sanders, Ralph. 1973. *The Politics of Defense Analysis*. New York: Dunellen Publishing Co.

Schilling, Warner, Paul Y. Hammond, and Glenn Snyder, eds. 1962. *Strategy, Politics and Defense Budgets*. New York: Columbia University Press.

Schlesinger, James. 1968. *Force Planning and Budgeting: The Issue of Centralized Control*. Washington, D.C.: Industrial College of the Armed Forces.

Spinney, Franklin. 1985. *Defense Facts of Life*. Boulder, Colo.: Westview Press.

U.S. Congress, House, Committee on Armed Services, Investigations Subcommittee,

Hearings. 1985. *Reorganization Proposals for the Joint Chiefs of Staff—1985.* Washington, D.C.: U.S. Government Printing Office.

———, House, Committee on Merchant Marine and Fisheries, Hearings. 1981. *Defense Sealift Capability.* Washington, D.C.: U.S. Government Printing Office. 1985.

———, Senate, Committee on Armed Services, Hearings. 1981. *Department of Defense Authorization for Appropriations for Fiscal Year 1982.* Washington, D.C.: U.S. Government Printing Office.

———, Senate, Committee on Armed Services, Staff Report. 1985. *Defense Organization: The Need for Change.* Washington, D.C.: U.S. Government Printing Office.

———, Senate, Committee on Foreign Relations, Hearings. 1982. *Situation in Lebanon.* Washington, D.C.: U.S. Government Printing Office.

———, Senate, Committee on Foreign Relations, Hearings. 1984. *Policy Options in Lebanon.* Washington, D.C.: U.S. Government Printing Office.

Taylor, Maxwell. 1960. *The Uncertain Trumpet.* New York: Harper and Brothers.

Weinberger, Caspar. 1984. *Annual Report to the Congress, FY 1985.* Washington, D.C.: U.S. Government Printing Office.

———. 1987. *Annual Report to the Congress, FY 1988.* Washington, D.C.: U.S. Government Printing Office.

PART III

THE CONTROL OF FORCE
AND THREATS

10

On Arms Control

MICHAEL D. INTRILIGATOR
AND DAGOBERT L. BRITO

This chapter identifies and analyzes key concepts in the area of arms control, specifically including its definition, goals, and approaches. Such an analysis is important inasmuch as the term *arms control* means different things to different people. Its definition, goals, and approaches have changed over time, and these concepts influence attitudes toward arms control. As discussed below, with certain conceptualizations of the term and associated goals and approaches, some people are supporters of arms control, whereas with other conceptualizations other people are skeptical about or even hostile to the notion.

To start with our overall conclusion, we believe that arms control, defined as various initiatives to promote strategic stability by reducing the chance of war, especially nuclear war, has had and continues to have an important role to play in national and international security affairs. At the same time, arms control requires reconsideration of, if not total rethinking about, both its agenda and its procedure in order to ensure its continued relevance.

DEFINITION OF ARMS CONTROL

We define *arms control* as *changes in the numbers, types, and qualities of weapons; changes in their configurations; and other modifications that affect their use or effectiveness in order to reduce the chance of war, especially nuclear war.* Over time the meaning of the term *arms control* has changed in rather profound ways. We identify three successive definitions. Our own

This chapter is a product of the UCLA Center for International and Strategic Affairs central research project "Alternative Approaches to Arms Control." We would like to acknowledge the valuable suggestions of Richard Bitzinger, Roman Kolkowicz, Edward Kolodziej, Patrick Morgan, Bennett Ramberg, and Randolph M. Siverson.

definition represents, in effect, a return to that of an earlier period, which we believe is the most appropriate one.

The original meaning of "arms control," specifically in the immediate post–World War II period, was virtually synonymous with disarmament. In this interpretation, arms control refers to reductions in weapons, particularly strategic weapons of mass destruction such as nuclear weapons. "Control" over "arms" was exercised by reducing their numbers, that is, limiting and reducing inventories of weapons. Some people still use the terms "arms control" and "disarmament" virtually interchangeably.

By the 1960s, the meaning of arms control had changed, particularly in Thomas Schelling (1960, 1966) and Schelling and Morton Halperin (1961). Their definition of the term involved any initiative that would reduce the chance of war, particularly nuclear war; reduce damage in case war did occur; and reduce the cost of defense. This definition allows for weapons reductions, but it also admits other changes that would promote strategic stability, such as changes in basing, in types of weapons, and other modifications that would reduce the chance of war. Schelling and Halperin even noted that in certain situations arms *increases* could be interpreted as arms control. Such a reversal of the prior interpretation of arms control as strictly weapons reductions was conditioned on the development of the deterrence paradigm (as developed in, among others, Brodie, 1946, 1959; Kahn, 1960, 1962; Brennan, 1961; and later discussed in Jervis, 1978 and Brodie, 1978).

According to the deterrence paradigm, stability in the sense of reducing the chance of war is achieved when each of the contending nations has enough capability to inflict unacceptable damage on the other side in a retaliatory second strike, after the other has inflicted the first strike (George and Smoke, 1974). If arms control seeks to reduce the chance of war and if such stability is achieved by deterrence then the operational implications of arms control are radically different from those for which arms control seeks only weapons reductions. Under the deterrence paradigm there should, for example, be a concern over the basing of weapons, leading to concern over bomber basing, as stressed in Albert Wohlstetter (1959); to the hardening of missile silos, and to the development of newer modes of basing strategic weapons, such as submarines, as stressed in Oskar Morgenstern (1959). Furthermore, if improvements in the survivability of strategic weapons are not sufficient to obtain adequate second-strike capability, then it may be necessary to deploy new types of weapons or additional weapons, precisely the case in which arms control calls for *more* weapons under the deterrence paradigm.

By the late 1970s, the meaning of arms control had once again changed, at least for some people. The Strategic Arms Limitation Talks (SALT) had begun in 1968 as a U.S.-Soviet dialogue on strategic weapons. This dialogue led to the 1972 SALT I and ABM treaties and to the 1979 SALT II treaty, which was signed but never ratified by the United States. Under the Reagan administration, the followup to SALT was the Strategic Arms Reduction Talks (START), which began in 1982. Partly as a result of the wide attention given the SALT/START process, including negotiations, summit meetings, signings of treaties, and debates over ratification, some people started to interpret arms control as strictly U.S.-Soviet negotiations on limiting or reducing strategic weapons. The early change in the interpretation of arms control from reducing the number of weapons to reducing the chance of war involved a substantial broadening in interpretation, for example, to include concern over types and bases of weapons, weapons survivability, and so forth. The later change in interpretation, restricting arms control to superpower negotiations, pointed in exactly the opposite direction. Confining arms control to bilaterally negotiated weapons reductions narrowed even the early interpretation, which allowed not only for bilaterally negotiated reductions but also for reductions stemming from unilateral actions or multilaterally negotiated agreements.

If arms control is limited to bilaterally negotiated weapons reductions and if such negotiated reductions are seen as minimal or meaningless, then it is natural to conclude that arms control does not work. Certainly, the titles of two recent papers reflect this idea of failure: "What Went Wrong with Arms Control?" by one of the intellectual fathers of arms control, Thomas C. Schelling (1985–1986), and "Farewell to Arms Control?" by Joseph S. Nye, Jr. (1986).

Debate over definitions is normally rather sterile, but in this case the definition of "arms control" turns out to be crucial inasmuch as it influences attitudes, perceptions, decisions, and outcomes. If leaders perceive that arms control is valuable, based in part on their attitudes as shaped by their interpretation of arms control, as in the 1960s and early 1970s, they will make certain decisions with regard to weapons, such as deployment of submarine-launched ballistic missiles (SLBM), hardening of missile silos, and the ABM treaty. Conversely, if they see arms control as ineffectual, based, in part, on attitudes as shaped by the interpretation of the late 1970s and 1980s, then they will make rather different decisions, as in the development of the B1 bomber, the United States' breakout from the SALT II treaty limits, and the launching of the Strategic Defense Initiative (SDI).

Our definition above represents a return to the definition of arms control used in the 1960s and early 1970s, which we believe to be the most relevant and useful definition of arms control (Intriligator and Brito, 1987). Such a definition is broad enough to encompass the earlier and later definitions in that it allows as one possibility weapons reductions and, as a further specification, weapons reductions based on bilateral negotiations. Furthermore, this earlier definition permits stability to be achieved via deterrence, particularly mutual deterrence, or via some other mechanism. Arms control, by our definition, is not the same as disarmament, which refers only to reductions or elimination of weapons. In certain instances, as already noted, arms *in-*

creases can be interpreted as arms control if such increases promote the goals of arms control. Nor is arms control, by our definition, the same as bilaterally negotiated weapons reductions, which is but one of several alternative approaches to arms control.

Our definition of arms control is consistent with the idea of seeking goals in one's arms policy that are seen as beneficial from the viewpoint of a single country, a pair of countries, or a group of countries. A country can individually or unilaterally reach certain goals through its arms policy. In terms of two or more countries, certain changes in arms may be seen as mutually beneficial in improving all sides through cooperation. Thus, one aspect of arms control is cooperation with other nations, including potential adversaries, in achieving certain goals, particularly in controlling potential conflict. Cooperation is possible between untrustworthy adversaries within a framework of partial information because it is to their mutual advantage. Arms control takes place in an adversarial context. When it involves two or more countries, it typically entails negotiations and bargaining in order to seek out preferred positions that yield an advantage to all participants. From a game-theoretical standpoint, potential mutual gains can be achieved through arms control which exploit the non-zero-sum character of the two-or-more-player game representation of choosing arms policies (Brams, 1985).

GOALS OF ARMS CONTROL

The goals of arms control are dependent on its definition. If, for example, arms control is defined as disarmament (or weapons reductions) as in the period immediately after World World II, then the goal is simply the elimination of weapons (or reduction of weapons stockpiles). If, alternatively, arms control is defined as bilaterally negotiated weapons reductions, as in the late 1970s and 1980s, then the goal is to attain agreements yielding such reductions, as in the SALT/START process. Sub-goals are organizing to negotiate, carrying out a successful negotiation, and signing and ratifying a treaty.

Given our definition of arms control, which is similar to that formulated by Schelling and Halperin in the 1960s, a reasonable set of goals for arms control are those also formulated in the 1960s. The first and foremost of these "canonical" goals, that of *strategic stability*, is *to reduce the chance of war, especially nuclear war*. The second goal, that of *damage limitation*, is *to reduce or to limit damage in the case war does break out*. The third, that of *cost containment*, is *to reduce the cost of armaments*.

In addition to these canonical goals, other aims may be advanced or influenced through arms control: (1) to reduce tensions and to act as a confidence-building measure; (2) to promote strategic and military objectives; (3) to promote international political objectives; (4) to promote domestic interests or to alter the domestic political climate; (5) to alter perceptions of adversaries; and (6) inasmuch as arms control initiatives have effects on alliances, to strengthen one's own alliance and/or weaken the enemy bloc. These other goals, however, are either secondary to the canonical goals or achieved through mechanisms other than changes in numbers and types of weapons.

When the canonical goals were formulated in the 1960s, it was emphasized that the goal of strategic stability, that is, of reducing the chance of war, should be the primary goal. The primacy of this goal is even clearer today. Given the devastating consequences of war, even a war involving only conventional weapons, but especially a war involving nuclear weapons, it is clear that avoidance of war is the critical objective. As to the other canonical goals, damage limitation is extremely difficult and costly, if it can be done at all, whether through passive defenses such as fallout shelters or through active defenses such as the SDI program. Thus, although it is still a reasonable goal, the nature of war technology makes it extremely difficult to realize. The last canonical goal is that of cost containment; but defense costs, at least those for the United States, are by no means high relative to the total economy. For example, the United States spends about 7 percent of its gross national product (GNP) on defense, and this fraction is lower than that for most prior periods. There may be greater pressure for cost containment in the Soviet Union, which spends about 16 percent its of GNP on defense.

Thus, of these various goals, *reducing the chance of war, especially nuclear war, must remain the primary goal*, and this will be the assumed goal in what follows. Accordingly, the *arms* in the term *arms control* will be taken to refer to weapon numbers, qualities, configurations, and so on, whereas the *control* will be taken to refer to control over their potential *use*, not simply their numbers or types. In particular, arms control will be identified as initiatives taken with the goal of reducing the chance of war, especially nuclear war. In terms of expected utility analysis, the primary goal of arms control is to reduce the probability of the war outcome, recognizing that, while it would also be useful to reduce the damage (disutility) associated with this war outcome and to reduce the cost of arms, these other goals are clearly secondary.

ARMS CONTROL: APPROACHES AND METHODS

If arms control is defined, as above, as changes in the numbers, types, and qualities of weapons; changes in their configurations; and other modifications that affect their use of effectiveness, and if the goal of arms control is to reduce the chance of war, especially nuclear war, then there are several alternative approaches to arms control. Although the approach frequently emphasized (or even used to define arms control) is arms control based on bilateral negotiations on limitations or reductions of weapons leading to treaties with verification provisions, this approach is but a particular instance of one of three broad approaches to arms control, namely, the *unilateral*, *bilateral*, and *multilateral approaches*.

The unilateral (or independent) approach involves the initiatives taken by a single country, with or without the expectation of reciprocity. If arms control refers to actions taken to stabilize the nuclear balance and arms control is not restricted to weapons reductions, then examples of unilateral arms control initiatives include the building and hardening of missile silos and the development and deployment of submarine-launched ballistic missiles. These examples, together with earlier bomber deployments, led to the creation of the triad of weapons that exists in both the United States and the Soviet Union and also in the United Kingdom, France, and China. These unilateral initiatives are arms control initiatives in that they change the types and configurations of weapons and in that they reduce the chances of war through deterrence. Another type of unilateral initiative which refers to potential changes in weapons qualities is restraint in the development or deployment of new weapons systems. For example, for many years the United States did not develop anti-satellite (ASAT) weapons, even though it had the capabilities to do so. Yet another example is the United States unilateral decision, made by President Nixon, not to produce biological weapons. These various unilateral arms control initiatives are often ignored, although they are extremely important. In fact, they are probably the most important arms control initiatives ever taken in the nuclear period to reduce the chance of war because they, together with weapons deployments, have jointly created the stability of mutual deterrence.

The bilateral approach involves formal treaties, mutual understandings, or parallel unilateral action, that is, unilateral actions taken simultaneously or consecutively by both sides. Examples of accords include the limited test ban (1963), which progressed from parallel unilateral action to a mutual understanding to, ultimately, a formal (multilateral) treaty. The SALT I (1972), SALT II (1979), and START (1982) negotiations form another example of bilateral arms control, which led to formal treaties.

Multilateral initiatives, as in the bilateral case, can be achieved through formal treaties, mutual understandings, or parallel unilateral action. Examples include the multiparty treaty prohibiting atmospheric testing, the three-party (U.S.-USSR-U.K.) negotiations on a comprehensive test ban (CTB) treaty, and the ongoing Mutual and Balanced Force Reduction (MBFR) talks. Another example is the Non-proliferation Treaty (NPT), involving over 130 countries. In addition to the NPT, other multilateral initiatives support the non-proliferation regime, such as the London Suppliers' agreement and the Zangger Committee. These multilateral approaches to non-proliferation are sometimes treated separately from arms control, but they are consistent with the definition of arms control advanced here and thus should be treated as arms control initiatives. By the same token, unilateral initiatives to prevent nuclear proliferation, such as requirements for full-scope safeguards or for return of spent nuclear fuel rods to the supplying country, should also be regarded as arms control initiatives. All are consistent with the broad operational definition of arms control as actions affecting arms that can reduce the chance of war.

All three approaches are influenced by, and to some extent also influence, domestic political factors. Domestic constituencies can influence attitudes toward these approaches, particularly political, economic, military, social, and intellectual leaders. For example, some leaders may be hesitant to use unilateral approaches without reciprocation, seeking a *quid pro quo* response to unilateral initiatives. Similarly, some leaders may oppose arms control measures on ideological grounds or may tie arms control measures to other steps through a process of linkage to gain certain advantages in other areas. Effective arms control requires either strong political leadership or a stable domestic consensus about the utility of arms control initiatives or agreements. Allies present yet another consideration for arms control, and some degree of harmonization of domestic, adversary, and allied interests is generally required for effective arms control.

Just as there are several alternative *approaches* to arms control, depending on the number of participants, there are several alternative *methods* of arms control, that is, the instruments by which arms control is achieved. The most frequently discussed method is probably reductions or limitations in the number of weapons, a method that long precedes the nuclear age. For example, the nine treaties stemming from the 1921–1922 Washington Disarmament Conference used precisely this method to limit arms in the hope of preventing war. For example, they adopted the 5–5–3 ratio of future capital–ship replacement tonnage for the United States, Great Britain, and Japan, respectively. In the nuclear era, this method forms the basis of the SALT and START approaches to arms control.

Another method of arms control, which also precedes the nuclear era, is that of agreements or decisions not to deploy certain weapons. In the nuclear era, three examples of this method are the ABM Treaty, which obligated the two superpowers not to deploy antiballistic missile systems beyond certain agreed-on numbers and types of locations; the unilateral decision not to deploy an ASAT weapons system; and the NPT, which obligates the nuclear non-weapons states not to develop or to deploy such weapons. A third method of arms control involves changes in types, bases, or configurations of weapons, that is, how weapons are deployed for use. Examples include the hardening of ICBM silos, the development of submarine-launched ballistic missiles, and the development of missiles with MIRV warheads—and also the possibility of deMIRVing missiles. A fourth method of arms control is that of limitations on testing. Examples include various test moratoria, the limited test ban, the partial test ban, and the threshold test ban, and involve unilateral, multilateral, and bilateral approaches. A fifth method of arms control is that of nuclear-free zones. Unlike the method that involves decisions or agreements not to deploy, which pertains to countries, the method of nuclear-free zones involves

Table 10.1
Alternative Approaches/Methods of Arms Control

Methods	Approaches		
	Unilateral	*Bilateral*	*Multilateral*
Limitations in numbers	Elimination of obsolete weapons	SALT I, II START	MBFR
Agreements/ decisions not to deploy	Restraint on ASAT	ABM Treaty	NPT
Changes in types, bases, or configurations	Hardened silos Submarine deployments	New system restrictions in SALT II	
Limits on testing	Unilateral moritoria	Threshold test ban	CTB
Nuclear-free zones	Norway Japan		Austria Seabed Space

decisions or agreements not to introduce nuclear weapons in certain designated areas. Examples include the unilateral decisions not to introduce nuclear weapons in Norway, Japan, and other states and the multilateral agreements not to introduce nuclear weapons in Antarctica, in Austria, on the seabed, and in space.

These alternative approaches and methods can be combined into a matrix of cross-classifications, as presented in Table 10.1. This table indicates some of the many possibilities for arms control. All of the cross-classifications are possible, and most can be illustrated by historical examples, as in the chronology of formal arms control efforts presented in Table 10.2. Unfortunately, many people still treat arms control only in terms of the bilateral approach—limitations/reductions in weapons cross-classification, as in the SALT/START process. Such a narrow interpretation of arms control accounts for some of the skepticism about or even hostility to arms control. The argument against arms control is that, since arms control purportedly refers to U.S.-Soviet negotiations on numbers of weapons and since purportedly these negotiations have not accomplished much, arms control does not work. This reasoning is flawed, and the conclusion is false. Arms control involves many possible approaches, as illustrated in the table, not just bilateral negotiations. As to the bilateral negotiations themselves, they have had important effects. Although strategic arms limitation agreements can lead to qualitative weapons improvements (Brito and Intriligator, 1981), the SALT and ABM agreements probably have been beneficial in providing predictability of the other side.

Table 10.2
Chronology of Major Formal Arms Control Efforts

1. U.N. Atomic Energy Commission, est. 1946
2. U.N. Commission on Conventional Armaments, est. 1946
3. U.N. Disarmament Commission, est. 1952
4. 1958 Experts Conference
5. 1958 Surprise Attack Conference
6. Nuclear Test Ban talks, est. 1958
7. Antarctica Treaty, 1959
8. Ten Nation Committee on Disarmament, est. 1960
9. Conference of the Eighteen Nation Disarmament Committee; Conference of the Committee on Disarmament; Committee on Disarmament, est. 1962
   a) Nuclear Non-proliferation Treaty, 1968
   b) Biological Weapons Convention, 1972
   c) Seabed Denuclearization Treaty, 1973
   d) Chemical weapons
10. Limited Test Ban Treaty, 1963
11. Hot Line Agreement, 1963
12. Outer Space Treaty, 1967
13. Latin American Nuclear Free Zone Treaty (Treaty of Tlatelolco, 1967)
14. SALT I—ABM Treaty and Interim Agreement on Limitations of Strategic Arms, 1972
15. Mutual and Balanced Force Reduction Talks, est. 1973
16. Threshold Test Ban Treaty, 1974
17. ABM Protocol, 1974
18. Vladivostok Agreement, 1974
19. Peaceful Nuclear Explosions Treaty, 1976
20. Helsinki Conference on Security and Cooperation in Europe, 1975
21. Conventional Arms Transfer Talks, est. 1977
22. Comprehensive Test Ban Talks, est. 1977
23. Indian Ocean Naval Arms Control Negotiations, est. 1977
24. Anti-Satellite Weapons Talks, est. 1978
25. SALT II, 1979
26. Radiological Weapons Negotiations, est. 1979
27. Environmental Weapons Treaty, 1979
28. Intermediate Force Reduction Talks, est. 1980
29. START Talks, est. 1982
30. Stockholm Conference on Confidence- and Security-Building Measures Agreement, 1986

Table courtesy of Bennett Ramberg, Center for International and Strategic Affairs, UCLA; used in his presentation to the UCLA Extension course "Rethinking Arms Control."

Furthermore, there is value in *negotiating* even without reaching an agreement. (Recall that the final "T" in both "SALT" and "START" refers to "Talks," not "Treaties.") Thus, the conclusion of this flawed line of reasoning—that arms control doesn't work—is false, since it stems from two false premises.

ARMS CONTROL: THE ROLE OF THE ARMS RACE

The *arms race* refers to the interactive acquisition of weapons between two or more powers, and conceivably includes both numbers and qualities of weapons (Richardson, 1960; Bull, 1961; Intriligator, 1964, 1975; Schelling, 1966; Rathjens, 1969; Gray, 1971, 1974, 1976; Brito, 1972; Intriligator and Brito, 1976; and Brito and Intriligator, 1985; see the survey of conflict theory in Intriligator, 1982). The nuclear arms race involves an interactive acquisition of nuclear weapons not only between the superpowers, but also among the smaller nuclear powers of the United Kingdom, France, and China. There are important interrelationships between the arms race and arms control, involving strategic considerations, economic factors, technology and technological change, perceptions, the role of the military, and political factors (Brodie, 1973). The arms race and arms control are, to a large extent, two sides of the same coin. The result of the combined effects of the nuclear arms race and a variety of arms control initiatives—unilateral, bilateral, and multilateral—is that the current situation is one of great stability against a premeditated attack by either superpower against the other. This strategic stability, that is, stability against a premeditated attack, stems from the current situation of mutual deterrence, in which each superpower has the ability to retaliate in a devastating second strike against a first strike of the other.

While there is strategic stability against a premeditated attack, the arms race itself exhibits instability. Factors such as heuristic decision rules about weapons levels or acquisitions and misperceptions of one's opponent's capabilities have led both to weapons procurements and to qualitative weapons improvements (Intriligator and Brito, 1985b). Ironically, the instability of the arms race reinforces the stability against the outbreak of war by enhancing deterrence. By adding to the capability of both superpowers to launch a second-strike counterattack, increasing the number and certain capabilities of weapons has enhanced deterrence against a premeditated strike (Intriligator and Brito, 1984).

As a result of the arms race, there are enormous stockpiles of nuclear weapons on both sides. These stockpiles are, however, fundamental to stability against the outbreak of war via mutual deterrence. Some have argued that the stockpiles could be cut considerably without sacrificing the stability of mutual deterrence. Nonetheless, there is considerable value in having not only a variety of types of weapons, as in the triad of three independent weapons systems, but also a large stockpile of each type of weapon. Both a variety of types of weapons and larger weapons stockpiles serve as a hedge against potentially destabilizing technological breakthroughs that could occur on either side. For example, the large number and variety of weapons of each type have served to offset the effects of substantial increases in accuracy. This increased accuracy is potentially destabilizing, and in recent years has actually put all fixed-site land-based missiles at risk. On the other hand, the presence of other types of weapons, particularly mobile and concealable weapons, such as submarine-launched missiles, has ensured a continuation of mutual deterrence. Large weapons stockpiles and the variety of weapons types in the triad reinforce contributions to strategic stability via mutual deterrence (Intriligator and Brito, 1985a).

The concept of stability is important in this context, but it has often been misinterpreted. The current situation is one of an unstable arms race, with no stopping point as each side builds additional weapons or creates additional weapons capabilities. At the same time (and partly as a result of this quantitative and qualitative arms race), there is considerable stability against a premeditated attack owing to fear of retaliation. An attack by either side would be suicidal and therefore irrational. There is thus an unusual juxtaposition of stability and instability, namely, instability of the arms race and, simultaneously, stability against a premeditated attack.

Nuclear weapons, which are obviously the cause of the problem of the possibility of nuclear war, can also help solve this problem, via the system of mutual deterrence, though less obviously. Their presence has fundamentally and irreversibly changed the global system. Since the knowledge of how to build nuclear weapons not only exists but cannot be destroyed, there is no way to eliminate nuclear weapons from the world. A completely disarmed world is probably a dangerous situation since in such a situation even a small number of nuclear weapons could represent a substantial threat without the threatened nation having the capability to retaliate. Indeed, nuclear weapons are probably most likely to be used in precisely such a situation, with a very small stockpile on only one side, as in the U.S. atomic strikes against Japan (Intriligator and Brito, 1981). For this reason, complete nuclear disarmament, interpreted as reductions in nuclear weapons stocks down to zero or near-zero levels, is extremely dangerous. It raises the probability of war and is therefore inconsistent with the paramount goal of arms control.

The arms race, defined as the interactive acquisition of weapons, especially nuclear weapons, is inconsistent with the goal of arms control, namely, strategic stability against the outbreak of war, if it increases the chance of war An example is an arms race involving low or zero levels up to relatively low levels of weapons that can be used to attack the other side without fear of retaliation and yet cannot be used to deter the other side.

Not all arms races are inconsistent with arms control. An arms race that increases the levels of weapons from relatively low levels that can attack but cannot deter to higher levels that cannot attack (because of the opponent's levels of weapons) and do deter is not only consistent with arms control, but can also be considered an arms control initiative in that it involves changes in levels of weapons that reduce the chances of war. Conversely, *dis*arming races can be consistent with arms control if they obtain or preserve the stability of mutual deterrence. However, a disarming race that went "too far" in reducing weapons levels down to the point at which mutual deterrence is lost would be inconsistent with arms control (Intriligator and Brito, 1984; for an opposing view, see Mayer, 1986, and for our response, see Intriligator and Brito, 1986).

Although the current situation between the superpowers is one of strategic stability based on mutual deterrence, there are other paths to nuclear war. Probably the greatest danger of nuclear war today stems from *inadvertent* rather than intentional war, in particular via accident, loss of control, undependable field commanders, escalation from a regional conflict, and the actions of third-party nuclear powers or sub-national groups. These inadvertent paths to nuclear war should be treated as part of the new agenda for arms control.

ARMS CONTROL: A NEW AGENDA

The strategic relationships between the United States and the Soviet Union have changed considerably over the post-war period. Furthermore, new nuclear powers have emerged, and technology has developed rapidly. Nonetheless, the bilateral arms control agenda is still basically the same as it has always been. It stems from the pre-nuclear period and even back into the nineteenth century and earlier, and focuses on limitations on or reductions in numbers of weapons. Such limitations or reductions are useful, particularly in improving the political climate, but they may have only a limited role to play in the current situation. Small reductions can improve the overall political climate and possibly reduce tensions, acting as confidence-building measures. From the arms control viewpoint of reducing the chance of nuclear war, however, they are largely meaningless. Conversely, large reductions could undermine the stability of mutual deterrence, which is reinforced by relatively large numbers of weapons on both sides. Furthermore, there are many more positive ways to improve the political climate than weapons limitations or reductions, such as joint projects in support of economic development or environmental protection both globally and regionally. Thus, the traditional bilateral arms control agenda of weapons limitations or reductions might usefully be supplemented or even replaced by new agenda items.

These new bilateral agenda items should address the principal current areas of instability, and they should be supplemented by related unilateral and multilateral initiatives.

The most immediate new agenda items should deal with the most important potential instability, which is probably inadvertent nuclear war. The period of instability resulting from lack of mutual deterrence occurred in the late 1950s and early 1960s, and culminated in the Cuban missile crisis of 1962.

Since then, the chance of an intentional nuclear war has probably declined as a result of the advent of such a mutual deterrence system. Over the same period, the chance of an inadvertent nuclear war has probably increased owing to the complexity of command and control, the growing sophistication of modern weapons and carriers, and the general difficulty of managing complex systems. Thus, the chance of inadvertent nuclear war has probably increased relative to the chance of intentional nuclear war.

Despite the growing relative importance of inadvertent nuclear war, there has been virtually no change in the arms control agenda. If arms control refers to initiatives that reduce the chance of war and if there has been an increase in the relative importance of inadvertant nuclear war as compared to intentional nuclear war, then this change should be reflected in the arms control agenda. Arms limitations or reductions do not address this issue. The problem of inadvertent nuclear war is largely a *systems* problem, reflecting the nature of weapons and how they are controlled, rather than simply a *numbers* problem, influenced by the number of weapons. It is not the case that each individual weapon has some probability of being used inadvertently, so the total probability of inadvertent use depends on the total number of weapons. Rather, the sytem for command and control is the likely source of a failure that could result in an inadvertent nuclear war.

Arms control initiatives designed to reduce the chance of inadvertent war must treat the problem of the potential failure of warning systems, of a potential loss of control by the national command authority, and of a potential escalation from a regional conflict (Kahn, 1965; Brodie, 1966). Although the probability of inadvertent nuclear war is undoubtedly small, still it is likely greater than the probability of a premeditated war. Accidents can and do happen, particularly at complex and large-scale human–machine interfaces, such as occur in the control of strategic nuclear weapons. Witness, for example, the accidents of the Challenger space shuttle and the Chernobyl nuclear power plant, two other complex large-scale human–machine interfaces. Of course, the chance of inadvertent nuclear war significantly increases in a time of crisis, but even without a crisis there is a chance of accident. There have been repeated accidents with warning and control systems. An example is the June 1980 incident at NORAD, the North American Air Defense command in Colorado, in which, without any crisis situation, radar operators incorrectly believed that they were witnessing a massive Soviet attack on all U.S. land-based ICBMs because a training tape was accidentally mounted on the computers. This type of accident is prototypical of accidents with complex systems, and it could have led to nuclear war under a launch-on-warning system if there had been (accidental) confirmation by a backup system.

Bilateral agenda items to deal with inadvertent nuclear war could include agreements in advance on how to deal with potential accidents or nuclear threats, for example, by irrational leaders or terrorists. Opponents might also agree not to deploy launch-on-warning systems, which could significantly raise the probability of war based on various human or technical mishaps. These bilateral agenda items could also be supplemented by reinforcing unilateral initiatives and multilateral agreements. Unilateral initiatives could include the elimination of weapons or warning systems that are vulnerable or accident-prone and improvements in C^3I (command, control, communications, and intelligence) to ensure control and to avoid false commands or communications. Multi-lateral agreements could extend communications in time of a potential crisis from the nuclear superpowers, via an expanded hotline, to all five nuclear powers (adding Britain, France, and China), so that any two, three, four, or all five could be in communication at all times. They could provide protection for all C^3I systems of nuclear weapon states. Multilateral agreements could also build on bilateral agreements on how to deal with potential accidents or nuclear threats and on not developing launch-on-warning systems.

The next group of new arms control agenda items are short-term items, dealing with, potential instabilities over the next five to ten years, especially the possible erosion of mutual deterrence. They involve actions to prevent such an erosion of mutual deterrence, since the current system of mutual deterrence constitutes the primary basis of stability against a premeditated nuclear war. Of particular importance are actions to avoid a possible decapitation strike, a possible breakthrough in anti-submarine warfare (ASW), or the deployment of anti-satellite systems. Bilateral agenda items could include agreements on anti-submarine warfare, anti-satellite systems, and anti-ballistic missiles. On strategic defenses, whereas a complete defensive shield would undermine mutual deterrence and hence could contribute to strategic instability, a limited strategic defense system could be valuable in defending retaliatory capability; in protecting the national command authority and C^3I; and in providing some degree of protection against accidents, third-party actions, and the like. Such a limited strategic defense system could be built unilaterally, but it would be preferable to develop and to deploy it on a bilateral basis, through U.S.-Soviet cooperation, given the mutuality of interests of both nations in achieving these goals. Thus, strategic defenses would be part of the bilateral agenda, with the goal neither that of developing a complete defensive shield nor that of no strategic defenses at all. Rather, the goal would be cooperative development of a system of active and passive defenses in order to protect both nations from accidents, from loss of command authority, and from deliberate or accidental strikes by smaller nuclear powers. This type of cooperation could be a useful confidence-building measure.

These bilateral agenda items could be supplemented, as in the previous group, by reinforcing unilateral initiatives and multilateral agreements. Unilateral initiatives could include actions to replace current vulnerable, fixed-site, land-based missiles by less vulnerable mobile and concealable missiles, such as long-range cruise missiles. The fact that these missiles are not verifiable should not interfere with their deployment. Indeed, if they are not verifiable, it means that they can be concealed, as in the case of submarines, and hence could survive a first strike. Thus, they could reinforce mutual deterrence by being available for a retaliatory strike. Multilateral agreements could build on the bilateral agenda to cover anti-submarine warfare, anti-satellite weapons, and limited strategic defensive systems.

Finally, the last group of new arms control agenda items are long-term items, referring to potential instabilities over the next ten years and beyond—specifically, the possible advent of destabilizing nuclear proliferation (Brito and Intriligator, 1978). Arms control initiatives in this area should be concerned not only with preventing nuclear weapons from falling into the hands of irresponsible leaders or sub-national groups, but also with preventing irresponsible decisions or a loss of control in current nuclear states. Bilateral agenda items could include further agreements on non-proliferation and agreements in advance as to how to deal with irresponsible leaders or decisions. These initiatives would be strengthened by unilateral non-proliferation measures, including stricter safeguards on spent fuel rods and by multilateral agreements that would extend the non-proliferation regime to cover the potential export of fissile material, nuclear facilities, or nuclear technology, from so-called second-tier suppliers, such as Argentina, Brazil, and India. When the non-proliferation regime was established, these states were presumed to be nuclear importer states, but they and several other states now have the capabilities to become nuclear exporter states. This recent change calls for further multilateral initiatives to strengthen the non-proliferation regime.

Pursuing all three categories of agenda items—*immediate*, to reduce the chances of accidental war; *short term*, to prevent the erosion of mutual deterrence; and *long term*, to control destabilizing proliferation—and using all three different approaches—unilateral, bilateral U.S.-Soviet, and multilateral—could represent a significant and reinforcing set of initiatives to treat the instabilities present or looming in the international system. Elements of this new agenda should also be pursued by a new multilateral arms control forum.

ARMS CONTROL: A NEW PROCEDURE

Bilateral forums for arms control have represented an important, but by no means the only, approach to arms control. Confining the negotiations to the superpowers could be defended in the past both on the grounds that at least one of the other nuclear powers, the United Kingdom, was represented implicitly through its close association with the United States and on the grounds that all three smaller nuclear powers—the United Kingdom, France, and China—had relatively insignificant stockpiles of nuclear weapons. The first argument does not apply to France and China, and the second, while true in the past, is only partly true today and will be less and less true in the future. The United Kingdom and France, and perhaps China as well, are planning substantial increases not only in their weapons stockpiles but also in their delivery capabilities (See Kolodziej, vol. 2, ch. 5). Under these circumstances, it is essential that these three powers participate with the United States and the Soviet Union in arms control negotiations—in a new five-nuclear-nations forum. No such forum currently exists. Although these five are the permanent members of the U.N. Security Council, the United Nations is not the appropriate setting for serious negotiations on arms control. The five are parties to certain multi-nation forums, but they cannot negotiate effectively there in the presence of other nations.

Such a new five-nation forum would, of course, be unwieldy, prone to political arguments and disputes, and much more complicated to manage and operate than the traditional two-party forum. For example, four of the five are potential adversaries of the Soviet Union. Nevertheless, there are precedents for successful multiparty forums, not only in the area of arms control, for example, the Stockholm Conference on Disarmament in Europe (CDE), but also in dealing with other global issues, such as economic and environmental issues. The essential point, however, is that all relevant parties should be represented. Excluding the smaller nuclear powers, especially China and France, creates problems and tensions that are themselves potential sources of instability, exemplified in the unwillingness of China and France to participate actively in the nonproliferation regime.

While such a new five-nuclear-power forum has been proposed before by, among others, former Canadian Prime Minister Pierre Trudeau and by Soviet General Secretary Mikhail Gorbachev, these earlier proposals have not included a new agenda for this new forum. Rather, they have involved the traditional agenda items. The new forum should also have a new agenda that is directed to current and potential future areas of global strategic instability. Indeed, one reason why such a forum has not emerged is the concentration on traditional agenda items, such as weapons cuts or limitations. This traditional agenda is an important reason for China and France's lack of participation in arms control negotiations and agreements.

Some of the agenda items for the new forum could involve the multilateral arms control initiatives presented earlier, which could result in gains to all parties. One agenda item might be communications involving, for example, an agreement on an expanded hotline connecting all five nuclear powers or any subset of these nations, and an agreement not to threaten the command, control, and communication systems of any of the parties. Another item might be accidents and nuclear threats, and would, for example, establish agreements or understandings on procedures to be followed by all five in crisis situations. A third item might be strategic defenses involving, for example, agreements on the extent of allowable strategic defenses; such agreements would build on the ABM treaty but modify it to include the other three nuclear nations and to allow for limited cooperative defensive deployments. A fourth issue might be non-proliferation, covering such points as agreements on nuclear exports or transfers of nuclear technology. Other agenda items would deal with other potential global risks, such as those due to other weapons of mass destruction, including chemical and biological weapons. Agreements in these areas could potentially lead to greater global stability without compromising national security policies.

This new procedure for arms control, in the form of a new five-nuclear-power forum, when coupled with the new agenda for arms control, could play an important role in achieving significant arms control results. The new forum, unlike present arrangements, would include all (overt) nuclear nations. Furthermore, treating several agenda items in one forum rather than in separate forums would permit bargaining to reach mutually satisfactory agreements or understandings.

ARMS CONTROL: A RESEARCH AGENDA FOR THE FUTURE

Given the definition, goals, and approaches of arms control as presented earlier in the chapter, the major challenge of future research into arms control is to identify new methods of arms control. The five methods summarized in Table 10-1 are certainly not exhaustive. Future research might focus specifically on new methods of arms control. The challenge to future research on arms control is not, in our view, that of defining limits or sub-limits on weapons, but rather that of identifying areas of instability and suggesting methods for removing these instabilities. We have suggested some of these areas of instability and methods for treating them on a new agenda and a new procedure for arms control, respectively.

The other important aspect of new research on arms control involves extensions to regional security, treatment of domestic political factors, and consideration of the role of non-nation actors. Most of the research that has been conducted on arms control focuses on arms control between the superpowers, the United States and the USSR. Yet some of the same issues, particularly the outbreak of war, occur at the regional level, whether in the Middle East, South Asia, or elsewhere. Useful research can be conducted on the subject of regional arms control, treating, for example, the role of the superpowers and the relevance (or lack of relevance) of superpower arms control concepts to the region and the role of the superpowers in the region. A second aspect of new research on arms control is the impact of domestic political factors on both the arms race and arms control. Political factors are frequently ignored, in part because arms control is usually treated by international relations specialists rather than by domestic political specialists. Such factors are often critical determinants of arms control in setting the agenda or in acting as a constraint. A third aspect of new research on arms control is the role of non-state actors, including sub-national groups, non-governmental organizations, terrorist groups, and multinational corporations, which are of growing importance both as sources of potential conflict and as entities that influence arms control initiatives.

CONCLUSION

Many people have become dissatisfied with arms control in recent years. Some have sought alternative solutions to the problem of nuclear weapons and the potential for nuclear war through utopian political solutions such as complete disarmament, world government, or a nuclear freeze. Others have sought alternative solutions via utopian miliary/technical solutions such as warfighting capabilities or a complete defensive shield to render nuclear weapons "impotent and obsolete." There are no easy alternatives, however, whether political or military/technical—or at least none in the near future. Arms control remains the best approach for dealing with the problem, but it has to be modified in both substance and procedure to make it a more effective instrument.

In terms of substance, a new arms control agenda might usefully move away from the traditional emphasis on weapons reductions or limitations in order to focus more directly on the basic instabilities themselves, specifically in the form of inadvertent nuclear war, the possible erosion of deterrence, and potential destabilizing proliferation. In terms of procedure, a new arms control forum involving all five nuclear nations could supplement or even eventually replace some of the present fragmented bilateral and multilateral forums as the principal medium for addressing the basic instabilities in the global system. Future research on arms control could expand on this new agenda and new procedure by identifying areas of instability and methods of treating them. In addition, new research on arms control could usefully treat regional security questions, the effect of domestic political factors, and the role of non-nation actors. The new agenda and new procedure for arms control, together with related future research on this topic, could help make the arms control process an effective instrument for achieving global and regional stability.

REFERENCES

Brams, Steven J. 1985. *Superpower Games*. New Haven, Conn.: Yale University Press.
Brito, Dagobert L. 1972. A Dynamic Model of an Armaments Race. *International Economic Review* 13:359–75.
————, and Michael D. Intriligator. 1978. Nuclear Proliferation and Stability. *Journal of Peace Science* 3:173–83.
————. 1981. Strategic Arms Limitation Treaties and Innovations in Weapons Technology. *Public Choice* 37:41–59.
————. 1985. Conflict, War, and Redistribution. *American Political Science Review* 79:943–57.

Brodie, Bernard, ed. 1946. *The Absolute Weapon: Atomic Power and World Order*. New York: Harcourt Brace.

————. 1959. *Strategy in the Missile Age*. Princeton, N.J.: Princeton University Press.

————. 1966. *Escalation and the Nuclear Option*. Princeton, N.J.: Princeton University Press.

————. 1973. *War and Politics*. New York: Macmillan.

————. 1978. The Development of Nuclear Strategy. *International Security* 3:65–83.

Brennan, Donald G., ed. 1961. *Arms Control, Disarmament, and National Security*. New York: G. Braziller.

Bull, Hedley. 1961. *The Control of the Arms Race*. New York: Praeger.

Daedalus. 1985. *Weapons in Space* 114: No. 2–3.

George, Alexander L., and Richard Smoke. 1974. *Deterrence in American Foreign Policy*. New York: Columbia University Press.

Gray, Colin. 1971. The Arms Race Phenomena. *World Politics* 24:39–79.

————. 1974. The Urge to Compete: Rationales for Arms Racing. *World Politics* 26:207–33.

————. 1976. *The Soviet-American Arms Race*. Lexington, Mass.: Lexington Books.

Intriligator, Michael D. 1964. Some Simple Models of Arms Races. *General Systems* 9:143–47.

————. 1975. Strategic Considerations in the Richardson Model of Arms Races. *Journal of Political Economy* 83:339–53.

————. 1982. Research on Conflict Theory: Analytic Approaches and Areas of Application. *Journal of Conflict Resolution* 26:307–27.

————, and Dagobert L. Brito. 1976. Formal Models of Arms Races. *Journal of Peace Science* 2:77–88.

————. 1981. Nuclear Proliferation and the Probability of Nuclear War. *Public Choice* 37:247–60.

————. 1984. Can Arms Races Lead to the Outbreak of War? *Journal of Conflict Resolution* 28:63–84.

————. 1985a. Heuristic Decision Rules, the Dynamics of an Arms Race, and War Initiation. In Urs Luterbacher and Michael Ward, eds., *Dynamic Models of International Conflict*. Boulder, Colo.: Lynne Rienner.

————. 1985b. Non-Armageddon Solutions to the Arms Race. *Arms Control* 6:41–57.

————. 1986. Mayer's Alternative to the I-B Model. *Journal of Conflict Resolution* 30:29–31.

————. 1987. *Arms Control: Problems and Prospects*. IGCC Research Paper No. 2. San Diego: Institute on Global Conflict and Cooperation, University of California, San Diego.

Jervis, Robert. 1978. Cooperation under the Security Dilemma. *World Politics* 31:289–324.

Kahn, Herman. 1960. *On Thermonuclear War*. Princeton, N.J.: Princeton University Press.

————. 1962. *Thinking About the Unthinkable*. New York: Horizon Books.

————. 1965. *On Escalation: Metaphors and Scenarios*. New York: Praeger.

Mayer, Thomas F. 1986. Arms Races and War Initiation: Some Alternatives to the Intriligator-Brito Model. *Journal of Conflict Resolution* 30:3–28.

Morgenstern, Oskar. 1959. *The Question of National Defense*. New York: Random House.

Nye, Joseph S., Jr. 1986. Farewell to Arms Control. *Foreign Affairs* 65:1–20.

Rathjens, George. 1969. The Dynamics of the Arms Race. *Scientific American* 220:15–25.

Richardson, Lewis F. 1960. *Arms and Insecurity*. Pittsburgh: Boxwood.

Schelling, Thomas C. 1960. *The Strategy of Conflict*. Cambridge, Mass.: Harvard University Press.

———. 1966. *Arms and Influence*. New Haven, Conn.: Yale University Press.

———. 1985–1986. What Went Wrong with Arms Control? *Foreign Affairs* 64:219–33.

———, and Morton H. Halperin. 1961. *Strategy and Arms Control*. New York: Twentieth Century Fund.

Wohlstetter, Albert, 1959. The Delicate Balance of Terror. *Foreign Affairs* 37:211–34.

11

On Domestic Controls

SAM C. SARKESIAN

The role of the military in politics and society has been part of the affairs of state throughout history. Interest in civil-military relations, however, tends to ebb and flow with the degree of world tension or turbulence within states. In the aftermath of World War II, an international environment emerged placing military systems in critical policy positions. Military power became a critical element in the ability of states to conduct external policy. The role of the officer corps in policymaking expanded, as did the importance of the military bureaucracy. Simultaneously, the power of the officer corps in domestic politics grew. Furthermore, superpower confrontations, continuing armed conflicts within former colonial areas, wars in the Middle East, and the dramatic increase in technological innovations in arms development reinforced the prominence of military systems and the military profession. In the main, civil authorities viewed these developments with some degree of alarm, not only in terms of international security, but also concern over control of the armed forces. As new states emerged in Africa and Asia in the 1950s and 1960s, they faced similar problems. But the problems were more acute, because these new states were characterized by fragile political structures and serious problems of internal instability.

These international developments were accompanied by the proliferation of studies on armed forces and society, with particular attention to the political role of the military in society and civilian control over the armed forces.

On the one hand, the increased study of military systems is a relatively new phenomenon because a variety of models, approaches, and empirical studies have developed an unprecedented degree of scholarly precision and

I wish to acknowledge the invaluable assistance provided by Robert Vitas, Department of Political Science, Loyola University of Chicago, in the completion of this work.

conceptualization. On the other hand, the study of the military and society is not new. Even before the time of Christ, attention to war and civil-military relations were included in studies of effective rule. In the *Republic*, Plato devoted a great deal of time examining the relationship between rulers and the nature of a well-ordered state. In the East, Sun Tzu addressed similar issues of war, the military, and the state.

Almost 2,000 years later, Machiavelli examined relationships among the military, politics, and rulers, arguing that rulers had to give serious attention to war and its conduct if they expected to retain control of their states. Carl von Clausewitz (von Clausewitz, 1976), the driving force of Western military thought, stressed the need to harmonize the relationships among the state, the people, and the military.

In the 1930s, with the onset of the Sino-Japanese War and as totalitarian states emerged in Europe, some American scholars became concerned about the nature of the military in such systems. It is in this context that Harold Lasswell (1941) formalized the garrison state thesis. Published before America's entry into World War II, Lasswell's study was a pioneering step based on the premise that the continuing threat of war would lead to the establishment of a garrison state as a response to external threats, and to subsequent erosion of liberal democracy as the society mobilized for war. Immediately following World War II, some scholars began to recognize that many states would be faced with different and more challenging problems in civil-military relations as a result of the changed world structure. Although primarily focused on the United States, these problems were seen as universal (Kerwin, 1948). The systematic study of the military and society, however, did not emerge until the late 1950s. Samuel P. Huntington (1957) and Morris Janowitz (1960) led the way. Somewhat earlier, Stanislaw Andrzejewski (1954) published a study of the military and society which was a harbinger of things to come, albeit cast in a formal sociological framework.

Since the publication of works by Huntington and Janowitz, studies of civil-military relations, military professionalism, and the military and society have become legitimate enterprises within a variety of disciplines and policy circles. This legitimacy has been reinforced by the creation of a number of organizations, such as the Inter-University Seminar on Armed Forces and Society, the William Isaac Thomas Center in France, and the Netherlands Society, whose purposes include the study of the military and society.

There seems to be little scholarly agreement, however, regarding theoretical constructs and substantive dimensions. According to Roman Kolkowicz (1985), these efforts are characterized by "conceptual unevenness, by a set of historically idiosyncratic circumstances, and by a certain professional parochialism." The purpose of this chapter is to identify the major themes and theoretical approaches to civil-military relations and military professionalism, as presented in the mainstream English language literature. The intent is to understand the state of the art, rather than develop new themes or theoretical formulations.

Although the boundaries of this study are not necessarily limited to scholarly efforts within the United States, the major themes in the literature are reflected in many of the writings of American scholars. This is not to deny the significant contributions to analytical studies by others (Howard, 1959; Vagts, 1959). It is also important to recognize that many of the earlier works were cooperative efforts between European and American sociologists (see, for example, Janowitz and Van Doorn, 1971). More recently, scholars from Third World areas have made important contributions to the study of armed forces and society (see, for example, Odetola, 1982). Yet, the availability of literature and the scope of scholarly efforts point to the United States as the necessary starting point. This should not be construed, however, as acceptance of Western models as universally valid. (This subject is discussed in fuller detail later in the chapter.)

Civil-military relations and military professionalism can be defined in several ways. Much has been written about the meaning of these terms. For our purposes, civil-military relations are defined as those relationships among the officer corps, civilian leaders, and major political groups which determine the political power and status of the officer corps, and the military's role in the political system.

Military professionalism refers to the corporate character of the officer corps, the degree of cohesion of the corps with respect to its role and purpose within the political system, and its leadership ability. Professionalism has to do specifically with the capability of the officer corps in defending the homeland against external and internal attack, in projecting power, and in coalition politics. The North Atlantic Treaty Organization (NATO), Soviet forces in support of the Ethiopian regime, and the use of naval forces to show the flag are cases in point.

There are a variety of ways to study the models, approaches, and themes in the scholarly research on armed forces and society. Certain strengths and weaknesses are associated with each. The framework used here is designed as a landscape in which a number of major approaches are identified. By identifying the approaches and linking them to some of the major published scholarship, the shape and substance of the subject can be sketched, leaving the reader to fill in the relevant details through further study.

ANALYTICAL FRAMEWORK

The framework for this study consists of three major approaches: systems perspective, military-specific, and disciplinary. Each of these approaches has several themes or sub-approaches.[1] There is no clear dividing line among them. By their very nature, they are interdependent in varying degrees, reflecting the state of the art as well as the complexity of the subject matter.

Nonetheless, a "critical mass" of reference points is associated with each approach, sub-approach, and theme. The study of military professionalism, for example, will invariably include attention to the political system as well as generalizations regarding the nature of that system. Yet, the primary reference point for such an approach is the military profession. Similarly, the study of the political system as it relates to the military role must include attention to military professionalism. To study the military profession, therefore, one must begin with an examination of the character of the political system.

THE SYSTEMS PERSPECTIVE

Civil-military relations from the perspective of the political system places importance on the character and dynamics of politics and the ideology of a particular system. The linking of civil-military relations to the nature of the system is based on the proposition that the military reflects society. Thus, for example, an open system gives rise, more or less, to a democratic military. It follows that the military must reflect the basic values of society and serve them accordingly.

Civilian Control Model

The basic formula in the systems perspective is civilian control. There are a number of variations, but the most important factor is that the degree of civilian control of the military is directly related to the character of the political system and the way power is achieved, distributed, and exercised by civilian leaders. In turn, there is a direct relationship between the characteristics of the system and the political orientation of the military profession. The relationship and orientation differ with each type of political system. For example, Huntington (1957, p. 2) has written:

The military institutions of any society are shaped by two forces: a functional imperative stemming from the threats to the society's security and a societal imperative arising from the social forces, ideologies, and institutions dominant within that society. Military institutions which reflect only social values may be incapable of performing effectively their military function. On the other hand, it may be impossible to contain within society military institutions shaped purely by functional imperatives. The interaction of these two forces is the nub of the problem of civil-military relations.

It follows that in the United States, the clearer the line between the civilian and military spheres, the more likely the military is under civilian control. The functional imperative is interpreted in objective terms and the societal imperative in subjective ones. "Objective" control of the military is a function of instrumentalities, administrative structures, and the decision-making process combined with an autonomous military profession. "Subjective" control is based on the sharing of outlooks and on compatible mind-sets between the military and society.

Military professionalism in open systems has clearly established civilian control mechanisms that create boundaries beyond which military professionals do not, or cannot, venture. This not only institutionalizes distinctions between society and the military, but it also compels the military to develop in specific directions. The profession is occupied with developing a military system primarily oriented to the battlefield as conceived in traditional terms (see for example, Weigley, 1977). Thus, the more professional the military, the less likely it will be involved in politics. This is the fundamental consideration in civil-military relations according to the civilian control approach. However, some proponents recognize the validity of a less rigid formulation (Sarkesian, 1975).

Recently, the civilian control approach has given birth to several themes revolving around the issues of convergence and isolation—whether the military is becoming more like society or moving away from it. Following the Vietnam War, with continuing dependence on a nuclear deterrence strategy, questions were raised regarding the development of the military system. These included questions of manpower, the relevance of high technology weaponry to low-intensity conflicts, the utility of nuclear weapons, the relationship of nuclear strategy to non-nuclear capability, and the capability of conventional forces to engage in unconventional conflicts. Many argued that "civilianization" of the military in the 1960s and 1970s was an important factor in eroding battlefield effectiveness (Walton, 1973). Others added that the military must be isolated from society in order to develop combat effectiveness (Hauser, 1973).

In other words, because of the Vietnam experience and the continual need to maintain an "adequate" military posture, some posited that the military had to renew its traditional values and return to the spirit of the pre-Vietnam profession, that is, maintain "distance" from society. This viewpoint was supported by a number of civilian leaders as a means of reinforcing civilian control and drawing clear lines between society and the military (Huntington, 1978; Peters and Clotfelter, 1978).

On the one hand, the military possessed an important role in matters of national security, involving it in domestic politics and policymaking (Sarkesian, 1975). On the other hand, many military professionals felt that the inability to bring the Vietnam conflict to a successful conclusion was a consequence of the failure of military professionalism, and the "spillover" of social issues into the military system (U.S. Army War College, 1970). The disregard of traditional military values, the increasing association with society, and the lack of military skills to engage in conflict were seen as culprits in diminishing U.S. military effectiveness. These problems were viewed as results of professional weaknesses stemming out of the Vietnam War, rather than the political system in general. Nonetheless, some of the most critical issues had their roots in the political system. Indeed, according to some, the social ills and turbulence of the 1960s and early 1970s within American domestic society were responsible for some of the most critical problems in the military at that time (Hauser, 1973). A common theme stressed the need to isolate the military from society. This theme further developed into a convergence-isolation perspective, as a number of scholars and military professionals saw a shift in the military to an "occupational" orientation and to a closer relationship with society. Similar issues emerged in all open systems (Moskos, 1973).

Comparative Themes

Comparative studies of civil-military relations based on the civil control approach are part of the growing literature. For example, William L. Hauser (1973) examines the French, British, and German armies in the post-World War II period to develop a framework for analyzing U.S. civil-military relations. Huntington (1957) studies the Prussian military and pre-World War II German, French, and Japanese civil-military relations as part of his analysis of U.S. civil-military relations. European scholars have contributed important studies to the comparative literature. For example, G. Teitler (1977) studied the evolution of professionalism in England, France, the Dutch Republic, and Prussia, combining sociological and historical themes with a comparative approach. There are many studies that focus on the military of a variety of countries (see Vatikiotis, 1961; Schmitter, 1972; Whitson, 1972; Baynes, 1972; and Martin, 1981). Illustrative of such works is Orville D. Menard's (1967, pp. 5–6) volume on the French Army, where he writes,

An army is an emanation of the nation it serves, reflecting social, political, and technological foundations. To study an army is to gain insights into the nation it serves because a nation and its army are interdependent. An army is not a mirror image of the nation, nor a microcosm—the nation writ small; it is, in organization, purposes, attitudes, and behavior, conditioned by the sustaining state.

Scholars have recently begun to seriously study civil-military relations in socialist countries, even though important work was done earlier on the Soviet military during Stalin's era (Herspring and Volgyes, 1978; Colton, 1979). Many of these studies focus on the military as an implementer of Politburo policy. Some of the more recent studies (Kolkowicz, 1985) challenge monistic perspectives, arguing that the civil control model regarding the Soviet Union is more complex and varied than earlier studies of the Stalinist military appeared to indicate.

Of particular interest in the studies of Soviet armed forces and society from Stalin to the present is the focus on party–military relationships. That is, the degree of party control exercised over the Soviet military is seen as the pivotal reference point. The state, as such, is generally on the periphery of civil-military relations.

According to Kolkowicz (1985), several models have emerged from the study of the Soviet military: the conflict model, the congruence model, and the participatory model. Each of these is identified with a specific scholar. The *conflict model* is based on the premise that there is a built-in conflict within the Soviet party–military–state triad (Kolkowicz, 1967). These relationships evolve from dynamic political conflict. This view represents a major difference from earlier approaches. The *congruence approach* is based on the view that the military and party elite are basically one, and, contrary to any conflict, a common mind-set determines the role of the party and the military (Odom, 1973). The *participatory model* is on the spectrum somewhere between the other two models, but tends toward the dynamic conflict model (Colton, 1979).

According to Amos Perlmutter and William M. LeoGrande (1982, p. 781), "These conflicting theories are not so much contradictory as they are complementary—once we understand the variegated nature of the party–army relationship." After studying the Soviet system and reviewing the Chinese symbiotic, and Cuba's fused, civil-military relationship, the authors conclude:

A party-dominant authority structure, a high level of elite integration, and a complex institutional relationship that combines elements of both subordination and autonomy—these are the relatively constant aspects of the party–army relationship in a communist system (p. 786).

Furthermore, the authors state, the military possesses an important role whenever there are intraparty struggles. In such conflicts, the army intervenes, not for itself but for one or the other party faction. "In times of crisis, the officers may well be the most strategic faction of the political elite, but they are still party men" (p. 788).

In addition to its political role, the Soviet Army plays an important role in supporting the existing political system and in ideological reinforcement. For example, Ellen Jones (1985, p. 291) notes the important role of the Soviet Army in adult socialization. She concludes that the "USSR's military is, in a very real sense, a civilianized institution."

It is clear that there exists some disagreement over the "models" of civil-military relationships in Communist states, particularly in the Soviet Union. Nonetheless, it appears that Soviet military professionalism has been strengthened over the years as a sense of institutional loyalty has evolved, professional autonomy developed, and the socialization role institutionalized.

But there certainly are limits to professional autonomy in the Soviet Union owing to the very nature of the system. The military is institutionally wedded to the party and recognizes the party's importance in maintaining military prestige and power. Although the military is seen as a partner in the party–military control of society, the military has a distinctly subservient political role in the Soviet Union. In such a system, the military is not apolitical, nor does it possess a clear political role other than its close marriage to the party. Indeed, the political role of the military is directed through the party rather than separated from it. Other Communist systems follow the Soviet model, even though they reflect some variations, as in China and Cuba. Thus, various models of socialist systems have evolved, each drawing somewhat different conclusions from the party–military relationship.

Developmental Approaches

As is the case with other approaches, there is a lack of agreement as to the correlation between a military perspective and the degree of development of a system. Development levels are generally used to distinguish three separate worlds. Labels such as the Third World are often used to separate the developing world from the First World (developed Western systems) and the Second World (developed socialist systems). However, it is inaccurate and misleading to place all states in the Southern Hemisphere in the Third World, since many differences exist within these areas. For example, development in India is considerably different from that in Chad. Argentine politics and economics are different from those of Tanzania, and so on. Moreover, states such as Israel and South Africa cannot be included in the connotative category of Third World as defined in the usual terms. In brief, political systems and ideologies vary within the Third World.

Although Western development models may be inadequate and inappropriate in studying the Third World, the categorization of Southern Hemisphere states as the Third World, or developing systems, is familiar in the lexicon of developmental studies. This categorization is utilized here as a means of providing an uncluttered formulation to focus on the literature and themes of the role of the military in developing systems, while recognizing the limitations of such a perspective.

The 1950s ushered in the development era. The breaking apart of colonial empires and the "winds of change" in Black Africa and Asia were signalled by the independence of Ghana followed by a variety of states in British and French colonial empires. As the development era accelerated, Western scholars began to examine the nature of economic modernization and political change. The general theme was based on the view that modernization and change were bound to create authoritarian-type systems, fragile institutions, and contending elites. In such systems, the most modern and politically powerful institution was likely to be the military (Finer, 1962). The failure of parliamentary systems in developing states would lead either to a one-party authoritarian or a Marxist-Leninist system.

In response to weaknesses in developing governing institutions, some scholars concluded that the military was a positive alternative (Johnson, 1962). However, Huntington (1965) noted that political change could lead to political decay. According to his argument, there was little in developing systems that could create viable governing institutions and provide for political mobilization and organization.

Many scholars concluded that the characteristics of the military were associated with modern institutions: bureaucratic, managerial, and ascriptive. The real progress in nation-building, according to their views, would rest on the ability of the military to perform its role as a modern institution providing education, skills, and leadership to the rest of society (Odetola, 1982). The military would bring with it the efficiency and strength lacking in most other social-political institutions. Moreover, the socialization function of the military and its linkage with other modern groups in the system would give it a commitment to modernity that is a requisite for developing systems. The military becomes a "heavy" institution in society, an institution viewed in positive terms.

By the end of the 1970s, scholars were taking a more critical view of the military (Nordlinger, 1977). Not only was there a recognition that the military had a political role, but also that military systems were not necessarily homogeneous. In a number of cases, the military was characterized by political divisiveness, as was the case in Nigeria in the late 1960s. Furthermore, a number of other scholars were of the opinion that little good emerged from military governments.

Ruth First (1971, p. 465) supported this view and argued, "The government of Africa, in the hands of politician-manipulators, or the less flamboyant but infinitely more parochial soldier-rulers, is not on the whole tyrannical, but bumbling. Time and again it makes false starts, and spreads false hopes." Others argued that in a number of instances, the military acted like any other interest group, pursuing its own self-interest while emptying the public treasury and stifling economic growth. Eric A. Nordlinger (1975, p. 210) reinforced this negative view of the military, writing, "Whatever else the foreseeable future may bring, two fundamental aspects of political life will surely not change: the soldiers will frequently wield their guns as praetorian soldiers, and they will do so on behalf of their corporate interests."

While recognizing the negative impact of the military on economic growth, some scholars, however, concluded that the military created political institutions and helped develop an environment for political development (Kennedy, 1974, pp. 56–57).

As military coups gave birth to yet more coups, praetorianism became a common phenomenon in developing states. Perlmutter (1978) argued that praetorianism existed where the boundaries between the military and civilian spheres were unclear and fragile governing elites existed, along with a constant change of one set of military elites for another. Military elites rule, in turn, was interspersed with civilian regimes. It is characteristic of a praetorian regime that the legitimacy of a ruling elite is based on who is able to rule, and not necessarily on abstract notions of legitimacy. Governing military elites were unable to solve the major problems faced by earlier civilian elites, and as the scholarship on development matured and became more sophisticated, the positive military image changed. Distinctions between political change and modernization evolved. In the first instance, there was little the military would or could do to establish modern governing institutions. However, in terms of economic modernization, the military could make some impact regarding order, investments, and corruption (Odetola, 1982).

Other scholars, however, saw the military as a contributor to political change and stability, and not very different from civilian politicians (Odetola, 1982, p. 185). Some scholars suggest that military rule can be a forerunner of democracy. J. Stephen Hoadley (1975, p. 206), for example, concluded in his study of the military in Southeast Asia, that "military management of politics provides the stability necessary for the development of indigenous democratic institutions that can replace those imposed by the colonial powers, and that the long-run evolution of democracy is thus possible."

Another stream of literature focuses on the causes of coups, the disengagement of the military, and the return to the barracks (Welch and Smith, 1974; Welch, 1976). While such studies are closely related to civil-military relations, their primary focus is on analyzing the causes of military intervention. That is, coups reflect civil-military relations of a particular kind. The same is true with respect to disengagement.

By the 1980s, the developmental approach to civil-military relations was in a state of transition. Not only were some military regimes replaced by civilian regimes through popular movements, but in some instances the military acquiesced to popular demands for changing one regime for another, as in the Philippines in 1986. Earlier, in Brazil and Argentina, military regimes gave way to civilian regimes, without bloodshed.

The developmental approach includes a variety of themes and approaches that are difficult to categorize. However, serious attempts have been made to do just that. In a recent analysis of the literature assessing the role of the military in developing areas, Laurence Radway (1982) identified four approaches: civilian control, professionalism, bureaucratic analysis, and political culture. But there is little agreement regarding a particular approach. This is well illustrated by the debates and disagreements regarding the cause of African coups d'etat, where scholars disagree not only over the proper research method, but also over the data used and its interpretation (Johnson, Slater, and McGowan, 1984). As Claude E. Welch cautions, "No single prescription for civilian control can be devised to apply to the scores of developing countries. Political systems are unique in their combination of circumstances" (1976, p. 313; see also Odetola, 1982, p. 22).

MILITARY-SPECIFIC APPROACHES

The evolution of studies on military professionalism parallels the study of political systems. Although of a later genre, as Huntington (1957) points out, it was not until the nineteenth century that the concept of an officer corps and professionalism emerged, mainly as a consequence of the evolution of the modern state and weapons. For the most part, military professionalism focused specifically on the "battlefield." In Western systems, the military profession was generally seen as separate from society and civilian concerns.

World War II marked a major turning point in American military professionalism. Until that time, the military was, more or less, a society unto itself with minimal identification with the larger society. It devoted its efforts solely to military tasks. This posture was reinforced by the "liberal" notions of American society which, in the main, accepted the military as a necessary "evil" that had to keep its distance from society (Sarkesian, 1981, pp. 15–16, 266–71). This had an important impact on the American military, often forcing military professionals to look to themselves for policy and strategic guidance (Kemble, 1973, pp. 202–3).

The challenges of World War II demanded significant changes in the nature of military professionalism and the military system. The military not only became involved in training large groups of citizens for a massive military machine, but it also became more influential in political and strategic circles. In the aftermath of the war, the prominence of the military receded but only temporarily. The onset of the Cold War, nuclear weaponry, and a host of international developments again placed the military profession in a prominent political position, reducing the historical gap between the military and society.

The Vietnam War and the American Military Profession

The Vietnam War proved to be another watershed for the American military and its people, crystallizing a number of dilemmas facing the American military profession. The Vietnam War also had international implications. It revealed the problems of any Western (open system) military profession in developing a capability to engage in "limited" wars and responding to changing domestic political forces. The critical question centered on the kind of military professionalism best suited for open systems in the security environment of the 1970s and beyond.

William L. Hauser (1973, p. 186) argued, for example, that the "Army cannot isolate itself from civilian society even if it wished to do so; on the other hand, it must somehow do so in order to preserve its necessarily authoritarian nature." Frederick C. Thayer (1973, p. 568) provided a different theme:

The concept of professionalism seems to demand that professionals themselves be constantly aware of the delicate balance they must maintain in their own behavior between autonomy and fusion. They cannot be so totally separated as to become the proverbial "society within a society," but neither can they afford total integration within the civilian overhead.

The Vietnam experience also precipitated a self-examination by the U.S. military. The U.S. Army War College Study (1970, pp. 28–29) found that many junior officers questioned the behavior and capability of senior officers. It also demanded a return to traditional professional concepts of duty, honor, and country. Many also agreed with the view that "we have democracy in this country but we have an autocracy in the military. And the public ought to be educated along these lines and that the military ought to stand up for what it has to have—and that is a disciplined force of people." In an empirical study of U.S. military professionalism, John H. Moellering (1973, p. 82) found that "Alienation from society, due to a variety of factors does . . . exist in the officers corps today. With the all-volunteer Army, a turning inward is likely."

The general conclusions of these studies indicated that the U.S. military in the 1970s was unhappy with itself, ambiguous regarding the relationship of the profession to society, and unclear as to the proper course of action. In brief, many military officers were concerned about the gap between professional standards and behavior, not sure of the proper political role of the profession with respect to the policymaking process and uncertain of how to reestablish acceptable relationships with society. In addition, "the evidence [showed] an underlying dissatisfaction with civilian perceptions of the military and the lack of civilian appreciation for the demands of the military profession" (Sarkesian, 1978, p. 42). Many officers felt that civilians had little understanding of the nature and demands of military professionalism and the sacrifices made by military men.

Elected officials in the United States were also concerned about the role of the military in determining policy. A number blamed the military for U.S. involvement in Vietnam and its unfortunate results. As a result, many concluded that the military had too great a role in policymaking. They focused on proper civilian control and supervision of the armed forces. Civilians, in general, and elected officials, in particular, sought to effect a better control system and civil-military relationships that would be in greater accord with liberal notions of democracy.

The Changing Nature of Western Civil-Military Relations

As a consequence of these changes in the profession, and between the military and society, a new set of civil-military equations emerged in the

United States. This was the case in all Western systems. The shift to a volunteer system in the United States, changing civilian attitudes regarding military service, and the belief that mass armies were unnecessary resulted in qualitative changes in civil-military relations and in the character of military professionalism.

Scholars and military professionals alike struggled to develop some "sense" of direction in civil-military relations and in military professionalism. What made the problem difficult was the recognition by many that the military had to engage in political give-and-take in order to acquire what it considered the wherewithal to develop and maintain military readiness. Huntington (1957, p. 345) recognized this trend early.

The apparent political role and visibility of the military in policy challenged previously held notions of "proper" civil-military relations. For many, such a role was contrary to the liberal view of democracy and the traditional patterns of military professionalism. Others argued, however, that political involvement by the military was a more realistic strategy and a tactical necessity. Nonetheless, a number of military professionals sought a return to traditional notions of civil-military relations and a military, if not isolated from society, at least separated from it (U.S. Army War College Study, 1970; Hauser, 1975).

The changing nature of the security environment and the prevalence of a "Vietnam syndrome" in the United States saw parallel developments in Western Europe. Although military professionalism in Western systems varies, it evolved from similar roots. That is, contemporary Western military professionalism is affected by contemporary wars, the demise of the mass army, and the values of open systems. Unconventional conflicts, small wars, and the nuclear environment have challenged traditional concepts of military professionalism. Unconventional conflicts, with their highly political content, complexities, and ambiguities, are neither easily incorporated into the traditional military professional mind-sets of open systems, nor do they fit into conventional views of war. It appears that only in the most unambiguous cases, with clear distinctions between war and peace, can coherent policies be designed and relatively clear boundaries be prescribed for military professionals.

It is the character of the contemporary period, however, that only rarely are conflicts unambiguous or distinctions between war and peace clear. As a result, for many military professionals of open systems, there are few cases of clear policies and strategies. Combined with a military system characterized by high technology weaponry, managerial and bureaucratic dimensions, and questions of professional status and functional utility, a new formulation of civil-military relations and military professionalism was necessary.

New Formulations: Search for Conceptual Coherence

The dilemma for the U.S. military profession in the aftermath of Vietnam— as for military professionals in all Western systems—was the development of an appropriate professional posture that could reestablish pre-Vietnam civil-military relationships and yet respond to the changing international security environment. New formulations emerged, primarily revolving around fusionist-purist approaches.

The purist approach, following the civil control model, presumes that civilian control is best achieved by the clear delineation of military and civilian spheres, where military professionalism is firmly rooted in apolitical mind-sets, and focused primarily on "military" matters and the battlefield. The purist, however, tends to recognize limits to the separation of the military from society, accepting this as a principle to insure military attention to the battlefield. This stance reinforces the notion of a liberal society.

In contrast, the fusionists argue that the more realistic formulation recognizes the military profession as an integral component of the political system which cannot be isolated from the political or social forces of the nation (Goodpaster et al., 1977). Moreover, they argue, it is unrealistic to assume that the military profession is not involved to some degree in the policy and decision-making process, no matter how indirectly. The key to understanding the military profession, therefore, is the degree of fusion. That is, what influence does the military profession possess in policy and decision-making processes? What impact does such an influence have on the nature and character of the military and the military profession? What are the major characteristics of the political system which the military serves? Finally, the fusionist approach should not be construed as an actual "fusion" of military and society. Rather, it is intended to show an inextricable linkage between the two. It is the strength of this linkage that is the critical factor in determining the nature of civil-military relations and the character of military professionalism.

The fusionist approach appears to be a more realistic formulation when seeking answers to the complexities of the relationship of armed forces and society. Although the fusionist approach may appear new for Western systems, it is not in developing systems and the socialist world. In these cases, there rarely has been a clear line separating the military, political institutions, and society. Indeed, after the initial euphoria of independence, most Third World countries came face to face with the realities of military involvement in society. Socialist states recognized relatively early the importance of the military in the political system, particularly in controlling society, maintaining internal order, and supporting the ruling elite.

From the Western perspective, the basis for the fusionist approach evolved from the post-World War II international environment regarding the utility of military force and changing domestic political attitudes. These were at work transforming the military establishment from a self-contained, inward looking system, to a more civilianized and complex one. Not only was the military becoming civilianized, but also society was being penetrated by the military (Lang, 1969, p. 22). Moreover, as Welch (1985, p. 194) writes, scholars should avoid simple dichotomization between "military" and "nonmilitary" or "civilian" systems in government. Many interactions exist. Military "participation" in politics is an accomplished fact in practically every country in the first, second, and third worlds.

A variation of the fusionist approach is the equilibrium model (Sarkesian, 1981, pp. 237–65), which is particularly focused on U.S. armed forces and society. The equilibrium model stresses enlightened advocacy and recognition of the political role of the military. According to this view, military professionalism is a function not only of military skill, but also of political education and comprehension of the broad scope of contemporary conflict, particularly unconventional conflict. Thus, military professionals are seen as participants in the formulation of policy and strategy which, by the very nature of contemporary conflict, requires a close military linkage to politics. The nature of open systems and the commitment of military professionals to the values of open systems establish the boundaries for military professional roles and the exercise of political power.

These boundaries, however, are based on dynamic relationships between the military profession and society, leading to an equilibrium model, which stresses civil control over the military and an absolute commitment of the military profession to their subordinate, yet important, status within the system. This relationship is dynamic and changes (seeking equilibrium between society and the military) as the nature of the sytem warrants and as international security challenges dictate. In brief, the military has a legitimate political role that is expressed primarily through the policymaking process. Equally significant, in light of the presumed relationship between the military and society, the military plays a role in socialization and the reinforcement of civic culture. The military can also express its attitudes, albeit indirectly in open systems, regarding defense policy and the positions of various politicians. The legitimacy of the military role, that is, the extent to which it can cross from the military professional dimension into the political, is largely determined by the ideology of the political system, its values and norms. Interestingly enough, the nature of the Soviet military profession (and socialist military systems in general) appears to follow the patterns described in the equilibrium model. Nonetheless, the models and approaches designed for the study of armed forces and society in any political system suggest that monistic approaches or universalistic models possess questionable validity.

DISCIPLINARY APPROACHES

Sociologists, political scientists, and historians have dominated the study of the military and society, though from different perspectives. Recently, anthropologists and psychologists have given serious attention to the subject. As pointed out earlier, disciplinary perspectives are generally subsumed within the systems and military-specific approaches. Nonetheless, it is important to identify the "critical mass" of disciplinary approaches, because their data and theoretical constructs differ in some respects from other approaches. It is also important to recognize the overlap and linkage among all of these approaches.

Huntington and Janowitz represent disciplinary as well as systems approaches. Huntington (1957, p. 3), a political scientist, writes: "the principal focus of civil-military relations is the relation of the officer corps to the state." It follows that the nature and character of officership and the control of the military are fundamental issues of civil-military relations. How this control is achieved and the dynamics between civilian and military values are important areas of research. Underlying Huntington's study is a political scientist's concern with state control over coercive instruments, legitimacy, and the proper functioning of the political system.

Political scientists are also concerned about the policy implications of civilian control. Policy, strategy, and the ability to wage war in differing environments across the conflict spectrum are prominent issues. These concerns also reflect popular issues such as nuclear freeze, nuclear winter, and arms control. Concern with such issues has also stimulated the involvement of a variety of professional groups, such as natural scientists and physicians. Although they do not necessarily concentrate on the role of the military and the issues of military professionalism (in open systems, in particular), their major concerns create an environment affecting the nature of military professionalism, albeit in a tangential and peripheral way. Perlmutter (1978) provides a cross-disciplinary perspective, synthesizing political science and sociology. Viewing the subject across the political spectrum, he attempts to provide a universal model regarding the political and governing role of the military.

Janowitz (1960) represents the work of sociologists in the study of civil-military relations and military professionalism. He notes (p. xii) that

this study is an attempt to describe the professional life, organizational setting, and leadership of the American military as they have evolved during the first half of this century. Treating the military profession as an object of social inquiry enables a fuller and more accurate assessment of its power position in American society and of its behavior in international relations.

Examples of sociological scholarship by European scholars include Jacques van Doorn (1975), Bengt Abrahammson (1972), and G. Teitler (1977). The political aspects of the military profession and the synthesis of historical, sociological, and comparative elements are characteristic of such scholarship. In the main, this scholarship suggests a very clear political role for the military and stresses the desirability of a professional system based on volunteers. Moreover, modern military professionalism is viewed as naturally evolving from the state of European political–military systems since the eighteenth century. These traditions contrast with the experience of the U.S. military.

In this respect, one of the better analyses of the literature and themes of armed forces and society from a sociological perspective is by Charles Moskos (1976). He concludes that there are three phases of conceptual development in the study of armed forces and society. The first phase was the period following World War II through the early 1950s, in which the military was seen as a "self contained entity with sharp divergences from civilian values" (p. 70). The second phase was the period of the 1950s and 1960s, when the military of Western developed systems was seen "as reflecting master trends towards societal bureaucratization with increasing overlap with civilian structures" (p. 70). The third phase, from the 1970s, appeared to be a return, to a degree, to the view that the military was divergent "from the civil format along with the demise of the citizen soldier. . . . In sum, present comprehension of armed forces and society is a return to a central concern with the phenomena of coercive force and its elaborations in social organization." With an extensive bibliography, the Moskos review is essential reading for those concerned with the sociological study of armed forces and society.

Historians have also made important contributions to the study of armed forces and society. As is to be expected, the historical perspective focuses on the evolution of the military profession and its historical relationship to society, much of it from a comparative approach. Historical studies are important for understanding the current state of the armed forces and society, since they provide the groundwork on which modern military systems rest. The work of Alfred Vagts (1959) provided an important reference point for historical studies, particularly in distinguishing militarism from the military way.

The historical method is best described by Martin Blumenson (1980, pp. 670–82). In a review of three books on the development of the modern military, Blumenson states that these books "describe and analyze the rise and development, over the past four centuries, of the modern military." He continues by pointing out what historical studies have concluded regarding the rise of the modern military profession, which is suffering from a "malaise . . . in search of a professional function and mission, as well as of social status and role." This was apparently the character of Western military systems in the early 1980s.

Anthropologists have only recently entered the field in a systematic way. The anthropological focus is primarily on the examination of tendencies toward conflict and studies of conflict control (Foster and Rubenstein, 1986).

Overall, disciplinary perspectives cut across other approaches. They broaden intellectual dimensions and provide critical analyses that are not usually adequately addressed in other approaches. However, disciplinary approaches tend to inject an intellectual bias that may ignore the perspectives of one or another discipline, thereby distorting the "realistic" character of civil-military relations and the quality of the military profession. As Welch (1976, p. 22) has written, "the heart of civilian control occurs within the corridors of government, far removed from the usual ambit of scholars."

POLITICAL REGIMES AND CIVIL-MILITARY RELATIONS

The study of civil-military relations and the control of military forces has not led to a theory or approach that is applicable to all systems. As this analysis shows, Western models dominated in the earlier period. More recently, a variety of non-Western approaches have emerged. This development has changed the scope and dimensions of comparative politics, challenging previously held notions about comparative theories and hypotheses. This has broadened the study of civil-military relations and military professionalism. In brief, the Western model may be inadequate and, in a number of instances, irrelevant to the nature and character of Third World systems. The notion of an apolitical military, for example, is unrealistic in the environment of political change and modernization that is characteristic of most developing systems. Equally important, later studies of Western systems have demonstrated that the military does wield political power in all systems, albeit often indirectly.

The analysis here indicates that there are several clusters of civil-military relations, each of which is generally associated with a particular kind of political system: open, closed-totalitarian, closed-authoritarian (Shils, 1965). The analysis also draws some general conclusions regarding the state of the military and politics.

The Military and Open Systems

The Western view of civil-military relations has traditionally rested on the notion that the military must be isolated from society and political dynamics. This did not necessarily mean "total" isolation, but rather one that legitimized the dominance of society and civilian leaders over the military leadership. This notion placed the military on the periphery of politics, producing an apolitical military. This view was reinforced by military professional education and socialization which accepted, as its core proposition, absolute civilian control of the military. Changes of political leadership were determined solely by democratic processes in which the military had little to say. While this view has been somewhat modified, the core principles remain unchanged.

It can be assumed from these propositions that in open systems, the more professional the military, the further it is removed from the socio-political dynamics. Control of the military is achieved, therefore, not only by the nature of the political system and the power of civilian leaders, but also by the values and norms of society, and the military ethos. Public attitudes and opinions regarding such military issues have an impact on the way civil authorities perceive, control, and supervise the military. Similarly, concern with legitimacy, credibility, and status drive military professionals and their bureaucracy toward accommodation with the fundamental principles of democracy, conditioned by civilian perceptions regarding the proper role and control of military forces. In brief, open systems institutionalize the principle of "power to the people" over the military system.

Closed Systems—Authoritarian

In authoritarian systems, the military is controlled by incorporating it into the political process and giving it a political role. However, authoritarian systems do not have "total" control over society. Governmental structures and party organs do not fully penetrate all societal groupings. In addition, there exists a degree of autonomy within certain sectors of society, which, in turn, can place some political pressure on the ruling elite. Military officers are visible within the political process, and the military system is closely linked with society and domestic politics. The power of political leaders is based on their ability to integrate the military into the political process and make it a component of the party in power. Concurrently, the military professional accepts, indeed demands, a role in the political process. Thus, the military in authoritarian systems can exercise a degree of independent political action, using this action as leverage to induce political concessions from the civilian leadership. This option is limited, however, by the political leverage of other groups.

Closed Systems—Totalitarian

Totalitarian systems (the epitome of closed systems) are systems in which political control by a small elite usually extends to, and penetrates, the most important segments in society. This is accomplished through government agencies, political party organs, and mobilization mechanisms. There is little, if any, room for political autonomy outside the controlling party. Power, prestige, status, and loyalty are usually achieved in and through the political party. Ideology plays a major role in legitimizing the existing system and placing all its components within the values and norms of the ruling elite.

The military system and profession become active agents of the ruling elite in closed systems. As such, the military is an institutionalized political organ as well as a military system. Control of the military is achieved through penetration of the profession by political agents, by the demand of political loyalty as the basis for rewards and promotion, and by the guidelines of a centralized ideology. In addition, the role of the military in governance and in the political party gives it a "stake" in the system. Finally, the military in such systems serves as an adult socializing agent reinforcing behavior patterns in accord with the views of the ruling elite.

A Summation

In open systems, the political power and role of the military in policymaking are minimal. In totalitarian systems, they are extensive, tempered by the fact that the military has an important stake in the system as it exists, and is closely controlled and supervised by the party and ruling elite. In authoritarian systems, the role of the military may be the most extensive and influential. But in some authoritarian contexts, civilian groups may provide an effective counterbalance, or at the least a competing force, to military power. In weak authoritarian systems, many of which are found in the Third World, political organs and government agencies may not be institutionalized to a point where they can provide an effective counterweight to the military. In such cases, the military becomes the "heavy" institution in the system and is placed in a coup-prone position. The same is true in weak Third World open systems.

In this respect, while military systems and military professionalism may possess some universal characteristics, in the main each military system is distinct in the way it serves society and how it relates to political authority. The military does indeed reflect society and vice versa. In this respect, the military has some political power in every political system. It is the extent of this power, the civilian control system, and the political dynamics between the military and civilian institutions that distinguish the military of one system from others. These appear to be the central factors in any systematic analysis of the control of military forces and civilian-military relations.

The Military and Politics

The military in every system possesses some political power. The extent of this power, how it is used, and its consequences are difficult to measure or analyze, except in the most obvious cases of military-dominant systems. Even there, however, civilian authorities exercise some power.

A useful template for the systematic study and analysis of civil-military relations and control of the military is the *political-military equation*. This equation consists of four components: political control (the locus of final authority over the military); value compatibility between military and society; organizational control (control of military organizations from within and without); and cultural patterns.

The substance and quality of each component are determined by the type and character of the political system (open or closed) in which the military functions. The legitimacy and credibility of the military system and the professional ethos are shaped by the nature and character of the respective political system. Thus, an effective civil-military relationship is achieved when each component of the political-military equation is compatible with and supportive of the other components.

Because of disjunctures between two or more elements in the political-military equation, serious incongruities can occur between the military and society. When this happens, it is likely that the military will assume, or at least attempt to assume, a more prominent role in politics and policymaking. It is also likely that civil control over the military will be diminished. How far this military prominence will progress is dependent on how quickly congruence can be restored.

The maintenance of congruence (or its restoration) is less difficult in developed than developing systems, though there is a measure of uncertainty in any system once a precedent of military intervention exists. The reason is that institutionalization of the four elements of the political-military equation is usually well advanced in developed as opposed to developing systems.

Applying the political-military equation to the analysis here results in three major categories of civil–military relations which reflect a particular kind of civil control of the military, or its absence. These are a civilian-dominant system, a system in equilibrium, and a military-dominant system. In civilian-dominant systems, the power of the military is minimal and its control by civil authorities is effective. A system in equilibrium is characterized by a relative balance of power between civilian and military institutions. The military-dominant system is the antithesis of the civilian-dominant system. These observations are the basis for developing an agenda for future research.

The Research Agenda

The scholarly literature on armed forces and society, and the prevailing models and approaches, raise a number of questions regarding the direction of needed research. There are at least two important considerations. First, model-building and hypothesis-testing need to focus on the political power of the military—specifically, how this power is achieved, maintained, and utilized. In addition, measures of military power need to be developed and comparative approaches designed for examining the power of the military in relation to those of other institutions. Furthermore, the impact of political power on the nature and character of the military profession needs to be analyzed in greater and comparative depth.

Second, a comparative approach to the study of armed forces and society must seriously examine the relevance of Western models, formulations from non-Western sources, and the relevance of alternative models and approaches to the study of the military and society. It is clear from the literature that much remains to be done in this area.

The nature of open systems, the changed international security environment, and the new dimensions of conflict challenge traditional views of civil-military relations and military professionalism. Moreover, scholarship emanating from Third World analysts may provide alternative concepts that are more attuned to the study of armed forces and society outside Western areas. Such scholarship tends to accentuate the internal political role and power of the military. These "new" dimensions are necessary to enhance the precision and sophistication of existing scholarship.

NOTE

1. For a description and definition of models, approaches, hypotheses, and so on, see James A. Bill and Robert L. Hardgrave, Jr., *Comparative Politics: The Quest for Theory* (New York: University Press of America, 1982).

REFERENCES

Abrahammson, Bengt. 1972. *Military Professionalization and Political Power*. Beverly Hills, Calif.: Sage Publications.

Ambler, John Steward. 1966. *The French Army in Politics*. Columbus: Ohio State University Press.

Andrzejewski, Stanislaw. 1954. *Military Organization and Society*. London: Routledge and Kegan Paul.

Baynes, J.C.M. 1972. *The Soldier in Modern Society*. London: Eyre Methuen, 1972.

Baynham, Simon, ed. 1986. *Military Power and Politics in Black Africa*. New York: St. Martin's Press.

Blumenson, Martin. 1980. The Development of the Modern Military. *Armed Forces and Society: An Interdisciplinary Journal* 6:670–82.

Cohen, Stephen B. 1971. *The Indian Army: Its Contribution to the Development of a Nation*. Berkeley: University of California Press.

Colton, Timothy J. 1979. *Commissars, Commanders, and Civilian Authority: The Structure of Soviet Military Politics*. Cambridge, Mass.: Harvard University Press.

DeCalo, Samuel. 1976. *Coups and Army Rule in Africa: Studies in Military Style*. New Haven, Conn.: Yale University Press.

Finer, S. E. 1962. *The Man on Horseback: The Role of the Military In Politics*. New York: Praeger. 2nd ed., Baltimore; Penguin Books.

First, Ruth. 1971. *Power in Africa: Political Power in Africa and the Coup d'etat*. Baltimore: Penguin Books.

Foster, Mary LeCron, and Robert A. Rubenstein, eds. 1986. *Peace and War: Cross-Cultural Perspectives*. New Brunswick, N.J.: Transaction Books.

Goodpaster, Andrew J., Samuel P. Huntington, et al. 1977. *Civil-Military Relations*. Washington, D.C.: American Enterprise Institute.

Hauser, William L. 1973. *America's Army in Crisis: A Study of Civil-Military Relations*. Baltimore: Johns Hopkins University Press.

Herspring, Dale R., and Ivan Volgyes, eds. 1978. *Civil-Military Relations in Communist Systems*. Boulder, Colo.: Westview Press.

Hoadley, J. Stephen. 1975. *Soldiers and Politics in Southeast Asia: Civil-Military Relations in Comparative Perspective*. Cambridge, Mass.: Schenkman Publishing Co.

Hogan, James J. 1978. Increasing Executive and Congressional Staff Capabilities in the National Security Area. Pp. 103–108 in Franklin D. Margiotta, ed., *The Changing World of the American Military*. Boulder, Colo.: Westview Press.

Howard, Michael. 1959. *Soldiers and Government: Nine Studies in Civil-Military Relations*. Bloomington: Indiana University Press.

Huntington, Samuel P. 1957. *The Soldier and the State: The Theory and Practice of Civil-Military Relations*. Cambridge, Mass.: Harvard University Press.

———. 1961. *The Common Defense*. New York: Columbia University Press.

———. 1965. Political Development and Political Decay. *World Politics* 17:386–430.

———. 1978. The Soldier and the State in the 1970s. Pp. 15–35 in Franklin D. Margiotta, ed., *The Changing World of the American Military*. Boulder, Colo.: Westview Press.

Hurewitz J. C. 1969. *Middle East Politics: The Military Dimension*. New York: Praeger.

Jacobs, James B. 1986. *Socio-Legal Foundations of Civil-Military Relations*. New Brunswick, N.J.: Transaction Books.

Janowitz, Morris. 1971. Rev. ed. *The Professional Soldier: A Social and Political Portrait*. New York: Free Press.

Janowitz, Morris and Jacques van Doorn, eds. 1971. *On Military Intervention*. Rotterdam.

Johnson, J. J., ed. 1962. *The Role of the Military in Underdeveloped Countries*. Princeton, N.J.: Princeton University Press.

Johnson, Thomas H., Robert O. Slater, and Pat McGowan. 1984. Explaining African Coups d'Etat, 1960–1962. *American Political Science Review* 78:622–40.

Jones, Ellen. 1985. *Red Army and Society: A Sociology of the Soviet Military*. Boston: Allen and Unwin.

Kemble, Robert C. 1973. *The Image of the Army Officer in America*. Westport, Conn.: Greenwood Press.

Kennedy, Gavin. 1974. *The Military in the Third World*. New York: Charles Scribner's Sons.

Kerwin, Jerome G., 1948. *Civil-Military Relationships in American Life*. Chicago: University of Chicago Press.

Kolkowicz, Roman. 1967. *The Soviet Military and the Communist Party*. Princeton, N.J.: Princeton University Press.

———. 1985. Civil-Military Studies: A Comparative and Interdisciplinary Approach. Paper delivered at the International Political Science Association World Congress, Paris.

Lang, Kurt. 1969. Technology and Career Management in the Military Establishment. Pp. 39–81 in Morris Janowitz, ed., *The New Military*. New York: Russell Sage Foundation.

Lasswell, Harold. 1941. The Garrison State and Specialists in Violence. *American Journal of Sociology* 46:455–68.

Lowenthal, Abraham F., and J. Samuel Fitch, eds. 1986. *Armies and Politics in Latin America*, rev. ed. New York: Holmes and Meier Pub.

Margiotta, Franklin D., ed. 1978. *The Changing World of the American Military*. Boulder, Colo.: Westview Press.

Martin, Michel. 1981. *Warriors to Managers: The French Military Establishment Since 1945*. Chapel Hill: University of North Carolina Press.

Menard, Orville D. 1967. *The Army and the Fifth Republic*. Lincoln: University of Nebraska Press.

Moellering, Lieutenant Colonel John H. 1973. Future Civil-Military Relations: The Army Turns Inward? *Military Review* 53:68–83.

Moskos, Charles. 1973. The Emergent Military. *Pacific Sociological Review* 16:255–80.
———. 1976. The Military. *Annual Review of Sociology* 2:55–77.
Nordlinger, Eric A. 1977. *Soldiers in Politics: Military Coups and Governments*. Englewood Cliffs, N.J.: Prentice-Hall.
Odetola, Olatunde. 1982. *Military Regimes and Development: A Comparative Analysis in African Societies*. London: George Allen and Unwin.
Odom, William. 1973. The Soviet Military: The Party Connection. *Problems of Communism* 22:12–26.
Perlmutter, Amos. 1978. *The Military and Politics in Modern Times: On Professionals, Praetorians, and Revolutionary Soldiers*. New Haven, Conn.: Yale University Press.
———, and William M. LeoGrande. 1982. The Party in Uniform: Toward a Theory of Civil-Military Relations in Communist Political Systems. *American Political Science Review* 76:778–89.
Peters, B. Guy, and James Clotfelter. 1978. The Military Profession and Its Task Environment: A Panel Study of Attitudes. Pp. 57–68 in Franklin D. Margiotta, ed., *The Changing World of the American Military*. Boulder, Colo.: Westview Press.
Pinkney, Robert. 1972. *Ghana Under Military Rule 1966–1969*. London: Methuen.
Radway, Laurence. 1982. The Political Role of the Military: Four Research Traditions. Paper delivered at the International Political Association World Congress, Rio de Janeiro, Brazil.
Sarkesian, Sam C. 1975. *The Professional Army Officer in a Changing Society*. Chicago: Nelson Hall.
———. 1978. An Empirical Assessment of Military Professionalism. Pp. 37–56 in Franklin D. Margiotta, ed., *The Changing World of the American Military*. Boulder, Colo.: Westview Press.
———. 1981. *Beyond the Battlefield: The New Military Professionalism*. New York: Pergamon Press.
Schmitter, P. C., ed. 1972. *Military Rule in Latin America*. Beverly Hills, Calif.: Sage Publications.
Scott, Harriet Fast, and William F. Scott. 1984. *The Armed Forces of the USSR*. 3rd rev. and updated ed. Boulder, Colo.: Westview Press.
Shils, Edward. 1965. *Political Development in New States*. The Hague: Mouton and Co.
Teitler, G. 1977. *The Genesis of the Professional Officers' Corps*. Beverly Hills, Calif.: Sage Publications.
Thayer, Frederick C. 1973. Professionalism: The Hard Choice. Pp. 564–69 in Frank Trager and Philip S. Kronenberg, eds., *National Security and American Society*. Lawrence: University of Kansas Press.
U.S. Army War College. June 30, 1970. *Study on Military Professionalism*. Carlisle Barracks, Penn.: U.S. Army War College.
Vagts, Alfred. 1959. *A History of Militarism*. New York: Meridian.
van Doorn, Jacques, ed. 1969. *Military Profession and Military Regimes: Commitments and Conflicts*. The Hague: Mouton and Co.
———. 1975. *The Soldier and Social Change: Comparative Studies in the History and Sociology of the Military*. Beverly Hills, Calif.: Sage Publications.
Vatikiotis, P. J. 1961. *The Egyptian Army in Politics: Pattern for New Nations?* Bloomington: Indiana University Press.

von Clausewitz, Carl. 1976. *On War*. Michael Howard and Peter Paret, eds. and trans. Princeton University Press.

Walton, George. 1973. *The Tarnished Shield*. New York: Dodd, Mead and Co.

Weigley, Russell F. 1977. *The American Way of War: A History of United States Military Strategy and Policy*. Bloomington: Indiana University Press.

Welch, Claude, E. 1976. Two Strategies of Civilian Control: Some Concluding Observations. Pp. 313–27 in Claude E. Welch, ed., *Civilian Control of the Military: Theory and Cases from Developing Countries*. Albany: State University of New York Press.

———. 1985. Civil-Military Relations: Perspectives from the Third World. *Armed Forces and Society: An Interdisciplinary Journal* 11:183–97.

———, and A. K. Smith. 1974. *Military Role and Rule*. North Scituate, Mass.: Duxbury Press.

Whitson, W. W., ed. 1972. *The Military and Political Power in China in the 1970s*. New York: Praeger.

12

On International Controls

HAROLD K. JACOBSON

In the popular view, the primary purpose of international organizations is to control the use of force as a means of settling disputes among states. Scholars might use a more formal term—international governmental organizations (IGOs)—and undoubtedly would maintain that these institutions have many additional functions, but they would agree that preventing war is a principal purpose of the United Nations and major regional international bodies. They would also believe that all IGOs, whatever their immediate purpose, could contribute to preventing war. Controlling the use of force is therefore a fair criterion by which to judge international organizations. What have international organizations done to control the use of force? How successful have these efforts been? These questions are the subject matter of this chapter.

HISTORICAL AND THEORETICAL BACKGROUND

Understanding why, when and how IGOs took on security tasks is a necessary preliminary step to analyzing the contemporary role of international organizations in controlling force. The ideas propelling IGOs into this field and the circumstances in which they assumed responsibilities were to establish an enduring goal; shape the character, procedures, and powers of the institutions, thereby influencing what they do today; and affect the way in which they are evaluated.

Plans for the creation of IGOs date at least from the inception of the multistate system in the seventeenth century. It was obvious to the political leaders and thinkers of the time that whatever benefits a decentralized international system comprised of sovereign states might bring, war among these states was possible and even probable. Many of these leaders argued, as their successors have since, that IGOs should be created to foreclose this possibility.

International governmental organizations have been a central feature of "peace plans" that have been advanced ever since the broad characteristics of the multi-system became apparent in the sixteenth and seventeenth centuries (Hemleben, 1943; Souleyman, 1941; Waltz, 1959). These plans generally placed limitations on the military forces available to states and provided that the centerpiece IGO would have military forces at its disposal. This IGO would use these military forces to compel states to abide by the commonly agreed upon rules and to stop states from breaking these rules. Limiting the military forces available to states was an essential aspect of insuring that the IGO's military forces would be powerful enough to accomplish their assigned task.

Since the control of military force is a core aspect of sovereignty, and sovereignty is the defining characteristic of the multi-state system, it should not be too surprising that these plans were stillborn. Starting in the early years of the nineteenth century, IGOs were created to facilitate economic interactions, not to implement peace plans.

As industrialization was applied to the development of weapons, and the potential human and material costs of war rose, the reluctance of states to create IGOs that would deal directly with security issues and thus military force began to diminish. The creation of the Permanent Court of Arbitration in 1899 was a pioneering, though modest, step. The carnage of World War I provoked states to go further and to establish the League of Nations, the world's first general-purpose IGO that could include potentially all states among its members. The league was also a limited attempt to apply the doctrine of collective security.

Woodrow Wilson, a political scientist before he became the United States president, was one of the clearest expositors and strongest proponents of collective security. Collective security is in essence an expansion and elaboration of the concepts presented in the peace plans. Wilson and others argued that collective security would be a superior alternative to the balance of power as a way of insuring security for states. Under a system of collective security, all states would agree to repulse any attempt to alter the agreed status quo through the threat or use of force (Claude, 1964). States would retain control of their military forces but could only lawfully use these forces for self-defense or, as directed by a central IGO, to repel aggression. In Wilson's view, the prospect of virtually all states uniting to defend a victim of aggression should be sufficient to deter any would-be aggressor.

However appealing Wilson's vision may have been, it has thus far proved unrealizable. There has not yet been a global status quo that could command universal assent as legitimately defining the borders of all states. Nor have most states been willing to subordinate their military forces to an IGO. Nevertheless, the doctrine of collective security remains an idealized goal against which the contribution of IGOs to controlling the use of force is often measured.

The Covenant of the League of Nations embodied the ambivalence of states about attempting to apply the doctrine of collective security. Member states pledged "to respect and preserve as against external aggression the territorial integrity and existing political independence of all Members" (Article 10). In the event of an aggression, the league council could recommend that states deploy military forces to implement this pledge (Article 16), but any league decision would require the unanimous vote of all members other than the parties involved. The league's founder states desired the protection that collective security could provide; they also wanted unfettered authority over where and how their military forces would be used.

To make aggression less likely, and the forces that could be deployed in support of collective security actions relatively more powerful, the covenant directed the league council to formulate plans for the reduction of all members' armaments. All members would be expected to implement these plans, which would be reviewed and revised every ten years (Article 8). If we put the task in the present idiom, we can say that the council was charged with formulating a global plan for arms control. These decisions would also require unanimity.

At the time, the theory of arms control was not as well developed as that of collective security, or as it would become in the post–World War II period. Two basic points—that smaller forces would be less able to conduct aggression and would lessen the requirements for extensive international forces— dated from the peace plans. In addition, as early as the waning years of the nineteenth century, there was concern that arms expenditures were excessive and mounting and should be limited. There was also a growing sense that some weapons had such horrifying effects that they should be prohibited or their use severely limited. Finally, there was a belief that arms races had erupted into war and that limits should be set to preclude their reoccurrence. Thus, as in the case of collective security, the ideas that went into the drafting of the League of Nations Convenant expanded and amplified those found in the peace plans.

Although these arguments for the regulation of armaments constituted an appealing case, they fell short of providing a practical plan for inducing states voluntarily to reduce or limit their military forces. Since states had to rely on their own military forces for their security, the level of these forces reflected their calculation of what would be needed to provide security. Given national self-reliance and sovereignty, could states be expected to entrust decisions about the level of their military forces to some external body? How could a state be expected to accept a lower level of military forces than its government considered prudent?

Putting these doubts aside, if unanimity among the league's members could be achieved, these key provisions of the Covenant of the League of Nations concerning collective security and arms control provided a blueprint for a centralized, hierarchical system for controlling the use of force in international relations. Although the covenent also gave the league authority to undertake other actions to limit the use of force, such as conciliation, mediation, arbitration, and judicial settlement, the key provisions concerning collective security and arms control were more novel and notable and fitted the idealized goal that grew out of Wilson's vision.

Judged by its efforts to bring about arms control and implement collective security, the League of Nations was a failure (Walters, 1952). The aspiration that the league could be the instrumentality for achieving arms control agreements proved fruitless. The league's Disarmament Conference, which began in 1932 and finally adjourned in 1934, produced few results. The inability of France and Germany to agree on levels for their military forces blocked progress. The farthest that the league went toward implementing collective security was to apply limited economic sanctions without success against Italy in the 1935–1936 Italo-Ethiopian crisis. In this crisis and others, the major states evidenced no enthusiasm for deploying their military forces for purposes that did not appear to them to involve their immediate vital interests, as they defined them. In contrast, some of the league's more modest efforts to limit the use of force, such as the publication of statistics on military forces, were more successful.

Nothing that was done through or outside of the League of Nations, however, could stave off World War II. This war, which was even more costly than its predecessor, produced renewed determination to prevent another, a determination that strengthened as the awesome power of nuclear weapons became apparent.

The United Nations was one product of this determination. In effect a refurbished version of the league, the United Nations was charged in its charter with achieving arms control and effecting limited collective security, as well as taking other actions to control the use of force in international relations. One important difference between the United Nations and the League of Nations is that the U.N. Security Council can decide to deploy military forces to resist a threat to the peace by the affirmative vote of only nine—including the five permanent members, China, France, the United Kingdom, the Union of Soviet Socialist Republics, and the United States—of the fifteen members of the Security Council. Unlike league decisions, U.N. decisions do not require unanimity. Officials who had worked with the league and scholars who had studied and thought about it contributed to drafting the U.N. Charter, and sought and gained this change (Goodrich, 1947).

In practice, achieving unanimity among the five permanent members of the Security Council has proved as elusive as achieving it among the league's entire membership. In 1950, when North Korea attacked South Korea, the United Nations ordered military actions that resembled the doctrine of collective security, but the Soviet Union was absent from the Security Council when the crucial decisions were taken, and the United States and South Korea provided the bulk of the military forces in the U.N. command (Goodrich, 1956). Eventually, the North Korean attack was repulsed, and the status quo was restored. Other than this instance, the United Nations has been no more successful in implementing collective security than was the League of Nations. Short of implementing collective security, however, the United Nations has made several important contributions to controlling the use of force in post–World War II international relations, as will be seen in subsequent sections of this chapter.

Another innovation in the U.N. Charter was recognition of a role for regional organizations in efforts to gain security. According to Chapter Eight of the Charter, the regional organizations, which were to be subordinate to the United Nations, could perform the same functions as the United Nations, including collective security. Important regional organizations have been created—for instance, the Organization of African States, the League of Arab States, the Council of Europe, and the Organization of African Unity—and they have undertaken numerous activities related to the control of force. They have generally not been subordinate to the United Nations, however, nor have they succeeded in implementing collective security. Moreover, their successes in arms control are limited.

Unexpectedly, the North Atlantic Treaty Organization (NATO) and the Warsaw Treaty Organization (WTO) were created to implement balance of power policies. These IGOs, as the discussion below suggests, have contributed to the control of force by being instruments of precisely the policy Woodrow Wilson wanted IGOs to end.

Though important arms control agreements have been achieved in the post–World War II period, the involvement of the United Nations specifically and IGOs more broadly in the formulation, negotiation, and implementation of these agreements has seldom been central (Bechoeffer, 1961; Jacobson and Stein, 1966; Talbot, 1979). Moreover, the arms control agreements have not led to reduced levels of armaments.

Drawing from this history, we can formulate the first answer to the question as to what IGOs have done to control the use of force: namely, they have not done what was originally expected of them. International governmental organizations have not performed the role traditionally assigned to them in peace plans or envisaged in the League Covenant and U.N. Charter. They have not implemented the doctrine of collective security. Nor have they been the focal point for arms control. Neither the league nor the United Nations has hierarchically directed global activities concerning security.

There are several explanations, the most important of which have already been indicated. The absence of a universally accepted status quo and the insistence of states—particularly the most powerful—on retaining freedom to decide for what purposes and when their armed forces should be used rather than automatically committing them to the service of an abstract principle have precluded the implementation of collective security. The insistence of states on determining the level of their military forces in the light of their own conceptions of their security needs has blocked arms control.

A second answer to the basic question of what IGOs have done is that the generally felt need to control the use of force in international relations has persisted and grown. IGOs have improvised and done what they could, even though this result has fallen short of their idealized role. Because of this improvisation, IGOs have performed many functions related to security and some of these have been unexpected. What has emerged is a multifaceted mixture of actions undertaken by different international institutions, a thoroughly decentralized rather than a hierarchical system.

The idealized prescription remains, however, and some activities undertaken by IGOs are directed toward creating conditions that could contribute to its eventually being realized. In the meantime, the activities of IGOs should be evaluated against a less demanding and more varied standard.

With this background, we may turn to a more detailed consideration of the activities that international governmental organizations have undertaken in the post–World War II period directed at controlling the use of force. First, we will consider what IGOs have done in disputes and armed conflicts. Second, we will examine the role IGOs have played in arms control. Then we will analyze the way IGOs have become factors in the balance of power. Finally, we will examine IGO activities that are less directly related to controlling force but could have a longer term impact.

CONFLICT MANAGEMENT AND RESOLUTION

Soon after the post–World War II era began, as it became clear that neither the United Nations nor any other IGO would be able to implement the doctrine of collective security, the search began for actions that IGOs could take when confronted with disputes and conflicts that would be relevant to controlling the use of force. The United Nations and other IGOs assumed several traditional tasks that had previously been performed by the League of Nations. They also invented new tasks, most notably peacekeeping.

IGOs can adopt resolutions and thus be instruments through which their members can express views about conflicts or situations that might lead to conflicts. These resolutions can express moral approval or disapproval, call for the cessation of violence, or recommend changes that might lessen the likelihood of violence. Depending on how sensitive states are to external opinion, such resolutions could affect their behavior. Throughout the post–World War II period the United Nations and other organizations have regularly adopted resolutions of this type.

IGOs can also provide a variety of dispute settlement services, such as good offices, conciliation, mediation, and arbitration. Executive heads can perform these services; indeed, it is one of their most prominent functions. Alternatively, IGOs can appoint individuals or panels to serve in an ad hoc capacity. The United Nations has frequently assigned such tasks to the secretary-general and other individuals. In addition, other IGOs have often provided these services (Gordenker, 1967; Rovine, 1970; Urquhart, 1972; Young, 1967).

Economic sanctions are another traditional instrumentality employed by international governmental organizations to affect and end disputes and conflicts. Economic sanctions, though less often imposed than less drastic actions, have occasionally been used by the United Nations and other IGOs (Renwick, 1981).

The United Nations' major innovation with respect to efforts to control the use of force has been the development of the concept of peacekeeping forces. First invented by then Canadian Foreign Minister Lester Pearson and U.N. Secretary-General Dag Hammarskjold for use in the Suez Crisis of 1956, peacekeeping forces are relatively small military forces, consisting of 5,000 or 6,000 personnel, that are interposed between hostile military forces to insure that the provisions of cease-fire agreements are observed. Such forces have been deployed in various Middle Eastern crises, in the Congo crisis, and in Cyprus (Boyd, 1971; Fabian 1971).

Peacekeeping forces can only be deployed with the consent of the belligerent parties; thus, the parties must be willing to stop hostilities. They may have exhausted available resources, become convinced that further warfare would be unlikely to yield significant gains, experienced severe pressures to cease hostilities from allies, or for some other reason decided that a cease-fire would be desirable. Agreeing to stop hostilities in response to the request of an international organization to which a state itself belongs can be a relatively graceful way to end a war. Furthermore, when border incidents have been a factor in the outbreak of hostilities, deploying a peacekeeping force can be hailed as a measure to correct the pre-war situation, one that could achieve the objectives for which arms were taken up. Peacekeeping forces have generally been comprised of military contingents from disinterested states, those that have had no immediate connection with or interests in the quarrel that led to the outbreak of hostilities. Military forces from the super- and great powers have generally been excluded; in contrast, such forces were preeminent in visions of how collective security would work. The objective of peacekeeping forces is to prevent warfare from recurring. Implicit in this objective is the fear that if warfare were to recur it might escalate and spread.

Scholarship concerning the role of IGOs in conflict management and resolution has become increasingly sophisticated. There are numerous case studies of particular episodes. Since more than 200 disputes have been referred to IGOs in the post–World War II period, aggregate studies have also become possible and have been undertaken. The most elegant of these studies have employed subtle criteria for measuring the success of actions undertaken by IGOs and have elaborated a comprehensive list of factors that might affect the chances for success (Butterworth, 1978; Haas, 1986). Using the criteria and the list of factors, they have developed persuasive generalizations concerning the conditions under which IGO actions have been successful.

Although the conclusions that emerge from this literature are substantial and rich, a broad generalization is found in Haas:

Relatively successful conflict management is possible when a major power and/or the Secretary-General mobilize support for a strong resolution authorizing civilian or military field operations. This tends to take place only when the issue dividing the parties involves decolonization or a dispute which is *sui generis* and does not grow out of a civil war. (Haas, 1986, pp. 27, 29).

Based on this generalization, analysts have argued that IGOs have played and can play an important role in managing and resolving conflicts.

Referring a dispute to IGO far from guarantees that it will be settled. Indeed, relatively few conflicts that have been referred to IGOs have been settled. Violence, however, has been abated in more than half of the cases, and the conflict has been isolated almost as frequently. IGOs can frequently put a conflict "on ice" in the hope that sometime, somehow it will be resolved without violence. This is a useful contribution to international security, even though it is not collective security as conceived by Woodrow Wilson and others. Because of the widespread longing for something as perfect as the idealized vision of collective security, however, there is a generalized sense that IGOs have fallen short. This sense often leads to ignoring IGO's real accomplishments.

ARMS CONTROL

In the years since World War II, IGOs have played on important, though not central, role in the regulation of armaments. Again, the role has been different from the centralized and controlling one envisaged in most peace plans and in the Covenant of the League of Nations.

Arms control and disarmament discussions have occurred within the United Nations since the organization was created. It has regularly adopted resolutions calling for arms control and disarmament. Although only a few agreements have actually been negotiated within the organization, it has approved several that have been negotiated elsewhere and has thus legitimized them. The United Nations' broad activities in this field have undoubtedly had an impact on the general climate of international relations. By keeping the issue in the forefront, they have made it impossible for governments to ignore it. They have heightened the popular desire for a world with fewer arms and have intensified the revulsion against nuclear weapons.

The small number of states that possess substantial nuclear arsenals has been one reason for the limited role of the United Nations in the post–World War II arms control negotiations. The nuclear weapons states, especially the

United States and the Soviet Union, have generally preferred a bilateral or limited membership framework rather than the United Nations, with its more than 150 members, for serious negotiations about nuclear weapons. As long as negotiations about nuclear weapons were conducted within the United Nations, no practical results were achieved. Subsequently, however, through trilateral, bilateral, and limited membership talks a number of significant results have been achieved.

A far-reaching regime against the proliferation of nuclear weapons has been created (Quester, 1981; Dunn, 1982). The principal elements of this regime are the Treaty Banning Nuclear Weapon Tests in the Atmosphere, in Outer Space and Under Water; the Treaty on the Non-Proliferation of Nuclear Weapons; the Treaty for the Prohibition of Nuclear Weapons in Latin America; and a U.N. body, the International Atomic Energy Agency (IAEA).

The first treaty was negotiated by the United Kingdom, the United States, and the Soviet Union in 1963, and endorsed by the United Nations later that year. It bans all but underground tests of nuclear weapons. It has been ratified by more than 110 countries. The second treaty was negotiated by the United States and the Soviet Union and then incorporated into a U.N. General Assembly resolution in 1968. Non-nuclear weapons states that adhere to the treaty bind themselves not to develop or acquire nuclear weapons, while nuclear weapons states pledge not to transfer weapons to the non-nuclear weapons states. More than 120 states have ratified this treaty. The third treaty makes Latin America a nuclear weapons-free zone. It was negotiated by the Latin American states in 1967 and endorsed by the United Nations that same year. All important Latin American states except Cuba have signed this treaty, and it is fully in force for all of those that have signed other than Argentina, Brazil, and Chile. IAEA was created by the United Nations in 1957. It provides technical assistance to developing countries concerning the development and use of nuclear energy. It serves as a framework for developing safety standards regarding the use of nuclear energy, and—most importantly for non-proliferation—it operates a safeguards system to protect against nuclear materials being diverted from peaceful to weapons purposes (Scheinman, 1987).

Whatever sanctions exist for application against states that are recalcitrant about accepting the various elements of the non-proliferation regime or violate the regime are primarily embodied in national law and national policy. Nuclear-supplier states generally insist that recipients of transfers of nuclear materials submit these materials to safeguards. U.S. law prohibits the United States from providing economic aid to countries that violate the non-proliferation regime. There are few sanctions that IGOs could impose.

Thus far, the non-proliferation regime has been more successful than is often acknowledged. Only six states, the United States, the Soviet Union, the United Kingdom, France, China, and India, have openly tested nuclear weapons or devices. Even if two or three more states—Israel, South Africa, and Pakistan—are capable of producing nuclear weapons, the number of nuclear weapons capable states is far smaller today than it was expected to be when the various elements of the non-proliferation regime were put in place in the 1950s and 1960s.

The two superpowers, the United States and the Soviet Union, have engaged in negotiations that have established limits on the growth of their nuclear arsenals. In the 1970s, the two most important agreements to result from these negotiations were the 1972 Treaty on the Limitation of Anti-Ballistic Missile Systems and the 1979 Treaty on the Limitation of Strategic Offensive Arms. Even though the second treaty has not been ratified, both sides have generally observed its broad terms. These treaties have since been supplemented by the superpower accord, ratified in May 1988, to eliminate intermediate- and short-range missiles.

Virtually the sole role of the IGOs with respect to these negotiations has been to encourage the superpowers to greater efforts. Not only have the superpowers wanted to settle their own affairs without interference from less powerful states, but once the negotiations became serious it became obvious that IGOs could do little to enforce arms control agreements between the superpowers (Ikle, 1961). The only meaningful deterrent to the United States or the Soviet Union violating a bilateral agreement between them would be the likelihood that the other side would take retaliatory action.

Another reason for the limited role of the United Nations in the post–World War II arms control negotiations has been the fact that the most substantial conventional military forces have been concentrated in Europe. As in the case of negotiations about nuclear weapons, the countries responsible for these forces, which include four of the nuclear weapons states, have preferred to conduct negotiations in forums that include only states that are located in the region or have military forces there, rather than to conduct them in the United Nations, where more than 120 additional states would be involved. The extensive negotiations that have occurred between NATO and WTO and in the broader framework provided by the 1975 Helsinki Agreement have yielded agreements on confidence-building measures, but have not yet produced agreements on force reductions. The United Nations has noted, endorsed, and encouraged these negotiations.

Those arms control negotiations that have been conducted within the United Nations have dealt primarily with subjects that could involve all states. These subjects include areas that the United Nations has termed the global commons, outer space and the deep seabed, and weapons that many states, not merely those with enormous industrial capacities, could develop and use.

The most important agreements to emerge from these negotiations have been the 1967 Treaty on Principles Governing the Activities of States in the Exploration and Use of Outer Space, including the Moon and Other Celestial Bodies; the 1971 Treaty on the Prohibition of the Emplacement of Nuclear Weapons and Other Weapons of Mass Destruction on the Seabed and the Ocean Floor and in the Subsoil Thereof; the 1971 Convention on the Prohibition of the Development, Production and Stockpiling of Bacteriological Weapons and on Their Destruction; the 1976 Convention on the Prohibition of Military or Any Other Hostile Use of Environmental Modification Techniques; and the 1980 Convention on Prohibitions or Restrictions on the Use of Certain Conventional Weapons Deemed to Be Excessively Injurious or to Have Indiscriminate Effects.

Since the early 1970s, negotiations have been conducted to strengthen the international legal restrictions against the use of chemical weapons. The 1925 Geneva Protocol for the Prohibition of the Use in War of Asphyxiating, Poisonous or Other Gases, and of Bacteriological Methods of Warfare is merely a no-first-use agreement. It does not prohibit the manufacture and stockpiling of chemical weapons, and it does not contain verification provisions. Even though private bilateral talks between the United States and the Soviet Union have supplemented the talks that have occurred within various U.N. bodies, especially the Committee on Disarmament, the differences between the two superpowers on verification have until now blocked an agreement.

According to the vision of peace plans and the Covenant of the League of Nations, the international system's centerpiece IGO—since 1945, the United Nations—would have been the main forum for negotiating agreements concerning the regulation of armaments and the principal instrument for enforcing these agreements. Some of the disappointment with what has happened since World War II stems from the lingering attraction of this vision. The disappointment can also be traced to the limited extent of the achievements so far, especially in view of the enormous dangers posed by modern weaponry. Judged against pre–World War II history, however, the accomplishments of the post–World War II period are impressive. More has been done to regulate armaments than in any previous historical period. No doubt the awesome character of modern weaponry has stimulated greater efforts than have occurred in the past. Following a decentralized, disaggregative approach, however, has arguably made progress easier to achieve.

IGOS AND THE BALANCE OF POWER

Until the post–World War II period, IGOs had been seen as instruments for controlling the use of force that would be an alternative to the traditional mechanisms of the balance of power. With the formation of NATO and WTO, IGOs became aspects of balance-of-power policies.

The North Atlantic Treaty could have been just a legal commitment, but in September 1949, just months after the treaty was signed, the signatory states decided to create a civilian and military structure. With the implementation of this decision, the alliance became bureaucratized and took on the form of an international governmental organization (Jordan, 1967). When the Warsaw Treaty was signed in 1955, the signatory states moved immediately to create an IGO. Since then, the two IGOs have been involved in the management of the two sides' military forces. This development has had significant, though often overlooked, consequences.

First, the rearmament of the two parts of Germany has been accomplished within the framework of the two organizations. This made it possible to conduct the process in ways that gave assurances to the allies and foes of both Germanies. Since the mid-nineteenth century, the issue of Germany's power and role in European affairs had been a continual source of dispute. Failure to agree on mutually acceptable terms for Germany's rearmament doomed the League of Nations' efforts to regulate armaments. The post–World War II solution has many negative features, but it has removed the issue as a source of serious contention in international politics.

Second, the bureaucratization of the alliances has predictably had a stabilizing effect on the military policies of the two sides. NATO and WTO have had an influence on the determination of the levels and types of military forces maintained by their member states (Jacobson, 1984). Like all bureaucracies, the two organizations have worked against the occurrence of sudden changes in their members' force postures. They have also worked to insure that the two military coalitions maintain roughly equivalent military forces. To the extent that a stable balance of power serves as a deterrent to war, NATO and WTO have contributed to controlling the use of force in international relations.

Third, NATO and WTO have provided a framework through which member states could exercise a moderating influence on their allies' policies (Fox and Fox, 1967; Halloway and Sharp, 1984). In particular, member states have counseled their allies to be cautious when pursuing military activities outside of the European theatre. They have urged their allies to conserve their military strength for preserving the East-West balance in the European theatre. They have also expressed their disinclination to be drawn into conflagrations outside of the European theatre because of their allies' military activities.

In these several ways then, involving IGOs in balance-of-power policies has enabled them to contribute to controlling the use of force and thus to peace, even though this is diametrically opposite to the mission that was traditionally foreseen for them. It must be noted, however, that the Warsaw Treaty Organization has also provided a framework for the Soviet Union to control political change within the regimes of its Eastern European allies.

INDIRECT CONTRIBUTIONS TO CONTROLLING FORCE

The direct contribution of international governmental organizations to controlling the use of force in international relations, while important, is, nevertheless, modest. The indirect contribution of IGOs may in the end prove more substantial. IGOs can be seen as conflict-avoidance mechanisms. To the extent that they can help states avoid conflicts that might escalate to the use of violence, they make a crucial, though indirect, contribution to controlling force.

IGOs can help avoid international conflicts in several ways (Nye, 1971). As arenas for cooperation among states, IGOs provide settings in which problems can be discussed at an early stage before the various parties' positions are fixed, when compromise and mutually acceptable solutions are still possible. When cooperation through IGOs occurs and is successful, beneficial activities can result; states will be reluctant to jeopardize these activities through conflicts with their partners. Cooperation can create incentives to avoid conflict (Mitrany, 1966).

Hopes of creating such incentives to avoid conflict were among the motives for the creation of the European communities: the European Coal and Steel Community, the European Atomic Energy Community, and the European Economic Community (Monnet, 1978). Indeed, some felt that the effects on the member states of joining together in the European communities would be even more powerful. In May 1950, Robert Schuman, the French foreign minister, launched the proposal to create the European Coal and Steel Community, which would place the production of coal and steel in France and Germany and the other member countries under a common authority. He said: "The solidarity in production thus established will make it plain that any war between France and Germany becomes not merely unthinkable, but materially impossible." (Carlyle, 1953, p. 316). The cooperation between France and the Federal Republic of Germany that has occurred within the framework of the European communities has certainly been one of the factors promoting pacific relations among these two states which have historically been involved in many violent conflicts (Russett, 1967).

Even if discussions in IGOs do not result in cooperation, they can nevertheless contribute to controlling force by making positions clear and thus help states avoid blundering into war (Alger, 1961). IGOs can develop norms to orient state behavior toward non-conflictual behavior.

Have IGOs made such contributions to conflict avoidance? IGOs have certainly undertaken all of the activities listed in the preceding paragraph. Since their contribution to controlling the use of force is indirect, tracing and measuring their effect are difficult tasks. There is evidence, however, that, as predicted, those who participate in IGOs develop a more complex and sophisticated understanding of international problems and cognitive change and social learning occur (Peck, 1979). It is also clear that as the number of international governmental organizations has grown, the relative incidence of interstate violence has declined (Jacobson, Reisinger, and Mathers, 1986). Surely other factors than the growth of IGOs have contributed to the decline in interstate violence, but it is not unreasonable to conclude that IGOs have played a role by contributing to conflict avoidance. This may well be the IGOs most substantial contribution to the control of force.

IGOS AND THE USE OF FORCE IN INTERNATIONAL RELATIONS

International governmental organizations were originally conceived primarily to prevent violence in international relations through control of the use of force. The peace plans that have been advanced by political leaders and thinkers from the sixteenth century to the present, including such notable figures as Immanuel Kant, William Penn, Jean-Jacques Rousseau, and Woodrow Wilson, have projected a central and hierarchical role for IGOs. In these plans, IGOs rather than states would control military forces. The implementation of these plans would have involved a direct, frontal attack on sovereignty, since having a monopoly on the legitimate use of force is a crucial element of sovereignty. Thus far, sovereignty has proved remarkably unassailable. A direct attack has not yet been fully mounted, much less succeeded. IGOs, however, have been created to serve a variety of purposes, including ameliorating conflict, and they have made significant contributions to controlling the use of force in international relations, though not those envisaged in the peace plans.

IGOs have helped control the use of force in international relations without making a direct assault on sovereignty. That so many different functions have been found for IGOs to perform short of breaching sovereignty is a testament to the strength of the desire for peace and the inventiveness of human beings when confronted with problems to which theoretical blueprints only vaguely apply.

The steps that have been taken so far point the road to the future. There is little sign that humankind will soon be ready to abandon the sovereign state system, but IGOs can contribute to controlling the use of force through modest, pragmatic, disaggregative, decentralized actions, building on the solid foundation of actions taken in the years since World War II. What has been done has not followed the prescription of the peace plans. Measured against the idealized prescription which these plans gave, the steps that have been taken fall short and are disappointing. Measured against what has been done in the past, however, the post–World War II actions are impressive and offer hope for more solid accomplishments in the future. They also suggest that in the immediate future legal, institutional, and multilateral prescriptions can provide only a partial answer to controlling the use of force in international relations.

CURRENT SCHOLARSHIP AND THE FUTURE

Scholarship has contributed substantially to what has been accomplished in the past, and scholarship can continue to contribute. The peace plans were an early form of scholarship about the contributions that international organizations might make to controlling the use of force in international relations. Scholarship in this tradition continues, most notably through such efforts as the World Order Models Project (Falk, 1975). The purpose of such work is to state broad goals and to outline new proposals for transferring authority and legitimacy from states to international governmental organizations. Such scholarship is visionary and hortatory.

Other types of current scholarship have had somewhat more modest ambitions. Some scholarship—still at the broad level of the international system—has been devoted to attempting to understand the conditions for the creation and maintenance of IGOs, and of patterns of cooperation among sovereign states. This scholarship is based on the hope that improved understanding will help policymakers and their constituents perpetuate and extend the cooperation that has already occurred.

Regime analysis is the most prominent among this school. Regimes are defined as "sets of implicit or explicit principles, norms, rules and decision-making procedures around which actors' expectations converge in a given area of international relations" (Krasner, 1983, p. 2).

In a seminal work, Charles P. Kindelberger argued that the existence in the international system of a hegemonic power was essential for regimes to be created and for cooperation to occur (Kindelberger, 1973). The core of his argument was that only a hegemonic power could or would bear a disproportionate share of the costs of the collective goods involved in the international cooperation. Although his book was about the interwar period, many other scholars applied his argument to the post–World War II period. In the years immediately after the war, the power of the United States was unquestionably several times that of any other state. In these years too the principal IGOs that undergirded the post-war order were created and the patterns of cooperation established, and it was clear that the United States bore a disproportionate share of the costs of the collective goods that all these regimes involved.

The question then arose, could these IGOs and the cooperation continue even though U.S. power declined relatively? Recent scholarship has argued that it could, that learning occurs and that incentives are established that make the continuation of IGOs and cooperation possible (Keohane, 1984).

Other current scholarship, following a tradition that dates from the 1930s, but using more modern analytical techniques, analyzes the functioning of contemporary IGOs (Haas, 1986). Much of this work is done under the sponsorship of international governmental and non-governmental organizations. The explicit or implicit assumption underlying this work is that a better understanding of how IGOs function will produce information that could be useful in making the institutions more effective. Even the most theoretical of the work of this genre has often found application.

All of these varieties of scholarship will and should continue. In addition, there are crucial gaps in scholarship that need to be filled. Very little is known about the domestic consequences of international cooperation and about the conditions within states that contribute to international cooperation (Putnam, 1988). Because international cooperation, as a consequence of growing interdependence, increasingly involves what formerly were exclusively domestic issues, filling this gap is essential to understanding the consequences and conditions of further international cooperation.

Another crucial gap is clarifying the relationship between interactions among states within and external to IGOs. If IGOs by themselves can provide only a partial answer to controlling the use of force in international relations, what then are the other elements of an effective prescription? What is the relationship, for instance, between the distribution of military force among states and cooperation within IGOs? Such questions are largely unexplored, yet they involve issues that are vital to understanding the nature and modalities of the contribution that international governmental organizations can make to controlling the use of force in international relations.

The broad issue covered in this chapter clearly provides ample room for creative and useful scholarship, scholarship that could contribute to peace, as past scholarship has demonstrably contributed.

REFERENCES

Alger, Chadwick F. 1961. Non-resolution Consequences of the United Nations and Their Effect on International Conflict. *Journal of Conflict Resolution* 5:128–45.

Bechoeffer, Bernard G. 1961. *Postwar Negotiations for Arms Control*. Washington, D.C.: Brookings Instition.

Boyd, James M. 1971. *United Nations Peace-Keeping Operations: A Military and Political Appraisal*. New York: Praeger.

Butterworth, Robert L. 1978. *Moderation from Management: International Organizations and Peace*. Pittsburgh: University of Pittsburgh, University Center for International Affairs.

Carlyle, Margaret (ed. for the Royal Institute of International Affairs). 1953. *Documents on International Affairs, 1949–1950*. London: Oxford University Press.

Claude, Inis L. 1964. *Power and International Relations*. New York: Random House.

Dunn, Lewis A. 1982. *Controlling the Bomb: Nuclear Proliferation in the 1980s*. New Haven, Conn.: Yale University Press.

Fabian, Larry L. 1971. *Soldiers Without Enemies: Preparing the United Nations for Peacekeeping*. Washington, D.C.: Brookings Institution.

Falk, Richard A. 1975. *A Study of Future Worlds*. New York: Free Press.

Fox, William T. R., and Annette Baker Fox. 1967. *NATO and the Range of American Choice*. New York: Columbia University Press.

Goodrich, Leland M. 1947. From League of Nations to United Nations. *International Organization* 1:3–21.

———. 1956. *Korea: A Study of U.S. Policy*. New York: Council on Foreign Relations.

Gordenker, Leon. 1967. *The UN Secretary-General and the Maintenance of Peace*. New York: Columbia University Press.

Haas, Ernst B. 1986. *Why We Still Need the United Nations: The Collective Management of International Conflict*. Berkeley: University of California, Institute of International Studies.

Halloway, David, and Jane M. O. Sharp, 1984. *The Warsaw Pact: Alliance in Transition*. Ithaca, N.Y.: Cornell University Press.

Hemleben, Sylvester John. 1943. *Plans for World Peace Through Six Centuries*. Chicago: University of Chicago Press.

Ikle, Fred Charles. 1961. After Detection What? *Foreign Affairs* 39:208–20.

Jacobson, Harold K. 1984. *Networks of Interdependence: International Organizations and the Global Political System*. New York: Alfred A. Knopf.

———, William Reisinger, and Todd Mathers. 1986. National Entanglements in International Governmental Organizations. *American Political Science Review* 80:141–60.

———, and Eric Stein. 1966. *Diplomats, Scientists and Politicians: The United States and the Nuclear Test Ban Negotiations*. Ann Arbor: University of Michigan Press.

Jordan, Robert S. 1967. *The NATO Staff/Secretariat, 1952–1957: A Study in International Administration*. London: Oxford University Press.

Keohane, Robert O. 1984. *After Hegemony: Cooperation and Discord in the World Political Economy*. Princeton, N.J.: Princeton University Press.

Kindelberger, Charles P. 1973. *The World in Depression, 1929–1939*. Berkeley: University of California Press.

Krasner, Stephen D., ed. 1983. *International Regimes*. Ithaca, N.Y.: Cornell University Press.

Mitrany, David. 1966. *A Working Peace System*. Chicago: Quadrangle.

Monnet, Jean. 1978. *Memoirs*. New York: Doubleday.

Nye, Joseph S. 1971. *Peace in Parts: Integration and Conflict in Regional Organizations*. Boston: Little, Brown.

Peck, Richard. 1979. Socialization of Permanent Representatives in the United Nations: Some Evidence. *International Organization* 33:365–90.

Putnam, Robert D. 1988. Diplomacy and Domestic Politics: The Logic of Two Level Games. *International Organization* 42.

Quester, George H., ed. 1981. *Nuclear Proliferation: Breaking the Chain*. Madison: University of Wisconsin Press.

Renwick, Robin. 1981. *Economic Sanctions*. Cambridge, Mass.: Harvard University, Center for International Affairs.

Rovine, Arthur W. 1970. *The First Fifty Years: The Secretary-General in World Politics, 1920–1970*. Leyden: A. W. Sijhoff.

Russett, Bruce M. 1967. *International Regions and the International System: A Study in Political Ecology*. Chicago: Rand McNally.

Scheinman, Lawrence. 1987. *The International Atomic Energy Agency and World Nuclear Order*. Washington, D.C.: Resources for the Future.

Souleyman, Elizabeth V. 1941. *The Vision of World Peace in the Seventeenth and Eighteenth Centuries*. New York: Putnam.

Talbot, Strobe. 1979. *Endgame: The Inside Story of SALT II*. New York: Harper and Row.

Urquhart, Brian. 1972. *Hammarskjold*. New York: Alfred A. Knopf.

Walters, F.P.A. 1952. *A History of the League of Nations*. London: Oxford University Press, 2 vols.

Waltz, Kenneth N. 1959. *Man, the State, and War: A Theoretical Analysis*. New York: Columbia University Press.

Young, Oran R. 1967. *The Intermediaries: Third Parties in International Crises*. Princeton, n.p.: Princeton University Press.

PART IV

SURMOUNTING FORCE AND THREATS

13

On Creating Security Systems

FRANCIS A. BEER

International security and insecurity define a central dimension of the modern world system. International security suggests peaceful change, whereas insecurity implies substantial violence. There is obviously a subjective, psychological component to security and insecurity (Lasswell, 1965). At the same time, objective factors—such as the past history of peaceful change and violence, the distribution of power and wealth, and other elements of the international system—are also important (see Deutsch et al., 1959).

Paradoxically, the world today is at once more secure and more insecure than in the past. On the one hand, there appears to be a long-run general historical trend toward the diffusion of peace. Wars have become less frequent, and the periods of tranquility between them are longer than they were in earlier times. At the same time, wars are more concentrated and severe. When wars occur, they are shorter, but casualties have increased both in absolute terms and relative to population (Beer, 1974).

This overall trend is not necessarily reflected in the histories of particular nation-states. In the United States, periods of major international peace have become more frequent and shorter. During the nineteenth century, peace periods between major U.S. wars extended from thirteen to thirty-three years. During the twentieth century, these peace periods became briefer, ranging from five to twenty-three years. Major wars necessarily have also become more frequent. The length of major wars shows no clear overall trend, although there is reason to believe that they have become longer in our own time. The war in Vietnam, lasting 141 months, was the longest in U.S. history. Major war casualties have increased absolutely, though not relative to population (Beer, 1983).

The work reported in this chapter was carried out in the Program on Peace and War, Center for International Relations, at the University of Colorado.

INSECURITY REDUCTION

One major approach to international security and insecurity has been to accept the international system as given and to try to alleviate its most extreme dangers. This position leads to a focus on insecurity reduction through policies of strategic deterrence, arms control, and the direct limitation of violence.

Strategic Deterrence and Arms Control

Strategic deterrence and arms control concentrate on the military sector of the international system. Strategic deterrence is "the threat to use force in response as a way of preventing the first use of force by someone else" (Morgan, 1977, p. 9). Such deterrence has been quite popular through history (see Naroll, Bullough, and Naroll, 1974), but the advent of nuclear weapons has given it a whole new dimension.

Historical precedents reinforce strategic deterrence. Thus, the traditional interpretation of World War II holds that strong Allied military capabilities and resolve during the 1930s would have helped keep the peace much more effectively than appealing to the higher values of democracy or Western civilization. Lack of Western military preparedness and commitment encouraged the Axis powers to move into areas like Czechoslovakia, Ethiopia, and Manchuria. Once World War II had begun in earnest, Western rearmament and resistance eventually slowed enemy advances and turned the tide, bringing victory for the Allies and a return to a relatively free post-war international order.

History also provides examples to buttress arms control. At the end of World War I, Germany and Austria-Hungary were labeled aggressors and were forced to pay heavy reparations through the Treaty of Versailles. Nevertheless, Kaiser Wilhelm II and Kaiser Franz Josef were no Hitlers. This conflict was one that nobody really seemed to want, fueled less by blatant aggression than by international instabilities (Aronson, 1986). Many observers of World War I believe that the spirited naval competition between Germany and Britain at the beginning of the twentieth century particularly encouraged the onset of hostilities (Art, 1973). Once war had begun, the speed of movement, the destructive power of weapons, and the German strategic position between two sets of major adversaries accelerated the military timetable. The German Schlieffen Plan hoped to turn the nightmare of a simultaneous two-front war into the more benign reality of two consecutive one-front wars. Under this plan, the Germans would first strike rapidly to the west, through the Lowlands into France. A quick victory there would free them to turn and move in full strength against the Russians in the East. In retrospect, it now seems inevitable that the military configuration that existed at the beginning of the twentieth century would put a major war beyond the control of any human being.

Highly developed offensive and defensive capabilities extracted a heavy toll in blood and treasure from the major European powers. The destruction of this war—the sacrifice of a whole generation—sent Europe into shock. In a sense, it never recovered. The Great War contradicted the whole liberal philosophy of human progress and perfectibility, and opened the door to nihilism. As a result of both world wars, the world position of some nations like Britain, France, and Germany greatly declined. Others, like Austria-Hungary, were dismembered. Western Europe, formerly a great civilization and the core of a Eurocentric world order, is now only one among many competing centers in the contemporary world system.

Strategic deterrence and arms control advocates apply the lessons derived from history to present problems of international security and insecurity (Neustadt and May, 1986). Proponents of strategic deterrence are adamant that no modern Munich must occur. As Thomas Jefferson suggested, eternal vigilance is the price of liberty. Nuclear preparedness and the military development of outer space are necessary to prevent a surprise first strike out of the blue, a present-day Pearl Harbor (Hybel, 1986).

Arms control enthusiasts focus their attention more closely on the parallels with World War I. Like Germany and England, both the United States and the Soviet Union see the other as aggressive, yet neither seems to want a nuclear World War III. Strong military competition, like the Anglo-German naval race, however, has a life of its own (Russett, 1983). Strategic weapons systems now include over 50,000 nuclear warheads (Arkin and Fieldhouse, 1985; cf. U.N. Secretary General, 1981), and new technology is rapidly moving the arms race into space. Contemporary "launch under attack" doctrine carries the same implication as did the Schlieffen Plan for rapid use of major force (Ford, 1985; Bracken, 1983). Arms control is necessary to prevent the twentieth-century world from following the self-destructive dynamic of nineteenth-century Europe.

Limitation of Violence

Strategic deterrence and arms control are two ways of reducing international insecurity. Other methods concentrate more directly on limiting international violence. These include the rational management of international crises that might lead to war, and of wars themselves once they occur. Restraint and the development of non-violent techniques may also be important.

Crisis Management. A crisis is a situation that has a high probability of resulting in war. The more serious the war is likely to be, the more serious the crisis will be. Crisis management implies special vigilance and control in such situations (Frei, 1982; Brecher, 1979; Hermann, 1969, 1972; Holsti, 1972).

The first step is to identify areas or nations at high risk of violence. One early social scientific attempt to do this was a survey of experts in January 1937. It ranked nations according to the estimated probabilities that they would go to war in the near future, and it appears to have been reasonably accurate (Wright, 1942–1965, p. 1478). Modern survey research, events–interaction data, and aggregate indicators offer possibilities for similar monitoring that might support national crisis management centers.

Special arrangements during routine periods may help to restrain crises when they erupt. These include crisis training for decision-makers, crisis communication networks, special provisions for accidents, avoidance of direct engagement of the military forces of major powers with each other, shunning of alerts and mobilizations for signalling purposes, increased reliance on conventional forces, and contingency plans for delayed rather than early launch of nuclear weapons. Such arrangements are most likely to be effective if conducted together with both allies and potential adversaries (Allison, Carnesale, and Nye, 1985; Blechman, 1985; Burton, 1969).

As crises evolve, high-level political committees can concentrate responsibility and detailed oversight. Under the direct supervision of the highest political authority, they may take charge of information gathering and analysis, elaboration of policy options, evaluation of contingency plans, and finally of actions taken. President Kennedy's handling of the Cuban missile crisis provides a good example of this procedure at work (Kennedy, 1969).

War Management. When war does occur, a conscious, organized effort at war management may help prevent smaller incidents of violence from turning into larger ones, keep limited wars limited, and preclude substantial wars from becoming total.

War management suggests the development of military plans that aim strictly at combatants rather than civilians. Furthermore, it implies the elaboration of battlefield command and control structures to contain violence. Remote monitoring devices, including the use of satellite surveillance, may enhance the integrity of political and military command and leadership. Training personnel in limited reaction should help to strictly control firing situations. Such surveillance and training might, for example, have prevented the My Lai atrocities during the Vietnam War (Goldstein, Marshall, and Schwartz, 1976).

War management also includes the recognition that both victory and defeat may be legitimate outcomes of a given war. Some wars may be fought for very small stakes or may only be winnable at enormous costs. The benefits and costs of particular conflicts should be weighed as carefully and precisely as possible during their progress, and steps should be taken to reduce and terminate wars as early as possible. A strategy of war limitation, together with specific planning and training, would make it easier for national leaders to cut their losses quickly in such situations (Beer and Mayer, 1986).

Restraint. Our discussion of crisis and war management has already suggested that restraint of violence is an important path to reducing international insecurity. Waging war has often seemed to be a device for creating peace. Traditional analysis of international relations has seen military intervention and preventive war as processes of conflict management. A big stick may not transform wolves into lambs, but at least it helps keep them out of the fold. Doctrines of military intervention or preventive war perceive violence as a good investment: A little now avoids more later. This was the logic of those who argued the need to stand up to Hitler much earlier in the 1930s. Similarly, international violence can supposedly work against domestic violence in other societies. Leaders of national states often see themselves in the role of world policemen. Thus, one of the justifications for U.S. intervention in the Third World during the post–World War II period was to avoid the bloodshed that would presumably occur following Communist takeover (Klare, 1972; Rostow, 1960). Military action, it was argued, would prevent the disease of violence from running its course. By similar reasoning, domestic violence might also limit war. Societies experiencing considerable domestic violence might be too preoccupied to undertake international conflicts. Either weariness or the pressures of domestic survival would limit external aggressive behavior (Beer, 1981: pp. 55–68).

The argument for military intervention and preventive war is not only plausible but also seductive. Force offers simple solutions to aggravating problems, for example, in the Middle East or Central America. Unfortunately, there is little evidence to support the belief that the cure is better than the disease. In fact, it may be worse. The therapeutic benefits of violence are far from certain. Thus, a recent study of the historical use of U.S. armed forces, without major war, found that they often influenced events favorably "from the perspective of U.S. decision makers—at least in the short term. In a very large proportion of the incidents, however, this 'success rate' eroded sharply over time." Such use of military forces "served mainly to delay unwanted developments abroad" (Blechman et al., 1978, p. 517).

Some theorists suggest that war produces subsequent resistance to violence (Richardson, 1960); yet even if this were true, such resistance would not logically extend beyond the geographical boundaries of prior violence. Even within those boundaries, it might be only a partial resistance. Resistance is also impermanent. Opposition to war in general would presumably fade with the passage of time, the blurring of memory, and the arrival of new, presumably non-resistant generations.

The future benefits of violence are problematic; the immediate costs— casualties and physical damage—are much more real. People are killed and injured; limited "brushfire" wars sometimes spread out of control, expanding dramatically in space, time, and weapons. It seems more prudent to shy away from using violence as a tool and, instead, to try and prevent it from breaking out or, once it has occurred, to attempt to limit it.

Non-violence. The limitation of violence implies a greater emphasis on non-violence as a warfighting technique.

Non-violence is as old as the history of religious leaders and movements. Traditions embodied by Buddha and Christ have inspired successful modern political movements and leaders. The Indian struggle for independence under the leadership of Gandhi and the struggle of the American blacks for greater equality under the leadership of Martin Luther King, Jr., are but two modern examples.

Non-violence cannot be used by all actors in all environments. Most human beings are different from Buddha, Christ, Gandhi, and Martin Luther King, Jr. The delayed benefits of non-violence, coupled with the substantial discipline required and pain incurred, are likely to make it a choice immediately beyond many of us. Some environments, like the twentieth-century British Empire and the United States, are more suitable for this kind of activity. Yet, even here, there are specific limits to applicability. Pacifism in the United States during World War II was so foreign to popular cultural ideas as to be simply unthinkable for most of the population. Non-violent attitudes were seen as cowardice, subversion, or even treason. In other environments, like Nazi Germany, non-violence seems even less appropriate. Pacifism may imply passivism, acquiescence, or even collaboration in violent acts by others. For example, many of the Jews incarcerated in the concentration camps of Nazi Germany during the 1930s walked docilely into the gas chambers and in some cases even helped capture others who attempted to escape.

Nevertheless, non-violence can succeed in appropriate situations. The expansion of knowledge about non-violent methods, training in them, and their application where possible would probably do a substantial amount to reduce both the incidence and casualties of war (Sharp, 1985, 1973; Seeley, 1982; Roberts, 1969).

CREATION OF SECURITY

Policies of insecurity reduction—strategic deterrence, arms control, and violence limitation—are proposed as major solutions to contemporary international problems. They appeal to most people because they deal directly with weapons and the use of force in international relations, and they promise practical results. They are limited, however, because they focus on immediately observable symptoms rather than on deeper underlying causes.

Policies of security creation go beyond exploitation or buffering of the existing international system. Such policies seek to reform, reconstruct, and ultimately to transcend the system, to shape the surrounding environment in such a way that it is stronger and less vulnerable to violence. They aim to change both the international superstructure and the international infrastructure, to tie the world together and break down divisions between its parts. They focus on balancing and restructuring the world system.

Balancing

International balancing is an attempt to rearrange the importance of, and relations between, the different levels of the system. The traditional view of international relations has been very state-centered. Historically, the international system has consisted of states with sovereignty, and only states could be subjects of international law. Balancing begins from the premise that the national level is overdeveloped and might usefully be constrained or even diminished. The international, transnational, group, and individual levels are too limited and might be enhanced.

World Order. World order proposals have a strong "top-down" emphasis. One strand of world order—world federalism—implies that the most desirable approach would be the creation of a single effective world government, perhaps modeled along the lines of modern federal polities, with lawmaking authority. If total unification is not possible, then a partial core union might serve as a growth center for the larger global enterprise (Clark and Sohn, 1966; Streit, 1949).

Failing such an ambitious solution, world order approaches the globe as a developing country and aims to forge strong superordinate strands of cohesion. World order implies support for continued international legal codification; signature and ratification of, and compliance with, multilateral treaties, agreements, and declarations; international courts and other attempts at adjudication, arbitration, mediation, and conciliation of conflicts and disputes; participation in, contributions to, and compliance with international organizations and collective decisions reached in them; development of and participation in international transactions, including trade; establishment of substantial global reserves of commodities in short supply such as money, food, and energy; and increased international communication through such means as diplomacy, travel, media, and education (Falk, 1975; Mendlovitz, 1975).

This aspect of world order, seeking to tie nations and peoples together through strands of cooperation, is valuable but partial. No connective bonds can hold together a world system whose other dynamics pull it apart. It must, therefore, be supplemented by other elements, one of which is international functionalism.

International Functionalism. International functionalism comes to the world system with less sweeping ambitions. International functionalists tend not to believe in grand solutions to world problems; instead, they take a more piecemeal approach. Following functionalist logic, nations and groups can best build international security by cooperating on specific projects, one at a time (Sewall, 1975; Lindberg and Scheingold, 1970; Beer, 1969; Mitrany, 1966; Haas, 1964). Such cooperation implies different regimes in different sectors. For example, one set of international cooperative arrangements may exist with regard to the law of the sea, another for trade in oil, and a third for nuclear weapons (Keohane, 1984; Krasner, 1982).

International functionalism may contribute to international security by confusing relations between enemies and transforming them, to some extent, into allies. For example, functionalism suggests that nations in different political blocs should develop cross-cutting activities involving economic assistance, trade, cultural, and scientific exchange. These relations involve the gradual growth of common interests that can soften the sharp edges of inter-bloc hostility and thereby lessen the structural tendencies to war. Sometimes trading partners may side together on specific issues, rather than always with their bloc partners. Cooperative tendencies should multiply as patterns of exchange and communication become more diffuse between Western and Eastern, Northern and Southern states.

Softening and Shrinking the Nation-State. The most controversial aspect of balancing involves softening and shrinking the nation-state, which has been the basic building block of the modern international system. The nation-state and nationalism have been, and will continue to be, central elements of the global system. They combine subordinate groups, with diverse identities and interests, into political communities with shared territory and aspirations. Yet the sharp edges of nations, like those of international blocs, increase the structural tendencies to violence. National aggrandizement is an important force leading to war. Expanding states exert lateral pressure on others that, feeling threatened, attempt to defend themselves (Choucri and North, 1975; Organski and Kugler, 1980).

Natural evolution and adaptation may limit national expansion. Over the course of history, many small tribes, fiefdoms, and principalities have combined into larger nations. This tendency is probably still continuing in many places. But some nation-states, like Austria-Hungary of the nineteenth century or the overseas European colonial empires, may have been too large. They have disappeared. Modern movements for national self-determination may further encourage the nation-state writ small (Kohr, 1978; Schumacher, 1973).

Constructive change may include broadening international leadership, so that it is less specifically tied to major nation-states. Historically, the political leaders of major powers have dominated international decision-making. Nevertheless, leaders of medium-size and smaller states have recently begun to play a more significant role. Smaller Western and Eastern European states as well as Southern nations have participated actively in the international arena. Officials from provincial or local communities have also begun to become active in international politics through economic attempts to increase international business and political activities, like sister city programs (Alger, 1977). International leadership need not be limited to political elites. The growth of international law, organization, transaction, and communication has given important international responsibilities to hosts of civil servants, businesspeople, educators, scientists, and artists. These developments have their own natural energy and should be encouraged.

We might reduce our concern for national security. Some analysts have suggested that we live in the age of the national security state whose dynamics work against international security (Herz, 1976; Barnet, 1973). National security in the dangerous world of interstate rivalry and violence requires both external and internal vigilance. Rivalry leads to war, and violence to repression. Such repression goes against the deepest aspirations of traditional democratic theory, which represents a reaction to absolute rule—an attempt to limit and confine it, to make it more rational, predictable, and routine. As states go down this road, their leaders become progressively freer of internal constraints on violence and simultaneously more prone to use it (Lasswell 1969, 1962, 1941). Movement in the opposite direction would involve greater political openness with particular emphasis on political participation, due process, and group and individual rights.

We might also give less attention to the claims of national interest. The national interest is the most important justification for war. Accepted theory suggests that states either should or do fight only or mainly in support of their national interests (Clausewitz, 1968; Morgenthau, 1951). While this proposition is widely accepted, it need not be taken uncritically at face value. The concept of national interest is widely used, but its meaning is not particularly clear. Beyond its focus on the material concerns of the nation-state, national interest presents no firm, objective guidelines for decision-making (Robinson, 1969). National interest need not always be the sole criterion for foreign policymaking (Wolfers, 1962). Furthermore, the national interest often works against the interests of higher and lower levels of political communities, which are called on to make sacrifices in its name. A broader conception of the goals of foreign policy would enhance international security by allowing more room for non-national and non-material aims.

We might also work at decentralizing national politics, economics, and culture. Although collective national enterprises may be required in many areas, specific regional and local activities, tailored to the interests of smaller communities, are also important.

Popular nationalism is one of the great forces leading to international violence. National bonding and the myth of the nation grip human beings all over the world and glorify the deaths of military heroes, soldiers, and ordinary citizens for their country (Kohn, 1965; Hayes, 1948; Cassirer, 1946–1967). This popular identification with the nation-state stands in the way of developing a broader pattern of overlapping international loyalties (Beer, 1985). No international community or ideal can compete with national symbols as justifications for foreign policy or personal sacrifice. Some progress in demythologizing the nation, and in identifying with other levels of community, would help to moderate the worst excesses of military zeal.

Group and Human Rights. Balancing at the lowest level of world system includes human rights—the protection and development of individual human beings. Our approach to the creation of security includes a premise that a strong and healthy system grows through the growth of its component parts rather than at their expense (Clark, 1977).

One of the most important human rights involves the freedom of association, people's right to form groups of their own choosing. These groups may safeguard religious, linguistic, and ethnic values dear to their members. We may think of these groups, through a derivative process, to be imbued with rights themselves. Nation-states themselves are examples of such groups. But groups binding people across and within nation-states deserve similar consideration. We see the rule most clearly in the exceptions—for example, genocidal campaigns waged against Armenians and Jews.

Another important human right is individual identity—clear status for individuals in the global system. While this seems obvious in theory, it is less evident in fact. Only recently have nations, and the few individuals making national decisions, begun to relinquish their monopoly as subjects in international law and as actors in international organizations and diplomacy. Ordinary people have always had clearer profiles in international economic, social, cultural, and scientific endeavors, and this pattern should further be imitated in politics. A good example of progress is the creation and growth of the European Court of Human Rights.

Human rights also include the enhancement of other major liberties, such as those enshrined in widely recognized documents like the United Nations' Universal Declaration of Human Rights and subsequent international covenants that codify civil, political, economic, social, and cultural rights. Such human rights can appear in a negative light, as individual boundaries that cannot be infringed upon by larger groups, including the nation-state. But they can also be seen much more positively as encompassing rights to the means for individual security and growth, the right to a fair share of global benefits, and the requirement to bear a fair share of the costs of its operation (Rawls, 1971).

Finally, an emphasis on human rights highlights the importance of individual interests, including what may be the most important individual right or interest, individual survival. These interests may be valid even when they seem to be opposed to the interests of larger groups. A basic human right would seem to be the right to calculate one's own interests, whether correctly or incorrectly. This right would include an assessment of one's obligations to the state and the possibility of conscientious objection to policies and actions that seem inappropriate (Walzer, 1970).

Restructuring

We have seen that security creation involves balancing relations *between* levels of the international system. A second major task of security creation is to restructure processes and activities *within* different levels of the international system. International restructuring includes demilitarization, as well as enhancement of equality and stability.

Demilitarization. The creation of security implies demilitarization at the international, domestic, and individual levels. It obviously means arms control but involves other elements as well. For example, international demilitarization means downgrading the law of war, at least those aspects of it that permit violence. This involves reducing the legal justifications for undertaking war and permissible wartime activities.

International organizations might place less emphasis on military tasks. International military peacekeeping has sometimes seemed to be an essential condition of international peace. Provisions for it appear in the U.N. Charter, and a host of U.N. peacekeeping operations have been initiated in various parts of the world (International Peace Academy, 1984; Rikhye, 1984; Wiseman, 1983). This approach might receive less attention in the future. Peaceful methods of settling disputes should become more important (Wehr, 1979).

The alliance aspects of international life might gradually be reduced. Regional military activity is suggested by Articles 51–54 of the U.N. Charter. Regional international organization is much broader than these alliances. The non-military dimensions of cooperation might receive greater attention, while military tasks could gradually be diminished. For example, the OECD might supersede NATO as a focus of Atlantic cooperation.

International demilitarization implies a real hesitancy in using techniques such as blockades and embargoes that withhold goods and services critical to the welfare of others. In addition, it entails explicit attempts to diminish international hostility. National leaders and media might try to avoid threatening gestures and words. They might work against international confrontation and personal hostility toward other leaders or peoples. Instead, they could attempt to carefully define and articulate specific issues of disagreement and reduce them.

National demilitarization involves subordinating the military sector of society. It means reducing standing armies both absolutely and relative to national populations, and lowering military budgets, in absolute numbers as well as relative to national productivity and expenditure. It suggests replacing the military draft with voluntary military service. It involves reducing secret police and clandestine intelligence activities. It includes efforts at domestic arms control, reducing armament levels of society in general. At the same time, it implies less police armament and more training in non-violent techniques. Finally, national demilitarization means reducing the use of military metaphors, analogies, images, and symbols in media and education.

Individual demilitarization also comprehends a number of elements. Individual demilitarization includes more comprehensive attempts to help those returning from wars and military service to readjust to civilian life. It also involves support for a more widespread recognition of the history and value of conscientious objection to war and violence. It comprehends refusal to undertake military service and the performance of substitute service. It includes resistance to paying taxes for military purposes and earmarking such funds for other uses. Conscientious objection has a long history in Western society. Many of the first communities in the United States were settled by conscientious objectors, and their legacy has been carried forward into modern times (Mameli, 1985; Seeley, 1982; Brock, 1968, 1972; Chatfield, 1973).

A strategy of individual demilitarization recognizes the aggressive dynamic of human beings. At the same time, it calls for the sublimation of aggressive behavior into less harmful ritualistic channels such as sports or socially constructive activities that can be a "moral equivalent of war" (James, 1958, p. 284).

A program of individual demilitarization accepts the necessity for conflict, struggle, and confrontation but refuses to endorse violence as an acceptable method for social change. It insists that the means used to produce social change are as important as the ends sought and searches for alternatives to violence as ways of producing progress. Individual demilitarization downgrades the use of violence or coercion to achieve or defend other values. It deemphasizes negative reinforcement such as punishment and threat. It stresses cooperation and consensus, with positive rewards and the promise of healthy, individual growth.

Equality and Stability. Restructuring the international system also means moving toward greater equality and stability. The ideas already presented for creating greater balance between levels of the system point in this direction. World order, international functionalism, denationalization, and emphasis on human rights also imply a more equal sharing of power, wealth, and knowledge—and responsibility. More groups and actors can participate actively in various dimensions of the world environment. As they articulate and defend their own particular concerns, they will also contribute their resources to the development of a shared human community.

International balancing also carries a stabilizing logic. Rapid change benefits some but not all. The losers from rapid and discontinuous growth may have a better chance to smooth the curve of change, as the world environment becomes more open and more densely interconnected.

A policy such as the one we are outlining obviously cannot be implemented all at once through a sudden, apocalyptic global revolution. Rather, it must take place gradually over time, through evolution. Revolutionary change is dramatic, but, by historical definition, it often carries with it a good deal of violence. The great revolutions of the modern world—France, the United States, the Soviet Union, China, the Third World—have been associated with important changes. Nevertheless, many beneficial developments might well have taken place without violent revolution. It is not clear, in any event, that violent revolution necessarily improves international security.

Constructive actions can and should be undertaken incrementally, in small pieces, as experiments. Policymakers should define their expected impacts in advance and then monitor the results to see if they achieve the anticipated results. If so, additional steps can be taken; if not, little will be lost. Whether the actions succeed or fail, policymakers will have a systematic basis for learning and innovation. They can subsequently try new and better policies aiming at the same end.

THE PROMISE OF INTERNATIONAL SECURITY

Our discussion has suggested a number of possible paths for limiting international insecurity and creating greater international security. Strategic deterrence and arms control are minimalist, narrowly defined, specific, short-term approaches. Limitation of violence includes various strands, some of which, like crisis management and war management, are easily applicable to specific situations. Other strands, like restraint and non-violence, are more difficult in the current context of international politics. Balancing the levels of the international system through world order, functionalism, denational-ization, human rights—and restructuring it by demilitarization, equalization, and stabilization—are obviously maximalist, difficult, and distant goals.

It is often assumed that many of the paths presented here are mutually exclusive; national security versus international security, strategic deterrence versus arms control, short versus long run, practical versus visionary. There certainly are trade-offs between them; yet some of the trade-offs may be more apparent than real. For example, our present discussion began with an ex-ample of the complementarity of perceived opposites, the contemporary growth of both international security and international insecurity.

We usually believe that advances in deterrence will set back arms control, or that progress in arms control or demilitarization will hinder deterrence. This is not necessarily true; indeed, deterrence and arms control may, to some extent, be preconditions for each other. If deterrence were completely assured, arms control might become easier in areas that were not deemed essential to national security. If arms control existed to a greater degree, deterrence might be more effective or less important.

The Strategic Defense Initiative offers a striking example of this comple-mentarity. Space-based strategic technology will be deployed primarily to provide deterrence (Jastrow, 1985). Yet much of it will also provide the ability to monitor and enforce arms control. Its vulnerability to attack will, in turn, require arms control measures to ensure its safety.

The short and the long run, the practical and the visionary, are not always at odds. Short run practical considerations are necessary for us to navigate the shoals and narrows of our present-day world, but we also need the vision of a fixed star to steer a course for the long voyage. Even if several of the approaches were mutually exclusive at the present time, they must not nec-essarily be opposed through all future time. Present contradictions may be resolved through subsequent deconstruction, recombination, and synthesis at a higher level.

We may think of a very complex process, or a large set of simultaneous processes, in which multiple actors attempt a variety of possible solutions to a great global problem. Existing reality, including both actors and environment, is continually dissolving and reforming in new, previously unimagined ways. An example is the way in which the League of Nations, United Nations, and networks of specialized agencies, regional organizations, and non-governmental international organizations have proliferated during a century of international violence, including two world wars and an armed conflict in Africa, Asia, Latin America, and the Middle East.

Some of the solutions proposed here will succeed at least partly; others will fail. We cannot, however, predict in advance which policies will fall in which category. If we could do so, we should have complete knowledge of the consequences of our action or inaction, and our problem would be either trivial or hopeless. The answer to this question lies in future evolution and learning.

Some of the paths that seem most realistic, modest, and practical may prove unexpectedly difficult, while others that seem fantasies may actually be realized. Who, in 1900, would have thought that the tough-minded European statesmen were wrong—and that the security meticulously guaranteed by networks of interlocking European alliances and undergirded with prestigious and powerful military establishments would fail as dramatically as it did in 1914? Who, at the apogee of royal elegance and imperial expansion, would have predicted a total restructuring of domestic and international politics—with the ruling houses of Europe virtually swept away? Who would have believed that the Russia of Czar Nicholas II would fall to a Communist revolution; that the Austro-Hungarian empire of Kaiser Franz Josef, whose political history went back centuries, would collapse and virtually disappear; that the proud and militaristic Germany of Kaiser Wilhelm II would be gutted and partitioned; that the British Empire, on which the sun never set, would shrink away to almost nothing.

Contemporary international insecurity is symbolized by a range of potential violence from central nuclear war to peripheral terrorism. The threat is very immediate. The promise of international security appears to us now only as a distant chimera. Nevertheless, a larger vision, a longer term agenda, may help decrease international insecurity and increase international security.

Survival and reform are not enemies. Both are important components of a comprehensive, coherent, and constructive international security policy.

REFERENCES

Alger, C. 1977. Foreign Policies of U.S. Publics. *International Studies Quarterly* 21 (June):277–318.

Allison, G. T., A. Carnesale, and J. S. Nye, Jr. 1985. *Hawks, Owls, and Doves: An Agenda for Avoiding Nuclear War.* New York: W. W. Norton.

Arkin, W. M., and R. W. Fieldhouse. 1985. *Nuclear Battlefields: Global Links in the Arms Race.* Cambridge, Mass.: Ballinger.

Aronson, T. 1986. *Crowns in Conflict: The Triumph and Tragedy of European Monarchy, 1910–1918*. Topfield, Mass.: Salem House.

Art, R. J. 1973. *The Influence of Foreign Policy on Seapower: New Weapons and Weltpolitik in Wilhelminian Germany*. Beverly Hills, Calif.: Sage Publications.

Barnet, R. J. 1973. *The Roots of War: The Men and Institutions Behind U.S. Foreign Policy*. New York: Penguin Books.

Beer, F. A. 1985. Multiple Loyalties and Alienation. In M. D. Ward, ed., *Theories, Models, and Simulations in International Relations: Essays in Honor of Harold Guetzkow*.

———. 1983. Trends in American Major War and Peace. *Journal of Conflict Resolution* 27 (4):661–86.

———. 1981. *Peace Against War: The Ecology of International Violence*. San Francisco: W. H. Freeman.

———. 1974. *How Much War in History: Definitions, Estimates, Extrapolations and Trends*. Beverly Hills, Calif.: Sage Publications.

———. 1969. *Integration and Disintegration in NATO: Processes of Alliance Cohesion and Prospects for Atlantic Community*. Columbus: Ohio State University Press.

———, and T. F. Mayer. 1986. Why Wars End: Some Hypotheses. *Review of International Studies* 12:95–106.

Blechman, B. M., ed. 1985. *Preventing Nuclear War: A Realistic Approach*. Bloomington: Indiana University Press.

———, et al. 1978. *Force Without War: U.S. Armed Forces as a Political Instrument*. Washington, D.C.: Brookings Institution.

Boulding, K. E. 1956. *The Image: Knowledge in Life and Society*. Ann Arbor: University of Michigan Press.

Bracken, P. 1983. *The Command and Control of Nuclear Forces*. New Haven, Conn.: Yale University Press.

Brecher, M., ed. 1979. *Studies in Crisis Behavior*. New Brunswick, N.J.: Transaction Books.

Brock, O. 1972. *Pacifism in Europe to 1914*. Princeton, N.J.: Princeton University Press.

———. 1968. *Pacifism in the United States: From the Colonial Era to the First World War*. Princeton, N.J.: Princeton University Press.

Burton, J. W. 1969. *Conflict and Communication: The Use of Controlled Communication in International Relations*. London: Macmillan.

Cassirer, E. 1946–1967. *The Myth of the State*. New Haven, Conn.: Yale University Press.

Chatfield, C., ed. 1973. *Peace Movements in America*. New York: Schocken Books.

Choucri, N., and R. North. 1975. *Nations in Conflict: National Growth and International Violence*. San Francisco: W. H. Freeman.

Clark, G., and L. B. Sohn. 1966. *World Peace Through World Law: Two Alternative Plans*, 3rd. ed. Cambridge, Mass.: Harvard University Press.

Clark, J. R. 1977. *The Great Living System*. Pacific Grove, Calif.: Boxwood.

Clausewitz, K. von. 1968. *On War*. A. Rapoport, ed. Baltimore: Penguin Books.

Deutsch, K. W., et al. 1959. *Political Security and the North Atlantic Area*. Princeton, N.J.: Princeton University Press.

Falk, R. 1975. *A Study of Future Worlds*. New York: Free Press.

Ford, D. 1985. *The Button: The Pentagon's Strategic Command and Control System*. New York: Simon and Schuster.

Frei, D., ed. 1982. *Managing International Crises*. Beverly Hills, Calif.: Sage Publications.

Goldstein, J., B. Marshall, and J. Schwartz. 1976. *The My Lai Massacre and Its Cover-Up: Beyond the Reach of Law?* The Peers Commission Report with a Supplement and Introductory Essay on the Limits of Law. New York: Free Press.

Haas, E. B. 1964. *Beyond the Nation-State*. Stanford, Calif.: Stanford University Press.

Hayes, C. 1948. *The Historical Evolution of Modern Nationalism*. New York: Macmillan.

Hermann, C., ed. 1972. *International Crisis: Insights from Behavioral Research*. New York: Free Press.

———. 1969. *Crises in Foreign Policy: A Simulation Analysis*. Indianapolis, Ind.: Bobbs-Merrill.

Herz, J. H. 1976. *The Nation-State and the Crisis of World Politics*. New York: David McKay.

Holsti, O. 1972. *Crisis, Escalation, War*. Montreal: McGill-Queens University Press.

Hybel, A. R. 1986. *The Logic of Surprise in International Conflict*. Lexington, Mass.: Lexington Books.

International Peace Academy. 1984. *Peacekeeper's Handbook*. New York: Pergamon.

James, W. 1958. *The Varieties of Religious Experience: A Study in Human Nature*. New York: Mentor.

Jastrow, R. 1985. *How to Make Nuclear Weapons Obsolete*. Boston: Little, Brown.

Kennedy, R. F. 1969. *Thirteen Days: A Memoir of the Cuban Missile Crisis*. New York: W. W. Norton.

Keohane, R. O. 1984. *After Hegemony: Cooperation and Discord in the World Political Economy*. Princeton, N.J.: Princeton University Press.

Klare, M. T. 1972. *War Without End: American Planning for the Next Vietnams*. New York: Alfred A. Knopf.

Kohn, H. 1965. *Nationalism: Its Meaning and History*. New York: Van Nostrand.

Kohr, L. 1978. *The Breakdown of Nations*. New York: E. P. Dutton.

Krasner, S. D., ed. 1982. *International Regimes*, Special Issue of *International Organization* 36:2. Cambridge, Mass.

Lasswell, H. D. 1969. *Psychopathology and Politics*. New York: Viking Press.

———. 1965. *World Politics and Personal Insecurity*. New York: Free Press.

———. 1962. The Garrison-State Hypothesis Today. In S. P. Huntington, ed., *Changing Patterns of Military Politics*. New York: Free Press.

———. 1941. The Garrison State. *American Journal of Sociology* 46 (January):455–68.

Lindberg, L. N., and S. A. Scheingold. 1970. *Europe's Would-Be Polity: Patterns of Change in the European Community*. Englewood Cliffs, N.J.: Prentice-Hall.

Mameli, P. A. 1985. The Evolution of the American Peace Movement in the Colonial Era. Unpublished M. A. Thesis. Boulder: University of Colorado.

Mendlovitz, S. 1975. *On the Creation of a Just World Order: Preferred Worlds for the 1990's*. New York: Free Press.

Mitrany, D. 1966. *A Working Peace System*. Chicago: Quadrangle.

Morgan, P. M. 1977. *Deterrence: A Conceptual Analysis*. Beverly Hills, Calif.: Sage Publications.

Morgenthau, H. 1951. *In Defense of the National Interest: A Critical Examination of American Foreign Policy*. New York: Alfred A. Knopf.

Naroll, R., V. L. Bullough, and F. Naroll. 1974. *Military Deterrence in History: A Pilot Cross-Historical Survey*. Albany: State University of New York Press.

Neustadt, R. E., and E. R. May. 1986. *Thinking in Time: The Uses of History for Decision Makers*. New York: Free Press.

Olson, M. 1982. *The Rise and Decline of Nations: Economic Growth, Stagflation, and Social Rigidities*. New Haven: Yale University Press.

Organski, A.F.K., and J. Kugler. 1980. *The War Ledger*. Chicago: University of Chicago Press.

Nye, J. S., Jr. 1986. *Nuclear Ethics*. New York: Free Press.

Rawls, J. 1971. *A Theory of Justice*. Cambridge, Mass.: Belknap Press.

Richardson, L. F. 1960. *Statistics of Deadly Quarrels*. Pittsburgh and Chicago: Boxwood and Quadrangle.

Rikhye, I. J. 1984. *The Theory and Practice of Peacekeeping*. London: C. Hurst.

Roberts, A., ed. 1969. *Civilian Resistance as a National Defence: Non-Violent Action Against Aggression*. Baltimore: Penguin Books.

Robinson, T. W. 1969. National Interests. Pp. 182–90 in J. N. Rosenau, ed., *International Politics and Foreign Policy: A Reader in Research and Theory*. New York: Free Press.

Rostow, W. W. 1960. *The United States in the World Arena: An Essay in Recent History*. New York: Harper.

Russett, B. 1983. *Prisoners of Insecurity: Nuclear Deterrence, the Arms Race, and Arms Control*. San Francisco: W. H. Freeman.

Schumacher, E. F. 1973. *Small Is Beautiful: Economics as If People Mattered*. New York: Harper and Row.

Seeley, R. A., ed. 1982. *Handbook for Conscientious Objectors*. Philadelphia: Central Committee for Conscientious Objectors.

Sewall, J. P. 1975. *UNESCO and World Politics: Engaging in International Relations*. Princeton, N.J.: Princeton University Press.

Sharp, J. 1973. *The Politics of Nonviolent Action*. Boston: Porter Sargent.

———. 1985. *Making Europe Unconquerable: The Potential of Civilian-Based Deterrence and Defense*. Cambridge, Mass.: Ballinger.

Streit, C. 1949. *Union Now: A Proposal for an Atlantic Federal Union of the Free*. New York: Harper.

U.N. Secretary General. 1981. *Nuclear Weapons*. Brookline, Mass.: Atheneum.

Walzer, M. 1970. *Obligations: Essays on Disobedience, War, and Citizenship*. Cambridge, Mass.: Harvard University Press.

Wehr, P. 1979. *Conflict Regulation*. Boulder, Colo.: Westview Press.

Wiseman, H., ed. 1983. *Peacekeeping: Appraisals and Proposals*. New York: Pergamon.

Wolfers, A. 1962. *Discord and Collaboration: Essays on International Politics*. Baltimore: Johns Hopkins University Press.

Wright, Q. 1942–1965. *A Study of War*. Chicago: University of Chicago Press.

Index

U.S., 139; and rivalry with other states, 5; scientific research in, 123; support for NATO in, 171
Franz Joseph, 280, 292
Front: changing definition of, 59–60
Frunze, Mikhail Vasilyevich, 69

Gabon: French military bases in, 154
Galtung, Johan, 104
Gandhi, Mahatma, 284
Gansler, Jacques S., 77, 102, 103
Garrison state thesis, 234
Geneva Protocol for the Prohibition of the Use in War of Asphyxiating Poisons or Other Gases, and of Bacteriological Methods of Warfare, 269
George, Alexander L., 114
Germany: arms production in, 100; British competition with in naval capability, 66–67; British misperception of as military threat, 31, 37; expansionism of, 3; military bases in, 152, 153, 154, 157; military bases of, 141, 148; rearmament of, 270; and rivalry with other states, 5; security dilemma for, 38–39, 40. See also West Germany
Ghana: independence of, 240; U.S. military bases in, 143
Gibraltar: military base at 140, 149, 154
Gilbert, Felix, 184
Gilpatric, Roswell, 33
Gorbachev, Mikhail, 228
Gorschkov, Sergei G., 140, 158
Great Britain: and Agadir crisis, 49; anti-Americanism in, 170; arms production and sales by, 75, 83, 85, 100, 105; competition with Germany in naval capability, 66–67; defense spending in, 131, 132, 136 n.3; and Falkland Islands conflict, 36, 111; as launching point for U.S. air raid on Libya, 139; military bases in, 140, 156; military bases of, 140, 141, 144, 154, 158, 159; misperception of German military threat by, 31, 37; nuclear deterrence in, 173; nuclear weapons of, 8; and rivalry with other states, 5; scientific re-

search in, 123, 126–27. See also United Kingdom
Greece: U.S. military bases in, 139, 143
Greenland: U.S. military bases in, 143, 149, 154, 156
Grenada, 149, 152, 160, 193, 199
Ground equipment production: in developing countries, 9. See also Arms production
Group of 77. See United Nations, Group of 77 within
Guam: U.S. military bases in, 144, 154, 156

Haas, Ernst B., 266
Halperin, Morton, 214, 216
Hammarskjold, Dag, 265
Harmel Doctrine, 182
Hauser, William L., 238, 243
Head, Richard G., 99–100, 104
Heisenberg, Werner, 66
Heisenberg principle, 14
Helsinki Agreement (1975), 268
Herz, John, 97
Hines, John, 69
Hitler, Adolph, 27, 28, 29, 37
H.M.S. Dreadnought, 66
H.M.S. Invincible, 67
Hoadley, J. Stephen, 242
Hoffmann, Stanley, 159, 168
Holland: military bases in, 152, 153; military bases of, 140, 141, 158; nuclear deterrence in, 173; and rivalry with other states, 5
Holloway, David, 101
Hong Kong: British military deployment in, 154
Howard, Michael, 165, 168
Hubbard, Frank, 70
Hughes, Thomas P., 132
Human rights, 287–88
Huntington, Samuel P., 17, 160, 184, 191, 234, 236, 238, 241, 243, 245, 248

Iceland: military bases in, 143, 152, 153, 154, 156, 157
Iklé, Fred, 65

About the Contributors

FRANCIS A. BEER is Professor of Political Science at the University of Colorado, Boulder. His publications include: *Peace Against War: The Ecology of International Violence.* (1981); *How Much War in History: Definitions, Estimates Extrapolations, and Trends* (1975); *The Political Economy of Alliances: Benefits, Costs, and Institutions in NATO.* (1972); *Alliances: Latent War Communities in the Contemporary World* (editor, 1970); *Integration and Disintegration in NATO: Processes of Alliance Cohesion and Prospects for Atlantic Community* (1969). He is currently working on the psychology of international violence.

IAN BELLANY is Professor of Politics at the University of Lancaster, England, and Director of the Centre for the Study of Arms Control and International Security. His most recent book (jointly edited) is *New Conventional Weapons and Western Defence* (1987). He is founding editor of the journal *Arms Control.*

DAGOBERT L. BRITO is the Peterkin Professor of Political Economy at Rice University. He has taught at the University of Wisconsin, Madison; at Ohio State University, where he was a professor of Economics and of Political Science and fellow of the Mershon Center; and at Tulane University where he was director of the Murphy Institute. His research interests include arms races and war, topics in public economics, and economic theory.

ROBERT L. BUTTERWORTH is Director of the Strategic Capabilities Assessment Center at the National Defense University on Fort McNair, Washington, D.C. His government service has involved work on intelligence and national security problems for the Pentagon, the White House, and the U.S. Senate. Before joining the government he was a member of the tenured faculty of

Political Science at the Pennyslvania State University. His most recent publication is "A Growing Dusk," an assessment of future intelligence collection
problems, in Roy Godson, ed., *Intelligence Requirements for the 1990s* (1988).

RICHARD C. EICHENBERG is Associate Professor of Political Science at Tufts
University and Director of the Ford Program in European Society and Western
Security in the Center for International Affairs, Harvard University. He has
lectured and published widely in the fields of public opinion, defense spending and comparative public policy. His most recent book is a 1989 study of
public opinion and national security in Western Europe.

ROBERT E. HARKAVY is Professor of Political Science at The Pennsylvania
State University, specializing in national security policy, arms control, and
U.S. foreign policy. He earlier served with the Atomic Energy Commission
and the Arms Control and Disarmament Agency. He has been a senior research
fellow at Cornell University, a visiting research professor at the U.S. Army
War College, and Alexander von Humboldt fellow at the University of Kiel,
Germany, and a Fulbright Research Scholar in Sweden. Professor Harkavy is
the author of *The Arms Trade and International Systems* (1975), *Spectre of
a Middle Eastern Holocaust* (1978), and *Great Power Competition for Overseas Bases* (1982). He is co-editor of several other books on national security.

MICHAEL D. INTRILIGATOR is Professor of Economics and Political Science
at the University of California, Los Angeles and Director of the UCLA Center
for International and Strategic Affairs. His major research interests are economic theory and mathematical economics, econometrics, health economics,
and strategy and arms control, and he has written or edited books and published research papers in all four fields. In strategy and arms control he is
the author of *Strategy in a Missile War: Targets and Rates of Fire* (1967) and
co-editor of *National Security and International Stability* (1983), *Strategies
for Managing Nuclear Proliferation-Economic and Political Issues* (1983),
and *East-West Conflict: Elite Perceptions and Political Options* (1988).

HAROLD K. JACOBSON is Director of the Center for Political Studies of the
Institute for Social Research and Jesse S. Reeves Professor of Political Science
at the University of Michigan. A specialist on international politics and institutions, he received his undergraduate education at the University of Michigan
and his graduate education at Yale University. He is the author of *Networks
of Interdependence: International Organizations and the Global Political
System* and the author or editor-contributor to eight other books. He has also
written numerous articles for professional journals.

EDWARD A. KOLODZIEJ is Research Professor of Political Science and Director of the European Arms Control and Security Project at the University
of Illinois, Urbana-Champaign. A frequent contributor to professional jour-

nals, he is the author of *The Uncommon Defense and Congress: 1945–1963* (1966); *French International Policy under De Gaulle and Pompidou: The Politics of Grandeur* (1974); and *Making and Marketing Arms: The French Experience and Its Implications for the International System* (1987). He is currently working on a study of comparative nuclear deterrence.

PATRICK M. MORGAN is Professor of Political Science at Washington State University. Among his publications are *Deterrence, A Conceptual Analysis* 2nd ed. (1983), and *Theories and Approaches to International Politics* 4th ed. (1987) as well as, with Klaus Knorr, *Strategic Military Surprise* (1983). In 1987–88, he was a visiting professor at Katholieke Universiteit Leuven and the College of Europe (Bruges) in Belgium.

JOHN RAINIER is a major in the U.S. Army and a faculty member in the Social Science Department at West Point. He is a specialist in military organization and force structure planning.

JUDITH REPPY is Associate Professor of Peace Studies at Cornell University and Associate Director of the Peace Studies Program. Her publications include *The Genesis of New Weapons*, ed. with F.A. Long (1980) and "Labour Use and Productivity in Military and Non-Military Related Industry," *International Labour Office* (1986). She is currently writing a book on military spending and the economy.

ANDREW L. ROSS is an Assistant Professor of Political Science at the University of Kentucky. His work has appeared in *Armed Forces & Society, Technology Review*, and a number of edited volumes. He is currently completing a book about military dependence and conventional arms production in the Third World.

SAM C. SARKESIAN is Professor of Political Science at Loyola University of Chicago. He is Chairman of the Research Committee of the National Strategy Forum and is Vice-Chair of the Research Committee on Armed Forces and Society of the International Political Science Association. He served as Chairman of the Inter-University Seminar form 1980–1987. Two of his most recent publications are *America's Forgotten Wars* (Greenwood Press, 1984) and *The New Battlefield: The United States and Unconventional Conflicts* (Greenwood Press, 1986). He is currently working on a book entitled *U.S. National Security Policy and Process*. Dr. Sarkesian served as regular army officer for more than twenty years.

JANICE GROSS STEIN is Professor of Political Science at the University of Toronto. She is co-author of *Rational Decision Making: Israel's Security Choices* (1967) and *Psychology and Deterrence* (1985). Most recently, she has published, "Extended Deterrence in the Middle East: American Strategy Reconsidered," in *World Politics*, April 1987. Her principal research interests are in strategies of conflict management, with particular reference to the Middle East.